Effective Professional Writing

Effective Professional Writing

Michael L. Keene
The University of Tennessee, Knoxville

D. C. HEATH AND COMPANY Lexington, Massachusetts Toronto

Cover design: Joanna Steinkeller

Published simultaneously in Canada.

Printed in the United States of America.

International Standard Book Number: 0-669-12419-2

Library of Congress Catalog Card Number: 86-81273

This book is dedicated to
all my family.

Preface

All over the country, students are turning to upper-division (or advanced) writing courses to provide them with the communication skills that they will need as professionals in science, engineering, business, government, and all of the other fields that college graduates enter. Such courses often carry titles like "Technical Writing," "Professional Writing," or "Business and Technical Writing," but they usually involve many more kinds of students and writing than their titles suggest. Students come to such courses with high expectations: that the writing assignments will be somehow "real" in ways that earlier writing assignments may not have been, or that writing problems that have plagued them for years can be solved in months.

Most important, these students seek a kind of knowledge that can be integrated into their professional lives. They are willing to work hard and often on their writing, and they frequently will seize the initiative to learn more than their teachers and texts initially present. The diversity of students, assignments, and kinds of writing, along with the students' expectations, place great demands on the teachers, texts, and syllabi in these classes.

Effective Professional Writing grew out of the success of one such class, a combination of what most academics would know as "Professional Writing," "Technical Writing," and "Business Communications." It can be most clearly defined in terms of the students for whom it is designed, the philosophy it is based on, the kinds of assignments the students perform, and the structure the book uses.

The Students

This book is intended for students who are juniors and seniors in widely varied fields of study—business, agriculture, science, engineering—who typically have not had a writing course since their freshman year and thus may have done little or no careful writing in one or two years. By this point in their college careers, most students have lived in the worlds of their major fields long enough that they have begun to internalize the concepts, vocabularies, and values of those fields. The only audience they have dealt with is the academic one; the only writing situation they have experienced is the classroom one.

The Philosophy

Effective Professional Writing has a definite philosophy: In order for students to become effective communicators in their chosen fields, the most important thing they need to learn is how to recognize and adjust to the differences between student writing and professional writing. As a result of always writing for experts—scholars who evaluate what they know based on what they write—these students lose the ability to communicate their fields' important subject matter to people outside those fields and to people who are not experts. The speaker or author who unconsciously assumes that an audience knows or cares as much about the subject as the speaker or author does usually fails in the attempt to communicate. Another common problem resulting from doing only classroom writing is the inability to see writing as *problem solving* for *decision makers*—a function practically unknown in student writing but very common in the professional setting.

Perhaps the major failing of new graduates entering business and professional life today is that many of them unquestioningly assume that all writing situations mirror the classroom one, and thus they fail to recognize the need to tailor their writing to different audiences, purposes, roles for writers, and communication situations. In order to improve this situation, students need explicit practice in such areas as audience analysis and adaptation, which many college courses spend relatively little time on.

Anyone writing a professional report with scientific, technical, or business subject matter is likely to feel the temptation to give in to the message (or content), to pour out the technical information onto page after page, with no regard for how the report's unique situation—its purpose, message, and audience, and the special role the writer plays in that particular context—should shape and guide the selection, presentation, and arrangement of that material. Teaching a strong concern for the communication situation helps restore both audience and purpose to their proper, balanced relationship with the message or content.

Although this book stresses all the traditional features of good writing—grammar, organization, style, and content—it does so, wherever possible, by connecting those features to the needs and values of each specific communication situation—to each specific purpose, message, audience, and role for the writer.

The Assignments

Effective Professional Writing offers instructors a wide variety of exercises and writing assignments to choose from. Depending on the teacher's choice, the typical papers in one semester may be a formal letter of introduction, a job-application letter and resumé, an extended definition-and-description report, a process explanation, a proposal, and a major report, but the chapters can lead to a number of other assignments, from progress reports and cases to problem solving. The text also provides for a variety of short speeches and presentations. In each case, the content of the student's writing is drawn from his or her own major field. The audience may be an executive/layman (the teacher), another professional in the student's field, the general public, scientifically educated nonexperts, or any of several possibilities created by the assignment or the teacher. In the book's later chapters especially, the purposes and processes unique to writing beyond college receive particular attention.

The Structure

This book is divided into five major sections:

Part I: An Introduction

Part II: Letters and Memos

Part III: Elements of Technical Reports

Part IV: Processes in Report Writing

Part V: Kinds of Reports

Part I explains the key differences between writing in classrooms and writing on the job. It also explains how to write in a clear, economical, straightforward style, and the ways in which working writers deal with the various challenges that they face in presenting their material effectively—that is, so that it does what they intend it to do. Part II is a short course in business correspondence, with special emphasis on writing successful job-application letters. Part III presents the building blocks of the kind of writing professionals do, the elements of which any report is constructed. Part IV describes the constructive processes by which those building blocks become effective communication. Part V presents typical kinds of professional reports.

In general, the sequence of chapters within each of this book's five Parts (and the sequence of Parts as well) proceeds from simple to complex and from basic to applied. Thus Parts I, II, and III present fairly basic principles and techniques of writing—from how to write letters with requests in them to how to explain processes. Parts IV and V deal with writing on a much more applied level —from how to design a professional report to how to write an effective proposal. Similarly, Parts I through III discuss writing from the student's viewpoint, whereas Parts IV and V focus on writing from the professional's point of view.

Effective Professional Writing is designed so that the chapters can be used in numerical sequence if you wish, straight through from 1 to 20. For a semester-length course, beginning with the business-writing chapters and then combining chapters from Parts I and III with chapters from Parts IV and V makes an excellent sequence. For schools on the quarter system, this book contains enough material for two courses—one that covers Parts I, II, and III, and an advanced course that covers Parts IV and V.

Acknowledgements

I want to acknowledge and express my appreciation for the support of all of the people who have helped me with writing this book—students, colleagues, reviewers, friends—all those who stayed with me through the whole project, as well as those who only made it part of the way. No one ever travels such a long road alone, and certainly I didn't on this one. Special thanks to Maxine Hairston, Merrill Whitburn, Greg Cowan in memory, and Ralph Voss—friends and supporters with heart as well as head. My gratitude, also, to the staff of D. C. Heath, especially English editor Paul Smith and production editor Bryan Woodhouse; their enthusiasm, advice, and good humor kept the book—and the author—on track. Very special thanks to Nancy and Amy Keene.

M. L. K.

Contents

15 Solving Problems 295

16 Using Research Libraries 312

19 Long Reports 373

20 Oral Reports 401

Appendix: Writing Better Sentences 413

Effective Professional Writing

Introduction

By your junior or senior year in college, you may well have begun to realize that you need to be able to write better (or differently) than you currently can. In the last two years of college, more and more classes require short reports, long reports, and term papers of all kinds. Some of you, such as those in engineering or management, may have already realized that throughout your professional life you will be reading and writing reports. For others of you, simply facing graduation and writing job-application (or law-school or medical-school application) letters brings the realization that all your life you may be held back by your inability to handle even a one-page business letter (much less a twenty-page report) quickly and effectively.

Just how important is writing to a professional? One professional engineer, a member of a large and successful consulting engineering firm, called here "XYZ Associates," wrote:

> There are two aspects to the role writing plays at XYZ Associates. Reports are the company's only product. Regardless of what level of talent we employ, or how sophisticated our analyses are, the primary conduit for us to reach our customer is through the interim (if any) and final report. If those documents don't satisfy the customer's need and place us in a good light, this company cannot be successful. The second aspect of writing's role follows from the importance of the first. Regardless of an individual's technical competence, if his writing ability is inadequate, his long-term value to the company, and therefore his salary and progression in the company, are limited.

This book is designed to help all of you—from all majors—learn how to handle the writing tasks you will face in business, industry, government, science, or whatever field you enter. This book can help you learn to solve your writing problems faster, more effectively, and with less stress. Everyone can profit by learning more and better communication skills. A middle manager in a high-technology manufacturing firm puts it more succinctly: "Anyone around here who can't write doesn't stay around here long."

PART I

An Introduction

Writing at work can be both more challenging and more rewarding than writing in school. But there may not be very much in your background (or the academic backgrounds of most students) that can prepare you for the demands professional life will make on your writing skills. This book's purpose is to give you the writing skills you will need when you leave college. Part I, the first three chapters, provides the groundwork in theory and principles for the rest of the book.

A recent article in *Consulting Engineer* vividly describes the writing problem engineering students face when they begin their professional lives. The same argument could be made concerning recent college graduates in nearly any profession:

> Many engineering managers assume that engineers hired right out of undergraduate or graduate school have adequate writing skills. After all, haven't all engineering graduates written the obligatory lab reports, freshman English essays, and long technical reports? No doubt some have. But very few have written technical writing that counts in ways that it does on the job. Few

> of these former students completed writing projects that were used to solve actual problems, were written for someone who paid for the project, or were written for readers often too busy to read the entire report.(1)

Another recent article adds depth to this picture. Two writing specialists at a major university surveyed 200 college-educated working people to find out how much of their time on the job they spent writing. The occupations of the people selected for the survey were carefully chosen to accurately reflect what government statistics say is the composition of the college-educated work force, and the other features of the study were equally carefully controlled. Here is one paragraph from their conclusion:

> When respondents were asked what percentage of work time they spend writing, 193 of the 197 who answered this question said that they write on the job. Furthermore, 145 of the 197 write at least 10% of their total work time or for four hours in a 40-hour week; 98 of the 197 write 20% of total work time or eight hours in a 40-hour week. People in professional and technical occupations—the types of occupations in which over half of college-trained people are employed—on the average write nearly 30% of total work time.(2)

This book is designed to help you learn to meet the writing demands that your post-college life will make on you. Chapter 1 explains in detail how college and professional writing are different in important ways. Chapters 2 and 3 begin the process of teaching you how to cope with those important differences, starting you on the way to becoming a more effective writer.

NOTES

1. William S. Pfeiffer, "A Short Course in Report Guide Preparation," *Consulting Engineer*, October, 1982, pp. 77–83.
2. Lester Faigley and Thomas P. Miller, "What We Learn from Writing on the Job," *College English*, October, 1982, pp. 557–569.

1

The Communication Situation

Everyone can profit from learning better writing skills. For a professional, good writing skills are *essential*. Whatever your profession—doctor, engineer, accountant, or wildlife biologist—once you have graduated you will rely more on your writing skills than you did while you were in college. Effective writing—and effective communication in general—is the lifeblood of business and industry (see Fig. 1.1). The main product (in some cases, the *only* product of many management organizations, research and testing laboratories, engineering firms, and financial institutions is written documents. In many companies the ability to write good, readable reports distinguishes those who move up the corporate ladder from those who don't. A just-graduated engineer may be surprised to find that 50 or 60 percent of each work day is taken up by reading and writing reports, or hearing and delivering oral presentations. It's even more surprising to learn that as one moves up the corporate ladder the percentage of time spent in such communication activities actually goes *up*.

1. Effective Writing

Consider a typical business morning:

> In the carpool to work you read the day's trade paper to learn the new trends. You get to work and check your mail, reading the letters that look

Figure 1.1 Lines of Communication

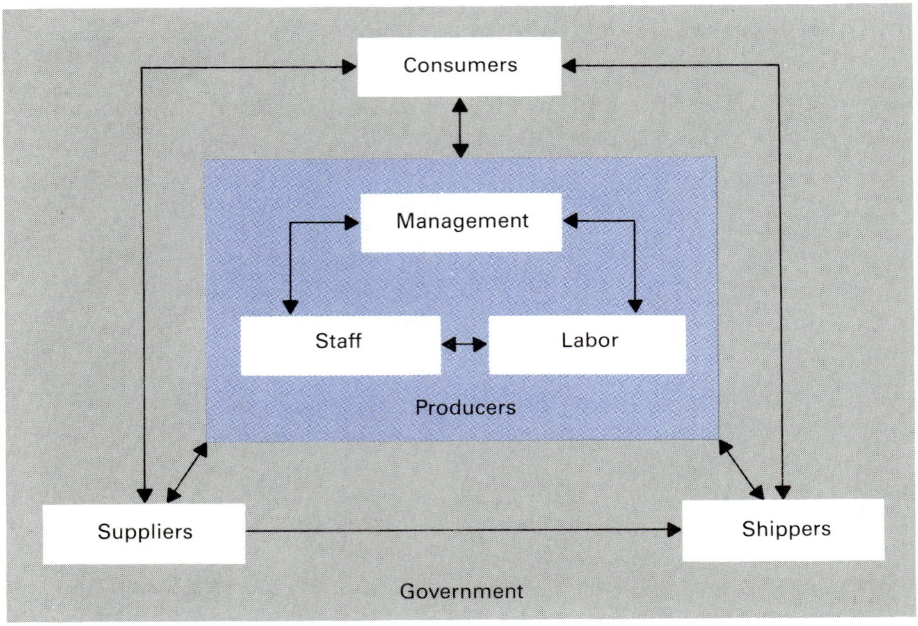

clear, simple to read, and easy to handle, putting the rest aside for later. You review your notes for the 10 a.m. meeting with the production staff. In the meeting you are vividly reminded that your boss is one of the most effective communicators you've ever met; he organizes his thoughts well and presents them clearly and effectively in both speech and writing. During the meeting you are put in charge of a subcommittee, and you realize this means you will have to write another thirty-page report. Preparing your last one took evenings and weekends for a month and nearly wrecked your marriage. You wish you could handle report writing as well as that person across the table. You're convinced you've got the know-how and the ideas you need to succeed, but you just can't communicate them effectively. Nothing you do ever looks as good on paper as it seemed in your thoughts.

By the time the meeting ends, it's 11:30 and you've spent the whole morning worrying over communication—especially writing. As the afternoon begins you dive into the stack of paperwork on your desk. Letters and memos to read and to write, reports to look over, and decisions to make based on all that written information.

Whether you are a doctor, an engineer, an accountant, or a wildlife biologist, if you wish to succeed in business, industry, government, or research, you will need to be able to communicate effectively. The goal of this book is to help you learn to do so.

1.1 What Is Effective Writing?

Effective professional writing gets its point across. It moves the reader in the direction the author desires. It *communicates*. If your goal is to convey information, then you will want to do so clearly and quickly. If your goal is to persuade, you will want the reader to follow your line of reasoning willingly.

Effective writing repays your reader for the time it took to read your report (or manual, brochure, letter, etc.). If your report is not effective, more than time has been lost. In professional life, wasted time is wasted money. If you waste your reader's time and money, you've wasted your own and your company's time and money as well. And no professional can afford that kind of waste.

1.2 Why Is Effective Writing Important?

In college you may pay a relatively low price for ineffective writing. If your reports take twice as long as they should to write, or if they never turn out nearly as well as you want them to, you may not feel you've lost too much. Your major may require little writing in college, and the effectiveness of your writing may rarely determine the course of your college career. If you do happen to receive a low grade on a writing assignment every so often, you may feel you have plenty of company among your classmates. You may also feel that as a student you are not expected to produce really polished writing but rather to focus on learning the subject matter.

Figure 1.2 For the client in Topeka, you are what you write.

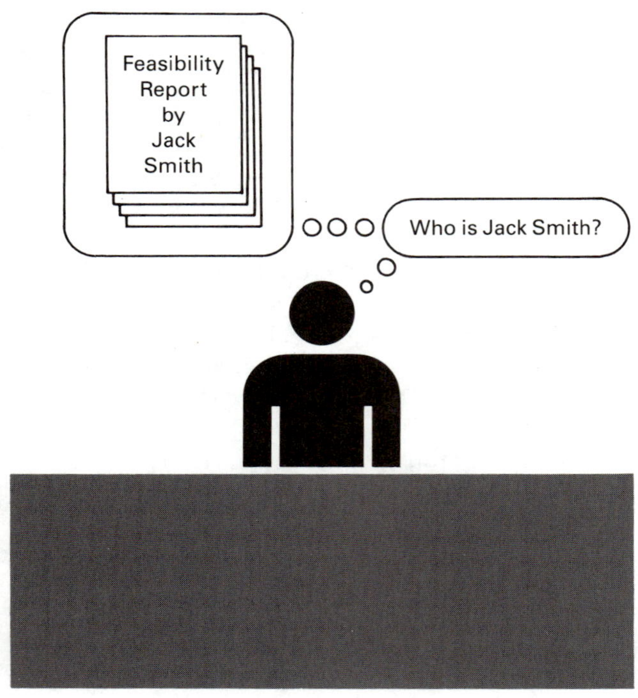

On the job all of that changes. From the moment you send in a job application letter and resumé, from the moment you stand up to introduce yourself in the first staff meeting, people around you are evaluating you and the quality of your work—and they do it largely on the basis of your communication skills. You get the job or you don't; you impress your boss that you are the best one to represent your company or you don't; you sell the customer or you don't; you get the contract or you don't. Therefore you keep your job—maybe get a promotion—or you don't.

In your professional life, the image of you projected by your writing and speaking is often more visible than you are (see Fig. 1.2). Thus you want your writing to be effective because it will reflect on both you and your employer. But you can do much more than this; you want your words to reflect the good quality of your thoughts. If you only think about avoiding major blunders in your writing, you're like a football team with no offense or a baseball pitcher with no fastball. There may be no more frustrating professional experience than to have a good idea but not be able to communicate it effectively in the written form your job requires. If you follow the suggestions offered here for developing effective writing skills, that kind of frustration may be one big professional problem you will never have.

2. College Writing Versus Professional Writing

The kinds of people you write for, their positions relative to yours, their reasons for reading, the kind of reading they do, and the images of themselves they want to see in your reports—in the writing professionals do, all these things are different from the way they are in the writing students do. Most of all, the people you write for and the situations you write in are *real* in a way college writing seldom is, and the way you adapt to your professional situation and your professional audience must reflect that reality.

What changes when you move from college writing to professional writing? It's easier to start by naming what stays the same. Generally you will still be writing within the same subject area (engineers write about engineering, accountants about accounting, and so on), although even that may not always be the case. But while the message, or content, remains the same, just about everything else about your writing changes. The purposes your writing serves, your audiences, and your own role as writer—all of these key elements of the communication situation change in important ways. It's popular among communication specialists to focus on four intangibles as keys to effective communication: audience, purpose, message, and writer's role. When you move from student writing to professional writing, at least three of these may change drastically (see Fig. 1.3).

3. Audience

During your college years you are always writing for experts—people who know more about your subject than you do. After college the roles are often reversed. Often *you* are the expert, writing to someone who knows much less about the specific subject than you do. Or you may be writing to your co-workers in the company—to equals. Or to total strangers. Or to technicians who work for you. These different audiences make demands on your writing skill that little in your experience as a student writer may have prepared you for. Your audience outside college is different from your audience inside college in at least these three important ways: its *kind*, its *position*, and its *role*. Professionals who are successful writers adjust to those factors almost automatically. If you continue to grow as a writer, the strategies shown in this book, which may require some effort on your part at first, will also become automatic for you.

The audience for your college writing is almost exclusively composed of experts. Those experts are in a position above yours (in the sense that professors are above students), they are part of the same organization (college, course) as you, and they usually carefully and actively read what you write (rather than glancing at it and passing it on).

Figure 1.3 The Writer's Universe

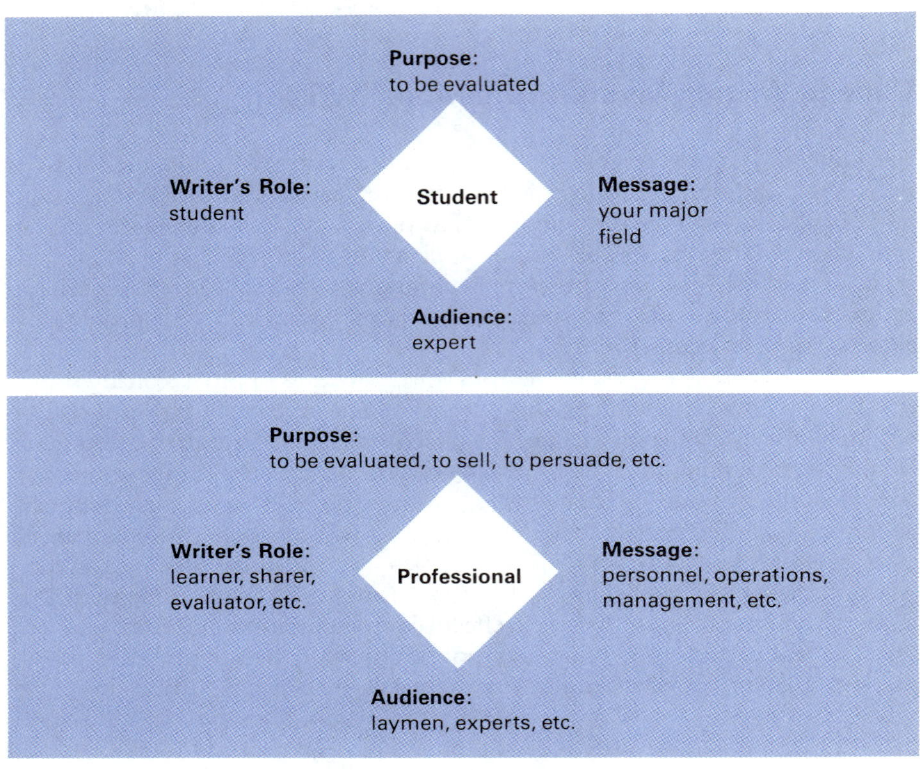

After college all of that changes. Your audience outside college could be experts, laymen, technicians, or executives—or a mix. They could be above you, below you, or on your level. They could be inside your company (internal) or outside it (external). And they could actively and carefully read your report, just skim it, or just file it. They may be persuaded by it, learn from it, pass judgment on it, or ignore it.

As a college student you may write for an engineering professor, a biology professor, or an accounting professor, but you're always a student writing for a professor. On the job, however, you may be an engineer trying to sell a construction proposal, a systems analyst writing instructions for people who work for you, a quality-control manager announcing a change in company procedures, or a field accountant writing up the results of an audit for official records. You had years and years to get used to the kind of writing required in school, and its kind was just about always the same. But the kinds of job-related writing you have to do may well change constantly, frequently allowing you little time to adjust. The effectiveness of your job-related writing often depends *directly* on whether you

Box 1.1 Different Kinds of Audiences

Layman: A person in whom you can assume no implicit knowledge or interest in your subject. *Examples*: The general public—people reading an account of how DNA works, or instructions for installing a garage-door opener, or a critical comparison of two products.

Expert: A person who has substantial knowledge, experience, and (probably) interest in your subject. *Examples*: An engineer reading an engineering report, a marketing professor reading a student's paper, a banker reading a financial statement, or a dietician reading a description of a new clinical diet for cancer patients.

Executive: Someone with decision-making power over your career. *Examples*: A store manager reading a suggested change in inventory procedures, a department head reading the product brochures of various copiers, or the president of the company reading your report.

Technician: The person who actually runs the machine or performs the procedure; a person with some hands-on knowledge of the subject, interested in it in a how-to sense. *Examples*: A secretary trying to figure out a word processor's user's manual, a maintenance technician reading a service manual, or a PFC reading a training manual.

have properly judged and adapted to the requirements of each different writing task. Over and over the focal point of that adaptation will be the audience.

Learning to write for different kinds of audiences in different roles requires learning audience analysis and adaptation. Because your college writing—all of your writing as a student—has been for one kind of audience in one role and one position, you probably aren't in the habit of considering these features. To help you sharpen your thinking about the kinds, positions, and roles of audiences in business and industry, the next three sections of this chapter list and explain them in detail.

3.1 Four Basic Kinds of Audiences

It is impossible to classify every kind of audience in business and industry, so the best one can do may well be to choose a simple, reasonably efficient scheme and then remember that it may need to be amended in some situations. The classification given here has become almost standard. We will use it throughout this book, with modifications to be explained shortly.

In this classification scheme there are four kinds of audiences: layman, expert, executive, and technician. (See Box 1.1.)

Each different kind of audience has its own characteristics and requires its own adaptations. For example, because laymen typically have no built-in interest

Figure 1.4 Different Points of View People in various "audiences" are looking for the answers to the questions that are most meaningful to them personally, which are different for each group.

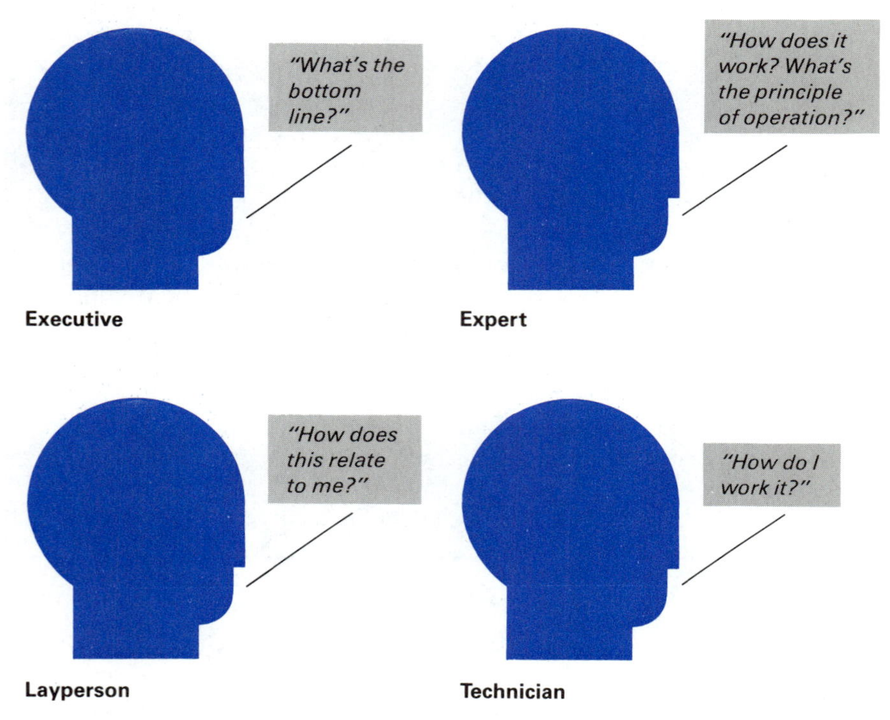

in your subject, you need to work on motivating them to read what you've written (see "Reader Benefits," Chapter 4, Section 2.4, for more on this). Experts, on the other hand, may have a great deal of interest not only in the conclusions you draw, but also (and especially) in seeing how you came to those conclusions (see Chapter 15, "Solving Problems," for more on this). Executives typically want to see the "bottom line" first, and only *after* seeing your conclusions and recommendations might they want to see how you arrived at them (see Executive Summaries, Chapter 12, Section 7). Technicians may not be interested at all in how you decided a certain operation needed to be done a certain way, but they will be very interested in exactly how the operation is to be done (see Chapter 11, Section 2). Each kind of reader brings a certain set of expectations to the act of reading (see Fig. 1.4), and for your writing to be successful you must anticipate and respond to them. Who the reader is, why the reader is reading, what the reader hopes to gain, and how you respond will vary with each kind of audience.

The strengths of this scheme—layman, executive, expert, and technician—are its simplicity and its comprehensiveness: it is easy to remember, easy to use, and fits most situations. Its weakness is that it names different characteristics for one kind of audience than for the others. It defines the executive audience in terms of the reader's role and position, the other three audiences by the reader's knowledge and interest. That is, a person can be simultaneously an executive and a layman, or an executive and an expert. Because your audience may fit more than one of these four types, the scheme needs to be slightly modified.

3.2 Complex Audiences

If your audience is one person who is both an expert and an executive, you have a *complex* audience. An engineer who has become president of an engineering firm is one example. Writing for such a reader would be different from writing for the company's vice-president, an MBA who came up through the company's accounting division. If you can recognize those complex qualities in your audience, the adaptation should be no more complicated than for a simple audience.

A particularly common complex audience is the layman/executive, someone who has no particular knowledge or interest in your subject but has decision-making power over your career. This kind of audience is more and more typical. Chemists in research labs have to justify their expenditures to an executive whose training and expertise are in accounting or management; engineers have to convince lawyers their projects are safe; and managers have to convince stockholders a merger is the sensible thing to do. If your writing class is being taught by an English professor, your audience is most likely a layman/executive. In all those cases the audience is layman/executive, and the adaptation is easy once the identification is correctly made.

3.3 Multiple Audiences

A *multiple* audience is one composed of several people who fall into different categories. There may be some executives and some technicians, some experts and some laymen, or any combination of types. Company newsletters are typically written for multiple audiences. So are a company's yearly reports. The information booklets the IRS sent out in the past are examples of bad writing for multiple audiences: by trying to write for everyone, the writers achieve clarity for no one.

In general there are three ways to adapt your writing to a multiple audience:

1. Write two or more separate versions, one for each audience.
2. Write for the common denominator—isolate characteristics held in common and work on those.
3. Compartmentalize your report—divide it into separate sections and clearly label them so the readers can find the sections they want easily and skip the rest.

Compartmentalization, which is usually the best method of adapting to a multiple audience, is discussed in more detail in Chapter 19.

4. Purpose

What purposes does your writing in college serve? to complete an assignment, to move ahead academically? to show a professor you've mastered some subject area, to be evaluated (and to receive a good evaluation)? What purposes does writing on the job serve? To get jobs (for yourself and your firm), to move ahead on the job, to keep records, to give orders, to make contacts, to gain personal satisfaction, to secure professional advancement—these are only a few of the purposes that apply to writing on the job. And each purpose, each reason for writing, makes its own special demands on how your writing needs to be done. Writing for record keeping (as in a typical quarterly progress report) is about as different from writing to persuade (as in a new product brochure) as night from day. And it is the change in *purpose* that keys all these differences—in tone, style, word choice, organization, use of visuals, degree of finish of the final document, and countless others.

Professionals do so many kinds of writing in so many situations that almost any generalization about purpose (such as "there are four purposes for professional writing") immediately has to be amended, made more complicated, and amended again. Having said that, we can then look at a *tentative* list of purposes for professional writing:

- To persuade
- To teach
- To inform
- To record

Of course no one piece of writing ever serves just one of those purposes—the same memo that requests your boss to buy you a new personal computer (a persuasive purpose) also informs the boss of your need (an informative purpose) and serves as a record you can refer to a week later when you haven't gotten an answer to your request. If the memo goes into detail about why you need the computer, filling your boss in on facts he or she doesn't otherwise know, then it also serves a teaching purpose. Thus in one ordinary memo we have all four purposes being served. Despite that, it wouldn't be hard to figure out which purpose was the most important (persuading the boss to give you a computer) and which one was least important (to keep a record of the request, perhaps).

Suppose, on the other hand, you were talking to your boss one day and happened to mention that you could really use a personal computer in your office, and that the boss said, "No problem, just put your request in a memo to make it official, and as soon as I get the memo I'll send through a purchase order." Think about how this *record-keeping* memo will be different from the other one that has to *persuade* the boss.

Another good example to consider here is the company newsletter. Is it fancy-looking, typeset on shiny paper, with lots of sophisticated visuals? Or is it plain-looking, word-processed and photocopied on cheap paper, with the only visuals cartoon sketches by the staff? *Purpose* explains these differences. The fancy one probably goes outside the company as well as inside it, and is probably used to represent the company to outsiders (and potential clients). Because it serves a persuasive purpose (whatever else it does), it gets the fancy, Class A treatment (see Chapter 13, Section 2.1, on various classes of documents). The plain newsletter, on the other hand, probably serves mainly the purpose of informing people within the company of key events (promotions, picnics, and problems); thus it gets the plain, Class C treatment.

Consider one last example of how purpose shapes a typical piece of professional writing, and of how purposes interact in complex ways: Susan Smith is a junior engineer with XYZ Engineering, a rapidly growing firm that specializes in geotechnical engineering—that is, figuring out if the ground below your proposed skyscraper is strong enough to hold it up. Assigned to the team of engineers who are testing the site for the new Wilson Towers high-rise apartment and condominium complex, she also will carry a large part of the burden of writing the final report to the client. She will write some parts of it herself, collect the parts other members of the team write, merge them into one document, shepherd the report through review by senior members of the team (and by her firm's management and its own editors), and keep an eye on the reproduction process. From her company's point of view, what are the purposes of the report, in order of importance?

1. First, Susan has to let her firm's client know the information it wants—the building can indeed be built, but with certain restrictions as to the type of footings that must be used. So she *informs*.
2. But she has to do it in such a way that the client believes what she says and acts on it (otherwise the report is a failure and Susan is in trouble). Therefore, in the report Susan has to be fully professional, both in the way she handles her technical tasks and in the way she communicates her results. So she has to *persuade*.
3. If the client lacks engineering expertise (maybe the client is a group of investment bankers and brokers), she also has to teach, to anticipate questions such as "why do we need this type of footings?" and answer them in terms and concepts nonengineers will understand—but without talking down to the client. So she *teaches*.
4. The report also serves as the record of her team's work, the tangible product for which the client paid a hefty sum of money. So she writes to *record* as well.

Thus her purposes, in order of importance, are to (1) inform, (2) persuade, (3) teach, and (4) record. Or at least, so we would guess by looking at the situation through our own eyes, and maybe by looking at the report.

From the point of view of Susan herself, however, the purposes of the report would fall in a different order of priority:

1. As a new employee and as one of a relatively small number of women engineers in the firm (a situation she hopes to help change), Susan is concerned with persuading the other members of the team that she is a top-flight engineer; she's more concerned with persuading people inside the company than outside it.

2. She wants to *inform* her client of the team's findings.
3. She wants to *record* the team's work.
4. She may forget that the report should also *teach* until one of her firm's managers sees a draft of the report and points out that she needs to explain the "why" with the "what."

Thus we see a different ordering of purposes when we look through Susan's eyes. From the client's point of view, the relative priorities of the various purposes would be different still.

Purpose is a complex aspect of the communication situation, one that merits concern at every level and stage of your writing. You may never be able to make your purpose, your company's purpose, and your reader's purpose exactly the same in every way, but you very much need to consider very carefully the relative importance of these four purposes in each writing situation.

5. Message

During college you write mostly about things in your area of subject specialization as it is traditionally understood. After college much of that stays the same, but some of it changes. Regardless of your major, you may find yourself writing about nearly anything at one time or another—personnel problems, company history, new products, management and operations, or the conference you just attended, to name a few topics. Following is a list (not a complete list) of some of the main areas you may find yourself dealing with. Remember that in each case any or all of the four purposes discussed in the previous section may be involved, and that any of the four audiences explained in Section 3 of this chapter could be your audience:

Science	Personnel
Technology	Sales
Business	Production
Government	Research & Development
Medicine	Operations
Education	Agriculture
Management	

Whichever one of these areas you work in, and however your college major fits into that area, you will find that there are certain ways of writing that are acceptable and others that are unacceptable. For example, in government writing people typically have a much higher tolerance for jargon (language that only a particular in-group can understand) than in science writing; the same person who in the first group would aspire to be a "change agent with positive feedback" would in the second group want to be a Principal Investigator.

Of course, each of the main categories of content has almost infinite subdivisions, many of them overlapping with subdivisions of other categories, and as you become more and more of a specialist in your subject you will inevitably learn more and more about how writing works in that field. It would be impossible to cover here all of the different varieties of writing, or even to point out all of the ways in which they differ. A few of the important ways are:

- the acceptability of jargon
- the degree of technicalness
- what constitutes an acceptable proof of a point
- how tactful the writing needs to be
- what other concessions are typically made to readers
- typical structures
- average sentence length
- use of visuals

The important point for writers making the transition from college to professional life to remember is that the content of your writing—specifically how well you have mastered your field—just doesn't exist apart from your writing, at least not as far as your readers go. If you write poorly, people will always suspect and challenge your subject knowledge; if you write well, your writing will be a major asset in your career.

6. The Writer's Role

"Student" may best sum up your role for the last ten or fifteen years. As your purposes, messages, and audiences change when you become a professional, your role as a writer also changes. After leaving college, each different writing situation you face will require you to size up your role anew. You may be writing a note containing complex instructions to your secretary, a report to your boss explaining a difficult work-related problem, or a letter to a prospective customer. In each case the role you play as a writer will need to change, and that change will combine with the particular audience, purpose, and message, to shape your final written product.

How many roles can writers in professional life play? Well, you might as well ask how many writers and how many situations there are. Not surprisingly, a list of typical roles looks a little like a combination of the lists of purposes, messages, and audiences. Typical roles include seller, buyer, persuader, reporter, subordinate, evaluator, teacher, consultant, complainer, peacemaker, sharer, even student, and the list goes on and on. You already have all the knowledge you need to recognize such roles; we all slide into and out of a variety of them every day. The trick is to apply to your writing the common sense and instinct that guides you through daily encounters. In your writing you have probably become so accustomed to playing the role of *student* that you no longer consider what role you are in as a

Exhibit 1.1 A Persuasive Passage

URANIUM ENRICHMENT REVOLVING FUND

Unlike most government activities, the uranium enrichment program produces revenue. The program interacts with the private sector by purchasing resources such as electrical power and by selling enrichment services. The long lead-time for constructing new facilities to meet the growing demand for enriched uranium requires that expansion decisions be made far in advance of the need for additional capacity. The business nature of this enterprise requires a more flexible financing system than is provided by the annual appropriations cycle of the federal budget.

To accomplish this objective, proposals by Senator Glenn of Ohio and Congressman Lujan of New Mexico are currently before Congress to establish a uranium enrichment revolving fund. While differing in details, both proposals make the following recommendations:

[Six recommendations are listed.]

If this legislation is enacted, substantial benefits in economy and efficiency will result:

[Seven benefits are listed.]

Source: U.S. Department of Energy, *United States Enrichment News*, November, 1980.

writer; now that you are moving beyond student life, you need to become accustomed to (1) taking a few minutes to size up the role you play in each situation, and then (2) adjusting your writing accordingly.

Four examples from actual reports will show you how these elements—purpose, message, audience, and writer's role—all interact in any one piece of writing. Exhibit 1.1 gives an example of writing to persuade.

Even though the persuasive quality of this is more low-key than you may be used to seeing in advertising, editorials, and other more openly persuasive communication, the passage still has a point it is trying to make. All of the elements—the point or message, the writer's role, the audience, and the persuasive purpose—are closely intertwined.

That same intertwining of purpose, message, audience, and writer's role can be seen in the examples given in Exhibits 1.2, 1.3, and 1.4.

7. The Communication Situation: The Key Intangible Elements

The key intangible elements of any professional communication situation are:

- Message: *what* do you need to say?
- Purpose: *why* do you need to say it?

Exhibit 1.2 A Passage to Record

BREATHITT COUNTY, KENTUCKY: PROFILE

Coal mining is the major industry in Breathitt County, employing 21% of the county's labor force. The county's population declined more than 30% from 1940 to 1970, but in the 1970s the population began to increase.

Almost all of the coal produced in Breathitt County is surface mined, using contour and mountaintop removal methods. There are 900 million tons of strippable coal reserves in the county. Most mining operations are small, and their numbers have declined in recent years, due to several economic and practical factors, including the costs of conforming to regulations.

The most common problems associated with surface mining in the county are erosion, flooding due to sediment-choked streams, acid drainage, and disposal of mine wastes. These are chronic problems, because traditionally there was no reclamation of mined land. It will take several years before the effects of new regulations on sediment levels become evident. Because mountain soils are thin, most soil material is likely to be removed during clearing of vegetation, and it is often difficult to find the two inches of topsoil cover required on reclaimed land. There is little usable land in the county, so many landowners would prefer that land be returned to a slope flatter than the original hillsides. In mountaintop removal operations it is permissable for the land to be restored to a level condition, and it is subsequently suitable for alternative uses, such as pasture.

Source: John Seddon and Carl H. Petrich, *Management of Public Impacts in Surface Mining*, ORNL/TM - 7672.

- Audience: *to whom* are you saying it?
- Writer's role: *what* is your *relationship* to this purpose, message, and audience?

Some people—natural communicators—adjust to changes in these elements intuitively. For most of us, however, the changes require getting used to; considering these as variables (outside of college) rather than as constants (as in college) takes some effort. The rest of this book shows you how to make the necessary changes in your writing, once you realize those changes are necessary.

These four elements are key intangibles in any communication situation, but there may also be additional factors that become important. Sometimes, for example, the time line you operate on to write your report may be such that it winds up controlling everything else you do. If you have only two days to tour a manufacturing facility, and your manager wants your report as soon as you get back, you may not have time to make as many adjustments in your final report as you know your purpose, message, audience, and role really require. Or you may

Exhibit 1.3 A Passage to Inform

A REVIEW AND EVALUATION OF THE LANGLEY RESEARCH CENTER'S SCIENTIFIC AND TECHNICAL INFORMATION PROGRAM: INTRODUCTION

The technical report is used by the National Aeronautics and Space Administration (NASA) and many research and development (R&D) organizations as an information product, a primary means for communicating the results of their research to the user. For calendar year 1980, NASA published 3,399 technical reports of which 612 were published by the Langley Research Center (LaRC).

As part of the review and evaluation of the Langley Research Center's scientific and technical information (STI) program, the technical report was examined to determine the organization of the report (sequential components), the language used to convey the information (language components), and the methods used to present the information (presentation components). The examination included a survey of the literature pertinent to the subject and an analysis of current usage and practices of publishers of technical reports. The results of the examination are presented in this report.

Source: Robert A. McCullough, Thomas E. Pinelli, Douglas D. Pilley, and Freda F. Stohrer, *A Review and Evaluation of the Langley Research Center's Scientific and Technical Information Program*, NASA Technical Memorandum 83269.

be only one writer on a team of writers producing a major report, and you may have to go along with the way they have decided to do it, even though your own analysis of the situation causes you to disagree with something about their approach. These are only two examples of ways other aspects of the communication situation—such as time problems and office politics—can in isolated instances become as important as these four key intangibles.

The important point to remember is that the time you spend putting a value on each of these variables for each particular communication situation and then deciding how to treat the situation based on those values may be the most important time you spend. The investment in terms of minutes is actually quite small, but the rewards in terms of producing effective professional communication are high.

7.1 Applying the Principles

Finding the answers to the following questions will help you improve your knowledge of each communication situation you find yourself in, and thus strengthen your ability to deal with each particular communication situation.

Exhibit 1.4 A Passage to Teach

VALUE OF THE ENERGY DATA BASE

2.3 General Approach to Measuring the Value of Information Products and Services

Value of information and information products and services can be measured from the viewpoint of several participants in the information transfer process, including searchers of secondary products and services, readers of primary products and services, the organizations that fund users, and all of society that is the ultimate beneficiary of energy information. At each level are two kinds of value. The first value of information is determined by what the consumer is willing to pay, and the other is derived through use of the information. Both perspectives depend to a large degree on the extent and purposes of use of information. It is assumed that the more information is used, the greater the value. This does not mean that extensive use of information about one research result necessarily yields greater value than less-used information concerning another research result. What it does mean is that the value of any valid information is enhanced by factors that increase the amount and extent of use of the information. The paradigms used throughout this report are totally based on this assumption.

Source: King Research, Inc., *Value of the Energy Data Base*, DOE/OR/11232 - 1.

- *What* do you need to say?
  What are the key points you need to cover? Are they the ones the audience will want you to cover? Is there a natural organization those points fall into? Will that be the best organization for your audience? What level of detail do you need to use? How does the occasion that brings your audience to read this need to affect what you write? What kinds of presentation techniques (use of statistics, use of visuals, use of argumentation, etc.) will your audience respond to most positively? most negatively? How do you need to adapt your vocabulary to this situation?

- *Why* do you need to say it?
  What do you want to happen as a result of presenting this message to this audience? What is there in this communication situation that joins your purpose in writing with that of your audience in reading—that is, what is in this report for them? What will be done with your report (or letter, memo, etc.) once it reaches its audience? Will it be read and routinely filed away, circulated widely, or argued over? How do all these factors shape your report?

- *To whom* are you saying it?
  What is your audience's vocabulary level? How willing are they to hear what you have to say? What is their relationship to you (customer, teacher, peer, public, subordinate, manager, etc.) and yours to them? What is their power relationship to you? Where do they fit into the audience classification scheme presented earlier in this chapter? What does your audience stand to gain from this report? to lose? What is your audience's age, sex, education, primary group membership (accountants, engineers-turned-managers, etc.), and pertinent special interests (personnel, inventory reduction, research and development, etc.)?
- *What* is your *relationship* to this purpose, message, and audience?
  What kind of person do you need to be in this report? formal or informal? reserved or outgoing? official or unofficial? demanding or conciliatory? statistical or rhetorical? Consider carefully who you want to be and who your audience wants you to be—can you find a compromise voice to adopt?

These questions highlight only some of the major considerations that need to go into doing professional writing successfully. If you were to combine all the considerations of audience, writer's role, message, and purpose into one equation, that equation would have to be different for each report. Thus the techniques you need to use to adapt to the situation based on your analysis of it are much more difficult to generalize about than are the analysis techniques. For any given situation, you will have to make unique adaptations. The following list shows only some of the major kinds of possible adaptations:

- Provide your readers with the right kind and amount of background.
- Avoid specialized terminology when not absolutely necessary.
- If you *must* use specialized words, define them.
- Use visuals to help clarify your message. If formulas, mathematics, and complicated diagrams are going to obscure rather than clarify, either simplify them or avoid them.
- Use plenty of specific examples.
- Meet your reader's standards for thoroughness and accuracy.
- Be sure to answer the obvious questions before they're asked.
- Make sure your reader understands the report's structure. Always remind the reader of what the report has done so far and where it is headed.
- Within reason, make sentences and paragraphs short. The more complicated your content is, the clearer your writing must be. Prefer subject-verb-object word order.

Successful professional communication always occurs within the context of a specific writer, message, purpose, and audience. Successful analysis of the communication situation (and adaptation to it) may not depend on understanding the theories presented here (or elsewhere). Many people are successful at communicating because they have developed an intuitive sense for one or more of the four key intangibles; often, such people cannot articulate exactly how they do what they do. But for the majority of writers making the difficult transition from writing in college to writing on the job, learning to analyze each new communication situation and adapt to it is essential to effective professional communication.

EXERCISES

1. Compare these two definitions. How do the assumptions the writer made about the reader's kind and amount of education, the reader's degree of knowledge and interest in the subject, the reader's purpose for reading the definition, and the writer's role differ between the two definitions? What other significant differences are there?

A.

magnet any body having the property of attracting iron; specifically, a mass of iron or steel having this property artificially imparted and hence called an *artificial magnet*;—called also, according to its shape, a bar magnet, a horseshoe magnet, etc. A magnet usually has two poles of opposite nature, situated near its ends. If a magnetized bar or needle (magnetic needle) is so suspended that it may rotate freely around a vertical axis, as a compass needle, the magnet will assume a direction nearly north and south. The end towards the north is called the north end, or north pole; the end towards the south, the south end or south pole. The earth is a magnet whose poles are not far distant from the geographical poles. . . . If a second magnetized bar or needle is brought near the first, the unlike poles will attract each other while the like poles will repel each other. When a magnet is broken in two, each part is a magnet; hence, each molecule of a magnetizable body, such as iron, is itself a magnet, and magnetization is essentially the arrangement of the molecular magnets in a practically parallel array. Soft iron may be temporarily converted into a magnet, by induction without contact, or by the influence of an electric current (in which case it is called an *electromagnet*).(1)

B.

magnet a body having the property of attracting iron and producing a magnetic field external to itself; specifically, a mass of iron, steel, or alloy that usually has two poles of opposite nature situated near its ends so that when brought close to a similar body the unlike poles attract each other while the like poles repel each other, and that in the form of a bar or needle (as a compass needle) suspended so that it may rotate freely around a vertical axis assumes a direction nearly north and south.(2)

2. In what ways are the audiences for the following excerpts the same? How are the audiences different?

A.

Chemist Douglas Covey felt very much at home in his laboratory at the Washington University School of Medicine in St. Louis. The maze of glass tubes, whirling centrifuges, and bubbling flasks seemed to be all he needed to carry on his work, the creating and testing of new drugs.

Then three years ago he met Garland Marshall, a professor of biophysics at Washington. Marshall told him about a totally new way to confront his molecules: face to face on a computer screen. Covey was skeptical. "Computers have absolutely nothing to do with my work," he said. Today he admits that he was dead wrong. He has become a true convert to computer chemistry.

Part of Covey's research is now done in front of a cathode ray tube, where he manipulates a joy stick and the computer keyboard as though he were playing some sort of electronic space game. At the flick of a wrist, lines of red, yellow, and green turn and twist before his eyes, each image conveying a bit of information about the electrical charges, structures, and volume of the molecules he may later make in the laboratory.

Covey is one of many scientists in universities and drug companies across the country who use computers before turning to their test tubes.(3)

B.

Everybody knows what arthritis is. Stiff knuckles, swollen knees, a morning when you can't get out of bed, the poignant and agonized shuffling of people who've made desperate, last-ditch trips to the soothing-and-perhaps-healing waters of the famous bathhouses in Hot Springs, Arkansas, in hopes of a cure.

A crippler without a clearly defined cause that respects no age, although it has always been looked on as one of the inevitable and irreversible consequences of aging—that's arthritis.

But there's exciting news emerging from a recently held gathering in Little Rock, just a stone's throw from Hot Springs' Bathhouse Row. More effective treatment, and maybe prevention, of the disease seems possible with trace minerals—copper and zinc in particular. (4)

C.

Any science fiction buff would recognize the creature: Neither plant nor animal, the protoplasm grows in the cool damp darkness of a rotting log. Then, cued by its mysterious inner clock, the blob oozes upward, toward the surface and sunlight, toward the world of open air—there to undergo an astounding transformation.

That blob actually exists, not in fevered imaginations but in our own woods and gardens. It's the thoroughly terrestrial slime mold, an often lovely organism with an unlovely name. Some five hundred species of this cousin to mushrooms confound zoologists and botanists alike with a life cycle that takes them from beast to beauty to beast again. They first resemble primitive animals that grow into shapeless, slime-coated masses called plasmodia, then change into funguslike spore-bearing "fruiting bodies," or sporangia. Thereafter, they begin the cycle all over. (5)

3. Write three pages to explain one of the following topics in three different versions, one version (one page) each for three of the audiences specified here:

   Audience 1: A curious twelve-year-old (you could be writing part of the script for an educational children's television program or doing an entry for a children's encyclopedia).

   Audience 2: A friend your age (this could come in a personal letter, or as an explanation your friend must understand in order to write his or her own paper on a similar subject).

   Audience 3: A college English professor who will grade your writing and place you in (or out of) Freshman English on the basis of its quality.

   Audience 4: A prospective employer who will use this writing sample to evaluate your writing skills (this would be part of a longer application form you are filling out).

   Topic 1: Why does a cold glass crack if you put boiling water into it?

   Topic 2: What happens to water after it goes down the kitchen drain?

   Topic 3: How does a color television work?

   Topic 4: How do you deal with an angry customer?

   Topic 5: How does an airplane wing work?

4. Carefully read the following five passages. Each is by the same author, each is on the same subject, and each is for a different audience.(6) As you read the passages, construct answers to these questions:
   - Who is the audience? How much do they know about the subject? Why would they read this piece?
   - Where could the piece appear (give a specific title)?
   - What is the purpose of each piece?
   - What is the writer's role in each piece?
   - What in the writing of each piece caused you to answer each question as you did?

A.

Recent studies have provided reasons to postulate that the primary timer for long-cycle biological rhythms that are closely similar in period to the natural geophysical ones and that persist in so-called constant conditions is, in fact, one of organismic response to subtle geophysical fluctuations which pervade ordinary constant conditions in the laboratory (Brown, 1959, 1960). In such constant laboratory conditions a wide variety of organisms have been demonstrated to display, nearly equally conspicuously, metabolic periodicities of both solar-day and lunar-day frequencies, with their interference derivative the 29.5 synodic month, and in some instances even the year. These metabolic cycles exhibit day-by-day irregularities and distortions which have been established to be highly significantly correlated with aperiodic meteorological and other geophysical changes. These correlations provide strong evidence for the exogenous origin of these biological periodisms themselves, since cycles exist in these meteorological and geophysical factors.

B.

One of the greatest riddles of the universe is the uncanny ability of living things to carry out their normal activities with clocklike precision at a particular time of the day, month and year. Why do oysters plucked from a Connecticut bay and shipped to a Midwest laboratory continue to time their lives to ocean tides 800 miles away? How do potatoes in hermetically sealed containers predict atmospheric pressure trends two days in advance? What effects do the lunar and solar rhythms have on the life habits of man? Living things clearly possess powerful adaptive capacities—but the explanation of whatever strange and permeative forces are concerned continues to challenge science. Let us consider the phenomena more closely.

C.

Familiar to all are the rhythmic changes in innumerable processes of animals and plants in nature. Examples of phenomena geared to the 24-hour solar day produced by rotation of the earth relative to the sun are sleep movements of plant leaves and petals, spontaneous activity in numerous animals, emergence of flies from their pupal cases, color changes of the skin in crabs, and wakefulness in man. These periodisms of animals and plants, which adapt them so nicely to their geophysical environment with its rhythmic fluctuations in light, temperature, and ocean tides, appear at first glance to be exclusively simple responses by the organisms to these physical factors. However, it is now known that rhythms of all these natural frequencies may persist in living things even after the organisms have been sealed in under conditions constant with respect to every factor biologists have conceded to be of influence. The presence of such persistent rhythms clearly indicates that organisms possess some means of timing these periods which does not depend directly upon obvious environmental physical rhythms.

D.

A deep-seated, persistent, rhythmic nature, with periods identical with or close to the major natural geophysical ones, appears increasingly to be a universal biological property. Striking published correlations of activity of hermetically sealed organisms with unpredictable weather-associated atmospheric temperature and pressure changes, and with day-to-day irregularities in the variations in primary cosmic and general background radiations, compel the conclusion that some, normally uncontrolled, subtle pervasive forces must be effective for living systems. The earth's natural electrostatic field may be one contributing factor.

E.

Everyone knows that there are individuals who are able to awaken morning after morning at the same time to within a few minutes. Are they awakened by sensory cues received unconsciously, or is there some "biological clock" that keeps accurate account of the passage of time? Students of the behavior of animals in relation to their environment have long been interested in the biological clock question. Almost every species of animal is dependent upon an ability to carry out some activity at precisely the correct moment. One way to test whether these activities are set off by an internal biological clock, rather than by factors or signals in the environment, is to find out whether the organisms can anticipate the environmental events. The first well controlled experimental evidence on the question was furnished by the Polish biologist J. S. Szymanski. In experiments conducted from 1914 to 1918 he found that animals exhibited a 24-hour activity cycle even when all external factors known to influence them, such as light and temperature, were kept constant.

5. Inventory your own strengths and weaknesses as a writer in terms of the factors discussed in this chapter. To what extent have you been prepared, by previous training and experience, to deal with the kinds of writing situations described in this chapter? Write a short report (250 words) based on this inventory.

6. Write a brief analysis of the audience for the sample long report at the end of Chapter 19. Look carefully at all of the evidence the report offers, both explicit and implicit.

NOTES

1. By permission. From Webster's *New International Dictionary*, Second Edition (p. 1480), © 1957 by Merriam-Webster Inc., publisher of the Merriam-Webster® Dictionaries.
2. By permission. From *Webster's Third New International Dictionary* (p. 1359), © 1986 by Merriam-Webster, Inc., publisher of the Merrian-Webster Dictionaries.
3. Marcia Bartusiak, "Designing Drugs with Computers," *Discover* (August, 1981), p. 47.
4. Bruce Fellman, "Zinc, Copper, and Arthritis," *Prevention* (November, 1981).
5. Douglas Lee, "Slime Mold: The Fungus That Walks," *National Geographic* (July, 1981).
6. From *Practical Technical Writing* by Ritchie R. Ward. Copyright © 1968 by Ritchie R. Ward. Reprinted by permission of Alfred A. Knopf.

2

How Working Writers Write and Revise

In general, people write in one of two ways: either they compose very slowly and revise very little or they compose very quickly and revise slowly. Few experts agree that one technique is inherently better than the other, although there is some evidence that slow composers more frequently have problems with writer's block. This chapter presents a sketch of how professionals write, and then examines some typical problems working writers face and how they deal with them. By improving your understanding of the process of writing, you can become a better writer.

1. The Writing Process

Many students typically approach writing a report as something to be done in one sitting: start with several clean sheets of paper, write until you finish, and then make a clean copy. Because the purpose of the whole exercise is to achieve a grade, and the teacher evaluates the finished product, it may seem natural for you to try to start at the end, with the finished product. But in the last ten years, writing teachers have stressed that writing is most accurately and effectively seen as a *process* with several stages or phases. The model of writing presented here puts those stages in the spotlight.

It's convenient to depict writing as a process with four stages: Plan, Write, Revise, and Edit. But as soon as we do that, it must be pointed out that these stages do not really have a 1-2-3-4 sequence. Their relationship is not linear but rather multiply recursive—they frequently loop back on one another (Fig. 2.1).

Unfortunately, it is difficult to discuss all four stages of the writing process simultaneously, despite the fact that research shows they happen that way. Remember when you read the following discussion that in practice the stages can loop back on one another at any time.

1.1 Planning

Planning includes everything from selecting a topic, to formulating ideas about it, to devising a structure for it. Most people who need to write as part of their jobs are not in the position of having to decide what to write about; in business, topics for writing present themselves as an integral part of the work. If your boss wants you to write a report on the tests of the C-2 cooling fan, the raw material of your report is there waiting for you. In such situations, your first task may be to formulate what you want to say about a topic that has already been determined, and then to find ways to make the words flow. Here are seven *invention techniques* you can use.

1.1.1 **Working from Notes, Not a Vacuum.** If you feel paralyzed when you face a blank sheet of paper, then don't begin that way. As soon as you get your writing assignment, begin keeping careful records. Save everything, from scribbles on scraps of paper to laboratory records. Begin your writing by gathering up all of this prewriting material; look for words, phrases, and sentences you can use. Build the skeleton of your first pages from that material.

Figure 2.1 The Composing Process. Each phase of the process typically loops back on the others.

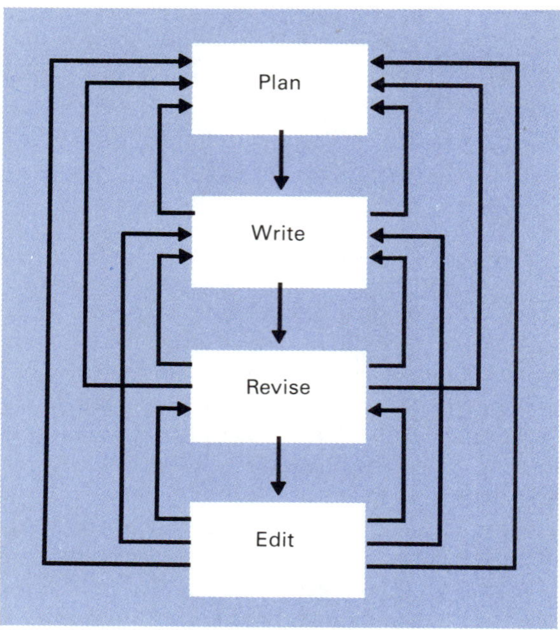

1.1.2 **Brainstorming.** In one way or another, most invention techniques derive from brainstorming. Briefly, brainstorming involves recording every idea that comes into your mind, not filtering out bad ones, not even trying to monitor which ones are better or worse. Later on, you sort your ideas out. If you are doing this alone, you may find that the time it takes to write out ideas slows you down too much; if so, try using a tape recorder to keep track of your thoughts.

1.1.3 **Questioning.** A more systematic approach to invention is called questioning. In the simple version of it, you answer the journalist's traditional questions about your topic: who, what, where, when, how, and why. Who did something, what was done, how, why, and when? Answering these questions may have helped more writers get started than any other technique.

You can improve on the journalist's questions by making and keeping your own set of questions. Start with the journalist's questions, but add more questions of your own to the list, such as

- What is the history of this?
- What is the future of this?
- What is it we're afraid will happen?
- What are the possible courses of action?

Figure 2.2 Cubing. Each side of the cube carries a different instruction.

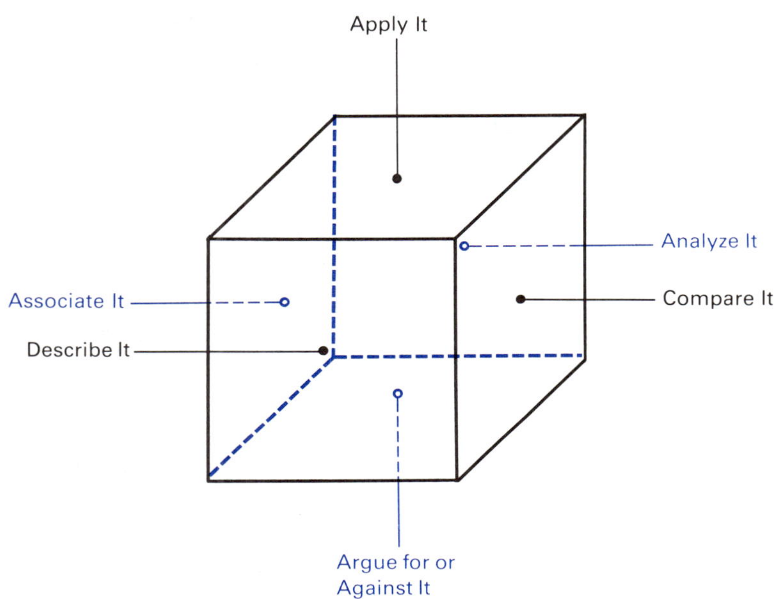

To use this technique, put your report notes aside and brainstorm questions about your topic until you have ten or twenty (or more) listed. Then start answering the questions and use the answers to make the beginnings of your report.

1.1.4 **Cubing.** A more organized form of questioning, called cubing, involves following very specific directions to get your writing started. Start with the image of a cube, as shown in Fig. 2.2.

Each of the cube's six sides carries a specific direction: Describe It, Compare It, Associate It, Analyze It, Apply It, and Argue For or Against It. Beginning with side one, you write as fast as you can following each direction for a set period of time (5-10 minutes). By the time you finish cubing, you will have several pages of ideas and comments on your topic. The only rule is not to stop writing; if you can't think of anything to write, write "I can't think of anything to write" over and over until you do. As with other invention techniques, you should try not to screen what you write. Don't select for good or bad, grammatical or ungrammatical, or smooth or clumsy—just *write*!

1.1.5 **Verbing.** An expanded version of cubing, verbing lets you make your own list of instructions to follow while you're inventing. Use a list of verbs, such as the one in Box 2.1, in the same way you use the instructions in cubing.

Box 2.1 Some Examples of Verbing Words

Build Up
Eliminate
Work Forward
Work Backward
Associate
Classify
Generalize
Exemplify
Compare
Relate
Commit
Defer
Leap In
Hold Back
Focus
Release
Force
Relax
Dream
Imagine
Purge
Incubate
Display
Organize
List
Check
Diagram
Chart
Verbalize
Visualize
Memorize
Recall
Record
Retrieve
Search
Select
Plan
Predict
Assume
Question
Hypothesize
Guess
Define
Symbolize
Simulate
Test
Play
Manipulate
Copy
Interpret
Transform
Translate
Expand
Reduce
Exaggerate
Understate
Adapt
Substitute
Combine
Separate
Change
Vary
Cycle
Repeat
Systemize
Randomize

Source: James Adams, *Conceptual Blockbusting: A Guide to Better Ideas* (New York: Norton, 1980).

1.1.6 **Looping.** Looping can be used as a spinoff from any of the other techniques discussed here. To do looping you must have one paragraph already written. This could be, for example, the paragraph from your cubing that you thought most opened up your topic. You then select (or ask a friend to select) the one line, sentence, or thought that is the central idea of that paragraph, begin a new piece of paper with that line, and write from there. The central idea is the thought that seems most interesting, worthwhile, pertinent, insightful, or otherwise worth expanding. You can do as many loops as you want. You can do three-minute loops, five-minute loops, or ten-minute loops. Most people find that after four or five loops they have found pretty much what they want to say.

1.1.7 **Outlining.** Many writers find that outlining is frequently the most effective way to start writing. An outline usually starts as a brainstormed list, and can end at any point you want it to. Remember that if you are outlining as part of inventing you can make the outline as finished or as rough as you want it to be. Working for your own purposes you do not need to worry about such rules as grammatical parallelism or "a B for everyA." But for any kind of document longer than a couple of pages, working writers usually produce some sort of outline, however rough. Then the report grows from there.

Nearly all invention techniques have certain qualities in common. Most often the goal is to help you be less selective about what to write and what not to write, to assure you not to worry about grammar, punctuation, spelling, and style while writing a first draft. Some people find it too restrictive to call such writing "first draft" and prefer to speak instead of a *zero draft*. In writing a zero draft, you want to write quickly and without detailed planning; you don't want criticism to interfere with creation. Another name for this activity is *freewriting*. The goal of all of these methods is to make a start, to get words on paper any way you can, in order to conquer the fear most people feel when confronted by a stack of blank pages.

1.2 Writing

Whether you do a long zero-draft or only an outline, at some point you will be ready to start putting words into sentences and sentences into paragraphs. That point may be determined by your own feeling of readiness or by the pressure of time. The readiness to begin this process, coupled with some sense of structure and movement toward a goal, characterizes the writing stage of this four-part model. Everything before that point is planning.

A number of factors can affect the writing stage adversely, especially fear and fatigue. Most people write better and more easily when they are not feeling threatened or tired. Unfortunately many students (as well as many professionals) find that the only time they have to write is when they have to work under exactly such adverse conditions. But to the extent that it's in your power, you should try to plan your writing project so that you do not have to work when you are tired or under pressure. This means starting well before your deadline, doing sufficient research, and saving style and grammar concerns for the revising stage. Writing when you are not fatigued means you should plan your use of time for days when you want to write, to allow yourself to write during quality time rather than "totally-exhausted-collapse-at-the-end-of-the-day" time.

Most writers are also sensitive to the medium and environment of their writing. Some people can only compose longhand, others only at a typewriter. Those of us who have made the switch to word processors generally will not write any other way. Some people need quiet, private surroundings, whereas others work much better in crowded, noisy offices or libraries. As your career demands more of you as a writer, it will profit you to know more about where and how you work best, so that you can structure your writing time accordingly.

Perhaps the most important generalization about the writing stage is the one behind this statement, made by working writers again and again: "The first time through I just try to get the subject down on paper, just to see if I've got enough data, and if I can handle what's there. Then after I finish that version I go back and start trying to make it good." As you become more and more experienced as a writer, you will probably learn to demand less and less of your early drafts. Your first written draft is an early stage, not a finished piece; grammar, punctuation, and spelling shouldn't be allowed to deflect or trap your good energy. The focus of your attention during writing should be primarily on content, on capturing and shaping the raw material. *The more aggressively you can approach your first draft, the more you can attack writing it, the better off you will be.*

1.3 Revising

In this model of the writing process, revising holds the key to quality. Although thorough planning will help you generate the right content, as a writer in a professional field much of the content of your writing will be predetermined. Thus composing can become a fairly routine process of "writing it up." The burden of making the report *good*, therefore, falls on revising. Doing a good job of revising requires three things:

1. The *time* to do a good job.
2. The *knowledge* to do a good job.
3. The *will* to do a good job.

This chapter can teach you how to revise effectively; developing the time and will to do so are up to you.

For working writers, revising is the key to successful writing. This chapter focuses on revising for clarity and content more than on revising for grammatical correctness (see Chapter 3 and the Appendix for more on this), but the two clearly reinforce each other in important ways. For example, it's hard to have consistently clear writing without consistently sound (grammatical) sentence structure.

Exhibit 2.1 shows a sample section from a technical report. By seeing both the first draft, with revision marks on it (Ex. 2.1a), and the final copy (Ex. 2.1b), you can see how a typical report changes from first to final draft.

Many of the changes in this report are clarifications of content. If we were to examine more paragraphs from other reports, we would see other kinds of changes. How can we account for the many different kinds of revisions this and other reports show? The first part of this section looks at revision from three different perspectives.

1.3.1 **Perspectives on Revision.** One popular explanation for revision describes it as *"seeing again"* (re-vision), an attempt to look with fresher eyes and fewer preconceived limits. The attempt is to gain a view of the document as a whole, to see whether it fulfills its purpose, to try to see the structure buried beneath the surface, to make alterations that will bring that structure into greater relief. The writer asks "Will this do what it needs to do? Is it right?"; looks for rough stylistic surfaces, ill-matched structures, or vague content, and tries to solve those problems. According to one school of thought, this revision on the global scale is something students often fail to do. Studies have shown that students and other inexperienced or struggling writers restrict their attention to individual words and phrases, missing the larger and more important problems that "seeing again" on a large scale could detect and solve.

Exhibit 2.1a Rough Draft of a Technical Report

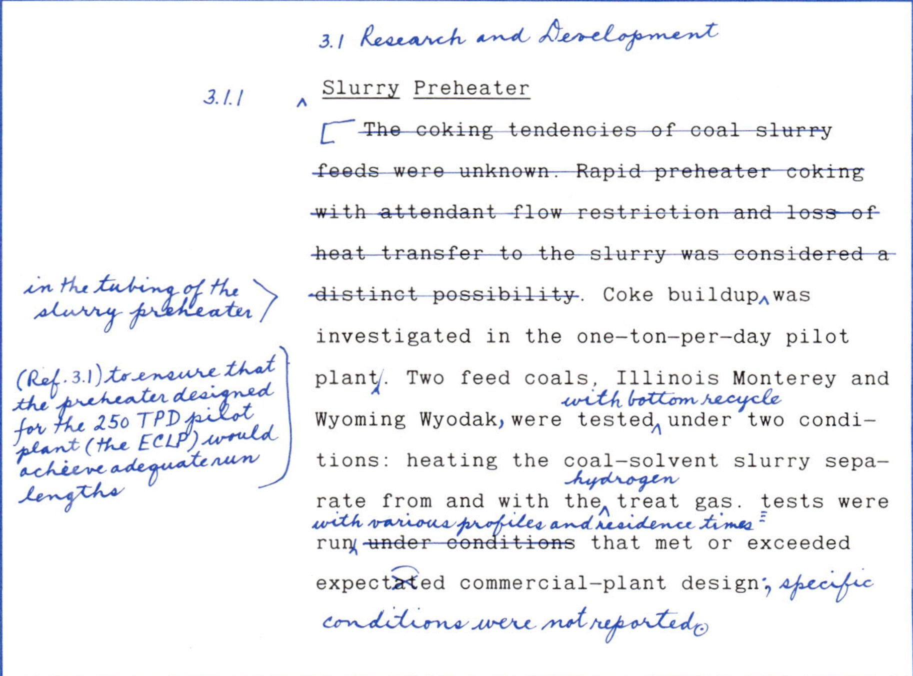

3.1 Research and Development

3.1.1 Slurry Preheater

~~The coking tendencies of coal slurry feeds were unknown. Rapid preheater coking with attendant flow restriction and loss of heat transfer to the slurry was considered a distinct possibility~~. Coke buildup in the tubing of the slurry preheater was investigated in the one-ton-per-day pilot plant (Ref. 3.1) to ensure that the preheater designed for the 250 TPD pilot plant (the ECLP) would achieve adequate run lengths. Two feed coals, Illinois Monterey and Wyoming Wyodak, were tested with bottom recycle under two conditions: heating the coal-solvent slurry separate from and with the hydrogen treat gas. tests were run with various profiles and residence times ~~under conditions~~ that met or exceeded expectated commercial-plant design; specific conditions were not reported.

Exhibit 2.1b Final Version, with Notes and Revisions Incorporated

3.1 *Research and Development*

3.1.1 Slurry preheater. Coke buildup in the tubing of the slurry preheater was investigated in the one-ton-per-day pilot plant (Ref. 3.1) to ensure that the preheater designed for the 250-TPD pilot plant (the ECLP) would achieve adequate run lengths. Two feed coals, Illinois Monterey and Wyoming Wyodak, were tested with bottom recycle of vacuum bottoms under two conditions: heating the coal-solvent slurry separate from and with the hydrogen treat gas. Monterey was also tested without bottom recycle. Tests were run with various temperature profiles and residence times that met or exceeded expected commercial-plant design; specific conditions were not reported.

1.3.2 **Processes in Revision.** Most working writers revise in many different ways and at many different times during the writing process. Five waves (or stages) of revision can be identified—revision for:

1. overall purpose and content
2. overall structure
3. paragraph structure and content

Figure 2.3 The Five Waves of Revision. Whether they occur in 1-2-3-4-5 order depends upon your point of view.

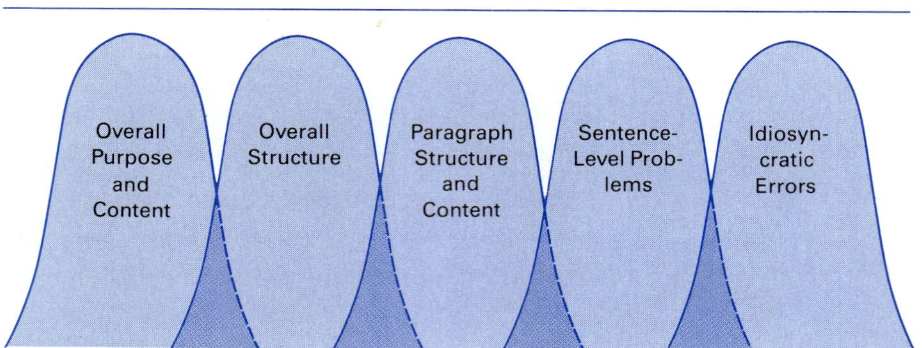

4. sentence-level problems
5. idiosyncratic errors

Like waves in the ocean, waves of revision follow one another closely and regularly, sometimes overlapping and sometimes intermingling (see Fig. 2.3).

1. Revision for Overall Purpose and Content. The first question to ask after you finish your first draft is whether the document serves its purpose. This is the broadest sense of asking whether your report is "right." If it's a proposal, does it contain the right elements to convince your reader to fund your project? If you're writing a final report, have you included all of the important information? Remember that *purpose* and *content* in this sense can be seen from two different points of view: that of the writer and that of the reader. You can't just ask if something is right, you have to ask if it is right for *this* audience. If your purpose in writing a first draft is just to get it all down on paper, the first step in revision is to make sure you've done just that. If you haven't, you should add or move large sections of the report until, in its large dimensions, it fulfills its purpose and has the right content.

2. Revision for Overall Structure. The second step in this ideal revision process involves checking the larger structure of your report. Make sure it has a beginning, a middle, and an end easily discernible to your reader. Suppose you've written a long report with five major sections: Why is the second one after the first and before the third, and why is the fourth not last? Your reader needs to see answers to those questions without having to ask them. Is your report's structure clearly one that will be as easy for your reader to follow as it is for you? If not, make whatever changes are necessary to attain that clarity of structure. This can be done by making structural changes in your report, adding more structural cues, or both.

A more specific form of this stage of revision requires looking at how each individual paragraph links with the paragraphs before and after it. Again, can your reader see the connection? Is there a clear reason why paragraph two is after one and before three? This form of structural testing is demanding and important, and if your report cannot meet this test, you need to work with the structure until it does.

3. Revision for Paragraph Structure and Content. In the third wave of revision, you need to examine the structure and content of each paragraph individually. Do the sentences in the paragraph proceed in an orderly sequence—for instance, from general to specific, or from specific to general? Are generalizations supported by specific examples where necessary? If you need to add, delete, substitute, or move sentences, this is the time to do it. Each paragraph should be a self-contained structural unit, and each paragraph should make a distinct contribution to the report. Ask yourself, "Does this paragraph help get the report where it needs to go?" If the answer is *no*, you may want to move (or drop) the paragraph.

4. Revision for Problems on the Sentence Level. Sentence-level revision proves again and again to be the best way to improve student writing. It may be that the quality of your *sentences* (their clarity, economy, and straightforwardness) tells your reader more about you as a writer (and reviser) than any other feature of your writing. Make these pointers part of your revision habits (see also Chapter 3 and the Appendix for more on this):

- Prefer active verbs to passive verbs, and strong verbs to weak verbs. Watch out for strings of passives or "is" verbs.
- Watch your sentence length and complexity: the longer the sentence, the simpler its structure needs to be.
- Prefer sentence openers to sentence closers, especially when they are critical to the meaning of the rest of the sentence.
- Prefer subject-verb-object sentence structures. Use other structures for variety, but let SVO predominate.
- Use words that end in *-tion* sparingly. Too many of them in any one sentence, especially when paired with a weak verb, make the sentence hard to read.
- Check for grammatical errors, such as sentence fragments and comma splices, that make the report difficult to read and understand.
- Be careful not to put long interrupters between subjects and verbs.
- Watch out for abstractions acting abstractly on other abstractions. Try to rephrase them in concrete terms; if you can't your reader will find them difficult to understand, as well. Can they be dropped without damaging the report?

As you mature as a writer, you need to try to become more aware of your style's strengths and weaknesses, and to learn which particular sentence-level revision techniques you need to pay the most attention to. If you really want to develop a clear, economical, straightforward style, you need to practice revision on the sentence level.

5. Revision for Idiosyncratic Errors. Idiosyncratic errors are those that may be unique to you as a writer. Such errors can be large-scale (you typically spend too long explaining background and delay getting to the point), or pervasive (you tend to overuse "is" base sentences), or of the one-word variety (you confuse *affect* and *effect,* or misspell *occasion*). All of us have errors we commonly make. To grow as a writer you need to keep a list of your typical errors, and as one stage in your revision process you need to check for and (and correct) those errors.

Checking for idiosyncratic errors in this way is especially important for people who are chronic misspellers. If you place yourself in that group, it may well be that you only regularly misspell 100 or 200 words. That number of words is easy to list and check for. There still will be words you misspell, but they will mostly be words you hardly ever use, and that unfamiliarity may itself bring them to your attention as words that you should look up in your dictionary. But with a list of your own most frequently misspelled words, you can work effectively toward eliminating those errors. There are also word-processing packages that automatically call your attention to spelling errors.

By applying the five waves of revision in sequence to the rough draft of your report, you can improve your writing. The five stages do not require you to *rewrite* your paper five times, only to *go over* your paper five times. Use the five waves of revision in sequence, working from the biggest units of your report to the smallest, from overall rightness down to individual words. The process is like tuning an engine, beginning with large-scale changes and working down to fine tuning. Or you can see the process as one like sculpting: first seeing a shape in a block of marble, then chipping away to achieve the large dimensions, and eventually making only the smallest of alterations.

1.3.3 **Gaining a Fresh Perspective.** Student comments about revision unite on two points: "I don't know how to," and "I can't tell when I need to." The five-wave process gives you a good start on the "how to," but does not address the problem of "when to." How can you see *when* your work needs revising?

In order to see the need for revising, you must somehow gain a fresh perspective on what you write. The *worst* possible situation is to write your report, revise it, and proofread it all at one sitting. Revision just cannot occur effectively in that context. The best way to gain a fresh perspective on what you've written, a perspective that will help you see where you need to revise, is to let time pass between writing and revising. If you finish the first draft Tuesday night, plan on revising it Wednesday. If you can get at least a night's sleep between writing and revising, you will be much better at revision.

Other ways to gain a fresh perspective include the following:

Typing: If you start with a handwritten draft and have the time to type an intermediate draft before the final copy, you may find that the places that need revising are much easier to see on the typed intermediate draft than they were in the longhand draft. Something about seeing the words arranged by the typewriter rather than by your hand makes problems easier to spot. Of course, word processing makes this technique especially easy.

Reading: You may find that you can detect problems better by reading your rough draft aloud: that is, your ear may be more critical than your eye. If you try this, it's important to read aloud and try to make the words make sense (the way a good newscaster does), rather than mumbling them.

Taping: If you have access to a tape recorder, try reading your draft as described above while you tape it. Then you can listen really critically on the playback. This will work especially well if you do not simultaneously read the typewritten copy during the tape playback but rather just close your eyes and listen for whether the report makes sense.

Sharing: All these techniques approximate ways to make yourself into someone else, a different person reading the report for the first time and trying to make sense of it. Professionals who write frequently do this by showing their manuscript to a friend (or an editor), just to see if it makes sense. Of course, if you are writing for a class there will be explicit limits on whether or how you share your paper with other readers. An informal survey of writing teachers shows that most do not mind (and some encourage) their students to show rough drafts to other students, with the stipulation that the reader not mark or correct mistakes. The reader responds only to questions such as "Does the thing make sense to you?", or "Do I need to explain more here?" Check with your teacher about whether you can use this technique and what limitations need to be put on it.

The five-wave process of revision presented here does not follow any one writer's particular revision techniques; such techniques are different for each person and each situation. This process is specifically designed as a way for you to learn to revise, based on experience working with students majoring in a number of different disciplines. Use the five-wave process on enough assignments to be sure you know how to handle each wave, and then modify the process to suit your own needs. If you work with it long enough to become competent at each technique, you will become a better reviser and hence a much better writer.

1.4 Editing

Once you're committed to a certain content and have decided that you just can't afford to add more material, you are ready to begin editing. This stage is similar to the revising stage, except that while you often move or take out words, sentences, or paragraphs, you almost never *add* anything. The first rule for editors of other people's writing is never to add anything, and it's also a good rule for editing your own material: If you keep finding places where material needs to be added, you're not ready to edit.

The editing stage involves rechecking every feature of the manuscript, from overall structure to sentence-level revisions. Now is the time to check style, grammar, spelling, and so on, which you were not concerned about while you were inventing and composing; checking these aspects of your report will help you produce as correct a manuscript as possible. Check also to ensure that the heading levels are correct, that the visuals are properly placed, and that the typing is accurate. Chapter 13, "Writing Reports in a Professional Setting," will present the process of editing in more detail.

Working as your own editor means you work as your own proofreader as well. If you do your own typing, you cannot proofread your report efficiently immediately after you type it. The more time you let pass between typing and proofreading, the better job of proofreading you can do. You can proofread best with a sharp pencil in your hand, actually pointing at each word. The slower you go the better. The list below is a good reminder of the most common proofreading errors:

1. Missing letters (*th* instead of *the*)
2. Extra letters (*the*" instead of *the*)
3. Transposed letters (*hte* instead of *the*)
4. Wrong letters
5. Missing words
6. Extra words
7. Transposed words
8. Missing spaces
9. Wrong homonyms (there/their, its/it's, to/too, affect/effect, cite/sight/site, etc.)
10. Missing punctuation
11. Wrong punctuation
12. Sentence fragments

Once again, the four stages of the writing process presented here are artificial divisions in what is for most writers a very intuitive and naturally unified process. But if you focus on each stage more than you have before, and become more conscious of what you are doing when you write, you will become a better writer.

2. Seven Problems Writers Face—and How to Deal with Them

All writers go through a version of the writing process, and all writers sometimes have problems. Here is a list of seven typical problems writers have, and how they cope with them.*

1. *Inspiration Versus Discipline.* It's always tempting to wait to begin until the winds of inspiration blow, but working writers can't afford to. If you want to finish your project, write on a schedule—a certain number of words or pages or hours per day on a regular basis—until you finish.
2. *How To Deal With Deadlines.* All writers must cope with deadlines, and few turn in their work much before the deadline. There are two main differences between amateur writers and working writers:

---

*These seven problems are based on original research conducted by Professor Maxine Hairston of the University of Texas at Austin.

- They set their own deadlines, independent of externally imposed ones.
- They extend their deadlines in both directions—not just pushing the deadline as late as possible but also expanding the time by beginning as early as possible. As soon as you receive an assignment, start on it in some way, if only by jotting down ideas on a note pad. Increase your writing time in *both* directions.

3. *Problems with Procrastination.* Writers often put off writing by straightening their desks, vacuuming the floor, or using a million other "creative avoidance" mechanisms. Working writers use this as part of their preparation for writing. Just as athletes limber up before exercising, so you can use a physical ritual (drinking a diet soda, sharpening a pencil) as a habit that tells your mind that it's time to write. Go along with starting-up rituals, plan them into the way you use your time—but then write.
4. *How Fast To Work.* You can't hope to work to standards if you try to do it all at once, especially at the last minute. Working writers work in stages, with the individual stages written either slowly with slight revision, or rapidly with great revision, but not at the last minute.
5. *How About Preplanning?* Most writers make some kinds of plans before they write, but they keep those plans flexible as they proceed. They view writing as a process *that generates some of its own best ideas* at the same time that they are writing down other, previously conceived ideas. Working writers stay alert for these new ideas and trust their intuitions about when to let those spontaneously generated ideas help shape the document in process.
6. *When To Revise.* Most writers revise *while* they write, and then revise again *after* they write. However, don't fall into the trap of doing so much revising while you're writing that your writing loses its momentum. Most writers learn to produce at least two drafts of anything they write, and there may well be more than two phases of revision involved in producing those two drafts.
7. *How To Deal With Problems.* All writers have problems with their writing at one time or another. Probably the most talked about problem is "writer's block." Working writers who have this problem usually also have developed routine ways of dealing with it, such as working on another part of the piece, writing on something else, talking the subject out into a tape recorder or to a friend, or going back and rewriting the last few pages up to the problem area. Working writers also have external ways of getting help; they turn to friends, family, other writers, or editors. When they need help, working writers seek it out, rather than just withdrawing into a blue funk and not producing.

Learning more about other people's writing processes (and about your own) can help you become a more effective writer. Not only do other people have the same kinds of problems you do, they've also worked out solutions to those problems. Writing can feel like a very solitary occupation, and being able to profit from the experience of other writers is a pleasant reassurance that other people have not only shared problems similar to yours but also overcome them.

EXERCISES

1. For practice with the invention stage, try the following exercise: Pick an everyday object (my favorite is a 32-oz. cola bottle) and write down as many questions about it as you can think of in ten minutes. Brainstorm the list of questions. Don't try for good questions, don't rule out bad ones, just try for quantity. Then do cubing with the bottle as your topic, giving yourself five minutes of writing time for each side of the cube. Finally, pick the cube passage that strikes you as most promising, and do three five-minute loops starting from it.

2. One of the ways to make it easier to write is to practice writing faster. For an exercise in fast composing, choose a simple process you know well (changing a tire, registering for classes, swimming freestyle, etc.) and see how full a description of it you can write in five minutes. Try this with three different processes. Once again, go for quantity of words and ideas, not quality.

3. The best way to learn revising is to do it. Take one of your earlier writing assignments from this class and recopy it, writing on every other line and only on the left half of the page. Now work through it with each of the five waves of revision. If you have access to colored pencils, use a different color for each wave. Finally, make a fair copy and hand both copies in to your teacher.

4. Another way to learn revising is to do it on someone else's writing. For this exercise, trade one of your earlier writing assignments with a classmate. Then proceed as in suggestion 3: Recopy the document, leaving lots of room for revision; put it through the five waves, preferably with a different color for each wave; make a fair copy, and turn in each version.

5. On the next writing assignment you do, try the five waves of revision. As you do it, keep track of what kinds of revisions you do: you may find it handy to classify them as substitution, deletion, addition, and reordering. Write a short analysis of the strengths and weaknesses of your own revision process, based on the results of that study.

6. Find five students in other writing classes and survey them about their writing processes, the problems they face as writers, and how they deal with those problems. Write a brief report summarizing the results of your survey and analyzing their implications. Attach to it as appendixes lists of the specific questions you use. Specify the audience you are writing to—other students, people training to become writing teachers, the general public, or other (specify).

7. Write a report in which you analyze your own writing process. The report should be presented in four drafts:
   1. the planning draft, including whatever initial notes you work from
   2. the first writing draft (the first full draft you write)
   3. the revising draft, either a middle-level draft or changes marked in a different color on the first draft
   4. the final draft with editing completed.

Try to achieve insight into your writing process, and try to show clear and methodical use of the four stages presented here. Specify your audience: your teacher, the public, a graduate student in English doing doctoral research on the writing process, or other (specify).

8. Choose one famous author (Hemingway, Sagan, etc.) and spend two hours in the library trying to find out about his or her composing process, what the problems were, and how the writer overcame them. A reference librarian can help you find interviews with your author. Write a brief report on what you found, in the same four different versions as described in Exercise 7. Specify your audience.

9. Choose two or three journals from your profession, and search back five years in each to see whether there have been articles published on writing problems in your profession. Write a report describing what you find. The context for the report is this: the faculty advisor in your major field is reluctant to accept the credit for this writing course as hours toward your major, and you want to use this report to demonstrate how important writing is in your field.

3

Readability: The Successful Interaction of Style and Audience

Ask a group of professionals from a variety of fields to describe in one word what single most important quality they look for in what they read and what they write, and the answer will probably be *readability*. Ask the same people what they mean by readability, or how it can be achieved, and you might well get as many different answers as there are people in the group.

Many different measures of readability in writing have been tried. Such factors as average numbers of syllables per word, average number of words per clause, and average number of unfamiliar words per 100-word unit have been tried as measures of readability. Still there is no agreement among communication professionals on what constitutes a fair measure of readability.

The weakness of all such quantitative measures of readability is that they fail to take the *audience* into account; a particular passage is readable *only* in relation to a particular audience's interaction with it. This chapter treats readability as the successful interaction of style and audience. Your words need to be arranged in clear, economical, and straightforward patterns; and your words need to be adjusted to the audience in terms of the vocabulary, concepts, and kind and amount of detail you use.

1. Clarity

In your writing as a professional, you should try to convey one and only one meaning. The kind of writing you do on the job is not meant to be expressive or open to interpretation. The writing you do on the job also needs to move along in an orderly way and to give the reader a clear sense of direction. Incorporating these qualities into your writing can help you establish a clear style.

Many times a sentence is not clear because the author has not reread it with an eye to whether it could mean two or more completely different things. Such *ambiguity* often happens because important details (those contributing to precision and exactness) have been accidentally left out of the sentence. The following sentences show some typical violations of clarity:

1. *Example*: "In its notice of proposed rulemaking, the Federal Trade Commission made it clear that they wished to limit advertising messages to children too young to understand their content."
   Discussion: The sentence can have two possible meanings that run counter to each other. Does the FTC want to limit the number of ads to which children are exposed, or does it want the ads to go only to children too young to understand them? Adding just one more detail can make the meaning clear: ". . . they wished to limit the number of advertising messages that are aimed at children too young to understand their content."

2. *Example*: The Industrial Distribution program here was established in 1956 and had its first graduate in 1958. The total enrollment is now 450 students, and last semester it graduated 105 seniors. At the Placement Center, the graduates had a choice of three job offers."
   Discussion: This paragraph seems to be saying that the program sent out 105

seniors to compete for a total of three jobs. The third sentence should read "At the Placement Center each of the graduates had a choice of three job offers." Careless wording of the sentence and the omission of two key words ("each of") changed the meaning of the paragraph drastically from what the writer intended.

Examples 1 and 2 were unclear because the writers accidentally left important details out of their sentences and then failed to reread the passages with an eye toward possible misunderstanding on the reader's part. A good guideline for that kind of rereading is this motto of successful writers and editors in all fields: "Anything that *can* be misunderstood *will* be."

Another common reason for loss of clarity is the careless use of abstract words in your writing, as the following examples demonstrate:

3. *Example*: "A major factor in determining acceptance or rejection of a loan centers around the concept of risk."
   Discussion: The sentence makes a reasonably simple thought needlessly hard to grasp because it uses abstractions instead of specifics—a *factor centers around* a *concept*. It might profitably be rewritten as "Loan officers determine acceptance or rejection of a loan application in part according to the degree of risk involved."

Some writers make careless abstraction a habit, using words like *concept*, *factor*, *aspect*, *facet*, and *centers around* over and over. The person who wrote the sentence in Example 3 followed it with this one:

4. *Example*: "This risk refers to the general picture that is portrayed by all the demand sectors for loans."
   Discussion: Now the concept the factor centered around is referring to a picture portrayed by sectors! Once again, to clarify that sentence would require introducing some tangible, concrete content, beginning with some people to perform the action in the sentence: "By 'risk,' people in the loan business mean. . . ."

Here are more examples of the loss of clarity through careless and needless abstraction and the lack of specifics:

5. *Example*: "Most of my communication skills lie in the verbal facets."

6. *Example*: "The art aspect of photogrammetry relates to the imagination and past experiences of the person working with the photographs."
   Discussion: *Aspects* and *facets* are two of the most overused and meaningless words around today. Often they combine with an equally popular but useless verb phrase, *relates to*.

7. *Example*: "The effect of decentralization in agriculture concerns itself with pricing efficiency and how accurately market news is reported."
   Discussion: Because the writer gives us an *effect* that *concerns itself*, it's hard to determine what the writer actually means to say, which is that the effect of decentralization in agriculture *depends on* pricing efficiency and the accuracy of market news reporting.

8. *Example*: "This area can be broken down into two questions."
   Discussion: As with the other examples, improving this unclear sentence requires introducing some specifics, including someone to do the breaking down and specific identification of the area: "The project engineer then asks two questions: Is the petroleum recoverable? What will recovery cost?"

There are many more ways to write unclear sentences than any book could list. You can find more examples and ways to improve them in the Appendix, "Writing Better Sentences."

2. Economy

When you're trying to improve your style, ask with each sentence you write whether you can say the same thing more clearly. But readers in business or industry demand more than clarity; they also want economy. Without making your writing too dense, try to say the same thing in fewer words. Choose words that will minimize the energy your reader will need just to decode your message. The next four examples show sentences that need revision for economy. (Because violations of economy are also violations of clarity, there is little point in debating whether this or that is a violation of clarity or a violation of economy. The important thing is to recognize that the sentence has a problem and to take steps to fix it.)

9. *Example*: "The area of communication I am interested in learning more about is along the line of technical reports used in industry and government."
   Discussion: This kind of writing characterizes the style of nearly any writer's first drafts. The meaning evolves in the writer's consciousness as the sentence proceeds out onto the page. The completed sentence then has a structure that may not be the most economical way to transmit that thought to the reader. Example 9 needs to be revised for economy, to take the clutter out of its structure and make its meaning clear: "I want to learn more about technical reports. . . ."

10. *Example*: "Effective communication is the key to the success of any project, whether in school, business, or between husband and wife."
    Discussion: By using grammatical parallelism, which means putting similar items into similar grammatical structures, the series of items at the end of the sentence can be shortened: "whether in school, business, or marriage." Look for chances to use parallelism when you have items in a series. You can tighten up the sentence even more by eliminating the verb *is*. One standard way of doing that is to change the basic form from "X is dependent on Y" to "X depends on Y." Another standard form for revising "is" verbs also works here: try flip-flopping the sentence, rotating it 180 degrees around the verb. The sentence that originally read "a . . . b" becomes "b . . . a," which requires changing the verb. Here, instead of "Effective communication . . . success of any project," we use: "Any successful project begins with effective communication, whether in school, business, or marriage." A 20-word sentence with

a weak verb becomes a 13-word sentence with a strong verb, and the writing takes on the kind of crispness and clarity that characterizes the best professional writing.

Many times the way you revise a particular sentence involves a combination of all of the methods discussed here: getting rid of extra words to reveal structure, revising "is" verbs, and being sensitive to places in which your first draft reflects the order of your thinking as it progressed rather than the order through which the reader's thinking needs to progress.

There will also be times when you will have to divide one sentence into two or more. This typically occurs in sentences that just try to say too much:

11. *Example*: "Legal liability is a difficult question consisting of many parts, with the most important being the parties to which the accountant has legal responsibility for unaudited replacement cost information and how much work the auditor can do without increasing his liability."
    Discussion: To improve this sentence, first establish a generalization and then support it with two examples: "Courts look at many factors to determine legal liability. The two most important are (1) the people to whom the accountant has legal responsibility, and (2) the amount of work the auditor can do without increasing his liability."

One last pattern for revising is especially helpful. Most sentences that begin with an "It . . . that" can be made more economical by deleting the entire construction.

12. *Example*: "It is a common occurrence with me that people tend to mistake my name for something else."
    Discussion: Deleting the entire "It . . . that" construction makes the sentence much more economical. All that needs to be saved out of the deleted part is one word to capture the thought's strength or frequency: "People often tend to mistake my name for something else." Depending on how strong a statement the writer originally intended to make, the *tend to* might also be deleted.

As with violations of clarity, there are more uneconomical ways to write sentences than any book can cover. Remember the patterns discussed above, and ask yourself this question: "Can I say the same thing more clearly and in fewer words?"

3. Straightforwardness

One of the most important qualities of effective writing on the job is straightforwardness. Within each sentence, does your writing say things in an order that makes sense, or do you carelessly require your reader to loop back to the beginning to understand the sentence? Violations of straightforwardness, like violations of economy, often occur in first drafts, when the writer is simultaneously writing down thoughts and formulating new ones. Sometimes a whole sentence can wind up backwards, as in the following example:

13. *Example*: "Soils are dynamic bodies having properties that reflect the integrated effects of climate and biological activity on the parent material at the earth's surface, which is modified by the topography of the landscape and the passage of time."
    Discussion: The sentence is too long, with too much involved in it. First we need to separate out its ideas:
    - Soils are dynamic bodies.
    - Those bodies have properties that reflect the integrated effects of climate and biological activity on the parent material at the earth's surface.
    - The earth's surface is modified by the topography of the landscape and the passage of time.

    Next we must ask what the logical order of the thoughts is. The whole sequence should be reversed here, to go from the general to the specific. The reader needs to be led from the most familiar concept—the changes in the earth's surface—to the least familiar—the dynamic properties of soils (which is also the point of the passage). The principle of leading your reader from the known to the unknown is crucial to establishing the straightforwardness of sentences, paragraphs, and reports. The quality of straightforwardness is established according to the *reader's* point of view: "As changing topography of the landscape and the passage of time modify the earth's surface, the parent material of soils at the earth's surface is affected by climate and biological activity. Those effects make soils *dynamic* bodies."

Just as there are recognizable patterns to use when you are trying to make your sentences more economical, so there are patterns that make sentences more straightforward. The next sentence shows a pattern you should recognize as not being straightforward, and you should use another pattern to fix it:

14. *Example*: "Explorations of the importance, physiology, economies, equipment, media, method, requirements during growth, what is happening now, and what the future holds for aseptic methods of propagation are included in the following report."
    Discussion: This sentence, like Example 13, is backwards. It conforms to a recognizable pattern, called *passive voice*. There are two basic voice patterns: active ("X does Y") and passive ("Y is done by X"). In Example 14, the sheer number of things that are having something done to them (explorations, physiology, equipment, etc.), combined with their being listed before the thing being done (they are included in the following report), makes the sentence difficult to read and understand. The thrust of the sentence is backwards. To become an effective writer you need to recognize such sentences and reverse their order: "The following report includes . . . ."

Examples 13 and 14 show sentences whose whole structures need to be turned around. Another kind of sentence that puts last the information that needs to come first is the "roundabout" sentence. It contains a phrase or group of words at the end that need to be at the beginning, while the rest of the sentence's order stays the same. Reordering is necessary when the phrase or group of words in question states the conditions under which the rest of the sentence occurs, as in the following example:

15. *Example*: "Initial attention pertaining to waveform analysis precedes the amplitude modulation discussion in order to provide background information."
Discussion: The "in order to . . ." needs to be first because it gives the preconditions for the rest of the sentence, the purpose behind it. Apart from those words, the rest of the sentence is also unclear; it needs an agent, a person to perform the action: "In order to provide background information, we will discuss waveform analysis before discussing amplitude modulation."

Another typical kind of roundabout sentence promises the reader to do one thing but then breaks the promise, as Example 16 shows:

16. *Example*: "The four main purposes of air traffic control are to prevent collisions between aircraft and ground obstructions; to provide for a fast, orderly flow of traffic; and to provide advice and information useful in planning and executing flights."
Discussion: If you say *four*, your readers will think it odd if you only list three. The clarity problem can be solved by the addition of a few key words: ". . . to prevent collisions between aircraft, to warn of ground obstructions, to provide for. . . ."

One last kind of roundabout sentence really baffles readers. This is the sentence with a head, a tail, and another head. It is actually one sentence that has overrun another:

17. *Example*: "Important fluid levels (gas, oil, etc.) should be checked, body condition, that the controls are functioning properly, and that the engine is running up to specifications are included in the preflight check."
Discussion: Here the writer forgot he had nearly finished one sentence and proceeded to finish another one. The sentence can be easily sorted out once one realizes it's mainly about the preflight check: "The preflight check includes. . . ."

You develop the habit of clear, economical, straightforward writing by building those qualities into your writing during *revision*. As you reread each sentence, watch for opportunities to enhance its clarity, economy, and straightforwardness. The practice sentences in the Exercises section at the end of the chapter will let you measure your ability to use revising to build these qualities into your writing.

4. Basic Audience Adaptation Techniques

Ensuring that your writing is clear, economical, and straightforward means *revising* it specifically for those qualities. When you write only for yourself (for example, in a private journal or in the first draft of a report) you need not worry very much about them. Creating a readable style only becomes important when you plan to show your writing to someone else. In that sense clarity, economy, and straightforwardness are audience-adaptation techniques, techniques that lead to the production of a readable style.

Style and audience interact in complex ways, made still more complex because of a third factor, *purpose*. These three elements have to work together for your writing to be as good as it needs to be. The product of the successful interaction of style and audience is a readable report that fulfills its purpose.

Changes in style mainly have to do with the way you express yourself. But making changes only in style—without changing content—will not necessarily produce writing that is readable for a specific audience. Without changing the fundamental truth behind what you're writing, there are three basic ways to adapt the content of your report to your specific audience; you can adjust:

- vocabulary
- concepts
- kind and amount of detail

The way you handle each of these features will subtly tell your reader whether he or she is your real audience. The key issue is whether you can resist the natural tendency to place your *own* needs, wants, and purposes as a writer above those of your readers. On the one hand, you naturally want to use the words that come into your mind first, to take knowledge of certain concepts for granted, to go into complete detail whenever you want to, and thus to fulfill your own purposes for writing, even if it means accidentally frustrating the reader's purposes. Your reader, on the other hand, naturally wants the vocabulary, concepts, and kind and amount of detail to be adjusted and customized just for him or her. Communication is difficult when reader and writer each clutch personal needs and purposes so tightly; the *report's* purpose can be fulfilled only when there has been a successful negotiation between the reader's purpose and the writer's purpose. Most of that negotiation takes place during the writing process, and the signs of its success include effective style and content adjusted to that specific audience.

4.1 Vocabulary

The most obvious way to adjust to your reader is by controlling the vocabulary you use. How much highly specialized language can you use? Consider this example:

> Aerodynamic tradition derives hydrofoil craft drag as a sum of drag coefficients to produce the drag polar which provides a convenient non-dimensional display of the most pertinent design features affecting craft performance. Coefficients for the drag polar are based largely upon empirical data. When consideration is limited to craft with fully submerged hydrofoils, and hydrofoil wave drag is represented in drag polar form, the total drag for such craft can be expressed analytically with a precision which matches that of the laboratory.(1)

A hydrodynamics expert can understand that fairly easily. For anyone else the specialized terminology makes comprehension difficult or impossible. Many professionals will tell you they wish their colleagues would use a less specialized vocabulary, and even experts often choose not to read a piece because its language is too dense. The question is, "If you really have something to say, why don't you say it so I can understand it easily?"

Specialized technical language becomes undesirable *jargon* when it interferes needlessly with the reader's process of reading and understanding. Identifying jargon is a little like identifying weeds: any plant growing in the wrong place can be considered a weed, and any technical term (or element of an otherwise restricted vocabulary) in the wrong place can be called jargon. Most problems with vocabulary in your writing will involve determining when you can and cannot use technical terminology. Whether you are being precise and professional or dull and pretentious depends partly on the words you use, partly on your purpose, and largely on your audience.

There are all kinds of jargon; every in-group has its own language. Newcomers to any professional field feel strong pressure to use specialized language to show that they are, in fact, insiders. Yet in every professional field there are people at the very top who speak and write in effective, plain English. Those people are admired and respected (and at the top of the profession) in part because of their abilities with language.

One of the interesting and rewarding things you can do to improve your writing is to become more critical of writing by people in your field. As you read professional journals, ask yourself how much of the specialized vocabulary you see is really necessary. Find out who the good writers in your field are, read their writing, and try to imitate it. Remember that in writing the test is effect, not what you prove about your membership in a particular group. Be careful not to use technical vocabulary inappropriately.

4.2 Concepts

Avoiding jargon is mostly a matter of being aware of what it is and how it blocks effective communication. A more subtle problem is using concepts your reader does not understand. Problems with concepts are harder to detect in your own writing than are problems of vocabulary, but they are equally disruptive to effective communication.

Whether your reader will really understand a concept or not is difficult for you to judge. Consider the following definition of plagiarism, written by a university lawyer at the request of a professor. The idea was to hand out to students a definition of plagiarism that would stand up in court. Here is the definition as the lawyer wrote it:

> Plagiarism definition: Any student who copies, reproduces, or in any manner presents the written work of another or others with the intent to cause any person to believe that such work is a product of the student's own mind and effort; or any student with knowledge that any work is that of another who submits same in a form which a reasonably prudent student would know is likely to induce a teacher or other person to believe that the submission is the product of the student's own mind or effort shall be guilty of Scholastic Dishonesty as that term is used in Section 34 of the University Regulations for 1984–1985.

Our attorney is writing for an audience that mirrors him in terms of knowledge, interest, and experience in reading legalese. Although courts and lawyers may understand that definition, students and faculty (outside of law school) generally do not. Is it the legalese that makes the definition able to hold up in court, or can the definition be rewritten for laymen in such a way as to make it clear to them and still hold up in court? If you didn't discuss this definition with a lawyer you probably would not realize that there are two concepts buried in the definition that would be critical in its courtroom use: *intent* and *reasonable prudence*. Any translation of the lawyer's definition into laymen's terms needs somehow to capture those concepts if it is to hold up in court. Here's how one writer dealt with rewriting the definition for a student audience while keeping the concepts intact:

> Any student who either:
> *Copies, reproduces, or in any other manner presents the written work of another person or other people with the intent to cause any person to believe that such work is a product of the student's own mind and effort,*
> Or who:
> *Uses what is known to be the work of another by submitting it in a form which a reasonably prudent student would know is likely to induce a teacher or other person to believe the submitted work is the product of the student's own mind or effort,*
> Shall be guilty of *scholastic dishonesty* as that term is used in Section 34 of University Regulations for 1984–1985.

The problems with the lawyer's definition of plagiarism are common to all kinds of writing for your profession. Under many vocabulary problems there lurk concept problems. The accountant who suggests that her client try "amortizing good will" has more than vocabulary to explain. And the computer-science technician who tries to explain the advantages of magnetic bubble memories to his employer cannot rest after explaining "magnetic" and "bubble" and "memory."

Concepts can be difficult to explain without long digressions. Imagine trying to explain "government by laws, not by people" to a European count from the Middle Ages, or "limited warfare" to a Crusader. Closer to home, ask a management professor to explain "management by objectives," or ask a wildlife and fisheries science professor to explain "maximum sustainable yield." But despite the difficulty of explaining key concepts to your readers, the ability to do so is one of the things that separates effective writing from ineffective, readable writing from unreadable.

4.3 Kind and Amount of Detail

Adjusting the kind and amount of detail you include may be the form of audience adaptation you are most familiar with already. In everyday conversation we automatically adjust the detail we include. You see your listener's attention start to drift away and you immediately hurry on to your point by cutting out details. Adaptation by paring detail is so easy some computers do it. In "Help" files or other settings, you can request a very basic text:

> *Efflorescence*. When a substance evolves moisture upon exposure to the atmosphere, the phenomenon is known as efflorescence. If the substance has a higher water vapor pressure than that of the atmosphere at the given temperature, water vapor is evolved from the substance.(2)

Or you can request more detail:

> *Efflorescence*. When a substance evolves moisture upon exposure to the atmosphere, the substance is said to be efflorescent, and the phenomenon is known as efflorescence. If the substance has a higher water vapor pressure than corresponds to that of the atmosphere at the given temperature, water vapor is evolved from the substance until the water vapor pressure of the substance equals the water vapor pressure of the surrounding atmosphere.
>
> Substances that are ordinarily efflorescent are sodium sulfate decahydrate, sodium carbonate decahydrate, magnesium sulfate heptahydrate, and ferrous sulfate heptahydrate. When the saturated solution of a substance in water has a water vapor pressure greater than that of the surrounding atmosphere, evaporation of the water from solution takes place.
>
> See *Deliquescence* for the converse phenomenon.(3)

How do you tell how much detail to include for any particular reader? You need to balance out two considerations:

1. How much (or how little) does your reader want or need to know?
2. How much (or how little) do you have to say to do justice to the subject?

When you feel those two considerations as forces pulling against each other, then you are becoming aware of audience analysis and adaptation as it must occur in order for you to become an effective writer.

Sometimes you want to do more and the reader wants you to do less; sometimes you want to do less and the reader wants you to do more. Unlike conversations, your writing cannot adjust as the reader goes along. You will have to determine the correct amount of detail the first time. That requires taking your reader's needs and wants into consideration mentally *while* you are writing or revising. It's not like playing chess against yourself in your head, but more like playing chess against someone else in your head. If you can do this successfully, the kind and amount of detail you use will tell your reader that he or she is at the center of your concerns as a writer. *Reader-centered writing* is readable writing. Its opposite, *writer-centered writing*, may be good for diaries, journals, rough drafts, personal letters, or avant-garde novels, but it is not effective in professional work. It sends the message that "I (the writer) am more important than you (the reader) are."

5. How Not To Write Gobbledygook

We've all seen gobbledygook—scientific, or government, or legal, or technical, or any kind of professional writing in which the use of jargon, generally poor word choice, and overly long sentence structures makes the writing unreadable.

The response of most readers to such writing is "Even if I could understand this, it's just not worth the effort." Different kinds of gobbledygook have different names—legalese, medicalese, Pentagonese, and so on. Here's an example of several kinds of Pentagonese rolled into one:

> Any fiscal planning subsystem requires considerable promulgation and synthesis at the division level to ensure efficacy of the relevant data base. Furthermore, the policy of redundant standardization performance implies anticipation of future growth dependence and preliminary evolution testing. Subsequent configuration finalization must function in concurrence with postulated hardware interrelationships and full utilization of integral criteria qualifications. While the purview of this office includes dissemination and characterization of functionally interwoven criteria subsystems, pertinent regulatory guidance, particularly the applicable concomitant sections of CFR 10.58.193, precludes furtherance of fiscal analysis considerations without high-tier functionality assurance. It is therefore necessary that triplicate submittals be availabilized for conceptual checking of utilization commonality.(4)

One way to discuss that passage's lack of readability would be to look at it in terms of clarity, economy, and straightforwardness, as discussed earlier in this chapter. Another way would be to look at it in terms of its audience—is there an audience who would read that and try to understand it? But there are some other criteria for readability that are not as general as audience or style in a broad sense. Although these criteria are generalizations, they provide several good rules of thumb for writers who want to avoid writing such gobbledygook as the passage just cited. These criteria remind you to check for sentence length, stacked nouns or adjectives, and abstract verbs.

5.1 Sentence Length

Frequently when a person produces an unreadable sentence, it will be unreadable in part because it is too long. For writers who are not professionals and who are dealing with complex subject matter, it seems that the longer the sentence the greater the chance that its structure will break down. Of course just what constitutes a sentence that is too long is a debatable point, but many writing specialists use a length of 17 words as a guideline. That is, while it is certainly possible to find very clear sentences longer than 17 words, or to find very unclear sentences shorter than 17 words, as a rule of thumb it's a good idea to look twice at any sentence you write that is longer than 17 words and make sure its structure really carries its weight. Generally that means using a subject/verb/(optional) object structure. (See the Appendix for more on this.)

5.2 Noun and Adjective Stacks

Some writers develop a habit of piling up modifiers in their sentences. This produces strings of words like "fully operationalized bi-directional real-time multiplexer" or "cantilever truss reinforcing gradient sloping beams," and it only takes a couple of phrases like that to tempt the reader not to read any further. When each sentence has two or three such groupings, you get a paragraph of solid, impenetrable gobbledygook. Two things characterize such phrases: the use of too many modifiers for any one phrase and the frequent use of nouns as modifiers. Avoiding the use of such noun and adjective stacks will make your writing more readable.

5.3 Abstract Verbs

One other key element contributes to the making of gobbledygook. The same writers who use overly long sentences and fill them with noun and adjective stacks also usually use weak and abstract verbs. Such verbs are forms of *to be*, *to have*, and other verbs such as *relates to*, *revolves around*, and *centers around*. Avoiding such verbs when they are not necessary to your sentence's meaning will help make your writing more readable.

This chapter has given you many different ways to make your writing more readable. Whether you focus your attention on clarity, economy, and straightforwardness or on controlling sentence length, avoiding noun and adjective stacks, and replacing abstract verbs, the goal is to produce more readable writing. A popular misconception about professional and technical writing would have you believe that it's okay for such writing to be really hard to read because the subject is really complex (or really technical). The principle here is something like "the harder something is to do, the less well you have to do it." Operating under a principle like that, human beings would never have made the ceiling of the Sistine Chapel a timeless masterpiece, or broken the four-minute mile, or eliminated polio, or walked on the moon. You should reject that principle and realize that the tougher the topic you are writing about, the more important readability becomes. As your topic becomes more difficult or more complex, your writing should become *more* readable, not less.

EXERCISES

1. Find a technical paper you wrote before entering this class. Revise it for clarity, economy, and straightforwardness. Turn in both copies.
2. Revise these sentences for clarity:
   a. My educational background basically centers around a B.S. degree in business administration as an accounting major.
   b. I spent two quarters studying the government securities market and three quarters of computer (Basic, Fortran, and Cobol) which will allow me to handle your data processing.
3. Revise these sentences for economy:
   a. It is my hope that this letter will allow you to have a better understanding of my writing.

b. The focal point of my interest is presently directed to achieving a major in Marketing with a double minor in Computer Science and Biological Science.
c. To elaborate, it should suffice to say that this is the only formal technical letter I have ever written.
d. It has been determined through research that the vaccination of adult cattle will nearly eliminate clinical disease.
e. The reason why I am taking this course is because it is required for me to graduate from the university.

4. Revise these sentences for straightforwardness:
   a. The position described in your advertisement of Sunday, October 4, 1986, in the *Washington Post* interested me very much.
   b. In response to your job opening notice concerning geotechnical engineers positions advertised in the Civil Engineering Magazine September 1986 issue, I am submitting my job application letter.
   c. In response to the letter you wrote Dr. Randall, I am applying for the position of Programmer/Analyst described in the aforementioned letter.
   d. By the time you finish reading this letter, statements related to past life, present thoughts, and future hopes should be clear.
5. Revise these sentences according to all three principles:
   a. If the insured exceeds the Benefit Limit due to a certain sickness or injury the insurance company will still pay additional money if you have a totally different sickness or injury from the one which caused you to exceed the Benefit Limit.
   b. Factors that cause a shift in demand curves are a change in the number of buyers, this is caused by population growth or an extension of the market, changes in the income of people and their tastes and preference for their product contribute greatly.
6. Choose any two of the following passages and revise them for clarity, economy, and straightforwardness to fit a layman/executive audience.

A.

The aim of the present work may be bracketed by a series of disjunctions. In the first place, the question is not whether knowledge exists, but what precisely is its nature. Secondly, while the content of the known cannot be disregarded, still it is to be treated only in the schematic and incomplete fashion needed to provide a discriminant or determinants of cognitive acts. Thirdly, the aim is not to set forth a list of the abstract properties of human knowledge but to assist the reader in effecting a personal appropriation of the concrete dynamic structure immanent and recurrently operative in his own cognitional activities. Fourthly, such an appropriation can occur only gradually, and so there will be offered, not a sudden account of the whole of the structure, but a slow assembly of its elements, relations, alternatives, and implications. Fifthly, the order of the assembly is governed, not by abstract considerations of logical or metaphysical priority, but by concrete motives of pedagogical efficacy.(5)

B.

Henry County is hereby authorized to incur indebtedness to the extent of not exceeding $700,000 in aggregate principal amount, and to issue its bonds in evidence of the indebtedness so incurred, for the combined purpose of constructing and equipping a new courthouse and a new jail in said county. Said bonds may be issued only after the question of the issuance thereof shall have been submitted to the qualified electors of said county at an election called for that purpose by the governing body of said county and a majority of said qualified electors voting at said election shall have voted in favor of the issuance of said bonds, which election shall be called, held, conducted, canvassed and may be contested in the manner provided by the then existing laws of the State with respect to elections on the issuance of bonds by counties, provided, however, that if a majority of the qualified electors of said county participating in the election on the adoption of this amendment shall vote for the adoption thereof then the approval of this amendment expressed by the vote in said county in favor of its adoption shall of itself authorize the issuance of the bonds, and in that event no additional election by the electors of said county shall be required to authorize the issuance of said bonds. In the event the majority vote in said county on the adoption of the amendment is against the adoption hereof, or in the event the majority vote at any election held in said county pursuant to the provisions of this amendment after its adoption is not in favor of the issuance of the bonds proposed at such election, the governing body of said county may from time to time call other elections hereunder on the issuance of said bonds, but not more than one such election shall be held during any period of twelve consecutive months. The power to become indebted and to issue bonds in evidence of such indebtedness shall be in addition to all other powers which the said county may have under the constitution and laws of the State, and any bonds issued pursuant to this amendment shall not be chargeable against the amount of indebtedness which said county may incur under the constitution and laws in effect prior to the adoption of this amendment.(6)

C.

Should purchaser fail to pay said indebtedness or any part thereof when due, or breach this contract, or should seller feel itself or chattels insecure, or if any execution or writ be levied on chattels or any purchaser's property, or a receiver thereof is appointed, or if a petition under the Bankruptcy Act or any Amendment thereof should be filed by or against purchaser, the entire unpaid balance shall at once become due and payable at seller's election, and seller may, without notice or demand, by process of law or otherwise, take possession of chattels wherever located, and retain all moneys paid thereon for the reasonable use of chattels and purchaser will pay for necessary repairs because of damage thereto.(7)

D.

Any person, firm, corporation or association or agent or employee thereof, who, with intent to sell, purchase, or in any wise dispose of, or to contract with reference to merchandise, real estate, service, employment, or anything offered by such person, firm, corporation or association, or agent or employee thereof, directly or indirectly, to the public for sale, purchase, distribution, or the hire of personal services or with intent to increase the consumption of or to contract with reference to any merchandise, real estate, securities, service, or employment or to induce the public in any manner to enter into any obligation relating thereto, or to acquire title thereto, or an interest therein, or to make any loan, makes, publishes, disseminates, circulates, or places before the public, or causes, directly or indirectly, to be made, published, disseminated, circulated, or placed before the public, in this state, in a newspaper, magazine, or other publication, or in the form of a book, notice, circular, pamphlet, letter, handbill, poster, bill, sign, placard, card, label, or over any radio or television station or other medium of wireless communication, or in any other way similar or dissimilar to the foregoing, an advertisement, announcement, or statement of any sort regarding merchandise, securities, service, or employment, who includes any false or misleading statements or assertions, shall be guilty of a misdemeanor.(8)

E.

For the preceding year or two, man has been witnessing a dynamic and explosive war of the newly developed schematic noise reduction systems, but the struggle is unceasing against a background of impending digitalization. From the digital point of view, binary playback is inevitable and the skirmishes over analog noise reduction merely a rearguard action to forestall obsolescence. The analogist, whose attitude is distinctly favorable, assumes that the three C's will anchor the digital Hun at bay for an equally elongated period: cost, complexity, and compatibility. And then there's vested interest. With untold billions of analog discs and tapes actively engaged in the world's household hi-fidelity systems, the conventional medium will, at ultimate, demise a lingering death of attrition many years after the successful launch of a home digital medium.(9)

7. Select a 100–150-word sample from one of the extracts from long reports in Chapter 13 or from the student report at the end of Chapter 19 and rewrite it for a lower-level audience. Begin by specifying the audience you are rewriting it for and the reasons they have for reading the passage.

8. You have applied for an entry-level job in your field of choice and now are one of the last three candidates. Your prospective employer has now asked each of the three final candidates to write a brief letter explaining your work-related communication skills (both writing and speaking). Write the letter, and remember to support any claims or generalizations you make. (In a short note on a cover sheet, explain to your teacher what profession you're planning to enter.)

NOTES

1. H. Raymond Wright, Jr., and Frank W. Otto, "Hydrofoil Craft Drag Polar," *Journal of Hydronautics* (October, 1980), p. 111.
2. and 3. This example was adapted from *Van Nostrand's Scientific Encyclopedia*, Fifth Edition (New York: Van Nostrand Reinhold Company, 1976), pp. 864–865. Reprinted by permission.
4. Used as an example of bad writing in Bill Minkler, "Let me speak to your computer," *Nuclear News* (Nov., 1980), p. 240.
5. Father Bernard Lonergan, *Insight*.
6. Amendment 237 to the Alabama State Constitution.
7. Part of a standard sales contract.
8. *Printer's Ink* model statute, 1945.
9. Robert Long, "Tape and Tape Equipment—A Time of Change," in *High Fidelity* (Sept., 1981).

PART II

Letters and Memos

Whether you're an engineer or an accountant, the business letters you write can make or break your day, week, month, or career. Many people new to the working world dread writing business letters, put off doing them, take time with them they can ill afford, and as often as not, wind up doing a poor job anyway. Try talking to a competent, trained professional about his or her problems with writing business letters. Beneath that smooth, professional surface, you often find a mass of anxieties and fuzzy ideas about how to write a good letter. Yet a professional in any field who cannot write effective business letters is like a tennis pro without a backhand.

What makes a business letter effective? There are two main factors:

1. It must do its job—fulfill its purpose—for both reader and writer.
2. It must be efficient for the writer; it must not take time or energy (or cause stress) out of proportion to its importance.The three chapters in Part II show you how to write effective business letters—letters that you produce efficiently and that get results.

The organization of Part II is a miniature of this book as a whole. There are too many different kinds of business letters to give specific attention to each individually: letters of inquiry, complaint, adjustment, good will, application, rejection, information, and reminder, to name just a few. Therefore these chapters first present principles that apply to all types of business letters. Then the needs that all business letter writers share get specific attention (for example, how to ask and how to say no). Finally, one most important kind of letter—the job application with resumé—is discussed in detail. The goal is to teach you the principles that will help you successfully adapt the basic patterns to your own needs.

A Note on Telephones

Every so often you hear, "I won't use letters; all my business will be done on the phone." It is an interesting idea, but hardly ever correct. Yes, telephones are an essential part of any modern professional's working day, but four closely linked points should be made about that:

1. Even if you set something up by phone, you almost always should write a letter confirming the arrangements. Not only does the follow-up letter bring to light or clear up any misunderstanding, it also provides a valuable record for future reference.
2. The phone is a tricky medium. Because you cannot see the person you're talking to, and because you cannot control what comes up and what doesn't (the way you can in letters), there are many complications inherent in the medium.
3. It is especially not a good idea to handle important matters *solely* by phone. Without the positive and negative feedback of body language or eye contact that go with direct face-to-face discussion, there are too many possibilities for misunderstanding, and too many possibilities for that misunderstanding to go undetected.
4. It is even worse to try to convey any kind of bad news over the phone; the impersonality that goes with the medium is almost insurmountable. If you must send a negative message, the phone should be your *last* choice. Use letters rather than the telephone, but prefer face-to-face over both.

It clearly is a good idea for people to use phones in their businesses, but plan on combining your use of the telephone with good, effective business letters.

4

Principles for Business Correspondence

1. **Proper Form in Correspondence**
   - 1.1 Basic Elements of Business Letters
     - 1.1.1 Margins
     - 1.1.2 Typing
     - 1.1.3 Heading
     - 1.1.4 Inside Address
     - 1.1.5 Subject Line
     - 1.1.6 Salutation
     - 1.1.7 Body
     - 1.1.8 Closing
     - 1.1.9 Supplement Line
     - 1.1.10 Second and Succeeding Pages
   - 1.2 A Note on Record Keeping
   - 1.3 Proper Form in Memos
2. **Principles of Business Correspondence**
   - 2.1 Solicited Versus Unsolicited Correspondence
   - 2.2 What To Do First and Last: Statement of Purpose and Action Closing
   - 2.3 "You" Attitude
   - 2.4 Reader Benefits
   - 2.5 Negative Messages
     - 2.5.1 Obvious Negative Messages
     - 2.5.2 Hidden Negative Messages
   - 2.6 Positive Emphasis
   - 2.7 Good Will
   - 2.8 Summary
3. **Business Goals and Human Goals**

   Exercises

Figure 4.1 The Force of Custom The writer violates custom to say one kind of thing; the reader may see the violation as a very different kind of statement.

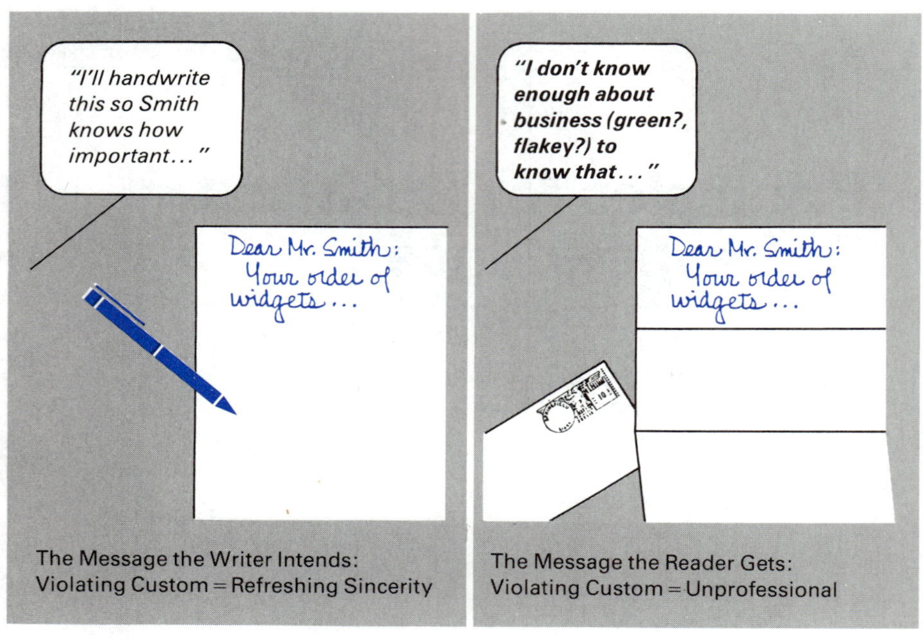

"I'll handwrite this so Smith knows how important..."
Dear Mr. Smith: Your order of widgets...
"I don't know enough about business (green?, flakey?) to know that..."
Dear Mr. Smith: Your order of widgets...

The Message the Writer Intends: Violating Custom = Refreshing Sincerity

The Message the Reader Gets: Violating Custom = Unprofessional

This chapter will give you a working knowledge of elements common to all kinds of business letters: proper forms and principles. Custom dictates how you deal with some of them. For instance, if you double-space your business letter instead of single-spacing it, or you write it in longhand instead of typing it, your letter may strike such an odd note when first opened that the message you intended to send may never really be considered. The message you are trying to send may be fine, but the message the reader gets may be only that you aren't really very professional. Figure 4.1 dramatizes the force of customary elements in business correspondence.

Although some elements of business correspondence seem to be dictated by custom and require only imitation of good models, others require considerable thought, vary from one person to another and from one situation to another, and create considerable debate among professionals. Chief among these may be the issue of negative messages, or how to say something the receiver may not want to hear. For example, how do you write a letter telling a customer that his account is past due and do it so that it increases the probability that he will pay up?

Anyone who has ever gotten an "account past due" letter knows the first impulse that races through the brain: "Well if they're going to get tough about it they can just wait another week or two." Maybe the only thing professionals agree on about negative messages is that there is no single right way to send them. Despite the philosophical nature of such concerns, the person who has learned how to transmit negative messages effectively, how to move the reader in a positive direction, will find that business and industry will reward that ability. Beyond that, the ability to use letters to gain people's cooperation and good will—even under adverse circumstances—is the mark of a fully effective communicator, a very special kind of person.

1. Proper Form in Correspondence

Maybe the best way to explain the importance of using proper form in your business correspondence is to compare it to having the right clothing and equipment for various sports. If you invite your friends over to play volleyball, and if they really are good volleyball players, they may not be impressed by your plastic volleyball and flimsy backyard badminton net (you need a leather ball and a very strong, very tight net made especially for volleyball). It may seem unfair to be judged by appearances, but the leather ball and special net really perform much better. Similarly, in business letters there is usually an important function behind the appearance, but only serious students of the subject may realize it.

What important functions could something like the placement and content of an inside address have? Some of these functions might be:

- to ensure that the letter goes to exactly the right person, even if the envelope has been thrown away
- to ensure that the person who receives the letter realizes you know his or her position in the firm
- to establish a certain level of formality or familiarity

Behind each of the following matters of form there are several good reasons. But remember, even if you cannot think of the reasons, the power of custom, of presenting a safe and familiar appearance, should not be dismissed lightly.

1.1 Basic Elements of Business Letters

The basic elements of form in business letters include the inside heading, inside address, subject line, salutation, body, closing, and supplement line(s). The following paragraphs explain each of the key points in detail. Exhibit 4.1 demonstrates one good form (unblocked) with each part labeled. There are a number of other popular forms for letters. Exhibits 4.2 through 4.5 show the block form, the military form (modified), the simplified form, and a typical letterhead form. The decision about which to use should be based on (1) which form you are comfortable with, and (2) which form you think will appeal to the reader.

1.1.1 **Margins.** Consistently use margins of 1 to 1 1/2 inches all around your page. The white space makes your letter more attractive visually, and it gives your reader a chance to make notes in the margins.

Exhibit 4.1 The Unblocked Form This is a very traditional letter form, still widely used.

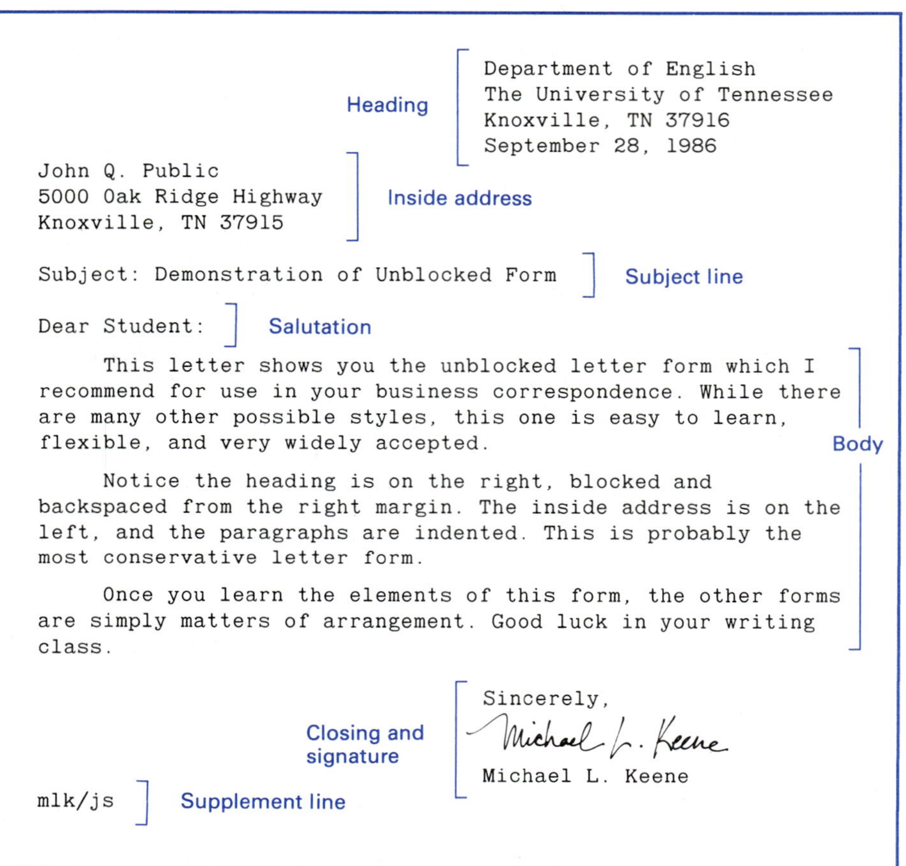

Department of English
The University of Tennessee
Knoxville, TN 37916
September 28, 1986

John Q. Public
5000 Oak Ridge Highway
Knoxville, TN 37915

Subject: Demonstration of Unblocked Form

Dear Student:

This letter shows you the unblocked letter form which I recommend for use in your business correspondence. While there are many other possible styles, this one is easy to learn, flexible, and very widely accepted.

Notice the heading is on the right, blocked and backspaced from the right margin. The inside address is on the left, and the paragraphs are indented. This is probably the most conservative letter form.

Once you learn the elements of this form, the other forms are simply matters of arrangement. Good luck in your writing class.

Sincerely,

Michael L. Keene

Michael L. Keene

mlk/js

1.1.2 **Typing.** Your business letter must be typed, on good paper (at least 20 percent rag content), using a clean typing element and reasonably fresh ribbon. Your letter should be single-spaced in blocks, with double spaces between paragraphs, and double (or more) spaces between heading and inside address, between inside address and subject line, between subject line and salutation, and between the body and the closing. For a one-page letter, you should try to arrange the spacing to put the body in the center of the page. If the letter is more than one page, use the entire page, leaving a bottom margin.

1.1.3 **Heading.** If you do not use letterhead paper, you should place your address and the date in a single-spaced block. If you abbreviate your state, use the Postal Service's official abbreviation. The heading should begin 1 to 1 1/2 inches down from the top of the page and far enough in from the right edge of the page for the right margin to be 1 1/2 inches. If you want to emphasize the date, skip one

Exhibit 4.2 The Block Form Everything begins at the left margin.

```
312 Left-Hand Canyon Road
Boulder, Colorado 47165
August 17, 1986

William Devereaux
Attorney
1512 Oak Terrace
Des Moines, Iowa 50321

Dear Mr. Devereaux:

As we discussed on the telephone yesterday, this letter
confirms my acceptance of the Johnsons' offer for my house on
Patterson Street. Their offer of $90,000 is just what I had
hoped the house would bring.

Please use the power of attorney I sent you to close the deal
at your convenience. Any time before the end of the month will
still keep me from having any problems with insurance, etc.
And as we also discussed, please deposit the check with the
B. F. Wilson office there in Des Moines. Charley Thomas of
that office handles my account and is expecting the check.

If you have any questions, call me at the number you have for
me here in Boulder. Thank you again for your help. Please also
send me a copy of the closing papers as soon as the deal is
finished.

Sincerely,
Kevin J. O'Farrel

Kevin J. O'Farrel
```

line between it and the rest of the heading. Most letterhead paper needs only a date typed in the appropriate place (see Exhibit 4.5).

1.1.4 **Inside Address.** The inside address tells the person opening the letter exactly who is to read it. This part should be at least double-spaced down from the heading, in a single-spaced block beginning at the left margin. It should include the reader's name (and title, if any), corporate affiliation, and address.

1.1.5 **Subject Line.** Many letter writers use a subject line between the inside address and the salutation to inform the reader of the point of the letter immediately. The advantage is that a reader, seeing the subject at a first glance, can decide whether to read the whole letter now, put it off until later, or route it to someone else. The disadvantage is that, to many readers, it makes the letter look like a memo

Exhibit 4.3 The Military Form (Modified) This form is very orderly, but too severe for some people.

```
Date:       April 10, 1986
To:         Wilson Parnell
            District Supervisor
            Acme Testing Labs
            1432 East Magnolia
            Norman, OK 73069

From:       E. C. Wyatt
            Regional Coordinator

Subject:    Shipment of Test Samples

Purpose. This letter is to confirm that I have received your
request for a change in the way we ship the test samples from
the lab here in Atlanta to you. As you suggest, beginning with
the May shipment we will ship by Rapid Express instead of
Acme.

Action. We will ship by Rapid Express, following our usual
policy of shipping on the first of every week. I hope the
change really does result in the cost savings you estimate. If
there are problems with these next shipments, just let me know
and we will find another shipper.

Thanks for the good suggestion.

                                    Sincerely,
                                    E. C. Wyatt
                                    E. C. Wyatt
                                    Regional Coordinator
```

and makes it seem too curt. If you choose to use a subject line it should be short; important words should be capitalized; and it should always be phrased positively.

1.1.6 **Salutation.** At least two spaces below the last line of the inside address (or the subject line, if you use one), you should greet your reader. Again custom dictates: Begin with "Dear Mr. Smith" or "Dear Sir" and end with a colon. Use a comma in place of the colon only if you are on a first-name basis with your reader. You should also be aware of the possibility that "Dear Madam" will match your reader better than "Dear Sir." And there may be times when you need to use "Dear Ms. Smith," although you may offend some people as much by using "Ms." as you do others by *not* using it. Custom has not yet firmly established a formal feminine singular greeting. Suppose your letter is to the editors of *Ms.* magazine; obviously "Dear Sir" would not do. To the extent that there is any established usage, it points to "Dear Mesdames," the French plural. Many professionals would say,

Exhibit 4.4 Simplified Form A growing number of people use some variation of this for all but their most formal business letters.

1212 North Avenue
Minneapolis, MN 35496

February 15, 1986

Wiscossett Town Board
Wiscossett, WI 54841

REQUEST FOR REAL ESTATE INFORMATION

My wife and I have often driven through your town on our summer vacations, and now we would like to consider buying a summer cottage on one of the lakes nearby. Will you please send us the names of four or five local realtors who deal in lake cottages around Wiscossett?

We are looking for a modest (2 bedroom, 1 bath) home, but it needs to have lake frontage, and it needs to be reasonably secluded. It need not be winterized.

Thank you for your assistance. I hope we will hear from you soon, and that we might in the future be among your neighbors.

Tom Parsons

Tom Parsons

however, that it would be better to avoid the problem somehow, such as using "Dear Editors." Another way to avoid this problem is to switch to the simplified letter form (see Exhibit 4.4), which does not use a salutation.

1.1.7 **Body.** The body of your letter should begin on the second line below the salutation. In the unblocked form, each paragraph should be indented. Normally your letter will be only one page long, which gives you enough space for three or four short paragraphs and the closing. In business letters, one-sentence paragraphs are fairly common, especially in the last paragraph.

1.1.8 **Closing.** Begin your closing at least two spaces below the last line of your last paragraph. Begin far enough to the left that the longest typed element in the closing ends at the margin. In most instances the traditional "Sincerely" is the right choice. Depending on the situation, you may wish to use "Respectfully submitted" or "Thank you," but be wary of stretching for a level of formal, eighteenth-century style the rest of your letter does not have with such closings as "Your humble servant." Leave enough room for your signature (three or four lines), then type your name. It is often a good idea to type your job title below your typed signature. Be sure to sign your name. Many people still believe ball-point signatures look tacky; certainly there is still no substitute for the appearance

Exhibit 4.5 A Typical Letterhead The centered letterhead combines well with an unblocked letter form. A left-side letterhead would work better with block or simplified form.

Thomson Heating, Inc.
1551 Laurel Lane
Duluth, Minnesota 54840
Phone (613) 841-4880

January 13, 1986

Gary Powers
Personnel Manager
Wallace Motors
Duluth, MN 54839

Dear Gary,

Thanks for sending the people from Ace Labs to us for their new heating and cooling equipment. We visited their plant last week, and it looks like we'll be able to do quite a bit of work for them.

I hope we have the chance to return the favor soon. In the meantime, if I can do anything at all for you, just give me a call.

Sincerely,

J. Thomson

Jim Thomson
Owner

a good fountain pen makes. Some fine-point markers also leave a strong and fluid line.

1.1.9 **Supplement Line.** In the lower left corner of the page, at least two lines below the typed signature and at least an inch up from the bottom, you may want to use another line (or lines), usually called a supplement line. Any or all of the following may be used. You may have typist's initials ("MLK/js"—typed for Michael L. Keene by John Smith). You may add an enclosure notation ("Enclosure") or a list of enclosures ("Enclosures: Final Cost Estimates"). There may be copy notations ("xc" has come to stand for photocopy; "cc" means carbon copy), and finally there may be a personalizing note or a postscript.

You would not normally want to use a "PS" in a business letter; you don't want to look like someone who has such last-minute changes of thought. If you think of something else important after the letter has been typed, you should probably retype it and incorporate the new material.

There is one very important exception to not using closing notes. Many business letters are recognized by the people to whom they are sent as form letters,

Exhibit 4.6 A Stock Letter Only the name is personalized.

Dear Jane Smith:

As you may be aware, we have recently acquired controlling interest in ABC Printing. Their facilities and personnel will be added to ours, and our customers will be better served by this addition.

While this should in no way affect your position in our company, we wanted you to hear the good news directly from us. The addition of ABC Printing should give us many more opportunities to make Consolidated Communications the leader in the field.

Sincerely,

Donna Banrow

Donna Banrow
Vice-President

db/js

with only names, titles, dates, and such inserted as they are needed. The letter shown in Exhibit 4.6 is one such stock letter.

While you may often use such a letter, fully aware the reader will recognize it as a form letter, you can ease your reader's feelings by adding a personalizing note as the bottom, as Exhibit 4.7 shows.

Exhibit 4.7 A Personalizing Note Such notes become more and more common as stock letters are used more and more.

should give us that many more opportunities to make Consolidated Communications the leader in the field.

Sincerely,

Donna Banrow

Donna Banrow
Vice-President

db/js

Forgive the form letter, Jane — there are just too many people to tell. Why don't you come by next week and we'll talk about some ideas I have for your next project?

Exhibit 4.8 A Continuation Page Second and succeeding pages begin this way.

```
Jane Smith                    2              November 13, 1986


and that is why the shipment as ordered never came through. I
suggest that in the future we accompany the shipments with
invoices clearly stating the type and number of parts shipped.
```

1.1.10 **Second and Succeeding Pages.** There will be times when you cannot say everything you need to say on one page. In those instances, place the following information one inch (six lines) from the top of the second (and any succeeding) page(s): At the left margin, the date. Then, 1 1/2 inches from the top of the page (three lines) below the name, page number, and date), continue the body of the letter. Business letters of more than one page should be paperclipped together, not stapled. Exhibit 4.8 shows a typical continuation page.

1.2 A Note on Record Keeping

Whether your letter seems important or not, you should always keep a copy, even if it is only an uncorrected carbon. Again and again this will pay off for you as customers lose original estimates, as you try to remember exactly what you said to prospective employers, or as someone questions the exact date your letter was sent. Too many people begin keeping copies only after several bad experiences caused by the lack of copies. You will have an advantage if you begin keeping copies now.

1.3 Proper Form in Memos

The nature of your audience tells you whether to use a letter or a memo: memos are in-house (sent to a person in your own firm or department), and letters are sent outside the firm. In some businesses and industries, be cautious about sending memos too many steps up the organizational chain of command. Obviously, a shipping room clerk would be ill advised to send a memo to the Chairman of the Board. Similarly, a student petitioning the Dean to count FORTRAN as a foreign language should send a business letter, not a memo. The following example shows one good memo form; there are many others (see Exhibit 4.9).

Remember that your choice of words and phrases creates as big an impact in memos as it does in letters. Choose the way you approach your reader carefully,

Exhibit 4.9 A Typical Memo Form Memo forms vary widely from company to company.

June 15, 1986

TO: Employee Members of "Basic Plus" Health Plan
FROM: Denise Walker, Program Administrator
SUBJECT: Extended Benefits for Families

From June 15 until July 15 you can increase the coverage on your immediate families to include dental care with no initial enrollment fee. For the average member, this means that for an extra $8/mo. your spouse and children living at home can have the same schedule of benefits for their dental care which you now enjoy.

Should you wish to take advantage of this limited offer, contact my office at Extension 5411. Remember, the offer expires July 15, 1986. Prompt action on your part will assure you of full dental coverage for your immediate family at a very low cost.

and avoid the temptation to dash off hasty, abrupt commands or complaints in memos. All the principles of business correspondence discussed in the next section apply to memos as well as to letters.

2. Principles of Business Correspondence

If the matter of proper form seems almost totally controlled by custom, and if that frustrates you because it leaves little room for your own creative thinking, take heart. The principles of correspondence are almost endlessly debatable. Depending on the situation, each principle applies in a different way and to a different degree. The principles are presented here in sequence from the least debatable to the most debatable. (As you might expect, the most debatable ones are often the most important.)

2.1 Solicited Versus Unsolicited Correspondence

From the reader's point of view, all business correspondence can be placed in one of two groups: *solicited* or *unsolicited*. Your reader either has or has not asked to hear from you. In terms of effect on the reader, this distinction is vitally important.

Most readers at least mildly resent unsolicited business correspondence, and in the face of that initial negative message your task as a writer is considerably tougher. Any letter that can follow its salutation with the three magic words, "As you requested," makes an initial good impression on the reader; everything else that letter does is easier.

Think of the way you read your own mail. Many of us first read the letters from friends and people we know, the letters we've somehow expected. Then later, when everything important has been done, we read the unsolicited mail. Thus if you want your letters to be as effective as possible, you want them to be solicited letters. You begin the body of the solicited letter with "As you requested" or "As we discussed on Thursday, August 12," or some such *contact phrase*. This phrase reminds the reader of earlier contact with you and helps create a favorable predisposition toward the rest of your letter.

Although your reader will mentally categorize your letter as either solicited or unsolicited, as the writer you actually have some freedom to move otherwise unsolicited letters into the solicited category. That is, from the writer's point of view the situation is not this:

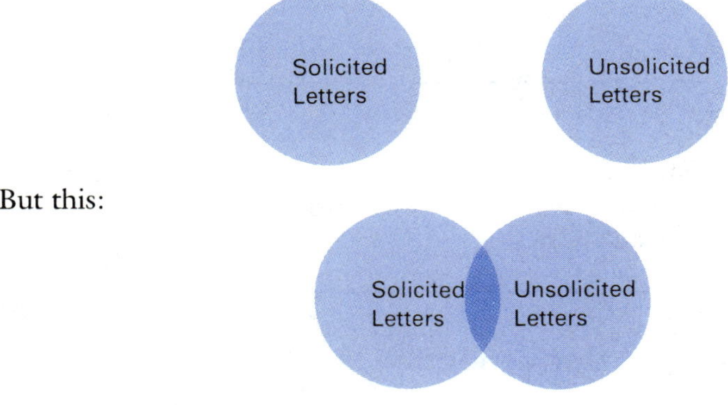

Although there will be times when your letter must be unsolicited, there are other times you can move it over into the solicited category. It is worth the effort to avoid sending unsolicited letters, perhaps by making an initial telephone call or by securing an introduction and reference from a third person who knows you both. Then you would have the contact phrases "As we discussed" or "Jim Smith in your Chicago office suggested that I contact you concerning. . . ."

In these and many other ways you can work toward moving your otherwise unsolicited correspondence to the solicited category. If you really must write unsolicited correspondence, remember that all the elements of the letter are precarious to handle because it is unsolicited (unless it is a "good news" letter, as discussed in Chapter 5, Section 1.4). In unsolicited correspondence, each principle is trickier to deal with. Reader benefits must be made clearer sooner: making your own purpose clear is more delicate; ensuring a return message is harder; *you* attitude makes a bigger difference; negative messages seem to be flashing red lights; maintaining a positive emphasis and good will takes more work; and the whole letter needs to be more persuasive.

2.2 What to Do First and Last: Statement of Purpose and Action Closing

Nothing aggravates people who receive business letters more than letters that "beat around the bush." State your letter's purpose plainly in the first paragraph—if possible, in the first sentence. Often you need to tell your reader not only why you are writing but also what you hope the reader will do in response.

Suppose you want to write for more information about a new word-processing software package you have seen advertised. You might begin your letter:

> I would like more information about the new PhraseMaster word-processing package.

Your letter would probably bring you a more satisfactory response if you detail specifically what you want the reader to do:

> I would like more information about the new PhraseMaster word-processing software. Would you please send me whatever brochures you have available, including. . . .

Adding the second sentence that lets the reader know exactly what you expect the next step to be increases the chances that the response you get will be the right one.

In a longer letter, you would put last the line(s) that lets the reader know exactly what needs to be done next. This principle—the action closing—is as important as putting the statement of purpose first. Even if a whole paragraph earlier in the letter detailed expected future actions, the last one or two lines restate briefly what you are requesting to be done.

The action closing, like all of the principles discussed here, can actually take many different forms. One of the most interesting—because it shows how precise the applications of these principles can become—is the "resale" ending. The concept of resale is borrowed from the field of executive selling. Any computer (or yacht) salesperson worth his or her hardware will try to end each encounter with a customer with resale, a phrase or line that lets the customer know exactly what will come next. It paves the way for future communication, providing the contact phrase that will make the follow-up communication solicited instead of unsolicited. In the simple letter we are discussing here, "I hope to hear from you soon" would conform to the principle of resale, but it would be better to give that line some impact: "Our office is considering purchasing a new line of equipment, and your product is one we want to consider very carefully. I hope to hear from you soon." This time the reason behind the resale is explicit.

A computer salesperson, writing an answer to a request for information, might add, "I will be in your city next week; why don't I call your secretary and arrange for us to go over these details in person? I hope to see you soon." Or a yacht salesperson, having just sold a 40-foot craft, would say something like: "Be sure to let us know if you have any problems; I'll call you in two weeks just to make sure everything is satisfactory." There are several reasons for calling on the client after the sale:

1. to make sure this sale will bring the client back for more
2. to sell accessories
3. to sell yourself to friends and co-workers of your client through that contact

To make your letters as effective as possible, open with a statement of purpose and close by making clear what you want your reader to do, using resale as appropriate to keep that communication channel open for future messages.

2.3 "You" Attitude

Employing a statement of purpose and the action closing in your correspondence explicitly molds your letter to satisfy both your needs and those of your readers. Using these elements fulfills the purpose of the letter, enabling it to do what you intend it to do. Another important principle of letter writing is to use "you" attitude. At its simplest, "you" attitude simply means using the personal pronoun *you* in business letters, but effective "you" attitude can be much more, including anything a writer does to demonstrate that the reader's needs, wants, questions, and concerns are matters of importance.

Maybe a teacher once told you a good letter uses at least as many *you*'s as *I*'s, or that you should try not to begin every sentence with *I*. "You" attitude is that principle, but extended to more than use of the word *you*. A simple courtesy letter (courtesy or good will letters are sent to reinforce and strengthen relationships; see Section 2.7) in two versions illustrates this concept. The first version has the opposite of "you" attitude, which some call "me" attitude. Notice that within the context of appreciation, this first letter actually does nothing for the reader, except perhaps to show how self-centered the writer is (see Exhibit 4.10). Exhibit 4.11 shows the same letter, rewritten to demonstrate "you" attitude. As you might expect, "you" attitude can be overdone. You must judge how much attention to your reader is enough.

2.4 Reader Benefits

"What's in it for me?" is a question you can count on your reader asking. "How does this concern me?" or "Why should I take the time to read this?" are other questions that the experienced writer explicitly answers. The more unsolicited your letter is, the more important it is to answer those questions before your reader has time to ask them. A good business-communication article begins this way: "Keep this article handy. It will be useful whenever you have to present statistical information in writing."

Exhibit 4.10 "Me" Attitude This makes the writer seem self-centered and needlessly ignores the reader.

```
Dear Jim,

     I want to tell you how pleased I was with your
presentation yesterday. I have seen countless such
presentations in my years with the company, and I can
truthfully say that it got me excited about the new sales
campaign more than any in a long time. Since the presentation,
several other people have mentioned to me that they agree with
me. Congratulations!

                                                Susan
```

Exhibit 4.11 "You" Attitude This makes it clear that the writer puts the reader's feelings over her own.

```
Dear Jim,

     You should be very proud of the good sales presentation
you made yesterday. Yours was more impressive than any this
company has seen in a long time. Several other people have
also commented on how well you did. Congratulations!

                                                Susan
```

Whenever your correspondence asks someone to do something, you need to explain why it is to your reader's advantage to do it—how it benefits the reader, why it is important. People usually take action faster if they understand how it benefits them or why it is important. Thus, instead of saying "Please mail us all forms pertaining to your third-quarter expenses as soon as possible," you could say: "In order to make sure you receive your reimbursement promptly, please mail us all forms."

Reader benefits can take either or both of these forms:

1. I can help you in the following way(s).
2. I identify with you in the following way(s).

The first option requires no particular explanation here; it is the stuff most reader

Exhibit 4.12 Two Kinds of Reader Benefits. The editor identifies with Mrs. White in the first line of the third paragraph, and then tries to help her.

XYZ Publishers
1512 Commerce Street
New York, NY 10012

Brenda White
1802 Lee
Oklahoma City, OK 73124

Dear Mrs. White:

Thank you for sending us your manuscript, The Search for Amelia, to consider for publication. You obviously know a great deal about your subject, and you present your knowledge quite clearly.

After due consideration, our editorial board feels we should not publish your book at this time. We simply do not feel that Amelia Earhart's disappearance generates the kind of public interest that can make publication profitable for us. What you set out to do is done very well, but you add nothing to generate new interest in the subject, and there is not enough interest in it currently to generate sales.

I remember at the start of my own career how unhappy I could be when I was told "It's well written, but not right for us." Let me encourage you to persevere, with this and other projects, but since you've told me you're a first-time author, let me give you two pieces of advice. First, before you invest the time and energy to write a book-length manuscript, do some preliminary groundwork, such as letters of inquiry, to see whether anyone will be interested in publishing what you might say on that topic. Second, you might consider hiring an agent, who would help your writing find its way to the right kinds of publishers.

Good luck with your career. I hope you will consider XYZ Publishers again in the future.

Sincerely,

John Wolfe

John Wolfe
Editor

benefits are made of. The second version of reader benefits can be very effective. Exhibit 4.12 presents a classic negative-message letter, impact of which is softened by both kinds of reader benefits.

Coming up with reader benefits usually requires only a moment's thought and an extra phrase on the writer's part, but their importance in terms of effect on readers cannot be overstated. Reader benefits tell your reader you care about him or her as a human being, a creature who deserves and responds to considerate treatment. Skillful use of "you" attitude and reader benefits gives your correspondence a tone of humanity and orientation toward the reader that will always make it more effective.

2.5 Negative Messages

So far, we have seen several examples of ways to make correspondence more positive through "you" attitude and reader benefits, but there are times when you simply cannot be totally positive: you may have to turn down a request, notify someone of a failure, or terminate a relationship. Any situation in which you send a message the receiver will not want to hear is called a negative-message situation. One of the largest bodies of literature in the field of business communication concerns what negative messages are and how they can best be handled. Because at times you cannot escape sending negative messages, we will discuss three different types: in this chapter, obvious and hidden messages, and, in the next chapter, those that require special structures for entire letters.

2.5.1 **Obvious Negative Messages.** When you know your reader will not be pleased with your message, you should take pains to minimize that unhappiness. Nothing is gained, and a great deal can be lost, by making people unhappy needlessly. There are several ways to soften blows; here are three different principles for handling negative messages:

1. A phone call is usually the the worst way to send a negative message. Do it in person if possible; as a second choice use a letter.
2. Always explain the reason for the negative message; if there is a positive side (or a reader benefit), be sure to emphasize it.
   Example: Not "We cannot ship your order," but "Due to the postal strike, we cannot ship your order. . . ."
   Example: Not "We have chosen not to hire you," but "Because of your lack of full-time experience, we have chosen not to. . . ."
3. To the extent that you can, cushion the negative message by putting neutral or good messages before and after it.

There is much more to dealing with negative messages than this, but before digging deeper into the subject, let us look at a classic negative message—a rejection letter—and see how it is handled by a professional (see Exhibit 4.13).

2.5.2 **Hidden Negative Messages.** Some negative messages are accidental on the writer's part and can be very harmful. Consider the following, taken from a brochure advertising a winter camp:

> For the first few years of our camp's existence we arranged programs for individuals as well as groups, but now we have turned our attention to serving groups exclusively so that we can offer this unique adventure to more people each year.

Exhibit 4.13 A Classic Negative-Message Letter Notice the ways in which the negative message (rejection of an application for a job) is softened by "you" attitude, good will, and reader benefits.

Agro-Tech, Inc.
P.O. Box 20598
Pocatello, ID 75220
March 15, 1985

Terry Bell
4239 Brazos Blvd.
Fiske, ID 77801

Dear Mr. Bell:

Thank you for sending us your application for the agricultural engineering position we advertised. We are always happy to receive applications from A&M graduates. Your credentials were especially good in terms of your education and agricultural background.

We received a number of applications from well-qualified candidates. Several of them had full-time engineering experience as well as agricultural backgrounds and excellent educations, and we have hired one of those experienced people. Therefore we cannot offer you a job at this time. We will, however, place your application on file, and automatically consider you for any position that opens up in the next six months. Of course you should feel free to re-apply for any opening we advertise that you feel is appropriate.

Positions such as the one you applied for are difficult to get right out of college. May I suggest that you look for an entry-level position with a local equipment company, and that you try us again when you have a year or two of work beyond college to support your application?

Thank you again for considering Agro-Tech. Best of luck in your job search.

Sincerely,

Jerry Bowen

Jerry Bowen
Personnel Manager

Those lines contain an example of a hidden negative message: the hint of past financial struggle. Although some readers may not notice it, others certainly will; they will wonder if the camp was not financially successful serving only individuals. Had the pamphlet's authors been watching for possible negative messages, they might have written:

In order to bring this unique adventure to as many people each season as we can, we serve groups exclusively. So get together with at least 7 of your friends. . .

Now the hidden (and needless) negative message, the hint of past financial problems, is gone. Hidden negative messages come in all varieties, and are likely to creep into your writing when you least expect them. In almost every instance, you can avoid them if you will just sensitize yourself to their presence.

So far we have considered negative messages as isolated elements in otherwise positive letters. But you often have to write a letter whose very essence is unavoidably negative. In the next chapter you will see how to write negative-message letters effectively—how to say no without losing customers, clients, and friends.

2.6 Positive Emphasis

Many statements can be phrased either negatively ("Your widgets will not be shipped until Thursday") or positively ("Your widgets will be shipped Thursday"). Although the strict meaning of such statements stays the same either way, their effects on your reader may be quite different. Maintaining a positive emphasis in your letters encourages your readers to make positive responses. To state the same idea another way: Whether the cup is half empty or half full may only be a matter of attitude, but if the person you are writing to is thirsty, it's better to say the cup is half full. The following example illustrates negative and positive emphasis:

Wrong (negative emphasis): You will be charged for each check unless you maintain a $300 minimum balance.

Right (positive emphasis): Checking is free with a balance of $300 or more.

2.7 Good Will

Applying good will in your business letters means considering your reader's needs and wants in ways that go beyond your own, and then responding to them. Although you may feel that saying "Your widgets will be shipped Thursday" does all you need to do, your reader will be much happier if you add what the reader really wants and needs to know: "Your widgets will be shipped Thursday, and you will receive them by Rapid Express Saturday morning." Here we clearly see the frequent split between the writer's needs (to notify the reader the widgets have been sent) and the reader's needs (to know when they will arrive). Effective business correspondence balances the reader's needs and the writer's, satisfying both, and thus accomplishing its purpose.

Wrong (no good will): We have received your application.

Right (good will added): We have received your application, and you can expect a reply in two weeks.

2.8 Summary

Box 4.1 summarizes the principles of business correspondence presented in this chapter.

Box 4.1 Summary of Principles of Business Correspondence

Solicited Versus Unsolicited Letters

"As you requested . . ."

Reader Benefits

"Keep this article handy–it will show you how . . ."

"You" Attitude

"Congratulations on your . . ."

Good will

WRONG: "Your order has been shipped as you requested."
RIGHT: "The widgets you ordered have been shipped as you requested and should arrive in about 10 days."

Buffer Negative Message

WRONG: "Your application has been turned down."
RIGHT: "Thank you for sending us your application. Choosing among so many qualified applicants is a difficult process, and choices are often made because one candidate offers something others do not, rather than because one candidate is better than the others. While we have chosen not to consider your application further at this time, we wish you the very best of luck in the future. We hope that you will continue to think of XYZ Corp. as future openings become available."

Positive Emphasis

WRONG: "You will be assessed a service charge . . ."
RIGHT: "Checking is free when . . ."

Purpose and Action Closing

WRONG: "I would like to request that . . ."
RIGHT: "Please call me at . . ."

3. Business Goals and Human Goals

Striking a balance between your needs as writer and someone else's needs as reader means paying a great deal of attention to human goals. Communication always goes from one human being to another, and all human beings have joys, fears, hopes, and frustrations which your writing must deal with. To ignore the human qualities of your audience is to send a clear negative message of a sort that often causes readers to take their business elsewhere.

A narrow focus on business goals produces this kind of letter:

```
Dear Sir:

We have received your order, and will ship it as soon as
possible.
```

There are times when such a curt note is all you need. This may be your only transaction with that person, or you may have to rush, or there may be a follow-up letter later. But it really doesn't take more time to be a little more human. This is especially true if your letter is a form letter, as routine correspondence usually is. Form letters are the least human letters of all, when they could easily be the most human. The same computer that printed out the letter above could just as easily turn out the one in Exhibit 4.14.

All of the principles described in this chapter share this one characteristic: they help you as a writer to see beyond your own needs to those of your readers. And as such, they show you how to go beyond the business goals of your letters to satisfy the human goals. The two are not opposites, for human goals wrap

Exhibit 4.14 Focus on Human Goals This uses the principles of business correspondence to satisfy human goals as well as business goals.

```
Dear Mr. Adams:

     Thank you for your order. We're happy you've chosen to
use our Superba Freeze-Dried Trail Mixes.

     We received your order on the 15th, and shipped the Trail
Mixes on the 16th. As you requested, the shipment was made via
Rapid Express.

     Should you have any questions, please call us at 1-800-
555-1234. We look forward to your continued business.

                                   Thank you,
                                   John Yary
                                   John Yary
                                   Catalogue Sales
```

around business goals. Satisfying both business goals and human goals, making each reinforce the other, is a secret not just for successful communication but for success in general.

EXERCISES

1. Revise the following sentences to eliminate negative messages:
   a. If we don't receive your payment by the 1st, you'll be billed an additional 5% late fee.
   b. I'm answering your last letter much later than I should.
   c. Unless you send us this information, we cannot issue your policy.
   d. Please don't hesitate to call if you have trouble understanding these instructions.
   e. I'm sorry I won't be here when you come to town, and so we won't be able to meet, but I hope we won't miss each other next time.
   f. Until you have received our authorization you are not to begin to get bids.
   g. If you fail to report for work as a result of any unauthorized job action, your position as a state employee will be jeopardized.
   h. If you took the test, as you claim, we have failed to receive your score.
   i. I wasn't in class yesterday. Did I miss anything important?
   j. It is true that my major area of study deals with large industries, but I will gladly work in a smaller company.

2. Revise the following sentences for positive emphasis:
   a. My major is General Industrial Technology, in which I have no particular area of specialization.
   b. My work experience has been limited to part-time jobs.
   c. During my five years of industrial experiences I have shuffled from job to job, each with increasing responsibility.
   d. I am interested in getting started in the engineering field and would like to start with your company.
   e. While I missed your recruiter on campus last week, I would still like to arrange an interview somehow.
   f. Our records show you did not return two of the twenty books you checked out.
   g. Four of the five samples you sent failed to pass the minimum standards.
   h. I hope to graduate this May.
   i. The project seems to have a good chance of success.
   j. We see no reason for you not to sign this contract.

3. Analyze the following memo's use of (or failure to use) the principles discussed in this chapter. Using your analysis, rewrite the memo so that it stands a better chance of accomplishing its goal (preventing a strike) by making better use of those principles.

OFFICE OF THE GOVERNOR

MEMORANDUM TO: All State Employees

I want you to know of my deep concern about reports of a possible strike by state employees if new labor contracts are not agreed to by August 21. Management is determined to reach agreement on new contracts that are fair to state employees and responsible to all the state's taxpayers. Irresponsible strike talk doesn't help collective bargaining for new contracts. It ignores the laws against strikes by state employees, and it ignores the law that provides for a fair contract through binding arbitration if the parties fail to reach agreement in bargaining.

All State employees should know just how seriously they may hurt their future if they participate in a strike.

- They would commit a crime—a felony under the state criminal code.
- They would forfeit the right to hold their state jobs—the law says they may not hold positions in the government.
- They would not only lose their pay but would lose their paid health and life insurance coverage and other fringe benefits.

We intend to abide by the law, and to enforce it in every practical way.

We have a deep interest in the well-being of all state employees and their families and I wanted you to be personally aware of the grave consequences of strike participation. I hope this entire issue will be resolved as the parties continue to work toward reaching a fair contract by August 21. That remains our uppermost objective.

Clayton James

Governor

4. Revise the following memo according to the principles presented in this chapter.

STATE UNIVERSITY

Computer Center

MEMORANDUM

TO: Dean Laura Bolt
College of Arts and Sciences

FROM: Steve B. Dickson, Director
Computer Center

SUBJECT: Funds for Instructional Use of Computer

Reference memorandum from Vice-President Knebel on this subject dated September 2, 1985 in which you were allocated funds in the interest of encouraging greater insturctional use of the computer, and my memorandum on this subject dated September 4, 1985, in which you were allocated supplemental funds from the CC to stimulate use of Dr. Knebel's allocation earlier in the fiscal year.

We have reviewed your accounts, and our records indicate that you did not spend at least one half of the Account 82122 funds provided by Dr. Knebel. Accordingly, the CC Suplemental funds allocated on September 4, 1985 are withdrawn. It is emphasized that this action does not in any way affect the allocation of funds from Dr. Knebel.

In the interest of stimulating use of your Account 82122 funds prior to the peak summer load, the Computer Center will again allocate supplemental funds for the Spring semester, 1986. Your CC Spring Semester supplemental allocation is an amount equal to 30% of one half of the total amount allocated to you by Dr. Knebel.

82122 Allocation for 82–83	Amount of CC Fall Supplement Used	YTD Expenditures	Amount of Spring Supplement Available
$7000	-0-	$1366	$1050

Balance Available for Use by 05/20/83*
$6684

Any unused portion of the CC Supplement will be withdrawn on May 20, 1986. *Please note that the CC supplementary allocations are in no way intended to limit the original allocation of funds from Dr. Knebel's office. It only provides an added bonus for spending the funds early.

SBD/js
xc: Dr. A. Knebel

5. The following memo is one administrator's response to the memo in Exercise 4. Write a brief analysis of its content. Will it be likely to increase the use of computer funds? Rewrite the memo to increase its likelihood of increasing the use of computer funds.

STATE UNIVERSITY
COLLEGE OF ARTS AND SCIENCES

Office of the Dean
MEMORANDUM

January 16, 1986

TO: Department Heads in Arts and Sciences
FROM: Laura J. Bolt, Dean
SUBJECT: Computer Funds for Instructional Purposes

Attached is a memo from Steve Dickson indicating that we have again failed to spend computer funds that were available to us.

```
Please forgive me for being so grouchy, but I have difficulty
in being sympathetic to complaints that we have insufficient
funds for instructional purposes when each year we fail to
take advantage of the available funding.

Attachment

xc: Vice-President Knebel
```

6. Using one of the business-letter forms presented in this chapter, write a formal letter of introduction in which you present yourself to your instructor. Here are some of the elements that you might include in such a letter:
   - What is the purpose of your letter?
   - What is your area of specialization? Within this area, what do you like to work on most? If you had a chance to study something in this area, what would you choose?
   - What are your plans for a job? What kinds of communication will be important to that job? Be as thorough as you can.
   - What kinds of communication will be important in your private life? In your home? At parties? At meetings?
   - What is your communication background? Include your experience in Freshman English, speech, debate, and dramatics.
   - What areas of communication would you like to work on most in this course? Why?
   - Why did you take this course? What is your honest attitude toward it?
   - Anything else you think it is important for your instructor to know about you.

   Caution: Do not use this list as a step-by-step guide to writing your letter, which will probably produce canned writing (like canned laughter); if everyone does this, all the letters in your class will be the same, reflecting the list but not your individuality. With the exception of the first item (purpose) the ordering of these items is not meant to be significant.

   Remember to analyze your audience for this assignment. Most students assume that readers know much more about what the students are writing about than they actually do. Be especially careful about that on this assignment. Write your letter for your instructor's *real* level of knowledge and interest, not the level you imagine.

7. Despite its best efforts, once in a while the Postal Service does some minor damage to a letter. When that happens, the customer will get the letter in a plastic bag, printed with a note like the one below. Read it carefully, and then come to class prepared to discuss how it uses the principles discussed in this chapter. Pay particular attention to possible ways it could be made better.

```
Dear Postal Customer

The enclosed article was damaged in handling by the
Postal Service.
```

We realize that your mail is important to you and you have every right to expect it to be delivered intact and in good condition. The Postal Service makes every effort to properly handle the mail entrusted to it; but due to the large volume, occasional damage does occur.

When a Post Office handles approximately one million pieces of mail daily, it is imperative that mechanical methods be used to maintain production and insure prompt delivery of the mails. It is also an actuality that modern production methods do not permit personal attention if mail is insecurely enveloped or bulky contents are enclosed. When this occurs and our machinery is jammed, it often causes damage to other mail that was properly prepared.

We are constantly striving to improve our processing methods to assure that an occurrence such as the enclosed can be eliminated. We appreciate your concern over the handling of your mail and sincerely regret the inconvenience you have experienced.

Sectional Center Manager/Postmaster

5

Patterns of Organization for Business Correspondence

Box 5.1 The Direct-Request Pattern

Paragraph 1: Request for information, services, etc.
Paragraph 2: Show why you need the information or service, and/or how you will use it.
Paragraph 3: State the specific action you want the reader to take.
Paragraph 4: Reader benefits (if possible) and "good will" ending.

1. Types of Letters or Memos

This chapter presents discussions and examples of letters in five broad categories that cover most types of business correspondence. We will look in detail at direct request, informative, persuasive, "good news", and negative-message letters or memos.* These patterns provide specific applications of the principles discussed in Chapter 4. Using these patterns (and the principles discussed earlier), you should be able to construct the kind of letter or memo you need for any particular situation.

1.1 Direct-Request Letter or Memo

For this discussion, assume you have a request you expect your reader to grant readily. The outline in Box 5.1 shows one good way to make such a request.

1.1.1 **Rationale.** If you are reasonably certain your reader will grant your request readily, you can save time by making the request right at the beginning. In the second paragraph, specify why you need the information (or services, etc.) in order to justify your request and to ensure that your reader will send you precisely the materials you need. Your third paragraph needs to make clear exactly what action you want your reader to take and explain any limitations and restrictions. (For example, if there is a time limit involved, explain the necessity for it.) Your "good will" closing and statement of reader benefits (if there are any) are especially important in this kind of letter or memo, because the rest of it concentrates more on what the reader can do for you than on what you can do for the reader. Exhibit 5.1 shows specific applications of the direct-request pattern.

Most job-application letters are a combination of the direct-request and the persuasive letter patterns. Because they are so important, they are covered in a separate chapter (Chapter 6).

---

*I am indebted to "Patterns of Organization for Business Letters" by Kitty O. Locker for much of the material in this chapter. The material is used with her kind permission.

Exhibit 5.1 A Direct-Letter Request Notice that the second paragraph tells the *why* of the request and the third tells the *what.*

Dear Sir:

Your ad in last week's Computer Times for a briefcase word processor has prompted me to write and request more information on it.

I am looking for a unit I can take on business trips and use wherever I stay. It needs to have battery power as an option, as well. It needs to be capable of sophisticated word processing and simple spread sheets, and it needs to be PC-compatible. But the two qualities that most attracted me about your computer are the built-in modem and the built-in printer.

Please send me a description of your briefcase word processor's capabilities. I would especially like information on its keyboard, compatibility, and what kinds of software packages are available for it. Obviously, I would also like to know its recommended retail price.

If this product is as good as it looks, my firm may well order quite a few. I hope to hear from you soon.

Sincerely,

1.2 Informative Letter or Memo

Assuming that your reader's attitude toward the information will be neutral, one good pattern for an informative letter or memo, the kind usually written in response to a request for information, is given in Box 5.2.

Box 5.2 The Informative Pattern

Paragraph 1: Provide the requested information and/or state the policy in question.
Paragraph 2: Explain how the information specifically touches on your reader's request, and/or how the policy applies to the current situation.
Paragraph 3: Present any negative factors (usually, areas in which the information or policy limits the reader's actions); try to show the motivation for these factors; retain positive attitude and positive emphasis as much as possible.
Paragraph 4: Reader benefits.
Paragraph 5: "Good will" ending.

1.2.1 **Rationale.** Responding directly to your reader's request in the first paragraph establishes your contact immediately. By answering the question asked earlier, you can help make the reader favorably disposed to the rest of your message. The detailed explanation in paragraph 2 is the meat of the letter, but do not get so caught up in presenting details that you neglect to explain the why's—especially if paragraph 3 will contain any negative messages. If your reader understands why the policy affects him or her in this way, everyone will get along better.

When you have negative messages that are incidental to a positive letter, be sure to keep them in perspective for the reader by placing them after the detailed policy explanation and before the reader benefits. Remember to show why these negative elements are necessary; the more negative messages you send, the more important following up with reader benefits is. If nothing else, reiterate the positive aspects of paragraph 2. For example, list several things the policy will allow the reader to do.

Your "good will" ending should convey to the reader the extent of your concern. Try to use that human concern to balance out the tendency in such a letter to sound too rule-oriented. Be sure to invite the reader to ask further questions if they come up; you might suggest a phone call to save time for your reader in the future. Exhibit 5.2 shows specific applications of this informative pattern.

1.3 Persuasive Letter or Memo

Persuasive letters or memos include a variety of kinds of correspondence, all of which have in common your expectation that the reader will initially disagree with your request, or at least will not be inclined to go along with it. You might be trying to persuade one of your local elected officials to change a policy or a vote, or you could be trying to persuade a corporate executive to schedule an appointment for you to demonstrate your product line. The basic pattern is given in Box 5.3.

1.3.1 **Rationale.** Try to disarm your reader's opposition by presenting the reasons for your request in the context of solving a mutual problem. This requires establishing a common ground between you and your reader. You can either try to

Box 5.3 Persuasive Pattern

Paragraph 1: Catch the reader's interest, establish mutual goal(s).
Paragraph 2: Define the problem you both share—the one that the reader's granting your request will solve.
Paragraph 3: Explain the solution. Show how any negative elements (cost, time, etc.) are outweighed by the advantages of the solution you propose. Present it not as *your* solution but rather as *the* solution.
Paragraph 4: Reader benefits.
Paragraph 5: State the specific action you want the reader to take.

Exhibit 5.2 An Informative Letter Notice the author anticipates unasked questions (for example, by providing the name of the nearest dealer).

Dear Ms. Eubanks:

Thank you for your request for information on our new Acme TravelWriter. I have enclosed brochures that should answer all your questions.

The TravelWriter weighs 1.5 pounds, opens for easy use on a lap or a desk, has a 128K memory, and a 6-character, 12-line amber screen. It uses either 120-volt AC current or an optional 12-volt DC battery pack (described in the enclosed brochures). The keyboard is standard, its size equal to that of most portable typewriters. Its built-in printer operates in its dot-matrix mode at 100cps and in near-letter-quality mode at 50cps. The unit comes in its own carrying case, especially designed to protect it from normal travel bumps and knocks.

Software available with the TravelWriter includes two word processing programs and five spread sheet programs. We expect to have additional programs (accounting, statistical modeling, graphics, etc.) available within the year. All these programs are PC-compatible.

Recommended retail price of the TravelWriter is $350; one word processing package comes with it for that price. Other software, the battery pack, and other peripherals are extra.

I hope this information leads you to give our product serious consideration. We believe there is nothing on the market that can come close to it for lightness of weight, high durability, and low price. The dealer nearest to you is Wilson Office Equipment, 1511 East Main Street, phone 555-1423. If you visit their store, you can see the TravelWriter and try it out for yourself.

Thank you for your inquiry.

Sincerely,

arouse the reader's interest in something *you* are interested in (the more difficult option), or relate your concern to something you know your reader is already interested in (the easier option). If you're writing to management, you can stress increased productivity; if your audience is labor, you can stress better working conditions. In this kind of letter, you must choose your approach carefully, striving for the right statement of the problem, the one with which your reader will identify and that will point your reader in the direction of the solution you propose.

After you have established the problem as something you are both interested in solving, define it in greater depth in paragraph 2. Be objective and detailed, using concrete examples to make your presentation vivid. You are trying to stir the reader to take action, so that in paragraph 3 you can show that, given the need for a solution, the one you propose is best.

Before you present your own proposal, briefly show why any obvious alternative solutions are unsatisfactory. Then present the solution you propose, but present it as *the* solution, not as uniquely yours. Show your reader that any clear-thinking person, once aware of the facts, must come to this same solution. Part of doing this includes answering the objections you know your reader will come up with. Do your homework ahead of time, and build into this part of the letter answers to foreseeable objections. For example, where will the money, or personnel, or equipment for this solution come from?

The reader benefits for this kind of letter should reinforce the common ground built in paragraphs 1 and 2. Explain the benefits that will come to those who solve this problem. Your last paragraph should specifically state what you want the reader to do; make sure that besides being moved to action, your reader will also know exactly the right action to take. Exhibit 5.3 gives an example of this persuasive pattern.

1.4 "Good News" Letter or Memo

1.4.1 **The Basic Pattern.** If you have good news to convey, you can assume that the reader's attitude will be positive. One good pattern to use is given in Box 5.4.

Rationale. When you have good news, place it first in the letter; then follow it with the details. Any negative messages should be subordinated into a middle paragraph. The reader benefits and "good will" ending should remind your reader that your interest goes beyond the message at hand, extending to the person who will read it. Exhibit 5.4 shows an example of this pattern.

1.4.2 **Courtesy or "Good Will" Letters.** The term "courtesy" (or "good will") letters names a widely varied group of letters including thank-you notes, congratulations, sympathy notes, season's greetings, and letters of welcome. They share these characteristics:

- These letters are never letters that *must* be sent.
- These letters almost never *require* answers.
- These letters always have as their major goal to create and build good will.
- Readers especially appreciate these letters *because* they are not necessary.

You send a good will note to strengthen your relationship with a person or a company. You should not try to do business in the letter; the good will is sufficient. Exhibits 5.5 and 5.6 tell you *how* to do these letters, but the most important element is *why* to do them: they epitomize business correspondence that has as its primary goal the satisfying of human needs.

Exhibit 5.3 A Persuasive Letter. Notice it is *our* problem and *our* solution, and that the letter is relatively informal (Jack and Bill went to school together).

Dear Jack,

After we talked on the phone yesterday, it came to me that there is a way to deal with our situation that we haven't considered, and it may well be the solution we both need.

I understand how frustrated you can get when your crews have to wait the results of our tests. But we cannot hurry the tests, or take shortcuts on these standards.

Let me suggest this: usually we receive your samples around noon on one day, and give you the results 48 hours later. Thus when we get the samples on Tuesday noon, we give you results on Thursday noon. But if we were to get your samples between 8:00 and 8:30 a.m., we could probably get you results by 5 p.m. the next day. And there would be a good chance we could get them to you at least part of the time considerably earlier, around noon. You see, we handle our work on a first-in, first-out basis, and we get most of it in around 9–10 a.m. By bringing in your samples earlier, you could get ahead of the pack, and get your samples back much earlier. That may well be the best solution.

This way you get the results you need, and we can get our own work started (and finished) earlier.

If this seems reasonable to you, give me a call and I'll alert our people in the lab that you're bringing the samples in earlier and expecting them to get the results out earlier. Fair enough?

Bill

Box 5.4 The "Good News" Pattern

Paragraph 1: Good News.
Paragraph 2: Details of good news.
Paragraph 3: Any negative elements (time limits, apparent inconsistencies, etc.).
Paragraph 4: Reader benefits.
Paragraph 5: "Good will" ending.

Exhibit 5.4 A "Good News" Letter Notice this letter contains no negative elements, and it goes out of its way to restore good will. The one possible negative message ("We regret we cannot . . .") is handled very carefully.

Dear Mr. Adcock:

Thank you for calling the error on your recent statement to our attention. As you suspected, we had indeed billed you twice for one night's lodging.

We have adjusted your bill to $38 the posted charge for one room, one night, one person. Since you sent the $38 with your last letter, your account with us is now marked paid in full, as the enclosed statement shows. We regret we cannot follow your suggestion of making your stay free, simply because of our billing error.

We hope you will accept our apology for this error, and that you will consider staying with us again during your next visit to St. Louis. We hope you will also accept the enclosed Special Guest certificate, which brings you one night's stay at any World's Inn for half price. It is our way of saying we appreciate your continued business.

Thank you again for staying at World's Inn.

Sincerely,

Exhibit 5.5 A Simple "Courtesy" or "Good Will" Letter Such letters are done solely to build good will; this one happens to be a thank-you note, but there are many other possible varieties.

Dear Vicki,

Thank you for the good job you did on the library tours for my advanced technical writing students last week. I appreciate the care and preparation you obviously put into it, and I admire your skill at presenting the material.

The students thought the introduction to the AIRS system and the OCLC was especially interesting and useful.

If I can be of any assistance to you, be sure to call on me. Thank you again for doing the library tour so well.

Sincerely,

Exhibit 5.6 A Bad Negative-Message Letter This letter may satisfy the writer's business goals, but it is destructive of the human relationship between the writer and the job applicant.

```
Dear Applicant:

     Thank you for your application. Unfortunately, we have
already chosen the person for that job. Good luck in your
continued job search.

                                      Personnel Manager
```

1.5 Negative-Message Letter or Memo

There will be times when you will know that your reader's attitude toward your message will be unfavorable. You may have to say no to a request, end a relationship, or raise a price. Remember that it is usually better to transmit such a message in person; the receiver will usually appreciate your dealing with the situation in person. But of course there will be times when you will need to use a letter. One good pattern for a negative message or memo is given in Box 5.5.

1.5.1 **Rationale.** It may seem to you that such a letter is a charade that does not fool anyone. In fact, it is not designed to fool anyone but rather to try to cushion a blow in a human way and to maintain as much good will as possible under the circumstances. You try to write the letter in a reasonably positive manner, not to deceive the reader into thinking it actually contains good news, but to show the reader your concern for his or her human feelings by buffering the negative message. Most experts agree you shouldn't introduce the negative message with "However" or "Unfortunately" or "I'm sorry, but . . ." because those phrases ring too false. (Although you should try to phrase the message as positively as you can, it is still going to be a negative message.)

Box 5.5 The Negative-Message Pattern

Paragraph 1: Establish good will. Then present positive aspects of your previous relationship with the reader.
Paragraph 2: Present reasons for the negative message. Then present the message.
Paragraph 3: Explain the positive aspects of the situation. Suggest alternatives. Re-establish good will if possible.

Exhibit 5.7 A Good Negative-Message Letter Notice the use of you attitude, positive emphasis, and reader benefits to cushion the negative message.

```
Dear Mr. Morgan:

     Thank you for your letter of January 15, 1981, regarding
employment with our firm. We are delighted that so many people
of your education and experience seek to work in our industry,
and particularly with as at Acme.

     The large number of qualified applicants made our hiring
decision depend upon a wide range of variables in addition to
education and experience. It is always difficult to choose
from among such good candidates, and this occasion proved no
exception. While we have selected another candidate to fill
the particular position for which you applied, we do
anticipate openings of a similar type in the future, and I
would encourage you to re-submit your application. Keep in
mind that knowledge and experience with computers can be a
determining factor for employment in this field, and anything
you can do to enhance your own qualifications in this area
would increase your potential in the job market.

     Congratulations on your graduation from State Tech
University, and good luck in your continued job search.

                                   Sincerely,
```

Compare the negative-message letters in Exhibits 5.6 and 5.7. One, without the pattern in Box 5.5, satisfies only business goals; the other, with the pattern, satisfies business goals *and* human goals. Which would *you* rather receive?

2. On Using Patterns

The patterns, rationales, and examples offered here demonstrate how to deal with typical business correspondence. If you want to grow as a writer, you should apply them with flexibility, using the principles of business correspondence explained in the previous chapter to tailor each letter to its particular situation. By combining principles, patterns, and audience analysis and adaptation, you should be able to write effective letters and memos. Remember the "myth of the 100-percent model": no single pattern applied unthinkingly will quite work anywhere. You must use your own intelligence and your own understanding of the specific writing situation (and of the *principles* behind these patterns). Blindly following *any* prefabricated plan in such a human situation is as foolish as having no plan at all.

3. Human Psychological Needs

Writing successful business letters means paying strict attention to your reader's needs. In many ways each reader will have specific needs that shape each letter you write. But there are certain qualities and feelings all readers seek, and certain qualities and feelings all readers seek to avoid. The pressures of the business world can tempt writers to be ruthless about ignoring readers' needs: the business goals of the letter may seem to dictate its content and structure. It's easy for any of us as writers to think only about our needs and not about those of our readers. But successful communication builds on shared needs, and the reader's share will always include the qualities described in Sections 3.1 and 3.2.

3.1 Qualities All Audiences Seek

All audiences, and especially all readers, seek to draw three feelings from a piece of writing: identity, stimulus, and security.

3.1.1 **Identity.** If you treat your reader as a unique individual you will be reinforcing his or her sense of identity, which is a very pleasurable experience for the reader. Think of the times a new acquaintance of yours breaks into a smile simply because you remembered his or her name; on the other side, think of the times you have been offended by not being treated as an individual. In general, the more your writing shows that it is tailored to fit exactly the person who is reading it, the better it will be received, because you are recognizing and reinforcing that person's identity.

3.1.2 **Stimulus.** No kind of writing is intrinsically boring. Some kinds of writing have more chances to be exciting than other kinds, but the responsibility of not boring the reader, like the responsibility for clarity, rests with the writer. In business correspondence, not boring your reader means asking yourself how much and what kind of detail to include and how to make your content easier to understand. This may mean putting the "bottom line" of a report at the beginning, or using a phone call and follow-up letter rather than a long, complicated letter that might be misunderstood. Certainly it means paying attention to sentence length and clarity, paragraph length, and overall length of the letter. In business letters it also means putting the purpose in the first paragraph.

3.1.3 **Security.** No reader wants to feel threatened by a piece of writing, and this is especially true when it comes to business letters and memos. For business letter writers, having proper concern for not threatening the reader's security means being careful not to include needless negative messages (and handling necessary negative messages carefully).

3.2 Qualities All Audiences Seek To Avoid

The opposites of the feelings all readers seek are those they seek to avoid: anonymity, boredom, and anxiety.

3.2.1 **Anonymity.** "Dear Occupant" mail makes readers feel anonymous. Canned laughter makes television viewers feel the show is anonymous, and canned speeches make the speaker, the occasion, and the audience anonymous. Being dealt with as a number, not a name, makes anyone feel anonymous. To keep your reader from feeling anonymous, build concern for your real audience into your letter.

3.2.2 **Boredom.** Writing for business and industry requires placing a premium on the reader's time and energy, especially in letters. The people who see your letters face a three-way choice: read it, route it, or skip it. If you write your letter carefully and organize it efficiently, your reader is more likely to choose to read it.

3.2.3 **Anxiety.** Remember the things that make you anxious when *you* are the reader: material that you cannot understand, that is not organized efficiently, that indicates that the writer considers his or her own needs to be more important than those of the reader. If you pay attention only to your own goals, your readers may well express their anxiety by consistently responding negatively to your letters. However, if you build shared goals with your readers, you can make them feel more secure and increase the probability that they will respond in the way you hope they will.

EXERCISES

1. For this exercise, you will write a variety of letters as either the student or the instructor in an upper-level technical- or business-writing class. The class carries a requirement for a twenty-page term paper. The following letters all concern negotiations between student and instructor on the topic for that term paper:
   a. As the student, write a direct-request letter in which you ask your instructor to approve a major report on a topic you suggest in the letter. For this assignment, you only need to choose a topic you know enough about to write these letters. The letter is pretty simple; you don't expect any problems getting the topic approved.
   b. As the instructor, write a letter responding positively to the letter in a. above, spelling out the term paper's requirements (get these from your instructor).
   c. As the instructor, write a negative-message letter turing down the request in a. above. Possible reasons for turning down the request include: the library doesn't have enough information; other students who tried that topic couldn't do it; there isn't enough time; the topic is too simple (or too broad); or there's no conceivable reason why anyone would be interested in such a paper. Be sure to offer alternatives.

d. Now, as the student, write a persuasive letter to the instructor, responding to the letter in c. above, trying to get the instructor to accept some modification of the topic you originally proposed, a modification that satisfies the objections in letter c.

2. The following letters involve a student (you) and a dean (Dean Smith). You request that the college's requirements for successful completion of two years' study of one foreign language be modified to allow you to substitute one year each of French and German. The dean refuses, you persuade, and offer the dean a compromise.
   a. As the student, write a letter requesting that you be allowed this substitution. Use your own major field of study—Dean Smith is dean of the college that department is part of.
   b. As the dean, refuse the student's request. Offer as your main reason the fact that in an era of declining educational standards, your university is determined to continue to turn out students with well-rounded educational backgrounds—and that means knowing foreign languages.
   c. As the student, write a persuasive letter trying to change the dean's mind. Feel free to offer a compromise.

3. You are the Customer Service Manager for Beta Boots, a major manufacturer of all sorts of boots. The recent popularity of Western boots caused Beta to hastily manufacture 50,000 pairs, and many of the people who have bought them have written in complaining that the boot's sole comes unglued from the rest of the boot. You have learned that it costs an average of $7.50 for a consumer to have them repaired locally. Your company has decided to offer each person who complains $3.75 toward repair: by the time the boots fall apart, half of their useful life is gone, so the company will pay half of the repair bill.
   a. Write a form letter to customers who have complained, attempting to persuade them to accept the $3.75 and let the issue end there. Obviously, you are also trying to salvage as much of the reputation of Beta Boots as you can.
   b. Write one very special letter to a very angry customer. This person (Mr. Samuelson) not only refused the $3.75 check, but also mailed back the boots. He now wants reimbursement for the $3.50 it cost to mail the boots, the $38.50 the boots originally cost, plus an additional $10 for "sheer aggravation." Your boss has authorized you to offer him a new pair of boots (an improved version of the originals) and the $3.50 postage but has made it very clear that he will not comply with the customer's other demands. Write a letter persuading Mr. Samuelson to accept the deal. Be very careful (Samuelson was *furious*) but very persuasive (you very much want the issue to end here).

4. You are a graduating college senior, and the chairman of your department has invited you to apply for graduate school and to accept a half-time teaching assistantship in that department. Write a letter turning down the invitation

but keeping open the possibility that at this time next year, after you've gotten a year's work experience, you may want to accept the invitation. Phrase your letter so as to keep the invitation open without making any kind of a firm commitment to apply next year.

5. You are the personnel manager of Acme Engineering Consultants, and David Powers has applied for a job as a Materials Testing supervisor, a position you recently advertised. He worked for you part time for the last half of his junior year and the first half of his senior year in college, but now you need to deny his request for a full-time job after he graduates. Your confidential reason for not hiring him is that he was only average in everything he did for you, always needing more supervision and guidance than anyone thought necessary. He was acceptable as a part-time employee, but you don't want him working for you on a full-time basis. The situation is complicated because you just hired a classmate of his for the job, and you know he will discover that. Write him a rejection letter that will maintain at least a reasonable amount of his good will.

6. Revise the following letter, eliminating the needless "I" attitude and replacing it with "you" attitude wherever possible.

128 W. 5th Street
Cedar Rapids, Iowa 53108
April 10, 1985

President
P.O. Box 90
Dubuque, Iowa 53110

Subject: Job Application

I believe I have the qualifications for the job offered by your firm in the April 8th Dubuque News and would appreciate strong consideration for the position.

I have the business skills that would be required for your firm and myself to excel. My academic background at the University of Iowa is a Bachelor of Science in Accounting degree with a strong achievement level in finance.

I think of myself as an energetic person with a strong desire to accomplish and do things correctly. Working together well with other people is the best way to solve problems and usually creates the optimum results.

Being a part of a creative company is one of the highest goals I plan to attain in my career. I would be proud to be a part of your firm. Would you please call me for an interview?

Sincerely,

6

Special for Job Seekers

(continued)

In the year before you finish college, you begin writing one kind of letter that is very important to you. Writing a poor job-application letter can be both personally frustrating and professionally damaging. (So can a poor graduate-school, medical-school, or law-school application letter.) If the letter fails to get you a position you are otherwise qualified for, that poorly written letter has also cost you money. Writing an *effective* job-application letter, on the other hand, can be more than satisfying and time efficient: the letter can bring you professional rewards for years to come (see Exhibit 6.1).

Can one letter really be worth twenty, thirty, or forty thousand dollars? Absolutely. If someone else gets that job but you have better qualifications, then your letter may well have cost you a year's salary. This may be your first real experience with the dollar value of good communication skills, especially of good writing. There are many other instances, but few focus so clearly on just one short letter.

This chapter provides you with the knowledge and strategies you will need to write an effective job-application letter—a letter that not only communicates

Exhibit 6.1 Your Job Application Can one letter really be worth twenty, thirty, forty, or fifty thousand dollars? Absolutely.

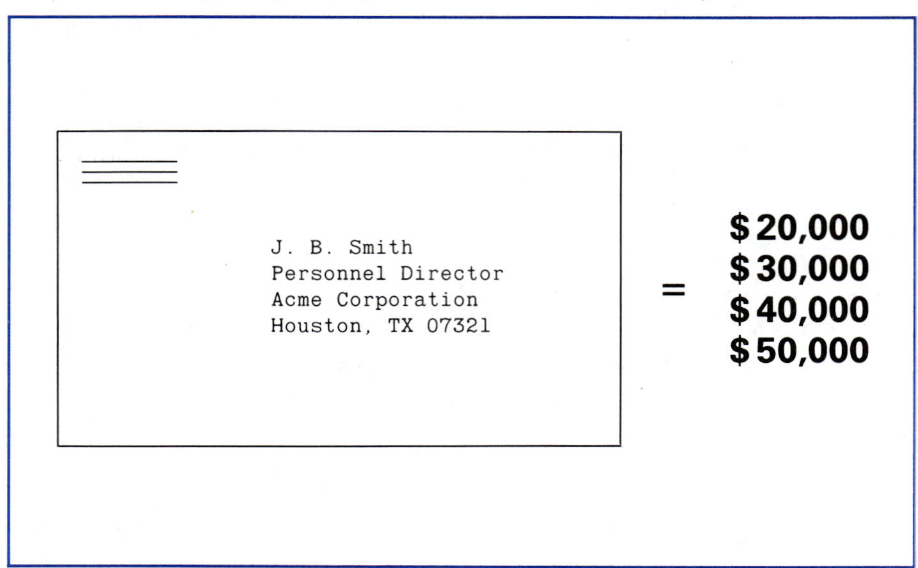

your individual qualifications but also gets you to the next phase of the hiring process. Besides the job-application letter, you will also learn to assemble an effective biographical resumé (also called a vita or data sheet) in one-page and multi-page formats, and a one-page qualifications sheet (or functional resumé). These various documents provide concrete examples of the key principles of business communication discussed earlier. Because this kind of letter is so important in your life right now (or soon will be), you need the precise focus on your audience those principles give you.

Although most college graduates use application letters at some point in their job searches, there are other approaches to finding a job. The percentage of jobs secured through personal contacts (many varieties of knowing the right person) runs from 50 to 90 percent. Some people go through interviews only, or interviews before letters. Some people use specialized types of resumes to go with particular interviews or letters. And some people use less direct methods of getting a job.

To make the most of your job search, you should keep your mind open to these other possibilities. But you will probably still find yourself at the point where nearly all of us have been—facing the single biggest writing problem of your senior year—the job-application letter.

1. Writing Effective Job Applications

What does a good job-application letter look like? Exhibits 6.2, 6.3, and 6.4 present three typical examples.

How do these letters differ from one another? The letter in Exhibit 6.2 uses another person's name as the contact phrase. The letter in Exhibit 6.3 comes from an applicant who has both work experience and academic training that exactly fit the job. Combining the qualifications from the first letter with the strong contact phrase of the second would produce the strongest possible letter. The letter in Exhibit 6.4 is a good letter but comparatively the weakest of the three. The writer has only academic training for the job and little relevant work experience. Because most students are probably in the same position as the writer of the third letter, this chapter will show you how such a person can make the most of the qualifications he or she does have.

How are these three letters alike? Each uses the same basic principles of business correspondence, adapted especially for job-application letters.

1.1 Basic Principles for Job Applications

The job-application letter is basically a persuasive letter of request. The following principles are important in your job-application letter:

1. Solicited versus unsolicited correspondence
2. Reader benefits
3. "You" attitude

Exhibit 6.2 A "Namedrop" Letter This technique will work only if Mr. Yount knows Dr. Joiner and respects his recommendation.

1402 Dale Street
Dayton, OH
45405
October 3, 1986

Mr. N. J. Yount
Recruiting Director
North American Producing Division
Atlantic Richfield Company
Post Office Box 2819
Atlanta, Georgia 30327

Dear Mr. Yount:

At the recommendation of Dr. Jerry Joiner, I would like to apply for the job of Professional Accountant in Atlantic Richfield's Accounting Development Program. I will receive my B.B.A. in Finance in December 1986, and will complete my concentration in Accounting the following May.

My course work at A&M fulfills the requirements listed in your announcement. I currently have a 3.34 grade point (on a 4.0 scale), with a 3.60 in my major. My training here included courses in Managerial Finance, Investment Analysis, Cost Accounting, Auditing, Income Tax, and Investment Accounting, among others. As your notice requested, I have enclosed an unofficial transcript with this letter.

In addition to my degree, I have work experience in areas related to this job. Currently I am working as the teaching assistant for Dr. Joiner's Advanced Accounting classes. By helping his students, I am developing a better understanding of the concepts of consolidated statement preparation, international accounting policies, and financial statement analysis.

The enclosed resumé will tell you more about my background. I look forward to the opportunity to talk with you about the contributions I can make to Atlantic Richfield's continued success.

Sincerely,

Jay Thomas

Jay Thomas

Exhibit 6.3 Letter from Applicant with Education and Work Experience A strong letter, but it could have been even better with a person's name in place of the "Dear Sir."

328 Krueger
San Rafael, CA 94901
February 1, 1985

Roth Young Food Specialists
5344 Alpha Road
St. Louis, MO 63103

Dear Sir:

I wish to apply for the food-technologist position for the development of dairy products announced in the January 1985 issue of Food Technology. In May I will graduate from State Tech with a double B.S. in food science and chemistry. In my food-science curriculum I have emphasized courses in dairy science, and from these classes (listed in my enclosed resumé) I have gained a thorough understanding of the principles and practices of dairy-product manufacturing.

Working as a technical assistant in a food-chemistry laboratory has taught me the scientific method of dairy-foods research and development. For my undergraduate project I developed a technique for isolating lipase, the chemical compound that makes milk go sour. This laboratory also gave me experience in the standard methods for chemical analysis of dairy products.

I have also worked as a technician in the food research and development laboratory of a large grocery chain. My responsibility was to determine the source of the problem in inadequate processes or defective products, to propose a solution to the problem, and to determine the economic feasibility and practicality of that solution.

I would be happy to come to St. Louis to meet with you at any time. I look forward to the opportunity to discuss the contributions I can make to Roth Young's continued growth.

Sincerely,

Sara Hayes

Sara Hayes

Exhibit 6.4 A Weaker Letter Presenting Only Weak Qualifications This applicant has only academic training, with little directly relevant work experience.

883 Cherry Street 211
New Orleans, LA 70117
February 2, 1985

Box DN-145
Wall Street Journal
1233 Regal Row
St. Louis, MO 63123

Dear Sir:

I would like to apply for a job as one of your staff consultants as advertised in the Wall Street Journal on Thursday, January 29, 1985. This May I will graduate from State University with a Bachelor of Business Administration degree and a specialization in Finance.

The curriculum at State includes an equitable mix of theory and practice combined to produce a good understanding of the fundamentals of business administration. In addition to my specialization in finance, my curriculum has included courses in basic managerial decision making, business simulation, marketing, business analysis, and accounting.

I have gained experience working at 1st Bank here in New Orleans twenty hours a week for the last year. My duties have included general bookkeeping, clerical work, and (my current assignment) working in the proof department. The enclosed resume provides more information about my work experience and my education.

I would be happy to come to St. Louis any time for an interview. I look forward to discussing with you ways I can contribute to your firm.

Sincerely yours,

Thomas Baxter

Thomas Baxter

Note: This chapter deals only with solicited applications—those written in response to a notice of a job vacancy. Unsolicited applications are rarely successful and difficult to generalize about.

4. Good will
5. Caution about unnecessary negative messages
6. Positive emphasis
7. Resale/action close

Exhibit 6.5 presents another sample letter, with notations showing its use of the principles. Briefly, here is how the letter uses each principle:

1. *Solicited Versus Unsolicited Correspondence.* The phrase "as described in the bulletin posted in the Geophysics office at State University" makes it clear to Mr. Armstrong that this letter is specifically aimed at that particular job; the letter is responding to a job notice sent out by the company. If Mr. Armstrong is like most readers of business letters, the fact that the letter is in that sense solicited gives him a much more favorable predisposition toward it.

Exhibit 6.5 A Strong Application Letter The letter's use of the principles for job-application letters is marked.

1902 Southwest Parkway
Apartment 735
College Station, TX
77840
February 5, 1985

Richard B. Armstrong
Senior Geophysicist
Texaco Incorporated
P. O. Box 430
Bellaire, TX 77401

Dear Mr. Armstrong:

I would like to apply for the position of geophysicist with Texaco as described in the bulletin posted in the Geophysics office at Texas A&M University. I will graduate from A&M this May with a Bachelor of Science degree in Geophysics, and I have worked the past three summers for major oil companies in various aspects of geophysical exploration.

[solicited versus unsolicited]

This summer work experience has guided my interest in exploration. The first summer I worked with Amoco Production Company interpreting gravity surveys with their gravity and magnetics group. The second summer I worked with Atlantic Richfield's Exploration Resources Group in Dallas preparing synthetic seismic logs using computers. This last summer I worked for Mobil in Dallas doing seismic interpretation, which I find to be most challenging.

[positive emphasis]

caution about unnecessary negative messages

good will

My classes at A&M give me the necessary background for this kind of work. These classes include Seismic Exploration, Geophysical Data Processing, Structural Geology, and Stratigraphy and Sedimentation. The enclosed resume gives more details about my education and work experience.

resale and action close

reader benefits and "you" attitude

I hope to meet with you when you arrive on campus for interviews March 3. I look forward to discussing with you the ways in which I can contribute to Texaco's exploration effort.

Sincerely,

Kim Solman

Kim Solman

2. *Reader Benefits*. The explicit reader benefits in this letter are in the phrase "the ways in which I can contribute." There are also implicit reader benefits throughout the letter: the reader (Mr. Armstrong) is getting exactly the kind of job applicant he wants. When you deliver exactly what the reader wants, that is reader benefits.
3. *"You" Attitude*. The phrases "meet with you," "discussing with you," and "contribute to Acme Oil" (at the end of the letter) focus the letter on the reader. Everything about the letter suggests it was written just for Mr. Armstrong.
4. *Good will*. Offering to go into more detail in the enclosed resumé alerts the reader to your having adapted just for this reader what goes in the letter and what is better left to the resumé. Some writers put everything, trivia and all, into their letters, and others only generalize. It is a courtesy to your reader to put in just the amount of detail he or she needs, and then remind the reader about the resumé.
5. *Caution about Needless Negative Messages*. It would be a needless negative message to claim "my classes give me the background for this job" without backing it up with specifics. To list all the classes here would also be a needless negative message.
6. *Positive Emphasis*. The fact that each of the summer jobs mentioned was with a different company, none of them with Acme Oil, doesn't faze this writer at all. She turns it to her advantage with a good positive attitude.
7. *Resale/Action Close*. It's clear what the writer expects of the reader; their next communication will be at an on-campus interview, for which the writer has apparently already signed up.

The careful use of these principles separates the letter written by a skilled writer from the letter written by an amateur. Of course, the biggest difference is in effect: one makes the most of your opportunity, and the other leaves your future to chance.

1.2 Basic Patterns for Job Applications

How are the sample letters in Exhibits 6.2 to 6.5 similar in their application of principles? Notice that they share the same four-paragraph structure (see Exhibit 6.6).

First Paragraph. The first paragraph contains the contact phrase that clarifies the letter's solicited nature and clearly states the purpose of the letter. The first paragraph also identifies the writer's single biggest claim to the job.

It is important to make it clear to the reader early in the first paragraph that this letter is solicited correspondence. Whether your contact phrase is "At the suggestion of. . . ," "As advertised in . . . ," or one of many others, place it in that first sentence. Also, get right to the point of the letter in the first sentence: apply for the job. "I would like to apply for the position of . . . as advertised in. . . . " is a good way to say it. Your reader will appreciate your good business letter sense and straightforwardness. Often the person who opens your letter only routes it somewhere else; getting right to the point at the beginning helps your letter find the right desk fast.

The rest of the opening paragraph should be a brief statement of your biggest claim to the job. "I have both college education and practical experience in . . . ." is probably the best phrase. Many new college graduates, however, can only say "I will receive my B.S. degree from XYZ University in May, 19 ___ ." Whatever your case, remember to put your best foot forward in the first paragraph; take your best shot first!

Second Paragraph. The second paragraph expands on your biggest claim to the job: academic training, job experience, or a combination of the two (whichever is best for the job). This may include a brief summary of your relevant background and a reference to more detailed information on the enclosed resumé.

If your college education is your biggest claim to the job, go into more detail about that education in the second paragraph. "As a management major, I took xx hours of management courses and xx hours of (whatever your second field of study is: computer science, accounting, etc.). These xx hours of management included. . . ." List a few of the most relevant courses, being sure to use descriptive titles: not "Management 4630," but "Theories of Organizational Behavior." If you haven't already done so, this is a good place to refer to your resumé: "Please refer to the enclosed resumé for more information on the courses I have taken that are relevant to this job." You can also refer to any extra bits of information that might connect your education with this job, such as "In my computer classes we used a Phrase Master 370/3601, which I know is the same hardware your company uses, so I should have no trouble adapting to. . . ."

Exhibit 6.6 The Conceptual Outline of a Job-Application Letter The letters shown in this chapter all share this underlying structure.

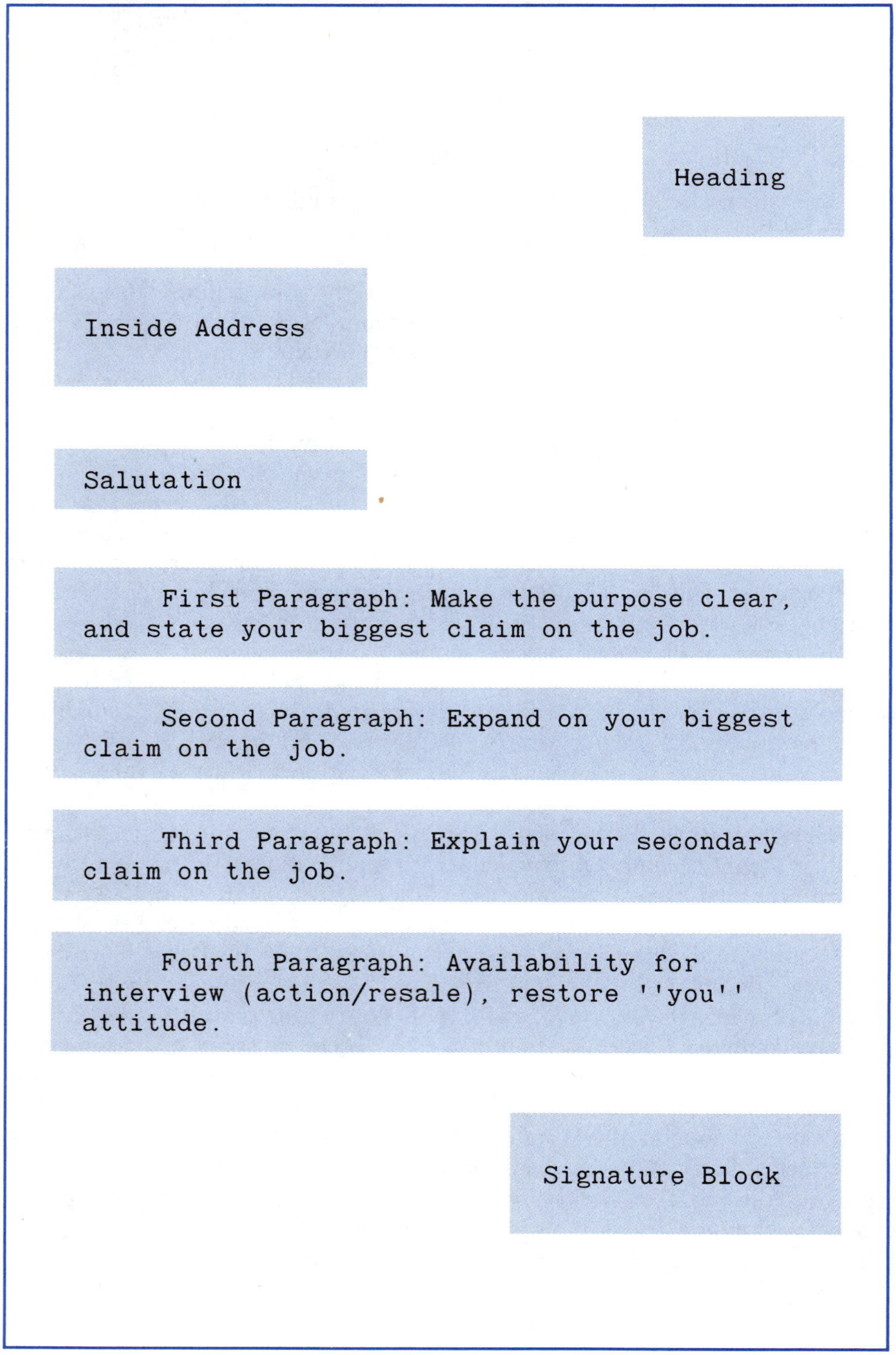

Heading

Inside Address

Salutation

First Paragraph: Make the purpose clear, and state your biggest claim on the job.

Second Paragraph: Expand on your biggest claim on the job.

Third Paragraph: Explain your secondary claim on the job.

Fourth Paragraph: Availability for interview (action/resale), restore ''you'' attitude.

Signature Block

Third Paragraph. The third paragraph explains your secondary claim on the job, typically either work experience or education. If you have education but no experience, finding a positive way to phrase this weaker claim is especially important.

Your reader may construe this paragraph—potentially the weakest—as a negative message; therefore, place it in the third paragraph, so it can have stronger buffer paragraphs both before and after it. If you have relevant work experience, even on a non-paying, volunteer basis, mention it positively here. If the only work experience you have is not relevant to the job you're applying for, bring it up here to demonstrate that you are capable of showing up on time, getting along with people, taking responsibility, etc. "Every summer since my junior year in high school I have held a full-time job for three months. Ranging from maintenance man to insurance salesman, these jobs have given me the ability to . . . and the confidence to. . . ." That may be weak, but it is better than applying for the job on the strength of your education alone.

Here is another good touch: "Through part-time jobs during the school year and summer jobs between terms I have earned xx percent of my college expenses." That is the kind of thing too many job applicants seem to apologize for when they should be proud of it. Most employers respect that kind of stamina.

Fourth Paragraph. In the fourth paragraph, mention your availability for an interview and make clear just what you expect the next step in the process to be. If you have inside information about what this company is looking for from its applicants and you haven't used that information yet, this is the place. Finally, you need a closing that restores the letter's "you" attitude and prepares you and the reader for the next stage of the process.

If the next step is an interview, you may want to bring the subject up by discussing your availability: "I am available for an interview at any time from March 15 on," or "I will be in Philadelphia for Christmas (from December 19 to January 12) and will call to arrange an appointment then."

At the very end of the letter, you need to turn the emphasis directly back on the reader with "you" attitude. "You" attitude is very difficult to achieve in a job-application letter because it naturally focuses on the writer more than on the reader. More than anywhere else, in the last lines you need to get the reader's needs and wants foremost. Here is one way to do that while also accomplishing the action closing and resale: "I look forward to the opportunity to discuss with you or a representative of your firm the ways in which I can contribute to your company's continued (success, growth, etc.)."

As with all the typical forms presented in this book, the best letter for you may be somewhat different. Yours may have two, three, four, or five paragraphs, and in rare cases (less rare if you've been out of school a few years), your letter may be more than one page long. Write the letter that strongly presents *you* as a competent, educated individual, and place that presentation clearly in the context of what you can do for that company. The sample letters presented here suggest the main elements of the most effective job-application letters, but don't rule out other possibilities. Use the sample letter discussed above to define the center of the set of all possible effective job applications, not to establish the boundaries on that set.

1.3 Questions Students Ask About Job Applications

The directions given here so far should give you a good basic letter. Of course, you have many questions; the following are the ones students ask most frequently:

Question: How do I say I'm qualified for the job? I really feel I can do a good job for these people, but where and how do I say so?

Answer: That's a tough question. The answers will vary from person to person, from job to job, and from profession to profession. What you want to watch out for is seeming to come on too strong. The way out of this is as follows. You would certainly not want to say something like, "I feel sure I can be the best lab technician Accu-Labs has," without giving the evidence to back that claim up (either before or after it), or "My combination of two years as a military lab tech. and four years' education in biology has given me. . . ." Because you must give the evidence anyway, why not just state it in a clear and suggestive enough way to make it inevitable that the reader will come to agree with your claim on his or her own, and then leave the claim unstated? Of course, to make that realization inevitable in your reader's mind takes writing skill, but the reward for that skill can be high.

Question: Do I really have to say, "I would like to apply for. . . ."?

Answer: Yes. Everyone in business and industry has bad reactions to letters that beat around the bush. A solicited letter of request should be carefully planned and straightforward.

Question: Why such a formal ending as, "I look forward to discussing. . . ."? Won't it be recognized as a stock ending?

Answer: Yes, it may well be recognized. But it is a comfortable, functional kind of formality, and that helps. And that particular ending works on your reader's psychology: many people who employ new college graduates have a bad attitude toward them. Some employers consider new graduates too "me"-centered and not enough company-centered, always asking "What will the company do for me?" rather than "What can I do for the company?" The phrase "the ways I can contribute to your company's. . . ." makes it clear that you are not "me"-centered.

1.4 Tactics and Strategies for Job Applications

Carefully consider every word in your letter not only from your point of view but also from that of your reader. Again, remember that anything that *can* be misunderstood *will be*. Use the words that will present exactly the right message, whether your reader skims the letter or carefully considers each word and phrase.

Three principles of business communication deserve special consideration in this regard:

1. Convey "you" versus "me" attitude.
2. Emphasize the positive rather than the negative.
3. Avoid unnecessary negative messages.

Although all of these have been discussed already, they are important enough to be re-emphasized, with specific application to the job-application letter.

1.4.1 **Convey "You" Attitude.** Try to build into every line of your letter your willingness to serve your employer. Show that you are much more interested in that than in having your employer benefit you. Check each sentence for accidental intrusions of "me" attitude that can easily be removed; be alert for chances to insert more "you" attitude.

Here are examples of "me" attitude turned into "you" attitude:

"Me" Attitude	**"You" Attitude**
"I know that the EDG Dept. is giving me the best possible training in the drafting profession."	"The Engineering Design Graphics Department has a national reputation for producing excellent draftsmen."
"This should be suitable to qualify me for your current job opening."	"This work experience should make me a strong candidate for the job you have advertised."
"I would like to tell you of my goals as a member of the construction industry."	"I can contribute to your company by. . . ."
"The job you have described seems to fit my desires perfectly."	Either omit this kind of statement entirely, or, if for you "desires" and "qualifications" mean the same thing, then you can say, "I have both education and training for a position in. . . ."
"I think my credits are more than sufficient to fill your job opening, and I look forward to employment by your company."	"I hope you find that the credentials I have listed here make me a strong candidate for the job you have advertised, and that I can have the opportunity to discuss with you the ways in which I can contribute to. . . ."

1.4.2 **Emphasize the Positive.** Word your phrases positively, not negatively. You want to describe your cup as half full, not half empty. Do not say things like, "I have not had any full-time jobs," but rather "through my part-time jobs I have earned 75% of my college expenses." Here are more examples of negative emphasis turned positive.

Negative Emphasis	**Positive Emphasis**
"While reviewing several job notices, yours caught my attention."	"I would like to apply for. . . ."
"During my five years of industrial experience I have gone from job to job, ..."	"I have five years of industrial experience at a variety of jobs, ranging from . . . to. . . ."
"My major is General Industrial Technology with no particular area of specialization."	"My major is General Industrial Technology."

"There are a few courses in my curriculum which deal with software systems."	"I have taken *X* hours of courses which deal with software systems, including ______, ______, and ______."
"My job experience is confined to summer jobs."	"Through my summer jobs I have been able to pay ___ percent of my college expenses."

1.4.3 **Avoid Unnecessary Negative Messages.** Many instances of negative emphasis like those discussed earlier can also be viewed as unnecessary negative messages. They are things you say that will strike the reader the wrong way, and on further examination you may find you do not need to say them at all. If you have no full-time work experience, leaving the whole subject of full-time experience out of your letter may be better than anything you could say that would begin with, "Although I have no full-time work experience. . . ." If the subject will not advance your cause, why bring it up at all?

Obviously, if you are asked directly about some such subject, you will need to respond honestly. But as long as you have the option of not bringing up such a subject, it is probably to your advantage to exercise that option.

Box 6.1 gives examples of typical unnecessary negative messages in job-application letters written by students. They do not require revision; rather, they should be left out entirely.

Your job application letters will never be exactly like the ones described above. In some ways, all job-application letters are the same, but in other important ways, they should all be different. Each one should reflect the unique person who sends it *and* the unique person and job it is addressed to. This brings us to the next part of writing effective job-application letters: analyzing your audience and adapting your letters to them.

Box 6.1 Unnecessary Negative Messages

1. I would like to get established within a company soon after I graduate.
2. I have been looking into several job prospects but so far I haven't got a job.
3. I wish to apply for this position to gain agronomic experience on an international level.
4. It is true that as a whole my major areas of study deal with large industries, but I will gladly work in a smaller company.
5. I am interested in getting started in the engineering field and would like to start with your company.
6. I am sorry this application is so late.
7. Although I missed your recruiters when they were here. . . .

2. Individualizing Your Application

The more you know about your audience and the more you adapt your letter to them, the more effective your letter can be. Your letter is already individual in the ways that mean the most to *you* because the key features of your life, ability, and personality are described in it. But to be really effective, your letter also needs to be individual in the ways that are most significant to your *reader*. That means you need to think about what kind of person your reader is—what he or she knows or doesn't know, needs or doesn't need, is or is not interested in. Carried to its logical extreme, this means that each letter you write for each job is different from every other letter you write. We will look first at ways to analyze your audience and then at ways to adapt your letter to that audience (short of writing a totally different letter for each job).

2.1 Visualizing Your Audience

To write a fully effective job-application letter, you need to visualize your audience. Try to visualize how your reader looks, dresses, talks, acts, drives, reads; get as clear a picture as you can. At the least, make the best guesses you can about your reader; at the most, get definite information. The more you can learn about your reader and store in your mind, the more your subconscious will do your audience adaptation for you.

If you are writing to a specific, named person (rather than "Box 152" or "Personnel Manager"), try to find out as much as you can about that person. If you are about to enter a professional field, you probably already know quite a bit about the kind of person who does the hiring in your field. Even such a stereotype can be useful here, if it helps you to visualize your audience.

The people who run professional advertising agencies do the most sophisticated audience analysis there is, and you can take advantage of it. Find a journal aimed at the kind of person you are writing to (such as a professional or trade journal in that person's field) and look at the people in the ads. Of course the people are professional models, but they are also the images your prospective employers have of themselves. If you have no other information to go on, write your letter as though it were to one of the people you saw pictured.

Successfully visualizing your audience gives your subconscious the chance to help you adapt your job-application letter (or any other document) to each particular audience. You also need to use the other analysis and adaptation techniques described in this book. There will also be specific characteristics about each job you apply for that will require your letter to be specialized.

You will probably still have questions that give you problems: Should I bring this point up at all? Should I make more of this item? Or should I omit it entirely? The answers to such questions can only come through knowing more about and visualizing your audience; do what you believe will have the best effect on your audience.

2.2 Avoiding "Dear Occupant" Writing

If you fail to do audience analysis and adaptation for your job application letters, you are probably doing "Dear Occupant" writing, the same kind of writing that offends most people who get mass-mailing advertisements. Writing to "Dear Sir" or "Personnel Manager" with no idea of who that person is or what that person needs is like dropping a pebble into a very deep, very dark well—you may never even know for sure that it even hit bottom. And you may never know if your "Dear Occupant" letters reached anyone, because they were never specifically aimed at anyone.

By now you have probably heard stories of people who graduated ahead of you and sent out 100 or 200 copies of the same job application letter. Those stories usually feature such details as having the letters done on good paper, with their inside addresses and salutations individualized by the word processor. The price is high, and those stories almost never mention whether that person actually got a good job, or whether any job at all resulted from the letter.

This shotgun approach to writing job-application letters usually backfires. As countless mass mail advertisers have found, it is practically impossible to be successful at simultaneously mass mailing and individualizing. Most people resent such letters—thus the descriptive phrase "junk mail."

The precise name for such a letter, one with only a word or two changed here and there before it is sent out to many different people, is *generic*. No employer worth his (or her) salt will be deceived by generic job-application letters. But the alternative, to write every letter fresh from scratch, may be impossible for you. There is an attractive middle ground between these extremes, however: Many students find that they can write two or three basic letters (the number depends on the range of jobs they are applying for) and then write the letters they actually send out based on those basic (or *modular*) letters. The letters sent out are composed of parts of the two or three basic letters, but they are individualized in more detail than just changing the receiver's name and address. The individualizing makes it clear to the reader that the letter is not mass produced. It may be one line in one paragraph, or a change in the order of paragraphs, or the creation of a brand new paragraph for that one letter.

An example will make this more clear. Here are the modular letters written by an accounting student who has a strong second emphasis in computers. She writes three basic letter: one (Exhibit 6.7) emphasizing her education and experience in accounting, another (Exhibit 6.8) emphasizing her education and experience in computers, and a third (Exhibit 6.9) emphasizing a combination of both. Following these examples, we will see what one of the letters she actually sent out looked like.

Some of the letters Ms. Jones sends out may be word for word like one of those above, but many of them will vary slightly. Exhibit 6.10 shows an example of a letter she sent out, based on the letter in Exhibit 6.9.

Most people find it very hard to write these basic letters starting from scratch because they're addressed to no one in particular. The way to do it is to write letters to your best job possibilities first, and then extract and modify your basic letters out of those specific examples.

Exhibit 6.7 A Basic Letter Notice how anonymous and weak this letter seems. It lacks the specific details that come with aiming it at one particular job, but it makes writing the specific letters go much faster.

Dear ________ :

I would like to apply for the position of Accountant which you have advertised in ________ . I will graduate this May from State Tech with a Bachelor of Arts degree in Accounting. I also have summer work experience in accounting.

My course work in Accounting includes courses in ________ , ________ , ________ , and ________ . I have also taken __ hours of courses in Computer Technology.

Each of the last three summers I have worked for Jones and Williams Agency, a local public accounting firm here in Los Angeles. The nature of my duties ranged from office assistant the first summer to assistant bookkeeper this last summer. Through these experiences I have learned more about how accountants actually work than college itself could ever teach me.

To provide you with more information about my work experience and education, I have enclosed a resumé with this letter. I can be in ________ for an interview any time at your convenience. I look forward to meeting you and discussing with the ways in which I can contribute to ________.

Sincerely,

Susan Jones

Susan Jones

Using basic letters still means you will have to type each letter separately. The changes from letter to letter will be too great for anything short of a word processor to handle. But by working from basic letters you will certainly be able to *compose* each letter much faster than otherwise, and these partially tailor-made letters are much more effective than mass-produced letters. You can also save the basic letters you wrote this year and use the best of them (the ones that get good results) again, with appropriate modifications should you want to change jobs.

2.3 Creating Yourself, Creating Your Reader

Why are individualized letters easier to write and more effective than mass-produced ones? The answer to this question contains the essence of the psychology of human beings as writers and readers. Most people who receive mass-produced

Exhibit 6.8 A Basic Letter This letter is anonymous and weak, like the one in Exhibit 6.7, but it brings out some interesting ideas about computers and accounting. It also shows the difficulty of applying for a job other than the one your degree leads people to expect.

Dear Mr. __________:

I would like to apply for the position of Computer Technologist you have advertised in the __________. My summer jobs have given me experience with many aspects of computer technology, and I have taken twenty-one hours of computer technology courses in college.

For the past three summers I have worked for Jones and Williams Agency, a public accounting firm here in Los Angeles. During those summers a major part of my duties has been to assist the firm's rapidly expanding computer operations. Thus I have had on the job experience with statistical analysis, interactive statistical processing, systems programming, and interactive computer graphics.

I will graduate this May from State Tech with a Bachelor of Arts degree, majoring in Accounting. This accounting background makes me especially aware of the business marketplace's needs and problems with computers, and that awareness should help me contribute to the field of Computer Technology. I can see the computers from the point of view of the accountant as well as the point of view of the computer specialist.

The enclosed resumé shows more about my education and work experience. I can be in __________ for an interview any time at your convenience. I look forward to. . . .

Sincerely,

Susan Jones

Susan Jones

writing of any kind resent the depersonalization they feel it brings. People want to be treated as individuals, to have their unique needs and desires taken seriously. But mass-produced, “Dear Occupant” writing creates a picture of a reader who is nameless, faceless, and characterless. For the reader, it is like looking in a mirror and seeing an empty silhouette staring back. Everyone you ever write to will have his or her own particular needs and desires. If you as a writer ignore the uniqueness of your reader, thus producing “Dear Occupant” writing, you risk having your writing ignored at best, actively resented at worst.

Exhibit 6.9 A Basic Combination Letter If she can find a job that asks for this combination of skills, this student stands a good chance. Here the combination of skills is unique and so strong it starts to make up for the fact that the letter still is not addressed to any particular person. But this would almost by itself define a particular job.

Dear Mr. __________:

I would like to apply for the position of Accountant which you have advertised in __________. I will be graduating from State University this May with a Bachelor of Arts degree in Accounting. In addition to the accounting curriculum, I have taken 21 hours of courses in Computer Technology. I also have summer work experience which combined accounting with computers, giving me the exact credentials your job notice called for.

My course work in Accounting includes courses in __________, __________, __________, and __________. Among my courses in Computer Technology were courses in COBOL, FORTRAN, ALGOL, BASIC, and Interactive Graphics. My overall grade point is 3.2 on a 4.0 basis.

Each of the last three summers I worked for Jones and Williams Agency, a public accounting firm here in Los Angeles. My duties ranged from office assistant to assistant bookkeeper. During those summers a major part of my duties was to assist the firm's rapid expansion of its use of computers. I gained on the job experience with statistical analysis, interactive statistical processing, systems programming, and interactive computer graphics.

The combination of accounting and computers in my background allows me to see computers from the point of view of accountants and accounting from the point of view of computer specialists. This perspective and my combination of abilities will, I hope, make me a strong candidate for the position you have advertised.

The enclosed resumé shows more about my education and work experiences. I can be in __________ for an interview any time at your convenience. I look forward to. . . .

Sincerely,

Susan Jones

Susan Jones

Exhibit 6.10 A Real Letter Based on the One in Exhibit 6.9 Once Miss Jones realized that her combination of accounting and computer skills was what really made her special as a job applicant, she went looking for a job that called for just that combination.

Dear Mr. Hermening:

I would like to apply for the position of accountant you have advertised in the Houston Post. I will be graduating from State Tech this May with a Bachelor of Arts degree in accounting. I have also taken twenty-one hours of computer-technology courses. My summer work experience has combined accounting with computers, so I have exactly the credentials you asked for.

My course work in Accounting includes the three standard accounting courses—cost accounting, managerial accounting, and accounting theory—among others. Among my courses in Computer Technology were . . .

(Except for the last paragraph, the rest of the letter follows the one in Ex. 6.9.)

The enclosed resumé shows more about my education and work experience. I can be in Houston any time for an interview at your convenience. I look forward to discussing with you the ways in which I can contribute to your agency's continued success.

Sincerely,

Susan Jones

Susan Jones

The reader you create in your writing needs to match your real reader's own best self-image, because that is what your readers will respond to most favorably. You may also find that your writing comes easiest and pleases you most when the image that it creates of you as a writer matches your own best image of yourself. If you are composing "Dear Occupant" writing, the kind of self-image you are creating may be so psychologically unpleasant to you that you actually find it hard to write. Skilled writers are those who not only have become conscious of their own styles but also have realized the value of style. Professional writers are those who learn to vary their styles easily and successfully, to create different implied writers and implied readers when the situation demands it. Just as you need to consider the reader your writing creates, so you also need to think about the kind of person it implies that you, the writer, are.

3. Effective Forms for Resumés

At some point in the job application process, nearly everyone has to prepare some kind of ordered visual presentation of abilities, education, and work history. This may be called a *data sheet*, a *vita sheet*, a *resumé*, or a *bio*; you may use it with your initial letter, at the campus interview, or at the on-site interview. You may also hear these kinds of documents classified as historical, biographical, or functional. Whenever you use such a document, and whatever you call it, this visual presentation is a vital part of your job application. It is something you will need to keep—and to update—the rest of your working life. If you wait to make one until the week before your first interview, chances are it won't be done nearly as well as it could be.

Three ways of presenting yourself on paper will be discussed here: the one-page resumé, the multi-page resumé, and the qualifications sheet. The most challenging of the three to produce is the multi-page resumé, and because all of the principles involved in it are also to a lesser extent involved in the shorter forms, most of the attention here will be paid to the multi-page resumé.

Each of the three forms presented below employs the same five principles:

- Placement on the page
- Typeface for emphasis
- Compartmentalization
- Psychological structure
- Audience analysis and adaptation

3.1 The One-Page Resumé

Exhibit 6.11 shows a one-page resumé in a popular format. It illustrates how to use each of the five principles listed above:

3.1.1 **Placement on the Page.** The most important material (name and professional goal, for instance) is at the top, in the most prominent position.

3.1.2 **Compartmentalization.** The document is divided into categories to suit the person it describes and the job he or she is applying for. Each compartment has contents adjusted for exactly those needs.

3.1.3 **Psychological Structure.** The document is designed to appeal to the psychology of the reader. The underlined items in the body (*Engineering Support Technician*, etc.) are set to catch the reader's eye as it scans the page. The most important and responsible job is listed first, not last. High school graduation is not mentioned; if he were applying for a job in his home town, it might well be.

3.1.4 **Audience Analysis and Adaptation.** The job Mr. Lynn is applying for is designing and building electrical equipment as part of a group. Thus it is no coincidence that his professional objective is worded that way. He has interpreted this to be a

Exhibit 6.11 A One-Page Resumé This is one of many popular possible forms.

MATTHEW LYNN

1431 Rudder Road Knoxville, TN 37920 (615) 577-5902	Single Age 25 Willing to Relocate
PROFESSIONAL OBJECTIVE	To participate in the design and building of sophisticated electronic equipment.
EDUCATION	Bachelor of Science in Electrical Engineering, The University of Tennessee, May 1986. Emphasis in Electronics and Instrumentation. Grade Point 3.0 (on 4.0 scale).
IMPORTANT COURSEWORK	9 hours in Electronics 9 hours in Instrumentation 6 hours in Computer Programming 8 hours in Physics 6 hours in Calculus 6 hours in Technical Writing
WORK EXPERIENCE 1984–1985	Engineering Support Technician, Petkus Corp., Tullahoma, Tennessee. Participated in development of production line tests and construction of sequential electronic test systems. Performed all Quality Control procedures during production.
Summers, 1981–1984	Electrician's Assistant, Welch Electrical Contracting, Tullahoma, Tennessee.
1979–1981	Framing Carpenter, Collier Construction Company, Tullahoma, Tennessee.
PERSONAL BACKGROUND	Matthew Lynn is a native of Tennessee. He enjoys travel, hunting, fishing, and camping. His other hobbies include gardening and home computers.
REFERENCES	Available upon request.

March 2, 1986

very down-to-earth kind of company, and that's how he presents himself in this one-page resumé.

3.2 The Multi-Page Resumé

With the multi-page format you can add categories, delete categories, move categories, and move items within categories, giving you more variables than can be fully discussed here. Exhibit 6.12 shows a good multi-page resumé; it uses each of the principles discussed earlier as follows:

3.2.1 **Placement on the Page.** Notice that this form uses headings centered within a wide left margin (as well as horizontal and vertical spacing) to achieve emphasis and divide categories. In the multi-page form the left margin headings are easier for a reader's eyes to follow than a series of centered headings would be. The most important items are placed in the most prominent positions—tops of pages, bottoms of pages, and left margins. The least important (or potentially negative) items are buried in the centers of pages. Thus the placement of items on the page appeals to the reader's psychology. To a greater degree than the shorter forms, the multi-page resumé organizes its information psychologically (to satisfy the reader) rather than logically (which may make sense only to the writer).

3.2.2 **Typeface for Emphasis.** One of the keys to success with a multi-page resumé is to use all of the resources of your typewriter to your advantage. Use words typed with all capital letters, initial capital letters, and underlining—each in a planned way. Combined with vertical and horizontal spacing, the varieties of typeface allow a skillful writer to guide the reader's attention across the page in the way most favorable to the writer.

3.2.3 **Compartmentalization.** The categories and subcategories used in the sample resumé may not be exactly those that will best reflect your own abilities and background. Also, the categories and subcategories—or the ordering of them—that work best for you on one application may not work best on another. Sometimes you need to enlarge a category, shorten it, move it to a more or less prominent position, introduce a category, or delete a category, all based on changes in your own qualifications or in the nature of the job you're applying for. Compartmentalization of the resumé allows you to choose how to present yourself to your reader. The kind of person you make yourself seem to be is (within the bounds of truth) completely optional.

3.2.4 **Psychological Structure.** The most important principle is to make the whole presentation a psychological sculpture, reflecting your reader's needs and interests rather than your own preconceptions. For example, it may never have occurred to you that from the reader's point of view it makes more sense to list your most recent work experience first, because it is usually closer to the job you're seeking, both in kind and in level of responsibility. Besides using reverse chronological order in work experience and perhaps in other areas, you may want to separate

Exhibit 6.12 A Multi-Page Resumé Such resumes can be adapted and modified almost endlessly.

TERRY WRIGHT

Box 253, Rudder Road Knoxville, TN 37919 (615) 577-4711	Single Age 21 Will Relocate
PROFESSIONAL OBJECTIVE	To become Production Control Manager, supervising the completion of industrial projects.
EDUCATION	Bachelor of Science in Engineering Technology, The University of Tennessee, May, 1982.
Courses in Major	Manufacturing Processes Industrial Safety Machine Production Technology Mechanics of Materials Statics and Dynamics Engineering Design Graphics (I & II) Plane Surveying (I & II) Statics and Strength of Materials Foremanship and Supervision Electricity and Electronics Communication for Industrial Personnel Computer Programming for Engineers
Supporting Courses	Purchasing Industrial Marketing Business Law Technical Writing Statistics
WORK EXPERIENCE (part-time, summers)	Air-conditioning repair technician, Johnny's Appliance and Parts, Knoxville, Tennessee. In addition to repairing air conditioning and all types of heaters, duties included inventory, billing, and book work.
1986	Designer and Draftsman, Ramtag (a division of Bemco), Knoxville, Tennessee. Duties included designing and drafting custom bakery equipment (tandem bun slicers, conveyors).
1984	Handyman, Taggart Research Division, Knoxville, Tennessee. Duties included over-hauling equipment and assisting in building construction.
1983	Carpenter's Helper, Pyramid Construction, Knoxville, Tennessee.

TERRY WRIGHT
(Resume, p. 2)

SCHOLARSHIPS and AWARDS	Through various part-time and summer jobs, paid for 80% of college education. Distinguished Student Award, 1978–1979, 1979–1980, for achieving a grade point 3.25 or better. Carl and Florence Wilson Scholarship, 1978–1979, for placing in the state Ready Writing Contest.
MEMBERSHIPS	American Society of Civil Engineers, student member Engineering Technology Society Intramural Sports: tennis, basketball, football Fellowship of Christian Athletes Knoxville Boys Club
REFERENCES	Mr. Joe E. Braberson, owner Johnny's Appliance and Parts 5423 N. Broadway Knoxville, TN 37925 (615) 523-8736 Dr. Tom Gunderson, Assistant Professor Department of Engineering Technology The University of Tennessee Knoxville, TN 37912 (615) 974-8015 Dr. James Hall, Associate Professor Department of Engineering Technology The University of Tennessee Knoxville, TN 37912 (615) 974-8023 Mr. William Hefflin Production Engineer Ramtag, Inc. 6897 Clinton Highway Knoxville, TN 37880 (615) 563-9880 Mr. Michael Hannert Foreman Taggart Research Division 6800 Oak Ridge Highway Knoxville, TN 37985 (615) 534-1885

your work experience into *full-time* and *summers*, or you may want to sort your experience by the kinds of duties you performed—clerical, supervisory, accounting, and so on. You need to decide what it is in your background that will most appeal to your prospective employer, and structure your resumé to bring that material into the forefront.

3.2.5 **Audience Analysis and Adaptation.** To give your resumé a structure that has a psychological appeal to your reader, you need to analyze the kind of person your reader is. Based on what you know and can learn about the profession, the company, the job, and the people who will do the hiring, what do you think your strongest points are? How can you emphasize those points? What else can you add that will help you get the job? Are there areas you are forced to bring up, but that you want to de-emphasize? How much detail do you need in each of the various categories? You need to think through these questions to make your resumé as effective as possible, and you can only answer such questions accurately if you analyze your audience.

Constructing an effective multi-page resumé never ends: whatever form you are happy with today, whatever form best reflects your unique qualifications today, you will probably want to change next week or next month, as your own image of yourself and the kind of professional work you do changes.

3.3 Questions about Resumés

Question: My grade point average isn't so hot. What do I do?

Answer: If you feel you must mention something about it on paper, try including only your grade point average in your major. Or place yourself in the appropriate percentile of your graduating class—"top 25 percent of class." Remember, as a negative message it may be better communicated orally than on paper.

Question: What about references?

Answer: Every professional handles references differently. Some include reference letters with the resumé, some put letters on file with placement services, and some prefer the employer to write or call the references. Whatever the case, you need to arrange with three to seven people at least to be prepared to write letters in support of your application if the need arises. Choose these people carefully; try to diversify your references so that each person will be able to speak to a different aspect of your individuality—weighted toward your professional abilities, of course. Don't hesitate to ask more people to be prepared to write letters for you than you may actually use. It is flattering to them, and the more people who know you are looking for a job, the greater the chances one of them will be able to help you as the contact for a possible job.

Question: My school's placement service has a standard form we all fill out when we sign up for interviews. Do I still need a resumé?

Answer: You need a resumé even more. Standardized forms, such as those used by placement services, tend to make everyone look the same. You want to come across as an individual. See if you can attach your multi-page resumé to that standardized form; if not, attach your short one. If even that isn't allowed, inquire about changing the placement director's policy.

Question: I've attached the resumé to my application, but I feel I need something to hand directly to the interviewers at the beginning of the interview. What do I do?

Answer: Read the next section—use a qualifications sheet.

3.4 The Qualifications Sheet

A new and different kind of one-page presentation of your abilities is called a qualifications sheet. Some people call it a functional resumé, as opposed to the historical or biographical form described above. The traditional resumé tends to look backward, telling what you *have* done. The qualifications sheet looks forward, telling what you *can* do. This lets you include the kinds of subjects you want to steer an interview toward, subjects that might not even be covered in the traditional resumé. A qualifications sheet is especially useful if your interviewer has already seen your multi-page resumé. As an elaboration of the professional-goals section of your resumé, the qualifications sheet lets you go into detail about exactly what you choose to have the interview to focus on.

The same principles of construction apply to the qualifications sheet as the resumé. Exhibits 6.13 and 6.14 show how typical good qualifications sheets look. Because these particular qualifications sheets are to be used in interviews, where the applicant's address is already available, they do not carry addresses.

4. Interviews

The best way to train yourself to handle interviews effectively is through mock (practice) interviews. Check with your placement service and the student chapter of your professional society for such interviews. The second-best way is to view films of interviews and to critique them. Also, some advice to help make your interviews more successful is presented in the following sections as answers to these questions:

What should be the *goal* of your interview?

What *preparation* is best?

What is a *script* for an interview?

What *questions* usually come up?

What *feedback* can be obtained?

There are two broad classes of interviews—those on campus or in some other neutral setting (such as a professional meeting) and those at the prospective

Exhibit 6.13 A Qualifications Sheet Notice the emphasis on skills.

Qualifications Sheet

JOHNNIE MACK SAMPSON

Bachelor of Science, Agronomy

Land Use Planning	Livestock Production Planning
Farm Equipment Design	Farm Equipment Construction
Farm Equipment Repair	Crop Production Planning

PROFESSIONAL OBJECTIVES

Short Term: To manage a large, production oriented farm or ranch, and to develop a high degree of professionalism for production and marketing of agricultural products.

Long Term: To own and operate a farm of about 3,000 acres around the Crowley, Texas, area.

PROFESSIONAL SKILLS

Farming

Experienced and qualified to operate most types of farm machinery including:

Tractors—I.H., 1066, 1486, 1566, 4166, 4366
Land preparation—moldboards and subsoilers
Cultivators—rolling and sweep
Cotton Stripper—John Deere 484
Planter—I.H., Cyclone 500
Combine—John Deere 7700

Shop Work

Metal Duplication—lathe, milling machine, drill press
Metal Forming—shear machine, Devorak iron bender
Metal Cutting—hand held torch, pattern torch
Welding—standard rod welder, wire welder

PERSONAL DATA

JOHNNIE MACK SAMPSON is 22 years old and a native Texan. He was born and raised on a six-thousand acre irrigated farm near Crowley. He is single and active in community activities such as Methodist Men and coaching a Little League softball team.

employer's place of business. The former is usually the shorter, and it is the one discussed here. But everything said also applies to the longer, on-site interview, just more so.

4.1 What Is the Goal of This Interview?

Interviewers typically have three goals:

1. To evaluate the candidate.

Exhibit 6.14 A Qualifications Sheet Notice what the "biography" adds to your picture.

Qualification Sheet

LINDA A. WOODRUFF

M.S. in Wildlife Biology

PROFESSIONAL OBJECTIVE

To work as a biologist conducting variable wildlife research in areas where the impact of man will alter habitat and adversely affect wildlife.

Professional Skills

Statistical Analysis	Plant Taxonomy
Computer Applications	Vegetation Sampling
EIS Preparation	Aerial Photo Interpretation
Technical Writing	Telemetry

EDUCATION

Master of Science, Wildlife Biology, The University of Tennessee at Knoxville, 1982. Strong background in botany, statistics, and computer science. Bachelor of Science, Magna Cum Laude, Wildlife Biology, The University of Tennessee, Knoxville, 1980.

Important Courses

Wildlife Biology—18 hrs.	Statistics—15 hrs.
Botany—12 hrs.	Computer Science—9 hrs.

EXPERIENCE

Graduate Research, University of Tennessee, 1981–1982
Graduate Research Assistant, University of Tennessee, 1980–1981
Supervisor, Youth Community Services, Knoxville, Tennessee, 1979
Research Assistant, Great Smoky Mtns. Wildlife Forest, 1978–1979

BIOGRAPHY

LINDA A. WOODRUFF is 25 years old, a native of Knoxville. She is single and willing to relocate. She enjoys backpacking, canoeing, cross-country skiing, sewing, and photography.

2. To stimulate the candidate's interest in the firm.
3. To maintain the candidate's good will.

You can increase your chances of success in interviews by making your goals compatible with the interviewer's goals. The candidate who goes in with one and only one goal—to get the job or go down in flames trying—risks too much emotionally to be able to survive more than two or three such encounters. That very single-mindedness also works against the candidate's success because it goes so strongly against the grain of the interviewer's goals. Go in trying to make a good accounting of yourself; tell yourself, "If I don't get the job, I still want to feel like I took my best shot, that they saw me at my very best." Aim for these goals:

1. To be evaluated at your best.
2. To stimulate the interviewer's interest in you and your ability to contribute to the interviewer's firm.
3. To build and maintain the interviewer's good will.

4.2 What Preparation Is Best?

As with goals, preparation that mirrors that of the interviewer is best. When you walk into the interview room, the interviewer will probably have a folder of information on you—professional goals, school background, letters of reference, application forms—and a good idea of just where you might fit into the firm's structure and how you might best contribute to the firm's success. You need at least as much information about each firm you interview with.

From resources in your library, your placement service, and other published sources you should try to find answers to questions like these:

What does the firm do?

What is its past and future?

Who owns it?

Who runs it?

Where are its various offices, branches, and manufacturing facilities?

What is its financial structure and status?

Who is the interviewer, and where does he or she fit into the corporate structure?

Where does that firm usually start entry-level employees (financially, geographically, and so on)?

The more homework you do for your interview, the greater your chances for attaining your goals.

The best preparation is that which tells you the most about what you need to know regarding the firm, the interviewer, and your possible contribution. Doing that kind of preparation should also increase your confidence in your ability to handle the interview successfully. And that by itself should be enough to repay the effort you put into doing the homework.

4.3 What Is a Script for an Interview?

Suppose that after you get your first paper back in class, you decide you want to talk with the instructor and explain that while you don't quarrel with the grade, you want her to know that the paper really isn't representative of your ability as a writer. You had tests in other classes to prepare for, which kept you from doing as well as you hope to in the future. That's your *script*. Or your teacher may call you in to tell you that if you don't start being more careful with written assignments, you'll fail the course. That's *her* script.

Failures in communication occur when two different scripts collide. Most interviewers have scripts for their interviews; in many cases the script was written down and the interviewer has it memorized. Exhibit 6.15 shows a typical script for a thirty-minute interview.

To be a successful job candidate, you should be sensitive to when the interviewer is following a script and try to adjust your own script accordingly. You need to have your own script—things you want to bring up, points you want to make. It will be different from the interviewer's script, but you don't want the two to clash. They must be compatible in order for the interview to be successful, for both you and the interviewer.

Exhibit 6.15 An Interviewer's Typical Script This one is for a thirty-minute interview (From Joan W. Rossi, "Making Your Students Interview-Ready," *The ABCA Bulletin*, September 1980, pp. 2–5. Reprinted by permission of Joan W. Rossi.)

THE INTERVIEWER'S PLAN

Objectives of the Interviewer:
1. Evaluate the Candidate
2. Stimulate the Candidate's Interest in the Firm
3. Maintain the Good Will of the Candidate

Structure of a Good Interview (30 min.)

Time	Interviewer's Activity	Interviewer's Purpose
	1. Reading Resumé	1. Notice grades, academic achievement, extracurricular activities

4-5 min.	2. General Comments –resumé –weather –"Why did you decide to study at _____?	2. Establish rapport Put candidate at ease Ask questions candidate can answer easily so he or she gains confidence
16 min.	3. Information Gathering a. Open questions requiring explanatory answers –"How do you spend your leisure time?" –"Tell me about your college experience." –"What courses did you like?"	3. Decide whether or not to ask candidate back for a second interview a. Determine candidate's motivations and habits
	b. Closed questions requiring short factual answers –How does a candidate act in certain situations? –Focus on past behavior	b. Determine if candidate's apparent attributes are reflected in reality
	c. Listening techniques –echo (repeat phrases) –eye contact –silence	c. Show acceptance
	d. Behavior observations –interested? –enthusiastic? –poised? –assertive	d. Pierce through candidate's nervousness to substance of what the candidate is like
5 min.	4. Answer Questions	4. Sell the organization
1 min.	5. Summary and Close	5. Tell the candidate when and how he or she will hear from the organization
4 min.	6. Write up Evaluation	6. Write while impression is fresh

Box 6.2 Ten Questions Interviewers Usually Ask

1. What are your short- and long-range professional goals and objectives?
2. Why are those your goals, and how are you trying to achieve them?
3. What are your professional goals for where you want to be five or ten years from now?
4. Why did you choose this career?
5. Why should we hire *you*? What specifically can *you* contribute to our company?
6. What qualities should a successful (engineer, accountant, etc.) possess?
7. Why are you seeking a position with *this* company in particular?
8. Do you have geographical preferences for your work? Why?
9. What do you like best about your field? Why?
10. What major problems have you encountered in your life (or education, or work experience), and how have you dealt with them?

Source: This list is adapted from the one reported by Frank Endicott in *The Endicott Report*.

4.4 What Questions Usually Come Up?

Of course there are too many possible questions to list here. Let's first focus on ten typical questions (see Box 6.2), and then look at five especially tough ones (see Box 6.3). There is no one right way for everyone to answer these questions that might come up, so you should rehearse your own answers to them.

Box 6.3 Five Especially Tough Questions

1. Suppose *X* happened. How would you deal with it? (*X* is some tough, work-related problem, typically a personnel problem.)
2. How well do you work under pressure? Give examples.
3. Which is more important to you, the amount of your salary or the type of job?
4. (asked of women, usually*) Why aren't you married?
5. (and also asked of women, usually*) When do you plan to have children, and how will that affect your job?

*If you think these last two questions are of questionable legality, you're right. The problem is that they still seem to get asked. Including them here is not meant to be a contradiction of the principle that people should be hired and promoted based on their abilities—with equity, not prejudice—but rather an acknowledgement of the reality that people *do* ask those questions, and wise job applicants will decide *in advance* how to deal with them.

Practice dealing with these and other foreseeable questions. They are often the ones that interviewers ask of each person interviewed, and are thus inevitable bases for making comparisons among candidates.

Remember that although you don't *have* to answer any question, failing to do so may jeopardize your chances at a job. Sometimes you can deal most effectively with a challenging personal question (like the last two in Box 6.3) by laughing it off or responding lightheartedly. Remember, too, that many times an interviewer will ask such questions just to see how you deal with tough situations. That is, the content of your answer doesn't make as much difference as the way you deal with the whole situation—being on the spot or being asked a possibly impertinent or insulting question. Thus *any* answer may be right, as long as it does not show you to be a person who cannot deal with tough situations.

4.5 What Feedback Can Be Obtained?

It's almost impossible to get feedback from interviews that fail. If you can find a class where mock interviews are done, you have probably found the best way to obtain feedback from your own interview behavior. Studies that have been done of interview failures point to these as some common areas in which candidates fail (see Box 6.4).

You can do an effective job of creating your own feedback. Right after each interview, while it's still fresh in your mind, jot down notes:

- What questions were asked that you hadn't anticipated, or that you didn't handle as well as you might have?
- What did you fail to say that could have helped you?
- Did you do enough homework, and was it of the right kind?

Use your answer to help you prepare for your next interview. See Box 6.5.

Box 6.4 Common Reasons Why Interviews Fail

1. Poor personal appearance.
2. Overbearing, overaggressive, conceited, or know-it-all behavior.
3. Inability to express self clearly.
4. Lack of planning for career, no purpose and goals.
5. Lack of interest and enthusiasm.
6. Lack of confidence and poise.
7. Failure to participate in activities.
8. Poor scholastic record.
9. Overemphasis on money.
10. Unwilling to start at bottom.

Box 6.5 An Interview Checklist

1. Have you focused squarely on making the best possible presentation of yourself?
2. Have you taken sufficient care with your personal appearance?
3. Have you done enough homework so that you can approach the interview with a strong, positive attitude?
4. Have you rehearsed answers for the predictable questions? for possible tough questions?
5. Do you have your own script for the interview, and are you prepared to be sensitive to (and adapt to) the interviewer's script?

Finally, although you almost never get feedback from an interviewer, be sure to give it. Send a courtesy letter to the interviewer, thanking him or her for the time and trouble. Remember not to do business overtly in the letter; it is designed primarily to build good will.

5. Other Methods of Finding Jobs

More jobs are acquired through personal contacts than through letters (although even personal contact jobs usually involve letters at some point). How can you place yourself in a better position for such jobs? First you need to have the personal contacts:

- Join the student affiliate of your major's professional association.
- Involve yourself in internship, co-op, or volunteer programs connected with your chosen profession.
- Become active in your school's government; make yourself visible.
- Get to know your teachers, and let them know you.
- Keep those professional relationships in good repair; don't be in the position of looking someone up after a two- or three-year total lapse in communication to ask for a letter of reference.

Once you have formed the personal contacts, let those people know you're looking for a job. Some students act as though looking for a job is something to be ashamed of; it's not. You didn't get fired—you graduated; people who graduate look for jobs. A nice way to let people know you're job hunting is to ask them to be prepared to be one of your references. You don't necessarily have to use that person's name on your resumé's list of references. What you're fishing for is the chance that your potential reference will know of an opening just right for you, and suggest you use his or her name in applying for it. Another possibility for letting someone know you're beginning to look for a job is to ask that person for advice: How can you best enhance your credentials as a job seeker, and what are that person's suggestions for successful job seeking in today's market?

EXERCISES

1. The Job Application. This assignment has very little of the classroom in it. It is designed to simulate the real job-application process as closely as possible.
   a. Find a job notice advertising an opening for the kind of job you can legitimately expect to apply for after you graduate. Make a copy of the notice. Now find a piece of advertising aimed at the kind of person the job notice asks you to write to. Make a copy of the advertisement. Think about what kind of person the advertisement is designed to appeal to. Can you create a psychological portrait of that person? Now write a letter applying for the job; include the job notice and the copy of the advertisement with your letter.
   b. Write a one-page resumé to go with the job-application letter in a., above.
   c. Write a multi-page resumé to go with the job-application letter in a., above.
   d. Write a qualifications sheet to go with the job-application letter in a., above.
   e. Assume that four weeks have passed since you sent in the letter in a., above, and you have not heard anything about the job. Write a letter inquiring about the status of your application.
   f. Assume the identity of the person you wrote to in a., above. Write a letter turning down the job applicant. Pay careful attention to human goals.

2. There are hundreds of books and articles that contain advice on how to write job applications and resumés. Find five to ten such pieces, and write a brief report summarizing the similarities and differences in their approaches. Consult the bibliography at the end of this book for ideas on places to look.

3. If your university has a job placement center, pay it a visit and learn the way the staff there recommends that students go about job searches. Ask specific questions, such as how many students with your major get more than one offer, how many interviews the typical student in your major has, what the biggest things to look out for in the process are, and so forth. Write a brief (300-word) report describing what you have learned.

4. Get the names of two or three students in your major field who have graduated in the last year or two. Contact each one and conduct a brief interview about his or her experiences in the job market and what lessons may be learned from those experiences. Write a brief report (150 words) detailing what you have learned.

PART III

Elements of Technical Reports

Every professional involved in the many different kinds of scientific, technical, and business writing has particular ideas about what the basic elements of that writing are. The six chapters in Part III describe key elements chosen because they are parts of nearly every report anyone writes in business and industry. Part III introduces the building blocks; Part IV describes key architectural processes you will need to put them together into finished reports, both during and after college. Part V presents examples and discussions of typical kinds of reports.

Chapter 7 addresses one of the most striking differences between school writing and the kind of writing professionals do: the highly visual quality of technical writing. School writing, especially essay writing, is often 100 percent verbal; there are only words on the page. Technical reports are often 50 percent verbal and 50 percent visual. The visual elements of professional writing include numerical items (tables, charts, and graphs) and pictorial items (photos, sketches, cartoons, and diagrams). Chapter 7 explains both varieties of visuals. Chapter 8 explains the use of headings, the single most important visual organizer in reports. Headings not only help cue readers into more efficient reading, but also encourage writers to write in a more logical, orderly fashion.

Most reports in business and industry have separate introductions. Some even have multiple introductory elements (such as an abstract, an executive summary, and an introduction). Chapter 9 presents an effective way of writing an introduction for any kind of report. It also explains fifteen different ways to write conclusions.

Definition and description are probably the most fundamental (and frequently used) skills any professional writer needs. Chapter 10 explains these important skills. Second only to definition as a required writing skill is narration, and in professional writing the ability to use narration to describe processes and write good sets of instructions is crucial to any writer's success. Those skills are explained in Chapter 11.

The final building block presented here is in Chapter 12, "Abstracts and Executive Summaries." These elements, only occasionally a part of college papers, are nearly always present in professional reports. Chapter 12 explains how to write them; it thus provides a good bridge into the second half of this book, which directly addresses the writing of reports in professional settings.

Treating such elements of writing as introductions, definitions, and processes as separate chapters in a book like this is a concession to the classroom situation the people who use such books usually are in. That is, your teacher may very well ask you to write a definition paper, a process paper, and so on. Once you leave college, however, the situation changes drastically. Usually you know only that you must write a report; its mix of definition, process, and so on, is controlled by its purpose as established by you and the situation you are writing in. This difference between school writing and professional writing is crucial. Here in Part III it is acknowledged in the writing assignments at the end of each chapter, at least one of which per chapter puts you into a real-world setting as a writer. Beyond that, the first three chapters in Part IV are especially designed to help you make the transition from school writing to professional writing. In particular Chapter 13, "Writing Reports in a Professional Setting," will help you to determine what mix of the various elements described in Part III you will need.

7

Visuals

Presenting your material visually can make your writing and your reports clearer, more attractive, and more frequently read. No other technique you can add with so little effort carries so great a reward as the ability to present material visually. Some writers only use visuals when the subject cries out for them; some use visuals in exactly the right places; and some use visuals whenever they can. This chapter gives you the know-how to use visuals in exactly the right places.

You decide when, how, and what kind of visuals to use based on your audience, your purpose, your subject, as well as the type of paper and the printing process used in the reproduction of your report. Many formats make the use of multiple colors too expensive; some audiences frown on all but the most restrained use of visuals. Some writers have access to sophisticated word processing, graphics, and printing equipment that makes visuals much easier. Some subjects need visuals more than others, and some audiences are better approached with visuals than with words. Successfully assessing all of these variables to achieve effective use of visuals distinguishes professional writing from student writing.

Visual presentations in reports can be divided into two types: presentations of pictorial likenesses (figures and illustrations) and presentations of numerical data (tables, charts, and graphs). Although the groups differ in appearance, the ways they are used are the same. This chapter first presents some situations in which using visuals would be recommended and then describes the two major types in more detail.

1. Uses for Visuals

Most students making the transition to writing as professionals need to learn to use visuals more often. The knack lies not so much in artistic skill as in seeing the *opportunity* and the *need* for a visual. In general, there are five possible situations in which you should consider using visuals:

- To clarify what you're saying.
- To get your point across with fewer words.
- To go into greater detail.
- To emphasize a particular point.
- To arouse interest.

Figures 7.1 through 7.5 illustrate these purposes.

Figure 7.1 A Visual to Clarify "Advanced lamilloy and shell-spar blade designs show a significant improvement over conventional." (Source: EPRI Journal, May 1980, p.42. Reproduced with permission.)

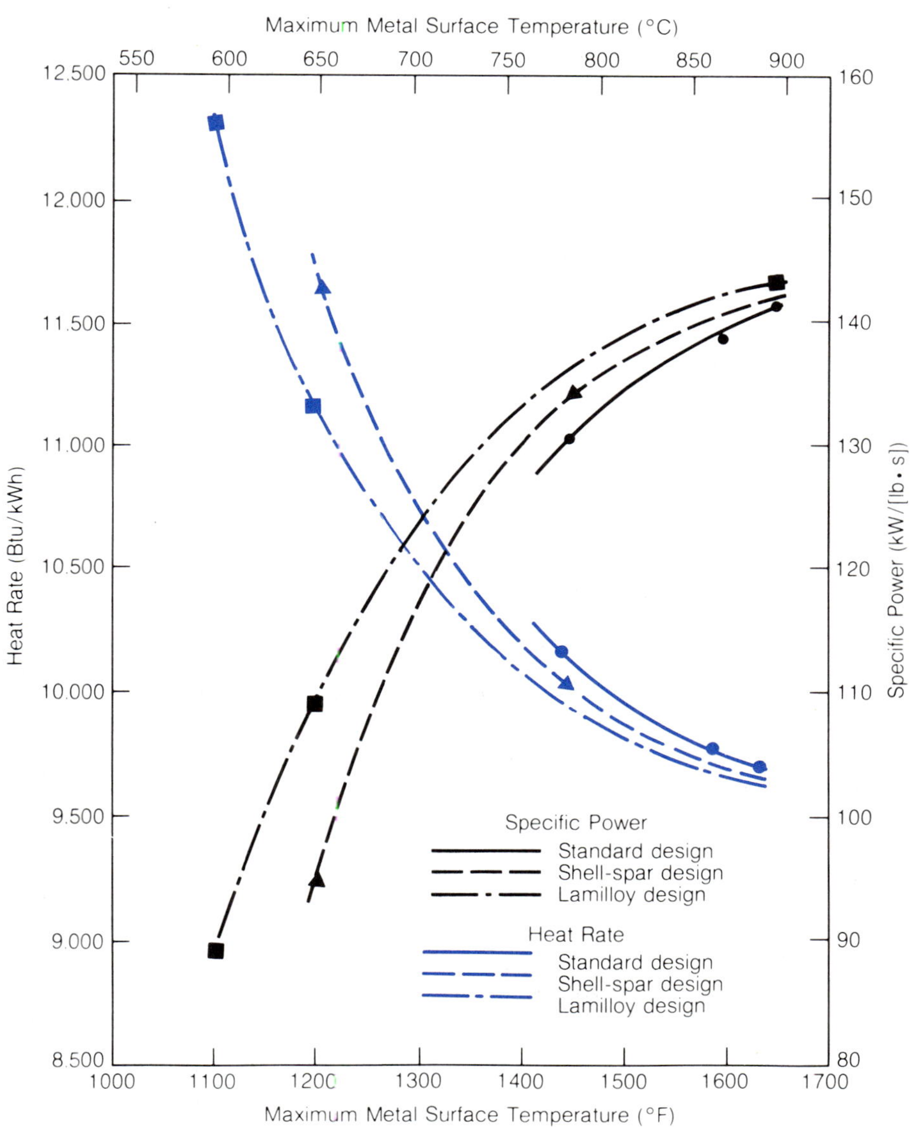

Figure 7.2 A Visual to Convey the Point Using Fewer Words How many *words* would it take to explain these arrangements? (Oak Ridge National Laboratory)

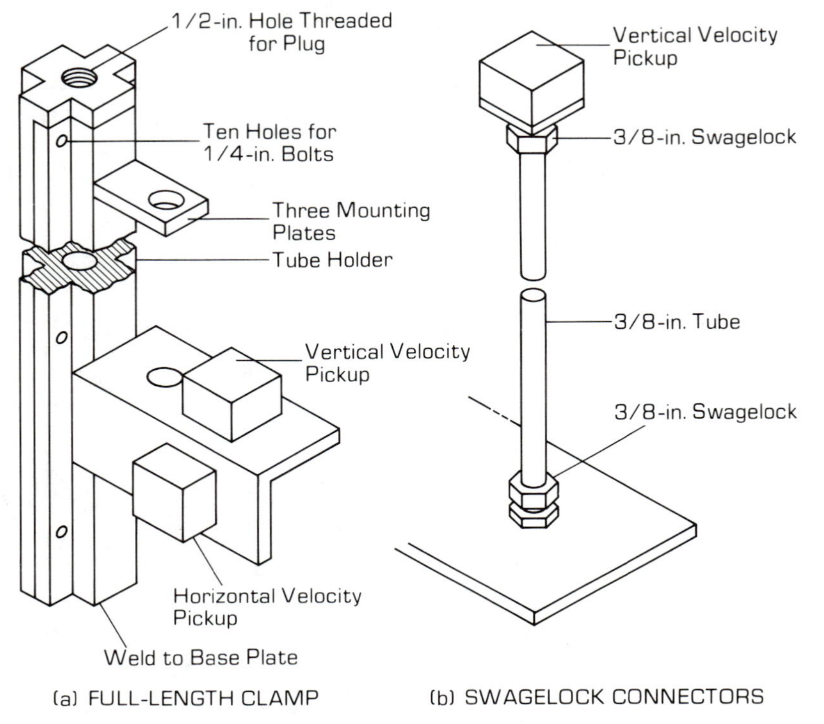

Figure 7.3 A Visual for Greater Detail This kind of detail almost can't be put into words. (Oak Ridge National Laboratory)

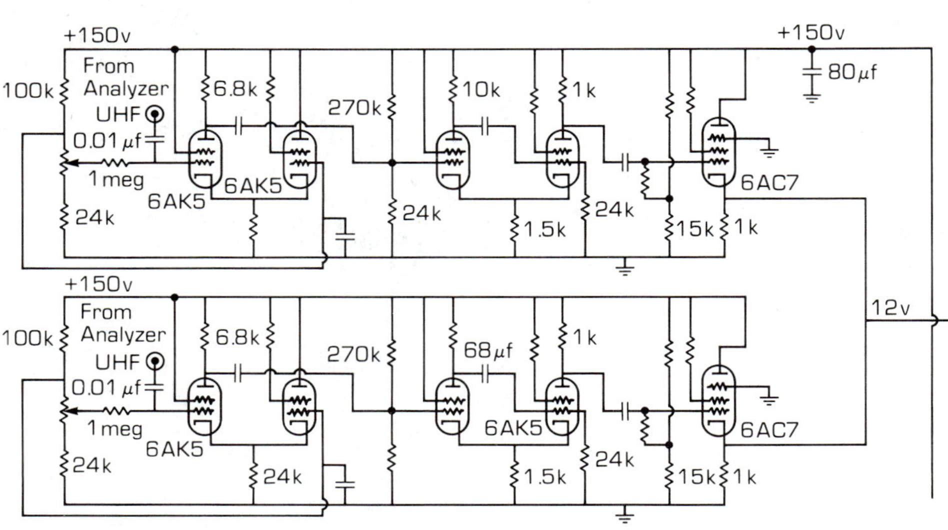

Figure 7.4 A Visual to Emphasize a Particular Point "Gamma Radiation of the Pool Surface Directly above the Reactor (16.5 ft. above Core)." (Oak Ridge National Laboratory)

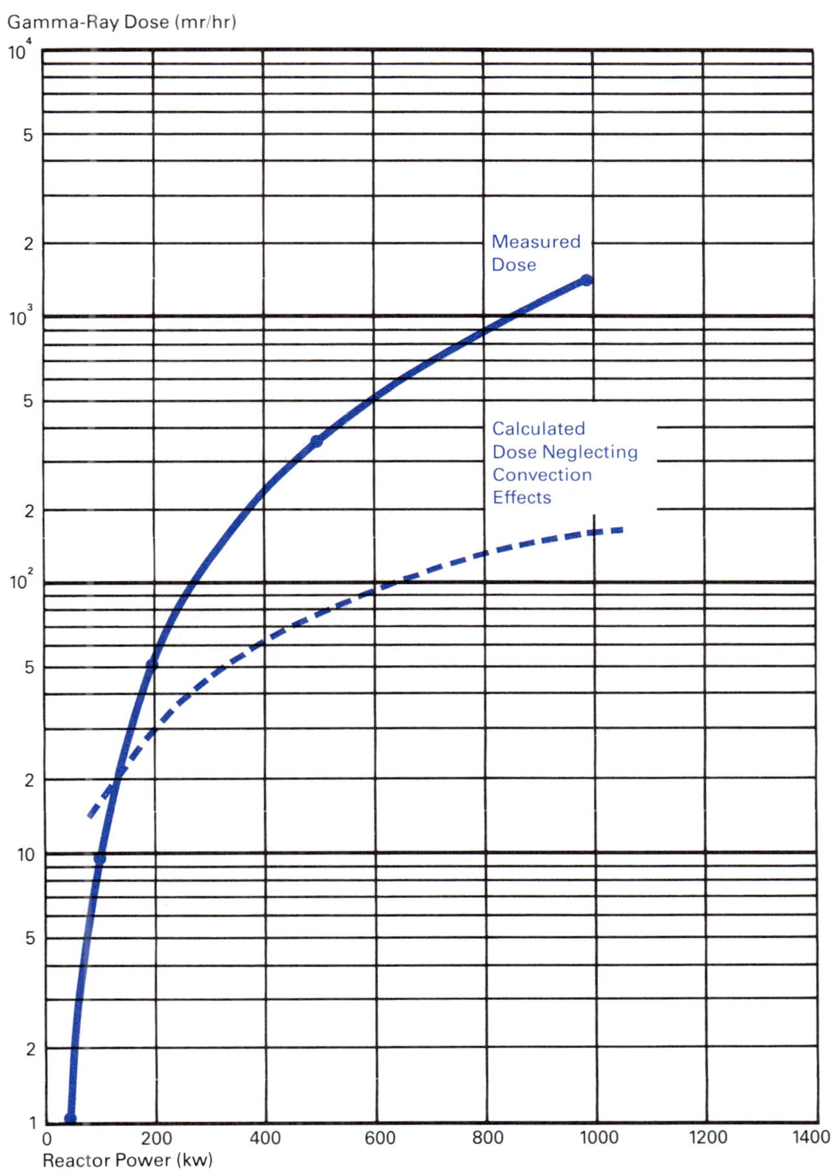

Figure 7.5 A Visual to Arouse Interest The value of an eye-catching and appealing logo is appreciated by professionals in all fields. (*Chemical and Engineering News,* Mar. 23, 1981. Reprinted by permission.)

28th Congress
International Union of
Pure and Applied Chemistry
August 16-21, 1981
Vancouver, British Columbia, Canada

Congress symbol shown above is an illustration by Freda Diesing of Haida Indian legend, "Raven finds mankind in a clam shell."

2. Kinds of Visuals

Many visuals present pictorial images; others are numerical. Consider the two ways of representing a human being, pictorial and numerical, that are shown in Figure 7.6. This distinction between pictorial visuals and numerical visuals is useful to the extent that it helps you learn about visuals; as you discover more about visuals and become more aware of their types, you may also find that they defy this simple, functional classification.

Figure 7.6 Two Ways of Representing a Human Being

(a) Pictorial

(b) Numerical

Joan Q. Average

Hemoglobin 12-14
Ht. 5′ 5″
Wt. 120-135
Hematocrit 42-44%
Fasting Blood Sugar 80-100
Cholesterol 80-220
Bilirubin less than 1
Age 22-38
BP 110/70
Pulse (resting) 70
Vision 20-20
Respiration 10-18
Shoe Size 6-9
% Body Fat 5-15
Triglycerides 60-120
Temperature 98.2-98.8

2.1 Pictorial Visuals

Included in the pictorial group are all likenesses and images of objects and ideas. Many writers avoid using pictorial visuals because they seem too difficult to produce. In professional settings, however, the visuals will be done most often by a professional artist, so that your lack of artistic ability shouldn't keep you from using visuals once you are on the job. As a student, if you are careful, pictorial visuals need not be difficult to produce. Even if you cannot draw, you can produce visuals of good quality. Here is a list of ways*:

- Cut it out and paste it in.
- Photocopy some other sketch of it.

*Remember, if you take the illustration or figure from some other published source, you must credit that source.

- Trace it.
- Simplify some other sketch of it.
- Computer-generate it.
- Farm the job out to a friend.
- Farm the job out to a pro.
- Learn to sketch adequately.

Few professional writers produce their own visuals, especially pictorial ones; they take the work to professional graphic artists. Only during college are you likely to have to do your own drawing. Figures 7.7 and 7.8 are typical pictorial visuals.

2.1.1 **Checkpoints.** With any kind of pictorial visual there are a number of points to check:

- Is the visual clear to the eye? Are its lines crisp?
- Is the amount of detail right for your reader?
- Is the visual balanced properly on the page?
- If the visual is a photograph, is it exactly in focus?
- If the visual is a photograph, does it have a good range of shades—i.e., not too much shadow?
- If you did not produce the visual yourself, is its source properly credited?

2.1.2 **Conceptual Visuals.** The strength of pictorial visuals lies in their power to evoke images, to suggest more than they say. Among the most interesting pictorial visuals are those that metaphorically represent their author's thoughts. Figure 7.9 shows some good examples of conceptual visuals.

Conceptual visuals dramatize an idea, not a thing. The importance of conceptual figures and illustrations lies in their ability to make abstractions real. If a key point in your report is abstract, you should consider illustrating it visually in order to give it clarity and impact. Figure 7.10 shows this technique.

2.2 Numerical Visuals

For convenience, visual presentations of numerical data can be divided into various types of charts, graphs, and tables. They are easier to use than pictorial visuals and, though less evocative, are more precise. Figure 7.11 shows a variety of numerical visuals.

Although all the generalizations about visuals that were made at the beginning of this chapter are true of both numerical and pictorial visuals, several specific occasions call for numerical visuals in particular. Use numerical visuals when you can:

Figure 7.7 An "Exploded" Drawing

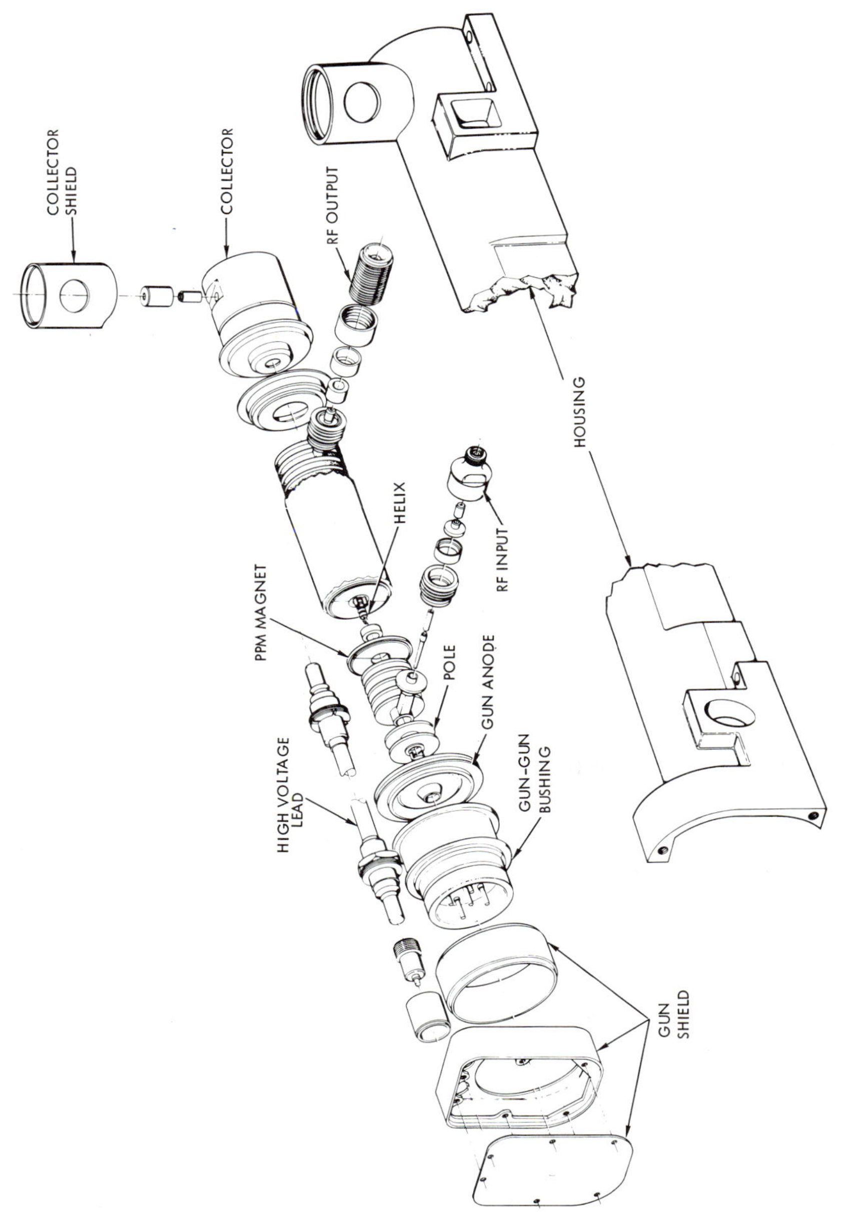

Drawing courtesy of Raytheon Corporation

Figure 7.8 A "Cutaway" Drawing

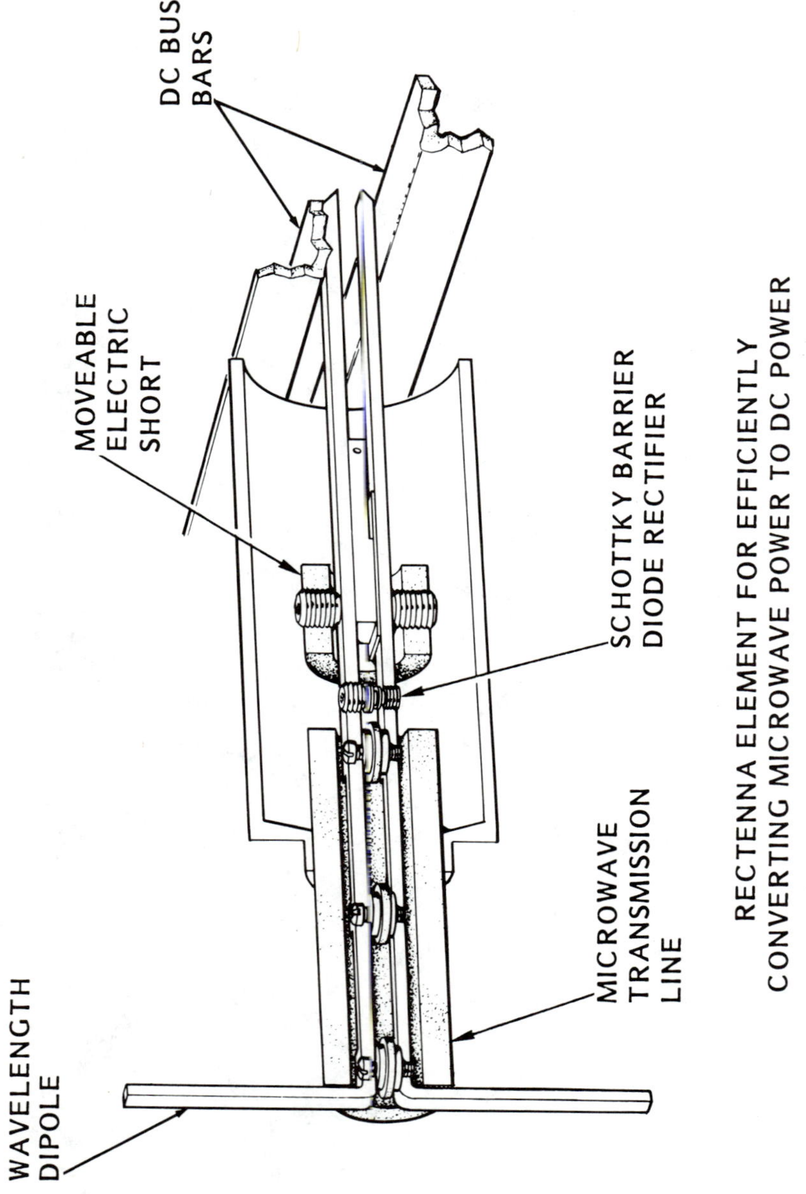

Drawing courtesy of Raytheon Corporation

Figure 7.9 Conceptual Visuals The first drawing introduces the report; the other drawings introduce sections. This scheme invites the reader into the text and unifies the report. (*Chemical and Engineering News*, Oct. 20, 1980, pp. 41-42, 45-46. Reprinted by permission.)

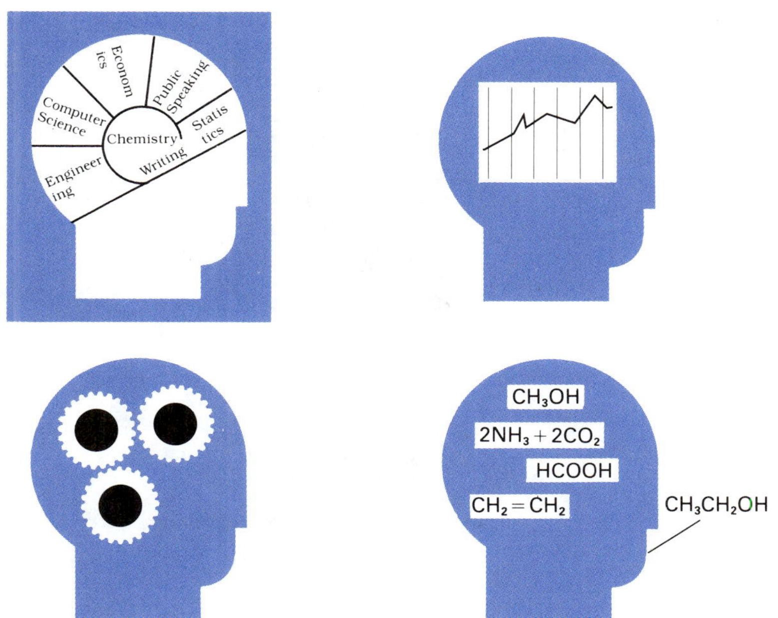

- make your reader understand more easily.
- make a comparison or contrast more vivid.
- pinpoint a specific detail more clearly.

2.2.1 **Checkpoints.** The content of any visual should be summarized in the text before it. You should avoid lazy introductions like this: "The information on 1985 earnings is presented in Table One below." If the information is important, its substance needs to be summarized in the text *before* the visual; don't force the reader to dig it out. Use the visual to reinforce (and maybe to expand) a point already made in the text: "As Table One shows, 1985 earnings are significantly lower in all categories than 1984 or 1983 earnings." Do not use the visual to *make* your point; let the visual *reinforce* the point.

2.2.2 **Graphs.** Making graphs is as much a craft as anything associated with effective writing for business and industry, but it is a relatively easy one if you're careful. A few basics can give you the skill to make a good beginning:

Figure 7.10 A Conceptual Visual: "The development should maximize the use of available funds." Conceptual visuals are especially effective for illustrating ideas.

"The development should maximize the use of available funds."

1. Be sure to give the reader the scale of the graph, and to indicate where the zeros are.
2. Be sure to operate within an acceptable range of precision.
3. Be sure your graph reads left to right and bottom to top.

There are more kinds of graphs than can be listed here. Figures 7.12, 7.13 and 7.14 show line and bar graphs, a scatter graph, and an isometric graph to show ranges.

2.2.3 **Tables.** Tables are very easy to use, and equally easy to misuse. Problems arise when a writer presents more information in the table than the reader wants or needs; as a result, important information may get buried. Be careful not to present your reader with a solid wall of numbers. Few readers care enough to ferret out the significant information from among the mass of data presented to them in such a table, and those who try often make mistakes.

In such a situation you need to either highlight the relevant data or present it first by itself and then integrated with the other data. Highlighting can be done a number of ways: by boldface type, by putting the material within its own box, or by color, as shown in Exhibit 7.1. When you present the relevant data first and

Figure 7.11 A Few Examples of the Many Different Types of Charts, Graphs, and Tables

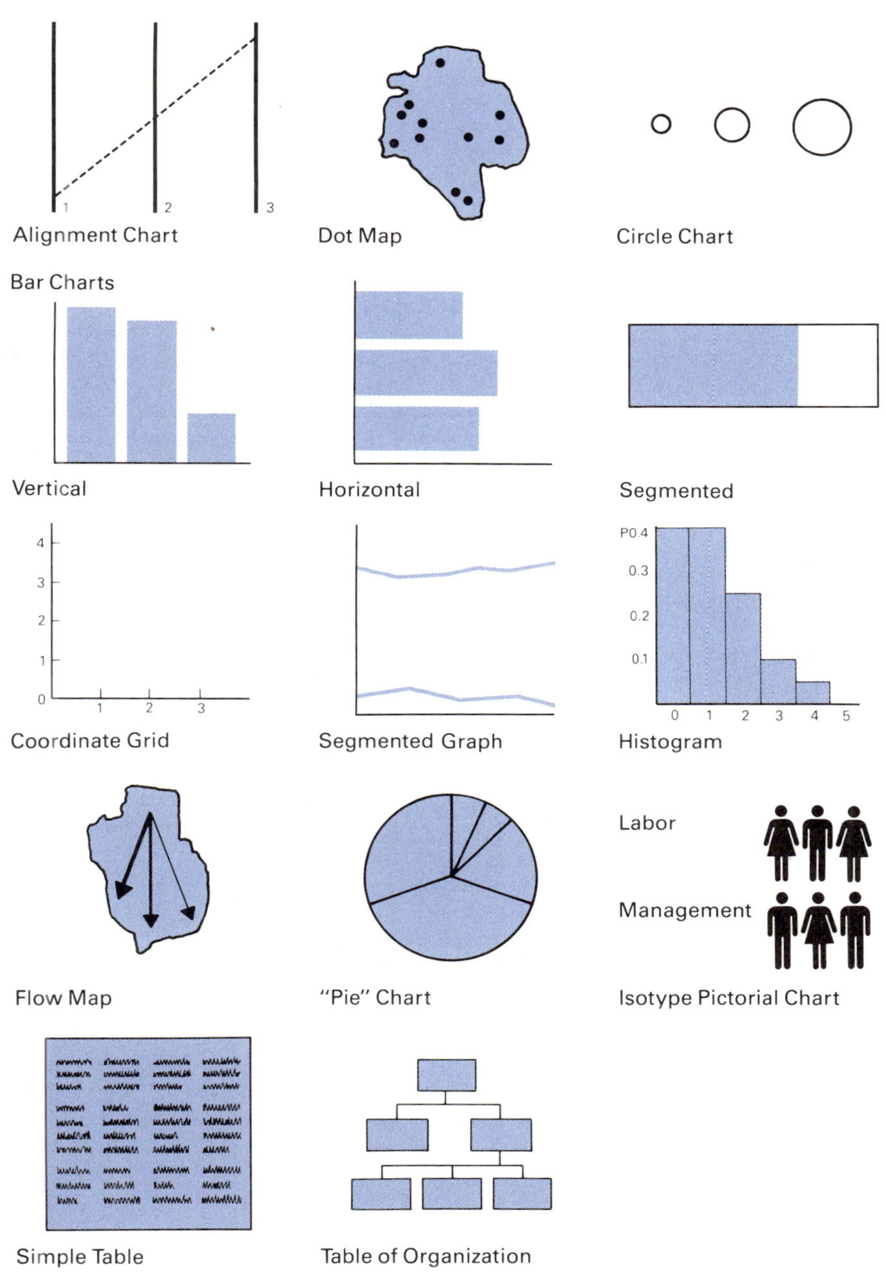

Figure 7.12 Line Graphs and Bar Graphs Used together, they are harder to understand but capable of carrying large quantities of information in a small space. (*Chemical and Engineering News*, June 8, 1981, p.43. Reproduced by permission.)

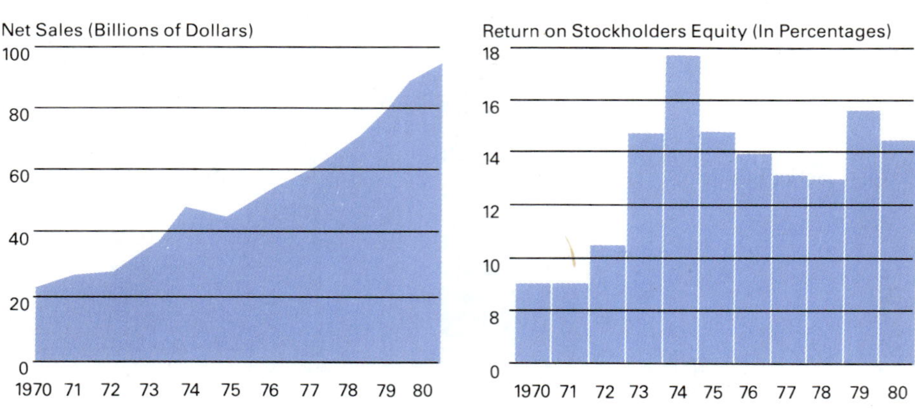

Figure 7.13 A Scatter-Graph Notice that the lines show interpolated relationships among the scattered data. (Oak Ridge National Laboratory—Fusion Energy Division Annual Progress Report, Period Ending Dec. 31, 1977, p. 135)

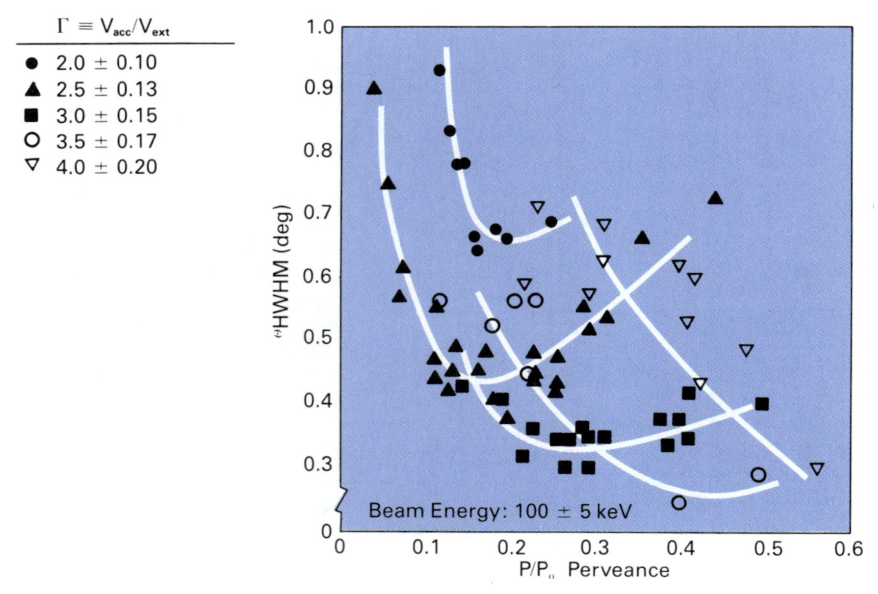

Figure 7.14 An Isometric Graph This sophisticated graph to show ranges can be generated only by computer. (Oak Ridge National Laboratory—Fusion Energy Division Annual Progress Report, Period Ending Dec. 31, 1977, p. 115)

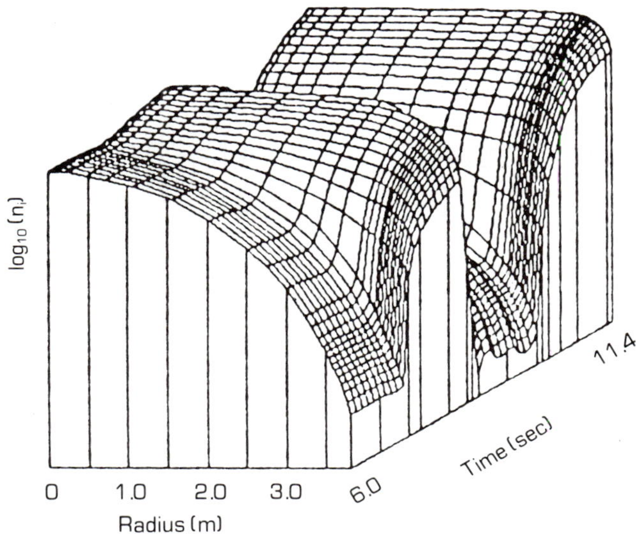

then place it in context with other data, you are doing a version of stairstepped visuals, discussed in Section 4.

2.2.4 **Charts.** Charts generally follow the same principles as other visuals. Again the key is simplicity. Be sure you are not presenting the reader with more information than he or she wants, needs, or can readily interpret. The key components in the chart can be emphasized by bold face, by color, or by simplification and stairstepping. Figures 7.15, 7.16, and 7.17 show flow, isometric, and isotype pictorial charts.

3. Guidelines for Visuals

Once you make the decision to use a visual, there are two important guidelines to follow—make it:

- a self-contained unit.
- accessible.

Exhibit 7.1 A Table Highlighted by Color

SUMMARY OF RADIATION DAMAGE IN STAINLESS STEEL STRUCTURAL COMPONENTS

	Neutron wall loading = 1.47 MW/m²		
Location	*Atomic displacement rate[a] (dpa/yr)*	*Hydrogen gas production rate (appm/yr)[b]*	*Helium gas production rate (appm/yr)*
First structural wall	20.9	913	276
Center of blanket	4.62	127	34.7
Rear of blanket	7.70×10^{-1}	7.43	1.91
Front of shield	2.16×10^{-1}	1.45	3.62×10^{-1}
Rear of shield	4.92×10^{-5}	1.11×10^{-3}	2.74×10^{-4}
Front of magnet coil	3.51×10^{-5}	5.13×10^{-4}	1.26×10^{-4}
Rear of magnet coil	6.26×10^{-9}	7.76×10^{-10}	1.67×10^{-10}

[a]Based on an effective displacement energy of 40 eV.
[b]Atom parts per million per year.

Source: Oak Ridge National Laboratory—Fusion Energy Division Annual Progress Report, Period Ending Dec. 31, 1977, p. 194.

The only exceptions to these guidelines are very small illustrations called "spot" visuals. Spot visuals can easily be incorporated into the text (see p. 163 for an example).

3.1 Visuals Should Be Self-Contained

All your visuals should be designed to be easy for readers to understand at a glance, at least on a superficial level, without having to refer to the report's text. Most experienced readers have learned that they can increase their reading speed and comprehension by quickly scanning the report before reading it; you should assume that *your* reader will do so, too. You want your reader to see the visual and, because it is self-contained, to have a good basic grasp of it without having to read the text.

There are three components to making your visuals self-contained:

- Frame each visual with sufficient white space.
- Identify each visual in three ways:
  1. Figure number
  2. Figure title
  3. A short explanation—either summarizing relevant points or focusing on the most important points.
- Keep your visual simple enough for a browsing reader to be able to grasp.

Figure 7.15 A Flow Chart Such charts are very popular for explaining computers. (Oak Ridge National Laboratory—INREM II: A Computer Implementation of Recent Models, p. 44)

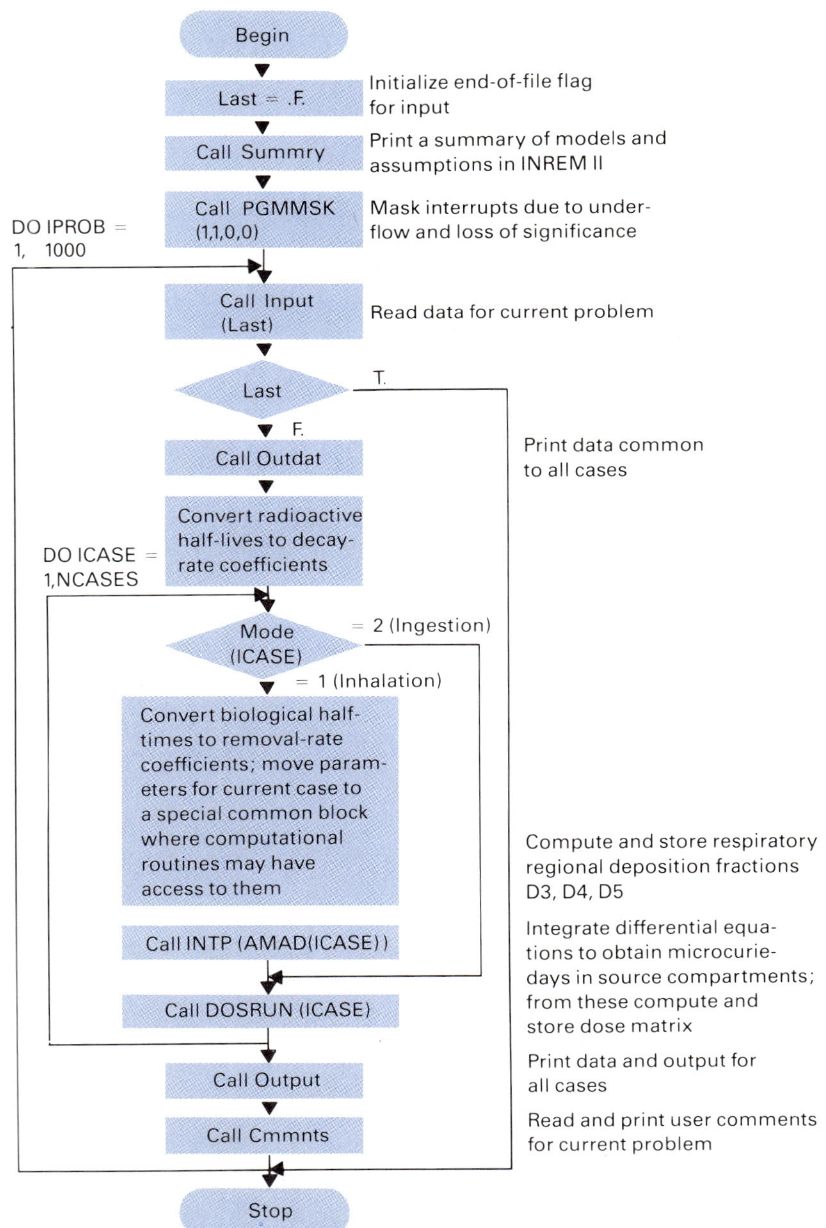
INREM II (Driving Program)
Begin
Last = .F.
Initialize end-of-file flag for input
Call Summry
Print a summary of models and assumptions in INREM II
Call PGMMSK (1,1,0,0)
Mask interrupts due to underflow and loss of significance
DO IPROB = 1, 1000
Call Input (Last)
Read data for current problem
Last
T.
F.
Call Outdat
Print data common to all cases
Convert radioactive half-lives to decay-rate coefficients
DO ICASE = 1,NCASES
Mode (ICASE)
= 2 (Ingestion)
= 1 (Inhalation)
Convert biological half-times to removal-rate coefficients; move parameters for current case to a special common block where computational routines may have access to them
Compute and store respiratory regional deposition fractions D3, D4, D5
Call INTP (AMAD(ICASE))
Integrate differential equations to obtain microcurie-days in source compartments; from these compute and store dose matrix
Call DOSRUN (ICASE)
Call Output
Print data and output for all cases
Call Cmmnts
Read and print user comments for current problem
Stop

Figure 7.16 An Isometric View Chart Because it combines the qualities of charts and graphs, it is treated under both types here. (Oak Ridge National Laboratory—Fusion Energy Division Annual Report, Period Ending Dec. 31, 1977, p. 15.)

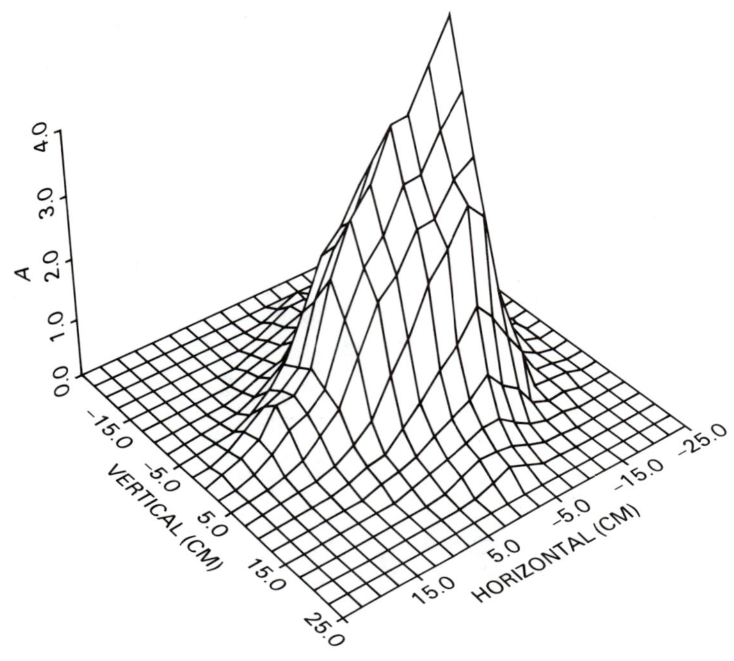

3.2 Visuals Should Be Accessible

Your visuals also should be clearly related to some nearby part of the report's text. Think of the reader who skims the report and finds an interesting visual. Will that reader be able to find the right section of the report's text to go with that visual? Will someone reading the report find the visual to go with the text?

To make your visuals accessible, follow these guidelines:

- Mention each visual in the text *before* the visual itself occurs. Your report should tell your reader when to consult the visual.
- Place each visual *as near as possible* to the material it illustrates, or tell the reader where to find it.
- Tell the reader in each section of the report that is supported by a visual *what to look for* in the visual.

Remember that the visual does not *eliminate* the need for words in your report but it can often *reduce* the number of words you need.

Figure 7.17 An Isotype Pictorial Chart Isotypes combine numerical content with visual impact. (*Chemical and Engineering News,* Nov. 23, 1981. Reproduced by permission.)

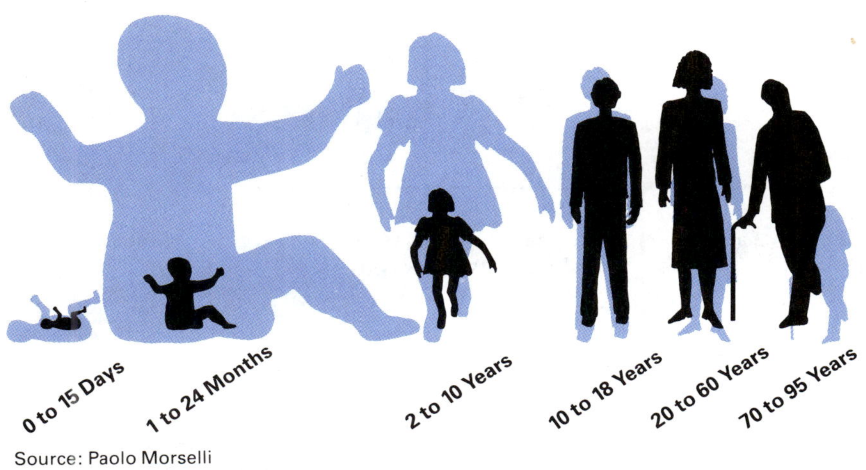

4. How To Adapt Visuals To Audiences: Stairstepping

There are many ways to adapt visuals to your specific audiences. Some were mentioned and shown in the earlier sections on charts and tables. One technique is especially notable because it so clearly shows the principles of audience analysis and adaptation in operation. Whenever your subject matter is especially complex, and you suspect it may dismay or mystify your audience with its complexity, you should consider stairstepping your visuals. Present a simplified version first, followed later by the fuller version (sometimes as much later as in an appendix).

Although there is no simple way to generalize about just when a visual is too complicated for any particular audience, one measure to go by is the "Magic Number 7 ± 2"; that is, any visual presentation of material is limited in its usefulness by the number of units the human brain can deal with simultaneously, often thought to be five to nine units (the problem, of course, is defining what a "unit" is). According to this theory, when your visual has more than seven to nine parts, you should consider stairstepping it. Figure 7.18 shows two stages of a stairstepped visual.

Stairstepping visuals also meshes well with another of the demands human beings, as information-processing systems, make on the structure of the information they process. Rather than presenting a mass of unsorted data (often called

Figure 7.18 (a) A Stairstepped Visual Here we see only the highest levels of the organization.

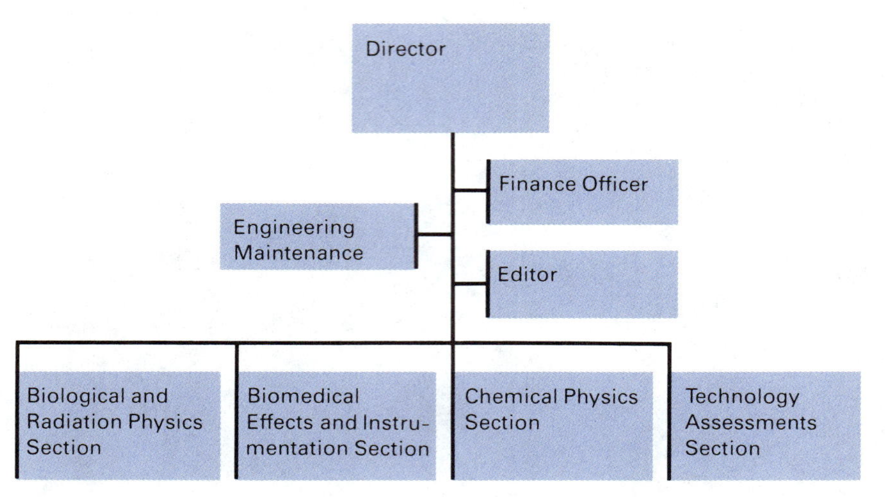

a laundry list), visuals that are stairstepped present a *hierarchically ordered* set or series of sets. Human beings, like most information-processing systems, handle hierarchically ordered information better than unordered information. (This is also true for textual information; see Exhibit 8.5 and its accompanying text.)

5. Where To Place Visuals

Although it may seem obvious that the best place to put a visual is right after it is mentioned in the report, that placement may not always be possible. Sometimes the visual has to go on a following page or at the end of the document, and sometimes the choice of where to place the visual is out of your hands. For these reasons, you need to consider carefully where to place your visuals and how to indicate that placement. The first step is to decide whether you are doing visuals in *publication style* or *manuscript-submission style.*

5.1 Publication Style

If your pages will go directly into print (as in camera-ready copy), you have control over where your visual will appear. In that case, it is usually best to put the visual right after its mention in the report. But what if the visual needs more room than is left on that page? Rather than squeeze it into the available space, place it at the top of the next page and resume the text after it. You might also

Figure 7.18 (b) Here we see the lower-level sections added.

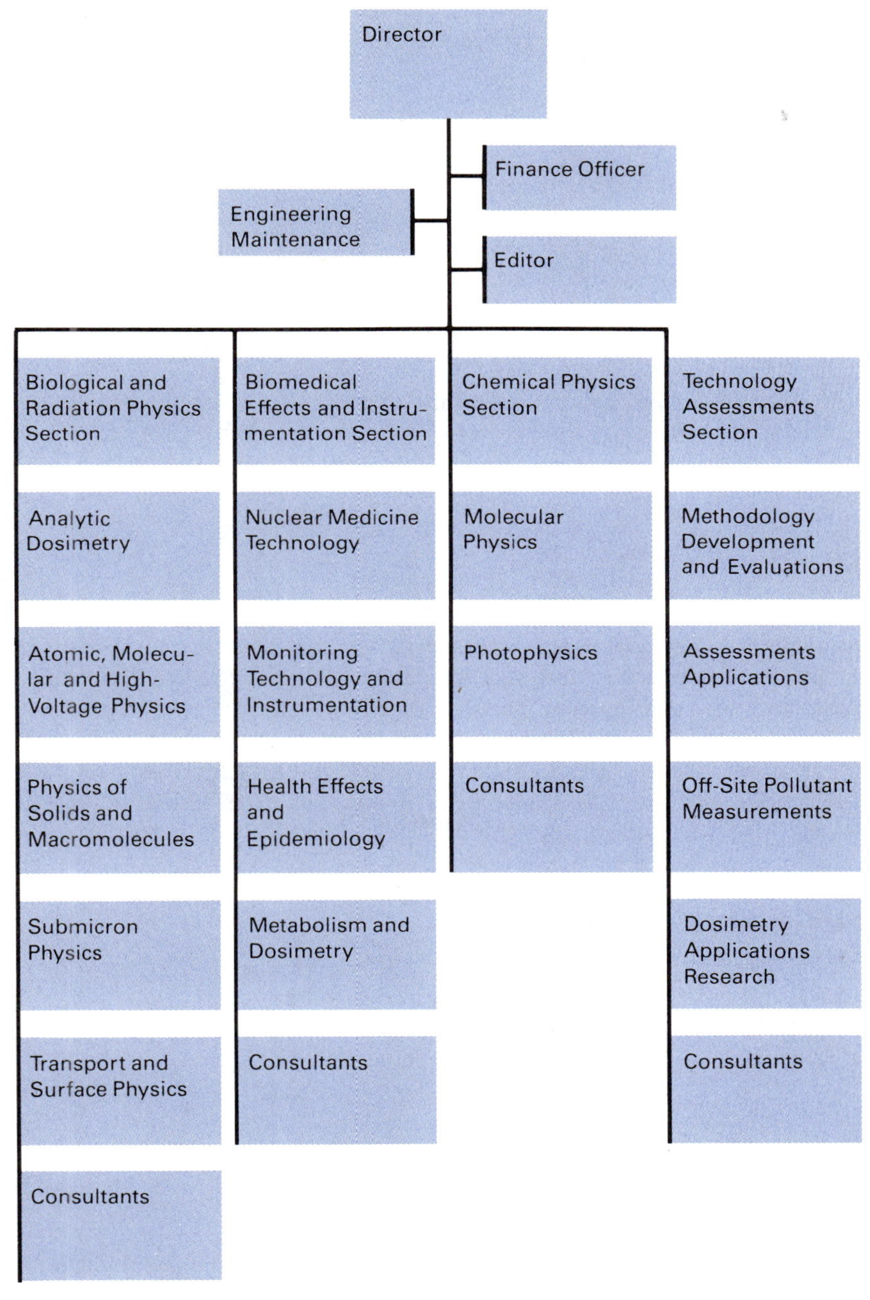
Director
Finance Officer
Engineering Maintenance
Editor
Biological and Radiation Physics Section
Analytic Dosimetry
Atomic, Molecu-lar and High-Voltage Physics
Physics of Solids and Macromolecules
Submicron Physics
Transport and Surface Physics
Consultants
Biomedical Effects and Instru-mentation Section
Nuclear Medicine Technology
Monitoring Technology and Instrumentation
Health Effects and Epidemiology
Metabolism and Dosimetry
Consultants
Chemical Physics Section
Molecular Physics
Photophysics
Consultants
Technology Assessments Section
Methodology Development and Evaluations
Assessments Applications
Off-Site Pollutant Measurements
Dosimetry Applications Research
Consultants

consider whether you should put every visual on its own separate page, with no text around any of them. Of course, that only works if each of your visuals is large enough to fill a page on its own. When you're preparing text to go straight into print, these matters will usually be specified by your editor.

5.2 Manuscript-Submission Style

Often the document you are preparing will go through some process of editing and typesetting before it is printed. In that case, you need to place your visuals somewhat differently. Put each visual on a page by itself following its reference in the text. Insert a note to the editor, indicating the ideal placement of the visual:

[Figure 10 here]

During the publication process, when the document is being readied for print, the visual will be placed as close as possible to that position.

6. How To Produce Visuals

Producing visuals can be very simple or very complicated. If you need complicated visuals (multidimensional or perspective drawings, for example) you should probably farm the job out to a graphics specialist. But as a student, depending on whether and how your writing will be copied, you can do a very competent job with a sharp pencil, a straightedge, some graph paper, maybe some colored felt-tip markers, and most of all, your own desire to produce a first-rate document.

If you are planning to produce your own visuals, adapt the following steps to fit your particular situation:

1. See the opportunity to use a visual.
2. Decide what kind of visual to use.
3. Decide whether or not you should or can use color.
4. Make a rough sketch (or find an example to follow).
5. Decide where to put the visual in the text, so that you can determine what size to make it.
6. Refine your rough sketch.
7. Copy it onto your page.
8. Check it—is it square with the page, not crowded, clear, self-contained, and accessible?

The most important point about using visuals is to make the commitment to use them. Will you use visuals in the right places and in the right ways? Your answer will be partly determined by your topic, your audience, and your time schedule. But a large part of your answer will be determined by your own desire to grow and improve as an effective communicator; many visuals are not so much a matter of "know-how" as "want-to." The spot visual below describes three levels of effort; which level is yours?

> There are three levels of effort:
> "I'll try."
> "I'll do my best."
> "I'll do whatever it takes."

EXERCISES

1. Choose three short factual articles from your local newspaper and produce sketches of visuals to illustrate them. You can assume the visuals are done for the same audience as the newspaper is written for. Try to use various kinds of visuals. Provide copies of the articles with the suggested placement of the visuals marked on them.

2. Zeno, the Greek philosopher, is said to have represented the way people learn in four stages of visuals: perception is an open hand, the mind's response is a partly closed hand, the mind's grasping of an idea is a fist, and knowledge is that fist enclosed in another hand. Divide one of the following processes into five to nine stages and produce sketches for conceptual visuals to represent each stage. Try to capture the same sense of rightness that Zeno's example shows.

Pollution	Writing a paper
Conservation	Import/Export
Gravity	Hysteresis
Consumer advocacy	Inertia
Corporate responsibility	Centrifugal force

3. Based on Table 7.1, produce sketches for *ten* different visuals representing the information the table contains. Assume an audience of taxpayers in general—people who are simply curious about how government money is spent.

4. You are a student intern in your university's Information Office, and you have been handed a copy of the report in Exhibit 7.2. Your task is to come up with ideas (including sketches) for five or ten visuals to illustrate the report when it is given to members of the local City Council. The purpose is to impress upon them the importance of the university's contribution to the local economy.

Table 7.1 House of Representatives Research Budget Requests ($ millions)

Agency	*1982 House appropriation*	*Administration request appropriation*	*1981*
NASA	*$ 6133.9*	*$ 6122.2*	*$ 5522.7*
R&D	4938.1	4903.1	4336.3
Research and program management	1100.0	1114.3	1071.4
Construction of facilities	95.8	104.8	115.0
EPA	*1201.5*	*1191.4*	*1351.0*
Salaries and expenses	583.7	582.8	553.7
Abatement, control and compliance	422.5	413.9	540.2
R&D	191.2	190.6	253.0
Buildings and facilities	4.1	4.1	4.1
NSF	*1103.5*	*1034.5*	*1022.4*
Research and related activities	1065.0	1020.1	946.7
Science and engineering education	35.0	9.9	70.7
Special foreign currency program	3.5	3.5	5.0
TOTAL	*$ 8438.9*	*$ 8347.1*	*$ 7896.1*

Source: *Chemical and Engineering News*, Aug. 3, 1981, p. 14. Reprinted by permission.

Exhibit 7.2 State University Contributions to the Capitol City Economy

No statistics are regularly available to show the monetary influence of State University upon Capitol City. The purpose of this report is to provide such statistics. Table 1 shows the estimated direct and indirect impact of University expenditures calculated for the 1984-1985 fiscal year. Column 1 of the table lists total University expenditures according to specific category. They are adjusted by estimated proportions of spending occurring in Capitol City (Column 2) and by the personal-income factor (Column 3). The resulting estimate of total local wages and salaries attributable to the University's direct expenditures appears in Column 4.

University expenditures increase not only local wages and salaries but also profits made by local suppliers of goods and services. Estimates of retained profits in the Capitol City Standard Metropolitan Statistical Area (SMSA) were calculated using a uniform 10 percent rate of return on all sales, and assuming that one-half of the resulting profits remain in Capitol City. Column 5 lists updated retained profit estimates. Total local income (sum of Columns 4 and 5) is listed in Column 6. Total 1984-1985 expenditures of $341.2 million translate into a personal income increase of $188.4 million. Total direct and indirect impact of University spending is calculated by multiplying the figures in Column 6 by a personal-income multiplier of 1.75; resulting figures are listed in Column 7.

Student expenditures also contribute to the local economy and are thus listed here. The Office of Student Affairs provided a total 1984-1985 figure for direct student expenditures of $132.8 million. University-related visitor expenditures provide another source of local income. The best estimate of these expenditures comes from a local Chamber of Commerce study; their figure of $25 million is used here.

Total direct and indirect impacts of University-related expenditures may thus be seen to be $423.1 million for the 1984-1985 fiscal year. Of that total, payroll expenditures made 62 percent, other expenditures 16 percent, student expenditures 19 percent, and visitor expenditures 3 percent.

TABLE 1 Estimated Direct and Indirect Impact of Expenditures of the University on the Capitol City SMSA Economy, Fiscal Year 1984–1985

Activity	*Total Spending Column 1*	*Proportion of Spending in the SMSA Column 2*	*Personal Income Factor Column 3*	*SMSA Wages and Salaries Column 4*	*SMSA Retained Profits Column 5*	*SMSA Personal Income Column 6*	*TOTAL Local Impact Column 7*
Payroll:							
State U.	$108,810,273	.90	1.00	$97,929,246	0	$97,929,246	171,346,180
System	10,188,516	.61	1.00	6,214,995	0	6,214,995	10,876,241
Ex. Station & Ex. Service	27,789,801	.32	1.00	8,892,736	0	8,892,736	15,562,289
Hospital	41,576,141	.90	1.00	37,418,527	0	37,418,527	65,482,422
Other Ex.							
Travel	9,615,584	.41	.06	236,543	197,119	433,662	758,909
Utilities	18,865,453	.94	.11	1,950,688	886,676	2,837,364	4,965,387
Communication	9,324,362	.93	.08	693,733	433,583	1,127,316	1,972,803
Supplies	37,735,967	.53	.66	13,200,041	1,000,003	14,200,044	24,850,077
Stores	30,267,701	.68	.39	8,026,994	1,029,102	9,056,096	15,848,168
Construc.	29,936,178	.69	.24	4,957,431	1,032,798	5,990,229	10,482,901
Other	17,058,420	.74	.29	3,660,737	631,162	4,291,899	7,510,823
Total	341,168,396			183,181,670	5,210,443	188,392,114	329,686,200

8

Headings

1. **Why to Use Headings**
2. **How to Use Headings**
   - 2.1 Four Levels of Headings
   - 2.2 Variations on the Four Levels
     - 2.2.1 Use a Fifth Level
     - 2.2.2 Use the Decimal System
   - 2.3 Talking Headings
   - 2.4 Other Visual Organizers
3. **Cautions About Headings**
   - 3.1 Stacked Headings
   - 3.2 Pronoun Reference
   - 3.3 Parallelism
   - 3.4 Frequency

   Exercises

One of the most immediately apparent characteristics of writing for business and industry is the use of headings and subheadings. Their presence does more than make this type of writing visibly different from other kinds of writing; it also signals important structural and psychological differences. Writing for business and industry is designed to be easy for readers to use, and that means the style must be readable and that the different parts of reports must be easy to find. Most readers will not read *all* of a report—only the sections he or she needs to read. Other kinds of writing stress an overall unity that writing in business and industry often sacrifices in favor of giving the reader ready access to particular sections. Using headings is the most visible method of furnishing that access. This chapter will show you why and how to use headings and discuss the common problems associated with them.

1. Why to Use Headings

Headings have four basic functions—two for the reader and two for the writer:

1. *To help readers find specific parts of the report.* Readers in professional settings want to be able to find *at a glance* the specific part of your report that most concerns them. Headings make that possible. Have you ever tried to find a particular part of a book or report, maybe while reviewing for a test, and spent much more time *finding* that section than you did *reading* it? Most likely that document did not make full and frequent use of headings and subheadings. One of the ways in which writers show their concern for the reader is by labeling specific parts of the whole with headings and subheadings, so that the reader can find those parts easily.
2. *To present your outline and organization to readers at a glance.* If your reader can understand the way you have structured your report and see the principle behind its organization, the time and energy needed to read the report will be reduced. Most working readers thumb through any multipage document before they decide whether or how much to read. If you handle headings properly, a reader thumbing through your report will see the headings and subheadings as a clear and logical outline of your presentation. That outline will be valuable for the reader's speed in reading and understanding the report.
3. *To ensure the writer's logical organization.* When you use headings you will find they make you think consciously and carefully about the structure of what you write. Does the structure make sense to you, and will it make sense to your reader? Does the organization that you (the writer) find comfortable to work with prove equally comfortable to your reader? Dealing with such questions is an important stage in the development of any writer, a stage that can come with the careful use of headings and subheadings.
4. *To announce new topics.* The ability to make smooth and effective transitions usually comes to writers only after much practice and hard work. With headings and subheadings, such transitions can be less important. Instead of having to lead the reader slowly and subtly from one topic to the next,

Exhibit 8.1 Four Levels of Headings Headings alert readers to a report's structural elements.

A-level heading → MAJOR HEADING

Xxxxxxxxxxxxxxxxxxxxxxxxxxxxxxxxxxxxxxxxxxxxxxxxxxxxxxxxxxxxxxx
xxxxxxxxxxxxxxxxxxxxxxxxxxxxxxxxxxxxxxxxxxx.

B-level heading → Minor Heading

Xxxxxxxxxxxxxxxxxxxxxxxxxxxxxxxxxxxxxxxxxxxxxxxxxxxxxxxxxxxxxxx
xxxxxxxxxxxxxxxxxxxxxxxxxxxxxxxxxxxxxxxxxxxxxxx.

Subheading ← **C-level heading**

Xxxxxxxxxxxxxxxxxxxxxxxxxxxxxxxxxxxxxxxxxxxxxxxxxxxxxxxxxxxxxxx
xxxxxxxxxxxxxxxxxxxxxxxxxxxxxxxxxxxxxxxxxxxxxxx.

D-level heading

Paragraph Heading.t.Xxxxxxxxxxxxxxxxxxxxxxxxxxxxxxxxxxxxxxxxxx
xxxxxxxxxxxxxxxxxxxxxxxxxxxxxxxxxxxxxxxxxxxxxxxx.

headings and subheadings can simply announce the change in topics. (See Chapter 9, Section 1.2.3, for information on the most common transitional devices.) Practice and hard work are still necessary, but headings and subheadings can help.

2. How to Use Headings

There are many different schemes for using headings and subheadings. This section explains how to use four different levels of headings, offers several common variations, and then discusses other ways to make your material's organization visible to your reader.

2.1 Four Levels of Headings

Many reports use four levels of headings, sometimes called *major headings*, *minor headings*, *subheadings*, and *paragraph headings*. You may find it less confusing to remember them as A, B, C, and D levels (where A is the major heading). Typically, the headings are indicated as shown in Exhibit 8.1.

The purpose of headings is to use the typography and the placement on the page (vertical and horizontal spacing) to alert the reader to structural elements in your report. You can reinforce the visibility of your headings—and make your writing more attractive visually—if you use the spacing above the headings to reinforce their levels of importance: skip five lines above an A-head, four above a B-head, and so on. Many writers emphasize the structural importance of A-heads even more by beginning a new page whenever one occurs. But the most visible characteristics of the different levels of headings are their typography (all capital letters, initial capitals, underlined, not underlined) and their left-right placement on the page.

2.2 Variations on the Four Levels

There are a number of ways to vary the four levels of headings. You can have five levels, delete a level, use the decimal system, use talking headings, or use any of a number of other kinds of visual organizers.

2.2.1 **Use a Fifth Level.** The four levels of headings presented here can be shortened to three or expanded to five. If you simply leave out the C or D level, you have three levels. If you use a heading that is centered, all caps, and underlined, you have five levels, and the new one becomes the A-level head.

FIFTH LEVEL

You can do the same with boldface type (students can either use rub-on letters or doublestrike with the typewriter):

FIFTH LEVEL

Or you can insert another level between the B and C levels, with initial caps, underlined, at the left margin. But keeping track of heading levels should not be allowed to draw too much of the reader's attention; if you use too many levels the complexity of the scheme may become self-defeating.

2.2.2 **Use the Decimal System.** In many fields, writers are encouraged to number the sections of their reports, either letting the numbers stand alone in the place of headings, or putting numbers in front of the headings. This common usage is illustrated in Exhibit 8.2. One method uses numbers and letters; the other uses only numbers. The combination of numbers and headings may be the most popular variation of this scheme and is used throughout this book.

2.3 Talking Headings

In your first draft of a report, you may well use general headings (*topic* headings) such as "Background," "Procedure," and "Results." (The sample DOE feasibility report structure uses such topic headings.) Your headings will be much more useful to the reader if in the finished version of your report you make them fully descriptive and specific. Rather than just name the topic, indicate what the section says about it. The four headings in Section 1 of this chapter, "Why to Use Headings," are talking headings. Here are three more examples:

Exhibit 8.2 Use of Decimal-Numbered Headings in Reports

(a) The Decimal System, One of Several Possible Varieties

1. MAJOR HEADING

1.1 SUBHEADING
1.1.1 *Minor Heading*
1.1.1.1 *Paragraph Heading.*

(b) Another Version of the Decimal System

4.0 SYSTEM DEFINITION AND BASELINE REQUIREMENTS

4.1 Functional Requirements
4.2 Performance
4.2.1 Reliability
4.2.2 Availability
4.2.3 Maintainability
4.3 Preliminary Assessment of Interface Requirements
4.4 Critical Elements
4.5 Constraints
4.6 Plans for System Tests

Source: Adapted from DOE sample Feasibility Report Table of Contents.

Background: Steady Growth From 1880-1950
Procedure: Survey of Industrial Growth Since 1950
Results: Economic Growth Slow or Totally Lacking

Specific headings such as these can do much more for your reader than the shorter, topic headings.

2.4 Other Visual Organizers

In the classroom, you can experiment with more techniques to visually organize the report for your readers. As with headings and subheadings, the point is to use the resources at your disposal to make your message reach the right readers in the right way. But before you use any of the following techniques you need to consider whether and how your writing is going to be reproduced (conventionally typed, word processed, photocopied, mimeographed, or photo-offset printed). As with other kinds of visuals, some of the techniques described here are possible only with certain types of manuscript reproduction. Most important, though, you should consider whether your specific reader may react negatively to less than common methods of visually organizing the text. If you are writing for the

Exhibit 8.3 Examples of Visual Organizers

☞ With those restrictions, here are several

Other Visual Organizers . Depending on the

method of reproduction and the NEEDS OF THE

AUDIENCE,

you can use pointers, → arrows ←, colored boxes,

colored type, h o r i z o n t a l s p a c e,

vertical space,

★★ stars, ALL CAPS, or **bigger type.**

Department of Energy, you probably cannot use any of these; if you are writing for a marketing agency, maybe you can (see Exhibit 8.3).

As you can see in the sampler in Exhibit 8.3 the use of too many visual organizers in one paragraph is a little disconcerting, but the careful use of one or two of those techniques is something too many practicing writers ignore. For the most part, though, you will have to rely on typographic variations that can be done on an ordinary typewriter, assisted by vertical and horizontal spacing.

3. Cautions About Headings

There are several conventions about using headings—*do's* and *don'ts* that you should be aware of.

3.1 Stacked Headings

Your headings will be more useful for your readers if you do not have one heading right after another, with not even one sentence in between them. This is another instance in which writing is designed for clarity more than for stylistic elegance. In most situations you should use at least one sentence between any two headings, even if the sentence is only a brief forecast of what is to come next (as with the sentence between Section 3 and Section 3.1). The exception occurs when one heading, such as the title of the report, is by itself on one page, followed on the next page by another heading, such as "Introduction" or "Executive Summary."

3.2 Pronoun Reference

It's not a good idea to use a pronoun in the sentence after a heading to refer to the heading. Consider this example:

Pronoun Reference. This is often a problem with headings. . . .

Exhibit 8.4 Grammatical Parallelism Notice the parallelism is broken each time a higher-level heading intervenes.

VISUAL ORGANIZERS

HEADINGS

How to Use Headings

  Typeface

  Spacing

Why to Use Headings

  Reader's Reasons

  Writer's Reasons

GRAPHICS

Different Kinds of Graphics

  Pictorial Graphics

  Numerical Graphics

Different Uses for Graphics

Rewrite the sentence to clarify the pronoun reference, even if it means repeating the words of the heading right after the heading.

> *Pronoun Reference*. Pronoun reference is often a problem with headings. . . .

If this kind of repetition bothers you, recast the sentence in question to move the repeated words away from each other:

> *Pronoun Reference*. Writers often have a problem with pronoun reference. . . .

3.3 Parallelism

To give your writing a polished look, make the headings on each respective level grammatically parallel to the other headings on that level (unless a higher-level heading intervenes). That is, balance a noun in one heading with a noun in the next heading on the same level, balance a noun plus prepositional phrase with a noun plus prepositional phrase, and so on. Exhibit 8.4 illustrates this use of grammatical parallelism.

Does every heading of any particular level have to be grammatically parallel to every other heading at that level? No, the rule is that intervention by a higher-level heading starts a new parallelism. That is, all the B-heads under the first A-head must be parallel to one another, but they don't have to be parallel to all other B-heads. In Exhibit 8.4, this is why the two D-heads under "How to Use Headings" must be grammatically parallel to one another but do not have to be grammatically parallel to the two D-heads under "Why to Use Headings."

3.4 Frequency

At first, you may have problems deciding just when to use a new heading or subheading. How frequently does your subject need to be divided? Of course

Exhibit 8.5 A One-level List It's difficult for anyone to comprehend such a structure without close study.

Definition of Accounting
Size and Importance of Accounting Profession
Governance of Accounting Profession
Pre-1800 History of Accounting
History 1800-1900
Problems with Financial Growth
Rising Professionalism
Accounting at the Turn of the Century
The Federal Government Increases Its Role
The Crash of 1929
Conflicting Government Policies
Role of Professional Organizations
The Era of Overruns
Current Controversies
The Future of Accounting

there is no one universal answer to this question; the frequency with which you use headings will depend largely on the nature of your topic, the length of your report, and the nature of your reader. Two general guidelines you can use to help you decide are:

- *Use a heading of some level at least every two or three pages*, if only to help the reader remember where in the report's structure he or she currently is.
- *Try to avoid having more than about seven headings on any one level without another, higher-level heading intervening*. That is, if your report has fifteen major sections, break it up into two or three larger segments. This is because of the human mind's limited short-term memory capacity, commonly thought to be seven (plus or minus two) units. Humans understand hierarchical structures better than long one-level structures. Exhibits 8.5 and 8.6 shows two versions of a report's table of contents which illustrate this principle.

EXERCISES

1. Describe and analyze the use of headings in a popular science magazine of your choice (*Omni*, *Scientific American*, *Discovery*, *Smithsonian*, etc.).
2. With careful attention to the need for parallelism, make a detailed outline (at least three levels of headings) of a report in which you define in detail a thing or a concept in your field for an executive/layman audience. The entries in your outline should function as the report's headings and subheadings.

Exhibit 8.6 The Hierachical Table of Contents This version makes sense at a glance.

The Accounting Profession Today
- Definition
- Size and Importance
- Governance

The Accounting Profession's Past
- History Pre-1800
- History 1800-1900
- Problems with Growth
- The Rise of professionalism
- The Turn of the Century

The Accounting Profession in This Century
- The Role of Government
- The Crash of 1929
- The Conflicts among Government Policies
- The Role of Professional Organizations
- The Era of Overruns
- The Controversies of Today

The Accounting Profession Tomorrow

3. Survey the top three professional or trade journals in your field and write a brief description and analysis of each journal's use of headings and subheadings. How do they differ, and which is most useful to you as a student?
4. Perform the survey described in 3 and write up its results into a brief report on the merits of using visual organizers in reports. Include the value of the full range of visual organizers—visuals, displayed lists, underlining, italics, etc.—in your report.
5. Assume you are a student hired as a summer intern in a local bank, and having taken an advanced technical writing course in school the previous year, you were surprised to see that the bank's reports were written without visual organizers of any kind. Your internship supervisor suggested you write a brief report on the value of headings, etc., as tools for better writing. The audience of the report is your internship supervisor (a middle-management person), but you're also aware the report may eventually go much higher up into the bank's executive structure.

9

Introductions and Conclusions

1. **Introductions**
   1.1 Qualities of Good Introductions
      1.1.1 Create a Context
      1.1.2 Establish the Purpose
      1.1.3 Forecast the Organization
   1.2 Writing Good Introductions
      1.2.1 Contexts To Use With *CPO* Introductions
      1.2.2 Times To Use *CPO* Introductions
      1.2.3 Using Mini-Introductions
      1.2.4 Adapting Introductions to Real Readers
2. **Conclusions**
   Exercises

Any piece of writing longer than one page should have special provisions for its readers simply because of its length. This is especially true for professional and technical writing, in which the writer puts a large amount of content in a small number of pages, and in which the readers tend to be busy, tired, and frequently distracted. If you want a reader at work to go beyond page one, you must make some special efforts in your writing. Some of these special efforts you have seen in previous chapters (such as paying attention to the real audience, employing "you" attitude, adding visuals, and using headings to organize the page visually). This chapter begins with the most important part of any piece of writing: the introduction. If your introduction shows special concern for your readers, the whole report stands a much better chance of being read. The second part of this chapter explains conclusions, another special provision that long reports make for their readers.

Here you will learn what makes a good introduction or conclusion, how to write a good introduction, and how to adapt your introduction to your specific audience.

1. Introductions

Readers usually form their first impressions of a report on the basis of their responses to the first paragraph they see. With written communications, as with people, first impressions are vitally important. In your own experience, haven't there been times when the first few paragraphs or first few pages of something you were reading put you off so much that you decided not to read the rest—or, at most, grudgingly and hastily to skim it? The same is true of readers in business and industry. They often have a deskful of other business, ringing telephones, and knocks on the door to attend to, a hundred distractions inviting them away from your work. If your introduction does not lead your working reader into the report and implicitly promise to make the content easy to understand, you must expect your words to remain unread.

If your introduction is too long, vague, hard to understand, or too far above (or below) the reader's level of knowledge or interest, you are saying to the reader, "I don't really care very much about you." That kind of negative message, once sent, is hard to retract.

1.1 Qualities of Good Introductions

Most successful writers seek to lead their readers from a general understanding of a subject to one particular point. For example, a report may seek to lead me from a general understanding of how fork lifts are used in lumber yards to a specific recommendation to buy one particular model of fork lift. Or the report may lead me from the need to remodel industrial buildings to take advantage of opportunities to save energy (a general understanding) to what should be done to one particular building (a specific understanding).

A temptation for many inexperienced writers is to dive right into their subjects, to begin with a recitation of facts, figures, and formulas. Those are, after all, the things that are right at hand when a professional begins to write. A good introduction, on the other hand, one that leads the reader from general knowledge into particulars, is generally not ready at hand; a good introduction has to be *made*. A good introduction does not consist of simply telling what you did, or simply relaying the facts; a good introduction moves the reader from a general awareness to specific points, and by doing so it unites the reader's purpose with that of the writer.

Any good introduction does at least three specific things for the reader—it:

1. *creates a context* shared by reader and writer.
2. *clearly establishes the purpose* of the report.
3. *forecasts the organization* of the report. In longer reports, this forecast of the organization often appears as a summary of the report.

1.1.1 **Create a Context.** Creating a context for your report means meeting your reader at a level of knowledge and interest in the subject you *both* share. This need to establish some common ground between reader and writer at the paper's opening expresses a basic principle of communication: for two people to communicate, their lives must touch somewhere, somehow. If their two worlds do not touch, they do not communicate. You are aware of this whenever you try to establish a conversation with a stranger. The first impulse is usually to establish some common ground. "What's your home town, major, hobbies?" are typical college conversation starters. Any answer that establishes some common ground usually leads to attempts to build on that ground. Suppose the two of you have the same home town. The next questions are "What high school did you go to?" or "Did you know. . .?" or "Who did you have for. . . ?"

These follow-up questions that attempt to build on the one point of shared ground lead to this theory's application to writing effective introductions: You can maximize your chances to communicate with your audience by establishing some common ground at the beginning of your report, and the more extensive that common ground is, the better your chances to communicate effectively (see Figure 9.1).

By making the most of whatever you have in common with the reader, you improve the chances for effective communication. By meeting the reader at his or her level of knowledge and interest in your subject, you become more able to lead the reader to the level you want in the report. To do this effectively, you have to gauge not only your reader but the professional community your reader is part of (scientists, technicians, government bureaucrats, engineers, and so on) and that community's values and attitudes toward your subject.

The first quality of a good introduction, then, is that it creates a context that unites writer and reader at the level on which their different knowledges of the subject most nearly coincide. The other two qualities of a good introduction, purpose and organization, also help ensure that writer and reader are coming into the subject with at least approximately the same goals.

Figure 9.1 Communication Possibilities The shaded area is the common ground between reader and writer established by a good introduction.

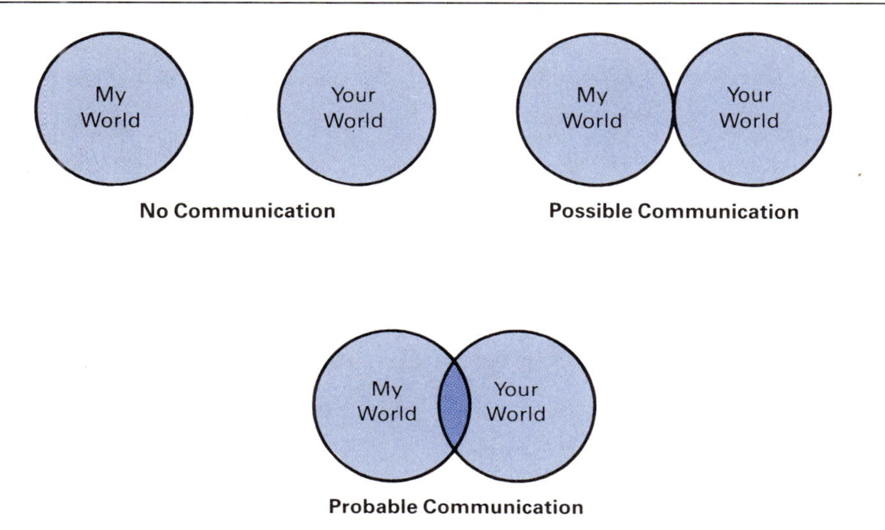

1.1.2 **Establish the Purpose.** Sometimes your statement of purpose is easily accomplished, as in "The purpose of this report is to explore the feasibility of expanding our operations into the Houston area." But behind such an apparently simple statement, important issues are being decided.

The phrase, "explore the feasibility of" means that the writer is, at least initially, leaving open the question of whether operations should be expanded into the Houston area. This open stance may or may not be what the reader expects. If the reader has strong expectations of a report that takes expansion into Houston for granted and presents a detailed plan for that expansion, this report's tentative opening will make that reader unhappy. Even if the report actually does present such a detailed plan, when the introduction doesn't establish a purpose that pulls together reader and writer into a common task, the reader's frustration may override anything else the report subsequently does. That is, the reader may not read the report at all.

The nature of the reader's purpose and its relationship to the writer's purpose are given their first explicit form by the opening statement of purpose. So although your statement of purpose may comprise only one line, you need to give its exact wording careful consideration. Be aware of whether it is talking about your purpose for writing the paper, the reader's purpose in reading it, or the way those two purposes interact to establish the paper's purpose.

1.1.3 **Forecast the Organization.** Your introduction should give the reader a clear idea of how the report is organized. The reasons for this are rooted in human psychology. Listeners and hearers understand incoming information more quickly and more efficiently if they first receive a brief idea of what they are about to hear and how it is organized. People who do lots of reading use a trick based on this principle to increase their reading speed: they read any abstract or summary printed with the text, glance at the table of contents to see the order of ideas, and leaf through the pages quickly, noting the sequence of headings and presence of figures or illustrations. Only then will an experienced reader actually start reading. By including in your introduction a forecast of the organization of the whole piece (or in longer reports, a summary) you can help your readers in the same way. For your reader, the shortest part of your introduction, the statement of organization, may well be the most important part.

1.2 Writing Good Introductions

The easiest way to learn how to write an introduction that includes context, purpose, and organization (a *cpo* introduction) may well be to observe how those three elements appear in each of the examples, taken from student papers, in Exhibit 9.1. Each student was asked to define something in his or her own field of study for a layman/executive reader (a technical writing teacher). Notice how each introduction, in its use of context, purpose, and organization, establishes a tone and approach the student feels is appropriate to that writing task. Notice, too, how those tones and approaches are different in each introduction.

These student-written examples show the kind of orientation that writing for a layman often requires. Of course, professional reports are often written for people with expert knowledge, and the introductions of those reports reflect that fact. The two introductions from professional reports in Exhibit 9.2 show not only how the tone varies with the changing audience but also how the forecast of organization can become a brief summary of the report.

Once you see how the forecast of organization can become a brief summary of the report, you can understand another adaptation to audience that shapes how reports begin: the use of an executive summary. This adaptation, especially useful in writing for decision makers, is discussed in Chapter 12, "Abstracts and Executive Summaries."

1.2.1 **Contexts To Use With *CPO* Introductions.** As the sample introductions shown here demonstrate, there are many possible contexts: the way things are usually done, the delivery of new information, the needs of some group of people, the response to a need, or the evaluation of a set of data, to name just a few. Whatever context you use, it should tell the reader the background or perspective from which the report should be viewed, and it should operate on about the same level as you judge your reader's knowledge and interest in the subject to be.

Some statements of context are used so often as to be recognizably recycled. This does not mean that you cannot use such a statement but rather that you should learn to use it carefully. A typical example is the high school graduation speech—or *crossroads* context: "Each of you has come to a crossroads in your life. . . ." If you use such a familiar image, you must either anticipate a ripple of recognition on the part of your readers, or you must weave the familiar image

Exhibit 9.1 Some Examples of *CPO* Introductions

DEFINITION OF THE NICOSIA CONSUMER BEHAVIOR MODEL

Buyer behavior models are usually divided into the two basic areas of *microscopic* and *comprehensive* models. In each area, several behaviorists have developed their own ideas as to how the consumer acts before, during, and after the time of a purchase. Through the use of several descriptive methods, I would like to describe for you one of the comprehensive models developed by Francesco M. Nicosia.

The Nicosia model of consumer behavior is a comprehensive look at what the consumer experiences during and after a decision process. . . .

DEFINITION OF AN INSECT

Many people often refer to any small, multi-legged creeping animal as a bug. Many of these "bugs" are not true insects but rather animals closely related to insects, such as spiders. Within this paper, I will present some of the distinguishing characteristics of insects so that you can be better informed and more able to identify them properly in the future.

Generally speaking, an insect is a small animal. . . .

THE DEFINITION OF AUDITING

American businesses have become so large and complex as to inspire awe and confusion in the average man or woman. As businesses grow larger and more complex, the public wants more and more assurance that businesses are acting honestly and openly in all their dealings. The one method of assurance to which we are looking with the greatest interest is the audit. My purpose in this paper is to use several definition techniques to help you understand what auditing is.

into the fabric of your subject so thoroughly that the image's familiarity is not immediately apparent. Box 9.1 lists fifteen such images; you can use it to suggest openings for your own introductions.

1.2.2 **Times To Use *CPO* Introductions.** You may find that once you have learned how to write this kind of introduction, you are tempted to use it everywhere. You obviously do not need a *cpo* introduction on a one-page business letter, nor do you want to use the same pattern at the beginning of every report you write.

In general, the need for a *cpo* introduction increases with the report's length and the reader's unfamiliarity with your subject matter. Any piece of writing more than a couple of pages long should make specific provisions to help readers deal with the quantity of content, and a *cpo* introduction does so very effectively. Similarly, the less familiar the reader is with the subject, the greater the psychological need for the sneak preview a *cpo* introduction provides.

Exhibit 9.2 Examples of Professional Reports with *CPO* Introductions

MANPOWER REQUIREMENTS AND SUPPLY FOR MAGNETIC FUSION ENERGY, 1981-2000

This study has been conducted to help the U.S. Department of Energy (DOE) complete a task assigned to it by the "Magnetic Fusion Energy Engineering Act of 1980" (P.L. 96-386). This law requires the Secretary of Energy to ". . . assess the adequacy of the projected United States supply of manpower in the engineering and scientific disciplines required to achieve the purposes of this Act, taking cognizance of the other demands likely to be placed on such manpower supply."

The law also requires that the Secretary make recommendations regarding the need for increased support for education in engineering and scientific disciplines.

This study focuses on estimating current employment and future manpower requirements for magnetic fusion energy until the year 2000. It also examines sources of labor for fusion energy and competing demands for the disciplines most important to the future growth of fusion energy.

DATA QUALITY IN THE 1978 & 1979 ANNUAL PATIENT CENSUS: AN ANALYSIS OF DATA EDITING PROCEDURES

Each year the Department of Medicine and Surgery and the Reports and Statistics Service, Office of the Controller, conducts a census of beneficiaries who are either in VA health care facilities or in non-VA health-care facilities under VA auspices. The census provides medical and administrative data on a cross-section of these beneficiaries for annual reports, program review, and planning purposes.

This report analyzes the procedures for editing data collected in the 1978 and 1979 censuses, with particular emphasis on the quality of data—i.e., determining whether data items are "good" or "bad" as judged by "high" or "low" error rates. The report begins with a description of the data collection and editing procedure, discusses error rates and their analysis, and ends with future research topics and a summary section.

1.2.3 **Using Mini-Introductions.** As your reports grow longer, the need to make special provisions to help your reader grows greater. The same principles that make *cpo* introductions necessary and effective also can be applied to key places *inside* your report. Every few pages, you will want to begin a new major subsection of your report; when you begin a new subdivision of your topic, you may want to use an *internal summary* and a *fresh forecast*.

Internal summaries and fresh forecasts recall where the report has been so far and remind the reader where it is going. They ensure that the reader and the writer are together at crucial places in the report. An internal summary is merely

Box 9.1 Some Useful, Standard Statements of Context

1. *The Offer of Something New:* "New developments in fiber optics have now made possible the smallest and least expensive. . . ."
2. *Historical Narrative:* "In the first 50 years of our company's history, we were known primarily for. . . . Now, however, with the increasing demand for new energy supplies, we find the marketplace demands that we change to. . . ."
3. *Comparison of Old and New:* "Until the recent increases in gasoline prices, efficient warehousing and distribution of our products was not a central concern of management. In recent years, however, the cost to us of moving products by truck has more than doubled. Therefore. . . ."
4. *Reference to Authority:* "Will Rogers' famous saying, 'I never met a man I didn't like,' could be taken as the motto for the image we want our salespeople to project."
5. *Crisis:* "Because of growing public awareness of the possibility that cigarettes do indeed cause serious health problems, our company's sales of cigarettes have ceased to grow. We now find ourselves at a crisis. . . ."
6. *Disappointment:* "When we first introduced our XZ-3000 model, we had great hopes that it would soon capture a large share of the market. Unfortunately. . . ."
7. *Opportunity:* "The failure of our competitor's XZ-3000 model presents us with a rare opportunity to. . . ."
8. *Challenge:* "These are the times that try men's souls. The summer soldier and the sunshine patriot. . . ."
9. *Blowing the Whistle:* "It is time to stop kidding ourselves into believing that our XZ-3000 model will. . . ."
10. *Adventure:* "Space—the final frontier. These are the voyages of the Starship *Enterprise*, whose five-year mission. . . ."
11. *Response to an Order:* "We are all aware that paper and printing costs are continuing to increase at an alarming rate. Because of those increased costs, our department's copying bill this quarter is 50 percent higher than last quarter's. The administration has decided that those bills can no longer be afforded. Therefore, in response to the administration's order, we are terminating all copying privileges. . . ."
12. *Revolution:* "The advent of digital transmission will revolutionize the telephone business, and it is the duty of each of us to be prepared for that revolution when it comes. Therefore, the following short courses will be offered to all employees beginning. . . ."
13. *Evolution:* "Since the founding of XYZ Corp. in 1880, the company has always changed to meet the changing needs of the times. This process of evolution and change has continued to today, and now. . . ."

14. *Confession:* "As Head of the Marketing Department for XYZ Corp., I have to confess that the government's predictions of a mild recession in the last quarter of this year had, for a time, not convinced me. But now. . . ."

15. *The Great Dream:* "I say to you today, my friends, that in spite of the difficulties and frustrations of the moment I still have a dream. It is a dream deeply rooted in the American dream. I have a dream that one day this nation will rise up and live out the true meaning of its creed: 'We hold these truths to be self-evident; that all men are created equal.' "*

*Martin Luther King's, "I Have a Dream" speech, delivered at the conclusion of the March on Washington, August 28, 1963.

a brief review of the main points that have been covered so far; a fresh forecast reminds the reader of what remains to be covered. The examples in Exhibit 9.3 come from the middle of long reports; notice the relationship among the internal summary, the fresh forecast, and the heading.

Internal summaries and fresh forecasts are easy to write. The only difficult point is to remember to use them and to decide whether they should be used before, after, or around your new subheading. That decision, however, is much less important than remembering to care enough about your reader to help him or her over the hurdles involved in reading your report.

1.2.4 **Adapting Introductions to Real Readers.** As the introductions shown so far in this chapter demonstrate, the kind and amount of detail you include in your introduction will vary depending on your audience, your purpose, your topic, the

Exhibit 9.3 Examples of Internal Summaries and Fresh Forecasts

As the comparison above has shown, the economics of some situations favors the use of solar over fossil fuels. Another factor must be considered, however, and that is the availability of solar energy systems.

MAJOR SOLAR DISTRIBUTORS

Information on availability of solar energy systems was received from Arkla Industries in Indiana, Helio Association in Arizona, and *Solar Energy Digest* in California. According to those sources. . . .

ISOLATION OF THE CHOLESTEROL

Centrifugation has prepared the plasma for the next procedure, which is isolation of the cholesterol from the plasma. The isolation entails three steps: saponification, extraction, and evaporation. . . .

Exhibit 9.4 Examples of Introductions Presenting Reader Benefits

DEFINITION OF THE NICOSIA CONSUMER BEHAVIOR MODEL

Buyer behavior models are usually divided into the two basic areas of microscopic and comprehensive models. In each area, several behavior theorists have developed their own ideas as to how the consumer acts before, during, and after the time of a purchase. Through the use of several descriptive methods, I would like to describe for you one of the comprehensive models developed by Francesco M. Nicosia.

The Nicosia model of consumer behavior is a comprehensive look at what the consumer experiences during and after a decision process. *As a consumer yourself, you will find that an understanding of the Nicosia model of consumer behavior gives you insight into your own purchasing behavior and into the ways that behavior can be taken advantage of by businesses.*

THE DEFINITION OF AUDITING

American businesses have become so large and complex as to inspire awe and confusion in the average man or woman. More and more, the public wants assurance that businesses are acting honestly and openly in all their dealings. The one method of assurance to which we are looking with greatest interest is the audit. My purpose in this paper is to use several definition techniques to help you understand what auditing is. *The more customers and investors such as yourself understand about the audit process, the easier business's public relations jobs will become and the more confidence the public will have in business's financial dealings.*

available space, and a number of other variables. One particular adaptation, *reader benefits* can give you an idea of the interesting and important ways *cpo* introductions can vary according to audience. For many layman audiences, you will do well to include a clear statement of reader benefits as part of your introduction. By telling your reader just what he or she can hope to gain from reading your report, you thus increase the chances that your report will be read and understood by your layman reader.

"Reader benefits" means an explicit statement of why your reader should read the report and of what your reader can gain from reading the report. Exhibit 9.4 shows two of the introductions shown in Exhibit 9.1, rewritten by students to include reader benefits (shown in italics).

2. Conclusions

Just as any document longer than a couple of pages needs an introduction, so such a document also needs a conclusion. Most readers remember best what they read last. The conclusion gives you one last chance to do what you want to do for your reader, to move your reader in the direction you choose. Twelve different techniques for conclusions are shown in Box 9.2

Box 9.2 Examples of Techniques for Writing Conclusions

1. *State the results of the investigation or study.* Of course, stating the results is what most readers expect a conclusion to do. Usually you will want to combine this technique with one of the others listed here.
2. *Recommend what action should be undertaken.* Although it is a fallacy that any recommendation report must *necessarily* end with the recommendation (see Chapter 14), this is another typical pattern for a conclusion. This pattern is also frequently combined with one or more of the others listed here (such as 5, 6, 7, or 8).
3. *Repeat the major points, for emphasis.* The longer and more complicated your report is, the more important it is to conclude by summarizing its major points.
4. *Briefly summarize the entire document.* Sometimes a report doesn't break down into major points very conveniently. In this case, you should write a summary to be used as a conclusion (Chapter 12, "Abstracts and Executive Summaries" will show you how to write a summary).
5. *Extend the implications of the current work.* Often your conclusion will go beyond the scope of your report proper, extending the report's temporal or causal sequence further than the range covered by the report's body (as in 6, 7, 8, and 9).
6. *State what the further problems or concerns might be and indicate how to deal with them.* One way of moving your report into the future is to foresee possible problems or events that could mean that the report's subject needs re-examination.
7. *Tell how to evaluate whether the process or action your report describes or recommends is proceeding properly.* Although presenting evaluative techniques in detail may be beyond the scope of your report, a brief description of them may be a real help to your readers.
8. *Describe alternative steps or troubleshooting procedures.* Another way to make your report more useful is to present as a conclusion a brief explanation of whatever alternative readings of the situation there might be, or of any particular actions that need to be taken, should the future course of events not go as the report suggests.
9. *Suggest other entirely different approaches.* Depending on how tentative or firm your report is, you may want to make your presentation of other approaches to the problem more detailed.

10. *Restate cautions and safety warnings.* Although it is never a good idea to have the necessary cautions and safety warnings *only* at the end of a document, in circumstances of extreme risk (or liability) it may well be a good idea to restate the appropriate cautions or safety warnings as part of your conclusion.
11. *Re-emphasize the importance of the topic.* This ending and 12 are less frequently used than 1-10 in scientific and technical writing and more frequently used in popularized science writing. Especially when writing for laymen, re-emphasizing the importance of the topic at the end of the document may be a good idea because laymen especially may not really be aware of it.
12. *Add a sense of an ending.* Most readers, especially lay readers, subconsciously expect the things they read to have some kind of an ending. Besides the more functional kinds of endings described in 1-11, you can add the *sense* of an ending by

- Ending with an appropriate quotation.
- Echoing a key phrase from the introduction.
- Adding an emotional appeal.

EXERCISES

1. Select five important topics or concepts in your field of study. For each one, write an introduction to a paper that will define each one of them for a layman/executive audience. Then rewrite each introduction for an expert audience.

2. Choose ten articles at random from your field's professional journals and examine their introductions. Do they conform to the principles described in this chapter? Write a brief report describing the way introductions are done in your field, based on these samples. (Be sure to turn in copies of the introductions with your report.)

3. Compare the types of introductions discussed in this chapter with five introductions from popularized science magazines (*Psychology Today*, etc.). How do the popularized science introductions differ from the ones in this chapter? What accounts for the difference? (Be sure to turn in copies of the introductions with your answers to these questions.)

4. Consider carefully the following professionally written introduction. What are its strong points? its weak points? Be prepared to discuss in class how to make it better. (The report has three chapters.)

Educational and Income Characteristics of Veterans
(March 1979)

This report focuses on three basic social indicators with respect to the population of male war veterans 20 years old and over. The analysis describes the attained education of veterans in 1979 and their personal and family incomes in 1978. These data are discussed in comparison with nonveterans within five-year age intervals.

Chapter 1, Median Family Income in 1978, shows the average income of families headed by veterans in comparison with that of families headed by nonveterans of similar age. Data are broken down by age of head and type of family, income status of the wife of the family head, and veteran status.

Chapter 2 discusses the personal income of individual men by age and by veteran status, with trend data going back to 1968.

Educational attainment of veterans is the subject of Chapter 3. The data demonstrate the relationship between years of school and median income of male veterans by their age. Data are also presented for nonveterans.

5. You have volunteered to assist your local zoo (on a volunteer basis) by helping produce a manual to guide the work of the many volunteers who help out at the zoo. The volunteers conduct tours for school groups, help stage special events (the spring zoofest, the oldest elephant's birthday, etc.), staff the children's petting zoo, help stage fund-raising events in the community, staff the information booths, and perform a variety of other functions. This manual will be especially useful for new volunteers who do not know the customary procedures and practices around the zoo, but it will also go to the "old hands," who once in a while need to be reminded that they can't rewrite policy on the spur of the moment to suit their own wishes. Your task is to write the introduction to this manual (100-150 words); invent any other information you may need (within the bounds of reason and common sense).

10

Definitions and Descriptions

Defining and describing may well be the most essential elements of technical communication. Even outside of professional life, it's difficult to have so much as a five-minute conversation without involving yourself in some kind of defining or describing—of your emotional state, tomorrow's weather, the management exam you just took, or the problems you're having with your nuclear engineering lab's weekly forty-page reports. As a professional, you'll find defining and describing at the heart of most of your writing.

This chapter presents fourteen ways to define and describe whatever you need to write about. The kind of task professional writing presents usually involves explaining to your reader just exactly what some object (or some abstraction) is; this chapter shows you how to do that.

Language theorists tell us that language establishes the meanings of words *contextually*, that except for the most common nouns (like *tree* or *door*) the meaning of each word in a sentence is established by the sentence it is in. Consider this sentence:

> I threw the gilhickie out the window.

Few people know with any certainty what a gilhickie is, but we can tell from the sentence that it is something (a) found indoors, and (b) light enough to throw out the window. We may also be able to speculate a little about what kind of thing one might throw out a window.

The more information contained in the sentence, the more of a definition of a gilhickie we can construct:

> Because it was beginning to smoke, I threw the gilhickie out the window.

Now we can construct a picture of a gilhickie as something that smokes when it isn't working properly. Add still more information, and we can construct a more precise idea of what a gilhickie is:

> Because it was beginning to smoke, I ripped the gilhickie from its mount and threw it out the window.

Now we're sure it's a piece of machinery bolted to the floor (but not too securely), something that runs, smokes when it isn't working properly, and can be thrown out the window.

Actually, *gilhickie* is a sailor's term for anything one can't think of the right name for. Rather than saying, "Hand me the thingamajig," the sailor says "Pass me that gilhickie." This example shows that the richer a language context a term is embedded in, the clearer its meaning will be. A good working knowledge of techniques for placing whatever you're writing about into a language-rich context will help you make your meaning clear in any kind of writing task.

The fourteen techniques examined in this chapter are divided into three groups: patterns at rest, patterns in motion, and indirect patterns. The examples used here come from a professional report, *Steam Turbines and Their Lubrication*, published by Mobil Oil Company; a few have been slightly rewritten to emphasize a particular pattern better. To see how all the techniques work together, you can find the first two pages of the actual report in Chapter 13, Section 2. Section 5 of this chapter contains a sample paper written by a student who was trying to use as many of these techniques as possible in one short report.

1. Static Patterns

These techniques treat the *X* being defined and described in a static and stationary way. Four techniques come under this heading: the formal pattern, explication, analysis (or division), and accumulation of detail.

1.1 The Formal Pattern

Usually seen as the fundamental definition technique, the formal (or logical) pattern has two stages:

1. First place *X* in a class.
2. Then differentiate *X* from the other members of the class.

You may already know this pattern, from courses in zoology or botany, as definition by *genus* and *species*.

In placing *X* in a class and then differentiating it from the other members of its class, be careful not to violate the basic logic by which definitions work; that is, do not make the definition either too broad (including too many *not-X's* in the class with *X*), too narrow (excluding some *X's* from the class you define), or circular (accidentally using *X* to explain *X*).

Too Broad. One way to go wrong with a definition or description is to include within *X* entities that are not *X*. For example, if you define an *irrigation system* as "anything that brings needed water to crops," you have accidentally included rain and snow as irrigation systems. The solution requires narrowing the explanation: "anything *man-made* that brings needed water. . . ."

Too Narrow. You can also err by excluding from *X* items that should be included within it. For example, if you define *point-of-purchase displays* as "any cardboard visual designed to be displayed with a product to increase its sales," you have accidentally excluded a number of types of construction (plastic, fiberglass) also common to P-O-P displays. Solve this problem by expanding the definition: "any visual media designed to be exhibited with a product. . . ."

Circular. A circular definition accidentally presupposes a knowledge of *X* in the explanation of *X*. This occurs by using some form of the words that name *X* to define it. For example: "A magnetic bubble memory uses magnetic bubbles to store memory." People who know what magnetic bubbles are probably do not need an explanation of magnetic bubble memory, but in any case, the explanation will not help someone who does not know what a magnetic bubble is. The solution is to add more information, being careful not to use forms of the words you're defining in the definition you're writing.

The following passage uses the formal pattern—without violating logic—to explain what a steam turbine is.

> The steam turbine is one of the world's most important prime movers. In a turbine, steam expands in stationary or moving nozzles from which it discharges at high velocity. The force of the high-velocity jets of steam causes the moving parts to rotate, thus making the energy in the steam available to do useful mechanical work—for example, to drive a compressor or generator. Steam turbines lead all other prime movers as the drive for electric-power generators. In addition, they are the versatile drives for many other machines, such as pumps, compressors, and mills of various kinds.

The first sentence places the steam turbine within a class (prime movers). The next two sentences differentiate it from other members of the classs by explaining how it works. The last two sentences differentiate steam turbines from other prime movers by pointing out their leadership as drives for electric-power generators and their versatility as drives for other machines.

This process of logical definition is typically represented visually by placing *X* in a class and then establishing boundaries between *X* and the rest of the items in the class (see Figure 10.1).

In an important sense, all of the following patterns are subcategories of this one: each pattern is a way to differentiate *X* from other objects, and could therefore be considered a second stage of the formal pattern. For example, our definition of a steam turbine uses process as one of the ways to differentiate steam turbines from other prime movers. As Figure 10.1 suggests, the smaller an original circle (or class) we initially place *X* in, the easier the second stage will be. The second stage of the definition uses a variety of techniques to draw the initial circle closer and closer—that is, define the class more and more narrowly, until it includes only the item or entity you are defining.

1.2 Explication

Explication consists of explaining the meaning of key words in a formal or logical definition. As such, it nearly always occurs in combination with a formal definition. The following passage uses explication by expanding on the meaning of the terms *reliability*, *trends*, and *automatic data processing*.

> In all of these services, turbine reliability has always been of prime importance. This term embraces both availability for service and the ability to perform satisfactorily in service for long periods.
>
> Modern trends are placing greater and greater premiums on reliability. These are trends toward larger sizes, higher pressures and temperatures, and toward the use of automatic data processing equipment for:
>
> 1. Logging and scanning of measured quantities and actuating alarms when necessary,
> 2. Computing performance and adjusting operation accordingly, and
> 3. Full automatic operation of plants in some cases.

Figure 10.1 (a) The First Stage of Logical Definition "First place *X* in a class."

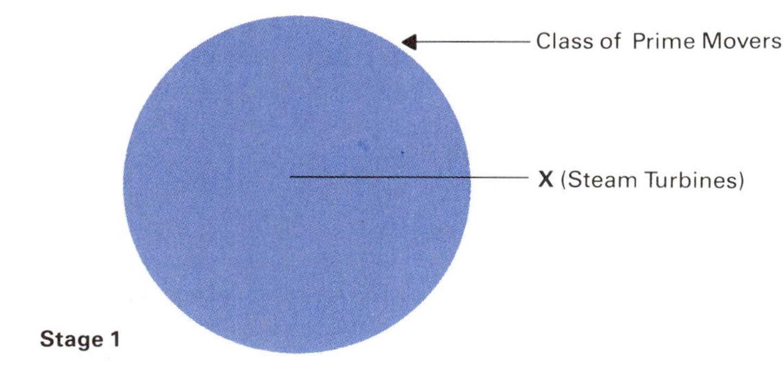

Figure 10.1 (b) The Second Stage of Logical Definition "Then differentiate *X* from other members of the class."

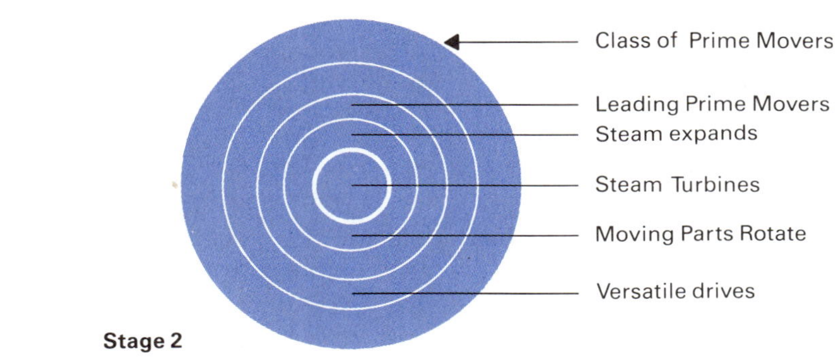

When you use explication, you may be tempted to grind through the several words pretty mechanically. Remember that giving in to such a temptation places your needs above those of the reader.

1.3 Analysis

Analysis (or division) means dividing *X* into its component parts. These can be either *X*'s natural parts (properly called its divisions) or its artificial parts (called distinctions). Sometimes these parts will coincide with the words discussed in an explication, but sometimes they won't. Often this technique will be supported by the use of a visual. Exhibit 10.1 gives an example of a professionally written analysis.

Exhibit 10.1 A Professionally Written Analysis

Among the most important of builders' efforts to achieve the reliability so essential to steam turbine applications is the provision of a lubrication system that will assure an ample supply of lubricant to all moving parts. The size of the turbine generally determines whether the system is simple or extensive and complex. Small turbines, such as those used to drive auxiliary equipment, are generally provided with ring-oiled bearings, other moving parts being lubricated by hand. Moderate-sized units, particularly if driving through reduction gears, may have both ring-oiled bearings and a circulation system which not only sprays oil to the point of gear mesh but also supplies oil to the bearings of both the turbine and the gear set. Large turbines are invariably provided with circulation systems that supply oil to all parts of the unit requiring lubrication, to the turbine governor mechanism, and for the operation of valve gear and safety controls. Generators and other equipment driven by turbines are often lubricated from the turbine circulation system.

You can see the several layers of analysis or division used in the passage clearly through the simple outline of it shown in Exhibit 10.2:

Exhibit 10.2 A Simple Outline of the Passage in Exhibit 10.1

Builder's efforts to achieve reliability include provision of a lubrication system, and the lubrication system's relative complexity is determined by the turbine's size.

I. Small turbines (such as those driving auxiliary equipment)
   - A. generally provided with ring-oiled bearings
   - B. other moving parts lubricated by hand

II. Moderate-sized units (especially driven through reduction gears)
   - A. may have ring-oiled gears
   - B. may also have circulation system
     1. circulation system sprays oil to point of gear mesh
     2. circulation system also supplies oil to bearings

III. Large turbines
   - A. always provided with circulation systems
     1. systems supply oil to all parts of the unit
     2. systems supply oil to the turbine governor
     3. systems supply oil for operation of valve gear and safety controls
   - B. often also lubricate generators and other equipment through turbine's own circulation system

1.4 Accumulation of Detail

Accumulating details may be the most common description technique. One merely adds detail to detail, with each making the reader's mental picture clearer. Determining which details to accumulate is critical; generally you should favor the ones that make *X* unique. Here is a paragraph built on accumulation of detail:

> Single-shaft, nuclear-powered turbines as large as 1200 mw are now in service. Cross-compound units (double shaft) as large as 1300 mw are also in service in nuclear-powered, electric generating stations. These large units operate at 1800 rpm. As a result of the tremendous impact on a system capacity when a 1200 or 1300 mw unit goes down for inspection or maintenance, the trend today is toward smaller, fossil-fueled units in the range of 400 to 700 mw operating at 3600 rpm.

2. Moving Patterns

Moving patterns involve placing *X* in some kind of larger *sequence*—of process, cause and effect, or time. This can happen four ways: explaining *X*'s process or operation, placing *X* in a sequence of cause and effect, explaining the history of *X*'s name (etymology), or explaining the history of *X* itself.

2.1 Process

If you define and describe *X* by process, you tell how *X* works or what it does. If your subject is a machine lathe, for example, you explain its principles and methods of operation. If your subject is inflation, you explain what is occurring that we call inflation ("prices are going up, each dollar's buying power is going down. . ."). Here is an explanation of how a steam turbine works:

> In a turbine, steam expands in stationary or moving nozzles from which it discharges at high velocity. The force of the high-velocity jets of steam causes the moving parts to rotate, thus making the energy in the steam available to do useful mechanical work—for example, to drive a compressor or generator.
>
> After it has expanded in the turbine, the steam usually exhausts to a condenser, which serves two purposes. First, by maintaining a vacuum at the turbine exhaust, it increases the pressure range through which the steam expands. In this way, it materially increases the efficiency of power generation. Second, it causes the steam to condense, thus providing pure, clean water for the boilers to reconvert into steam. This simple cycle—water to steam, power generation, and steam to water—forms the basis on which most steam-power plants operate.

2.2 Cause and Effect

Placing *X* in a causal sequence can help your reader understand it. What causes *X*? What is the effect of *X*? The following passage discusses the cause of turbine reliability—correct lubrication—and the effect of improper lubrication.

> Correct lubrication plays a major role in achieving reliability and low maintenance cost. High quality Mobil turbine oils, including world-famous Mobil DTE 797 Oil, have unusual ability to protect against wear and to resist deposit formation. Deposits may cause faulty operation of hydraulic elements, lack of lubrication, and overheating. Downtime for repairs or cleaning of lubrication systems is kept to a minimum with proper lubrication.

2.3 History of the Term

Sometimes the word for *X* has an interesting and revealing history. For example, Smackover, Arkansas, got its name from the way the French settlers' name for the place sounded to ears unfamiliar with French; thus, the French name for the settlement, *Chemin Couvert* (covered road), became Smackover. Such information is more readily available than you might think; it can usually be found in the nearest dictionary.

Remember that when you're discussing the word rather than using it, you need to mark that fact for the reader by underlining the word. The paragraph below explains how a particular part of some steam turbines got its name.

> When shutting down large turbines, it is necessary to keep the rotors turning for sufficient time to assure uniform cooling. If this is not done, uneven cooling may cause a distortion and bowing of the shaft. A *turning gear* is, therefore, provided on turbines of over about 10,000-kw size to rotate the spindle at 1 to 100 rpm during the cooling period.

2.4 History of the Object

Your aim in giving the history of *X* is to provide your reader with a richer and more readily meaningful context, thus enhancing the explanation. Even though its history may not be crucial, many people will feel more comfortable with a new item if they know a little about its history.

> The actual "growing-up" era of the steam turbine took place after 1899. In 1900, turbines of 1000 and 1500 kw were built. By 1905, at least ten turbines of 5000 kw were in service, and between 1906 and 1909, turbines of 7500 to 14,000 kw were installed. After this period, sizes increased at a rapid rate: 20,000 kw in 1911; 30,000 in 1913; 50,000 in 1917; and 60,000 in 1924. In 1929, a 208,000-kw cross-compound turbine was installed, and this remained the largest turbine for many years.

3. Indirect Patterns

When you use indirect patterns of defining and describing, you explain *X* by describing or relating something else to it.

3.1 Elimination

Sometimes the easiest way to explain *X* is to tell what it is *not*. That is, you pick the other objects (*Y*, *Z*, and so on) closest to *X*, those with which it might be easily confused, and you clearly differentiate them from *X*. In this way, by paying close attention to the items that surround *X*, you help your reader understand *X*. The following passage explains what a "properly refined petroleum lubricating oil" does by explaining first what can happen if one does not use such an oil.

> Thick, surface-separating films cannot be maintained at all times in the lubricated elements of steam turbines and associated equipment. For example, during shutdown, the thick oil film in journal bearings is squeezed out of the pressure area and some metal-to-metal contact is made. On starting (unless oil lifts are used), friction is high and some wear occurs. This condition of ***boundary lubrication*** continues at least momentarily until speed is high enough to develop a thick fluid film. Boundary lubrication may exist in other situations where speeds are low, loads are high, or lubricant supply is restricted.
>
> A properly refined petroleum lubricating oil has considerable natural anti-wear value, or *film strength*, under boundary-lubrication conditions.

3.2 Analogy

Analogy, or the making of figurative comparisons, is one of the most neglected but potentially useful techniques in writing for business and industry. By creating one well-chosen figure of speech, you can suggest more and deeper meaning in fewer words than you can with almost any other pattern. For example, one business analyst wrote that the American automotive industry is like a sleeping dinosaur—either just resting, or hibernating through bad times, or on its way to total extinction. The problem, he said, is that we just don't know which of the three options is right. Although figurative language may be underused in some kinds of writing, that may only make the well-chosen analogy more effective when it does appear.

> The force of the high-velocity jets of steam issuing from the nozzles of steam turbines may be utilized in two ways. If the nozzle is fixed and the jet directed at a movable blade, the jet's *impulse* force pushes the blade forward. If the nozzle is free to move, the *reaction* of the jet pushes against the nozzle, causing it to move in the opposite direction. Both these actions can be observed when using the ordinary garden hose. Many commercial turbines use both impulse and reaction principles.

Exhibit 10.3 An Example of Comparison and Contrast

> To reduce rotative speed while maintaining efficiency, the high velocity may be absorbed in several steps, which is called *velocity compounding*. In some turbines this is accomplished by two rows of moving blades between which is placed a row of stationary blades that reverses the direction of steam flow as it passes from the first to the second row of moving blades. Other ways of accomplishing velocity compounding involve redirecting a steam jet so that it strikes the same row of blades several times with gradually diminishing velocity.
>
> Another method of reducing rotor speed while maintaining efficiency is to decrease the velocity of the jets by dividing the drop in steam pressure into a number of stages. This is called *pressure compounding*. Each stage consists of a single row of stationary nozzles and a single row of moving blades, and the method is equivalent to mounting several single-stage impulse turbines on a common shaft. In large units, velocity compounding is usually employed in the first pressure stage and pressure compounding in the remaining stages.

3.3 Comparison and Contrast

If you move from comparisons that are imaginative to comparisons that are literal, you move from analogy to comparison and contrast. The passage in Exhibit 10.3 compares several ways of reducing the rotating speed of turbine blades while maintaining efficiency, and along the way makes a nice comparison between small and large turbines.

3.4 Examples: Naming

Few explanations are complete without examples. Many a writer of cloudy passages has learned to write reasonably clear explanations by learning to provide two or three good examples to support each important generalization. Here is an example:

> In many instances, efficient turbine speed is higher than that of the machine being driven. This may be the case, for example, where a turbine drives a direct-current generator, paper machine, centrifugal pump, blower, fan, or sugar-cane crusher. Under these circumstances, reduction gears are used to connect the high-speed turbine to the driven unit.

3.5 Examples: Pointing Out

To make a really effective definition and description of *X*, you need to tell your reader where to find an example of *X*. That is, you point one out. In the example in Exhibit 10.4, the writer gives a preliminary explanation of bearing lubrication, and then tells the reader where to find a better explanation.

Exhibit 10.4 A Passage Pointing Out an Example

Oil supply passages are provided in the housing and in the bearing shells through which a copious supply of oil is furnished from the circulation-oiling system. This oil is delivered to axial grooves and chamfers at the horizontal split, sometimes to both sides and sometimes only to one side. The grooves distribute the oil along the length of the bearing, and the chamfers assist in the formation of a film of oil between the journal and the bearing.*

*A complete discussion of bearing lubrication will be found in the Mobil publication "Plain Bearings—Fluid-Film Lubrication."

3.6 Examples: Showing

Despite the fact that it's such an obvious way to explain something to someone, using pictures and illustrations is as neglected a pattern as analogy. The illustrations in Figure 10.2 are from the page that faces the table of contents of *Steam Turbines and Their Lubrication*; anyone who looks at the table of contents also looks at these visuals.

This chapter organizes fourteen patterns according to a functional classification scheme, not necessarily a logical one. Depending on what you are writing about, one pattern may be pretty much like another, or one pattern may be exactly right and another totally inappropriate. Because of this, it is important that you go beyond looking at a particular pattern and debating whether it is comparison and contrast or analogy (to pick two patterns that often are hard to tell apart); the goal is for you to be able to *use* the patterns.

4. Adapting Definitions and Descriptions

At this point your instructor may be preparing to ask you to write a definition and description report in order for you to get intensive practice with using a variety of different developmental techniques. After college, although you will need to define or describe in nearly everything you write, the kind of thing you are asked to write will more likely be an annual report, period progress report, newsletter, sales promotion, design report, or procedures manual, to name only a few of the kinds of professional and technical documents. Nonetheless, most of what you will be doing is defining and describing.

In all of these kinds of writing, from academic exercise to multimillion dollar proposal, you need to be very careful to balance your purpose with that of the reader. The balance you strike between reader's and writer's purposes will determine how you handle two key aspects of your report—its organization and its level of complexity (and abstraction). Before you can determine what method of organization or what level of detail and abstraction may be right, you need to think about reader's purpose versus writer's purpose.

Figure 10.2 Cross-Sections of Steam Turbines (Reproduced by permission, Copyright 1965, 1981, Mobil Oil Corporation)

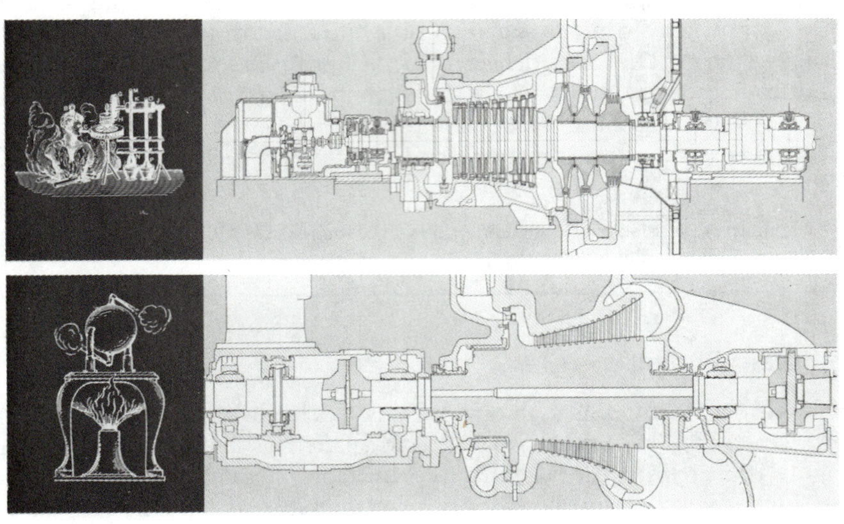

4.1 Reader's Purpose Versus Writer's Purpose

The conflicting demands of reader's versus writer's purposes always concern writers in business and industry. The tugs and tension between them are the forces you feel when you write. *Your* purpose as writer always must be balanced against your *audience's* purpose as reader(s). It is natural for any writer to want to tell everything he or she knows about a subject, just as it is natural for any reader to want to know only what directly concerns him or her. Writers are often not particularly aware of the amount of background a reader may need to be able to understand a document, or of the order of elements the reader needs to be able to understand with a minimum of difficulty. Readers, on the other hand, are especially aware of their need for background, and particularly impatient with writers who have not provided it. Similarly, writers tend to use most those words with which they are familiar, while readers resent writing that contains too many unfamiliar words. A thoughtless writer may tend to deal with his topic at a level most comfortable to him, without regard for the reader's inability to handle the topic at that level of abstraction. Being aware of your reader's purpose in reading, including his or her level of interest and knowledge, can help you avoid these problems.

4.2 Organization

If your writing takes its reader sufficiently into consideration, it will be reader centered, not writer centered. The way many writers work, first drafts tend to be writer centered—in vocabulary, amount of detail, level of abstraction, and organ-

Exhibit 10.5 A Writer-Centered First Draft

MEMORANDUM

To: Jim Hanson, Shipping Room Mgr.

From: J.R. Reed, V.P.

Subject: The shipping room mess

Date: 3/23/83

While you were on vacation I had occasion to come down and inspect the shipping room, and I was really shocked at what I saw. There were uncoded packages and parts of shipments all around, equipment not properly stored, not properly maintained. I couldn't believe what I was seeing, or that you let the shipping operation be so messy.I think that an operation like that needs to be neat and orderly with all equipment properly maintained and all shipments assembled in an orderly way. Not only does sloppiness increase the chances of losing shipments, but it also is a considerable safety risk to the people who work there.I shouldn't have to take my time to tell you things like this. My desk is covered with my own work, and it's a shame I have to do yours too.

ization. In their first drafts, most professionals who write just try to get the content down on paper. At that point, the best way for the ideas to be organized is whatever way they happen to come out, just so long as they all wind up on paper. First drafts reflect the order of thought that allows the writer to put words on paper most easily. What the reader needs, however, is a report written following the order of thoughts by which he or she can most clearly understand it. Ideally, the later drafts of the same piece of writing are progressively more reader centered, as the writer gains enough control over the material to adjust it to someone else's needs.

If you view the writing process as one of only two stages, such as creating and criticizing, it's easy to see the first—creating—as centering on the writer's need to get the subject down on paper somehow, and the second—criticizing—as centering on the reader's need to understand what has been written. The reader's need to understand, and in a broader sense, the document's overall effect on the reader, should be among your primary concerns when you criticize and revise your writing. Make sure the organization of your report builds from a base the reader will understand, and that the order of facts and concepts will be logical to the reader.

Exhibits 10.5 and 10.6 show the first and the second versions of the same simple memo. Between versions, the writer balances his initial concern with his own purpose against his growing awareness of what the reader wants, and will get, out of the memo.

Exhibit 10.6 A Reader-Centered Second Draft

MEMORANDUM

To: Jim Hanson, Shipping Room Mgr.

From: J.R. Reed, V.P.

Subject: Improving conditions in the shipping room

Date: 3/23/83

While you were on vacation I went down to the shipping room to check on the status of a delivery. What I saw there wouldn't have pleased you. There were packages and parts of shipments all around the room in no apparent order, and much of the equipment apparently had been left wherever the last user had finished with it. The equipment also didn't look like any maintenance had been done on it since you left.That kind of sloppiness increases our chances of confusing a shipment or having an on-the-job accident. I know that's not the way you like to run your shop. When you get caught up from being away, let's get together and review your policies on neatness and safety and try to come up with a way to keep those standards up even when you are not there to supervise them.

As Chapter 9, "Introductions and Conclusions," discussed, the temptation for writers is to jump right into the middle of a topic, reciting facts and figures with no preliminaries. The problem with this approach is that most readers need to know the background before they can make anything out of those facts and figures. That background is so familiar to the writer that he or she may forget to include it, but the reader absolutely must have it. The rest of the report must build in a similar manner, taking into account the information the reader needs to have, and not simply following the order of items the subject had in the writer's mind when he or she first put the report together.

4.3 Level of Complexity and Abstraction

Decisions about the appropriateness of a passage's level of complexity or abstraction cannot be made sensibly without knowing your audience; language that is too abstract or complex for one audience, message, or purpose may be just right for another. Consider the definition in Exhibit 10.7: Is it right to ask whether it is too abstract or complex without specifying what kind of audience it is aimed at?

Which sections of this definition are abstract? Some readers will find the first sentence difficult because it has a quality (velocity) changing according to another quality (time rate). The second sentence contains a concept (vector quantity) that may be unfamiliar to some readers and make the passage difficult, and the logic

Exhibit 10.7 A Definition Written at a High Level of Abstraction and Complexity

> *Acceleration*: the time rate at which a velocity is changing. Because velocity, a vector quantity, has both magnitude and direction, acceleration is also a vector quantity and must account for changes in both magnitude and direction of velocity. The velocity of a point or an object moving on a straight path can change in magnitude only; on a curved path, it may or may not change in magnitude, but it will always change in direction. This condition means that the acceleration of a point moving on a curved path can never be zero.

Source: From *Encyclopaedia Britannica*, 15th edition (1980), Micropaedia, Volume I, p. 48. Reprinted by permission.

of that sentence (because velocity has both magnitude and direction, and velocity is part of acceleration, then acceleration must also account for changes in both magnitude and direction) certainly will give trouble to anyone who had problems with the concept of "vector quantity". The logic becomes more complex with the next sentence ("The velocity of a point or object. . . ."), which provides a specific example of the previous sentence's point. The inference that can lead a reader to the last sentence from the previous two is still more complex, the result of an abstract reasoning process.

Some readers may have problems of the sorts detailed above; at least in the view of the editors of *Encyclopaedia Britannica*, most of their readers will not. What is too abstract or complex for one reader may suit another perfectly.

To adjust that definition of acceleration for a reader with less of a background in physics would involve alterations in more than just the words used in the passage; the concepts themselves would have to be simplified, or in some cases left out. The example would have to be more concrete, and able to stand on its own without reference to the theory in the abstract explanation. But again, we cannot really be specific about adaptation without specifying an audience and its purpose in reading the definition. If we can assume the audience for the *Britannica* is composed of college graduates, then we can see how concepts like "vector quantity" and abstract chains of logic may be appropriate. For an audience with only high school education, a better definition might well start out with "*Acceleration* means any change in an object's speed along its current path." The definition may then go right into a specific example, such as a rocket taking off, and explain that its increase in speed along its path is its acceleration.

Determining the proper levels of complexity and abstraction for a document requires that you know its audience and their purpose in reading it. Most writers save adjusting the levels of complexity and abstraction in their writing for some stage of their writing beyond the first draft. As Chapters 2 and 3 showed, making your writing readable is most properly a concern during revision.

All aspects of the document, from sentence length to overall organization, come into play when you are measuring and adjusting its levels of complexity and

Exhibit 10.8 A Passage with a Chain of Weak Verbs

DISINTERMEDIATION

Almost everyone borrows money at one time or another. Sometimes qualified borrowers are unable to get a loan because funds just are not available. This is because of disintermediation. Many people do not know what disintermediation is or how it works. However, since it affects anyone who borrows money, it is useful to have an understanding of the subject. Disintermediation is an economic process. More specifically, it is a monetary decision. When investors withdraw their savings from financial intermediaries to make investments elsewhere because the ceiling interest rate is lower than the interest rate offered on securities, disintermediation has occurred.

abstraction. One of the most important such aspects is the kind of verbs you use. Especially when you write a passage that defines and describes something, it's tempting to make nearly every verb a form of *to be*. The few that are not are usually either forms of *to have* or they are in passive voice (the form "A was hit by B" rather than "B hit A"; see the Appendix, Sections 2.1 and 2.2, for more explanation). Such a chain of weak verbs makes your passage needlessly abstract; nothing ever *does* anything to anything. Consider the example in Exhibit 10.8; the weak verbs are circled and connected.

The connected, circled words make a chain of weak verbs. The effect of that chain is to flatten the writing, taking away both life and precision of meaning. Three or four weak verbs in a row is bad enough, but you can easily find such sequences that go on for pages in many reports. Only the most determined reader will hack through this kind of deadly dull language, and it's deadly dull mostly because of the weak verbs.

The way to deal with such strings of needlessly weak verbs is to revise them out. Chapter 3 presents much more detail on revising weak verbs. The same passage, this time revised to strengthen the verbs, is shown in Exhibit 10.9.

Successfully dealing with issues such as organization, levels of complexity, and abstraction is crucial if you are to write effective definitions and descriptions. The combination of the right variety of techniques with the proper balance between reader's purpose and writer's purpose puts your definition or description on the track towards success. Any writer involved in writing an extended definition may be tempted to let his or her purpose as a writer—to get everything necessary into the definition and description by using the words and ideas that seem most convenient—prevent the fulfillment of the reader's purpose. In this kind of writing, as in any other kind of writing that professionals do, remember that purpose and audience go together, that in adapting your message to your reader you must be sensitive to fulfilling the reader's purpose. Combining the reader's purpose and the writer's purpose establishes the document's purpose.

Exhibit 10.9 The Passage in Exhibit 10.8 Revised with Stronger Verbs

DISINTERMEDIATION

Almost everyone borrows money at one time or another. Sometimes—because of disintermediation—qualified borrowers cannot get loans because funds just are not available. Many people do not recognize disintermediation or know how it works. However, since it affects anyone who borrows money, an understanding of the subject can help anyone who borrows money. Disintermediation is an economic process that occurs when investors make the monetary decision to withdraw their savings from financial intermediaries and to invest their money elsewhere. This usually occurs when the interest rate offered on securities exceeds the ceiling interest rate offered by financial intermediaries.

5. Some Sample Definition-and-Description Reports

The paper in Exhibit 10.10 was written by a business student for an advanced technical writing class. The assignment required the student to use as many of the different techniques presented here as possible, but to work them into a readable paper. Following this student-written example is a short section of a piece of professional writing (Exhibit 10.11).

Exhibit 10.10 A Definition-and-Description Paper

A Definition of <u>Selling Short</u>

The term "selling short" indicates a specific type of trade made in a financial marketplace. Although selling short can be done in either the stock market or the commodity futures market, it will be explained here only in the context of commodity futures. One only sells short in a market that is trending down, so the first part of selling short is accurately forecasting the price of a commodities market. To sell short successfully, one sells a given commodity at the current market price and then buys it back later at a lower price.

The origins of the term, "selling short" are obscure. Since the action involves selling, the first word's sense is obvious. "Short" is used in the expression in the same sense as "getting caught short." When one sells short, one runs the risk of getting caught without enough of the product to deliver—one is short of the product.

To understand selling short, one must first understand certain particulars about the commodity futures market. It is made up of 65 different commodities which may be divided into four basic categories: metals, meats, grains, and financials. Some of the commodities which make up these four groups are gold, silver, platinum, paladium, zinc, pork bellies, hogs, cattle, corn, oats, soybeans, U.S. T-bills, U.S. T-bonds, British pounds, and the Standard and Poor 500 Stock Index. Each commodity is traded in a specific contract size. For example, silver is traded in either 1000 oz. or 5000 oz. contracts. Each contract trades in specific increments. Silver trades in cents per pound; so a one cent move in silver is worth either $10 or $50, respectively.

All these markets are traded at a certain fixed time in the future. Each contract is deliverable during a certain specified month. For example, if one is trading December 1984 silver, that means one has control over a contract of silver which is to be delivered in December, 1984. By selling short a contract of December silver, the seller commits himself to deliver either 1000 or 5000 ozs. of silver in December. That commitment is cancelled when the contract is bought back. Buying back means purchasing the same contract of the given commodity at the prevailing market price and at the same exchange on which the short was sold.

The profit in selling short occurs when the commodity is bought back at a lower price than the one for which it was sold. A loss occurs if the commodity is bought back at a higher price. So if one sells short 1000 ozs. of December silver at ten dollars an ounce and buys it back at nine dollars an ounce, the end result is a profit of $1000. On the other hand, if the commodity is sold at ten dollars and bought back at eleven, the result is a $1000 loss. Figures 1 and 2 demonstrate the two trades.

Selling short is the exact opposite of the more popular type of trading—buying long. "Buy low, sell high" is the advice every new kid gets on Wall Street. Yet the amount of money to be made on the short side is in direct proportion to the amount made on the long side. Despite this fact, Wall Street traders and the American public are much more reluctant to sell short than they are to buy long. Selling short is like betting against the man shooting dice who has just had five successful passes: the odds are he is not going to have a sixth. There is money to be made betting the shooter's luck runs out.

One particular type of trader tends to go short more than anything else—the Hedger. As distinguished from a Speculator, the Hedger has some interest in the commodity beyond that of making money from fluctuations in its price. For example, a soybean farmer will use the commodities markets to hedge his soybeans, thereby insulating himself against the risk of price fluctuations during the growing season.

Suppose the farmer anticipates that in September of 1983 he will harvest fifty thousand bushels of soybeans. His cost per bushel is three dollars, so anything more than three dollars per bushel is a profit. The current market price, in

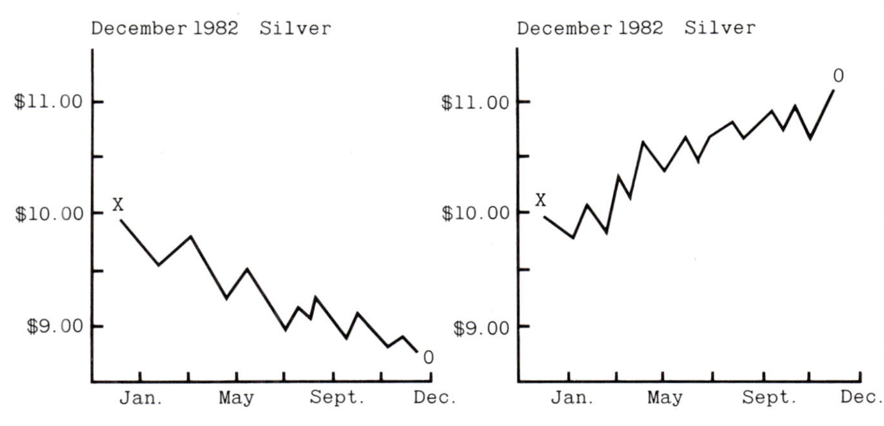

Figure 1.
Going short in a down-trending market.
X = point where contract was sold-short
0 = point where contract was bought back.

Figure 2.
Going short in an up-trending market.
X = point where contract was sold-short
0 = point where contract was bought back.

November of 1982, is six dollars a bushel. The farmer would like somehow to lock in that six dollar price for his next year's crop. So the farmer goes to the Commodity Markets and sells short 50,000 bushels (or ten contracts) of September 1983 Soybeans. He has committed himself to deliver 50,000 bushels of soybeans at six dollars a bushel in September of 1983 to an unknown destination for an unknown buyer.

In September of 1983 the market price of soybeans is four dollars a bushel. The farmer buys back his 50,000 bushels and sells them to a specific buyer in his part of the country. He executes both trades at four dollars a bushel. So by selling short in the commodity markets the farmer has increased his profit by two dollars a bushel. He has made $100,000 that otherwise would have been lost in price fluctuations.

The practice of selling short first appeared in the U.S. during the early 1700s. It was introduced by European merchants engaged in the cotton trade. If they were happy with the price they paid for a shipload of cotton they would offer the farmer an option on his next crop. For a small deposit they would have the right to buy the farmer's next crop at current prices. If prices had declined by the time the merchants returned, then they forfeited their deposit and paid market prices for their cotton. If prices had gone up, then the merchants exercised their option and bought their cotton at last year's prices. Since the farmer was supplying the complementary side of the option, he was essentially going short. If the price declined he made a little extra because he

```
got to keep the merchants' deposit. If the price went up he
lost a little, but he still sold his cotton at a price that
was acceptable to him.
    There are many commodity exchanges throughout the world on
which one may sell short. The most important domestic
exchanges are the Chicago Board of Trade, the Chicago
Mercantile Exchange, and the New York Mercantile Exchange.
Internationally, important exchanges are located in Zurich,
London, and Hong Kong.
```

Source: Used with the permission of Robert Vogel.

Exhibit 10.11 A Sample of Professional Writing

WHAT IS A ROBOT?

If you walk into the Nissan truck factory in New Smyrna, Tennessee, expecting to see shiny androids like C3PO assembling parts, you will be severely disappointed. The modern, industrial robot has far more in common with an ordinary piece of machinery than with a human. This only makes sense, since robots are machines. An example of a robot at work is shown in Figure 1-1 [Figure not included here.]. This industrial robot is trimming plastic dashboard components by moving them under a high-power laser. What is the difference between this robot and any other piece of automated machinery? Why is this machine called a "robot," not just an "automatic dashboard trimmer"? The robot is a special kind of automated machine. A robot can do not only this particular job of trimming, but it can be programmed and retooled to do many different jobs. This programmability and versatility is why all robots are automated machines, but all automated machines are not robots.

There is only one definition of an industrial robot that is internationally accepted. It was developed by a group of industrial scientists from the Robotics Industries Association (formerly the Robotics Institute of America) in 1979. They defined the industrial robot as ". . . a reprogrammable, multifunctional manipulator designed to move material, parts, tools, or specialized devices through various programmed motions for the performance of a variety of tasks." Let's take a close look at this definition to see just what it implies.

The first key word is *reprogrammable*. This implies that a robot is a machine that can not only be programmed once, but can be programmed as many times as one likes. Many electronic devices we use every day contain computer chips that are programmable. Programs are written on the chips of digital watches, for instance, that instruct them to do such things as play "Dixie" as an alarm. These programs cannot be easily changed, however. There is no allowance for input by the owner. You cannot, for example, put a song of your own into the watch when you get tired of waking up to "Dixie." The programs are "burned in" by the manufacturer. A robot, however, contains a program that is accessible, that can be changed, added to, or deleted, as the user chooses. A robot can have many programs to do different things in any sequence whatever. And, of course, to be programmable, a robot must have a computer that can be fed new instructions and information. The computer can be either "on board," which means the computer console is mounted on the robot itself, or it can be "remote," which means the computer that controls the robot can be anywhere you like as long as it can communicate with the robot.

The next key word in the RIA definition is *multifunctional*, which implies that the robot is versatile, that is, can perform more than one task. The same industrial robot used for laser cutting in Figure 1-1 could, with a simple change of end tooling, also perform welding, painting, or assembly operations.

The third key word is *manipulator*, which implies that a robot has a mechanism of some sort for moving objects for the performance of its work. It's the manipulator that separates a robot from a computer, just as it's the reprogrammability and versatility that separate a robot from other kinds of automated machines.

Finally, let's consider the meaning of the phrase *various programmed motions*. This implies that the robot is dynamic; that is, it is characterized by continuous, productive activity.

Although this definition may seem very broad and somewhat ambiguous, it does serve to separate industrial robots from, for instance, fixed-sequence automated machinery, or from multifunctional machines, such as food processors, that are equipped with interchangeable parts to perform various tasks, from blending sauces to grinding beef. It also removes robots far from the realms of science fiction, since any anthropomorphic (humanlike) characteristics a robot may or may not possess are merely a matter of efficacy.

From this perspective, then, the robot can be considered a major advance in the logical progression in the development of automated machines. We have moved from building machines that can do one job with human control to machines that can do many different jobs without any human control. The first industrial revolution has been said to be the start of an era of general industrial use of power-driven machines. The modern industrial renaissance may be called an era in which we are building machines capable not only of building other machines, but also of repairing and "reproducing" themselves.

Source: From *Robotics: A User-Friendly Introduction*, by Ernest L. Hall and Bettie C. Hall.

EXERCISES

1. For practice in the different techniques presented in this chapter, choose one of the following terms and explain it in the fourteen different ways discussed in this chapter. The explanations should be on a level your classmates can understand, but they need not be worked into one continuous piece of writing.

Fusion	Bluegrass music	Torque
Gravity	Credibility	Space shuttle
Libel	Conspiracy	Amortization
Spring	A liberal education	Software

2. For practice in the different techniques, choose one of the following and explain it in seven different ways, again with your classmates as audience. Then work the seven patterns into a well-written short report (300-500 words).

Concrete	Slag
Steel	Generally accepted accounting principles
Lathe	Prime interest rate
Enzyme	Containerization
Protein	Petri dish
Limit slope	Inertia

3. Choose an object or a concept in your field and define and describe it at length (500-750 words) for an executive/layman reader. Be careful to choose something you know well enough to write about without reliance on secondary sources, especially textbooks. Use a *cpo* introduction (see Chapter 9) and make the reader benefits explicit. Use as many of the fourteen techniques discussed in this chapter as you can; where you are consciously using a particular technique, write its name in the margin. Use at least one visual. Pay attention to your reader's purpose. Concentrate on producing a unified and clear piece of writing, rather than mechanically grinding through the various techniques.

4. One of the most common uses of definition and description in business and industry is to describe a situation. This may be a need for closing down an unsuccessful venture your company has been involved in, a problem with the manufacture or marketing of a product, or any of countless other situations. The writer's task generally is to get to the heart of this intangible subject and describe it in such a way as to give readers a good understanding of its complexities. For this exercise, use the techniques described in this chapter to give your classmates—in written form—the description of a situation. Although your teacher will probably give you more specific guidance as to what situations you can choose to describe (possibilities include historic events

or current controversial issues), this assignment usually works best when students choose things going on currently on or near the campus—something you can dig into a little yourself without having to do much library research. Maybe your campus has an ongoing traffic problem, or there are disputes over dormitory visiting hours, or there is a dispute about increasing student fees. Find some such current local situation and write a definition and description of it, with your classmates as the audience. Do not try to argue for one or another solution; what you are doing here is presenting a 500-word background report. Describe how this situation came about (historically, causally, etc.) and what its component parts are. Again, try to use as many of the fourteen techniques as you can, but don't give in to the temptation just to grind through them one after another.

5. Choose seven paragraphs from among those in the sample long reports from Section 5 (do not use paragraphs discussed as examples in this chapter) and explain the structural pattern(s) in each. Use the patterns described here as much as you can; where they don't fit, explain the new pattern. Write up your results into a short (300-500 words) report. Be sure to identify carefully which paragraphs you are discussing.

6. You are in your first year on a new job and, in casual conversation, have mentioned a new concept or piece of equipment in your field. Your boss overheard the conversation and has asked you to write a short (500-750 word) report explaining the concept or equipment to the boss. Your boss has 20 years' of experience in the field but generally does not keep up with new developments, choosing to leave that up to new employees, such as you. You want your report to be as professional as possible, so be sure to make full and frequent use of visuals.

11

Writing Instructions and Descriptions of Processes

One of the most common situations any working writer faces is the need to describe a process. Chapter 10 presented *process* as one of a number of techniques used in the larger context of explaining what something is. This chapter explains how to describe a process when you must explain how something works or how something is to be done. You may need to explain how a process works in general terms for an executive/layman audience. Or you may need to write a set of very specific directions or procedures with a layman, technician, or expert audience in mind. The two kinds of tasks are closely related, but the differences in purpose and audience mean big differences in the ways the processes are written up.

Because certain principles underlie all process descriptions, and because there are so many different kinds of process descriptions, this chapter has two main divisions: *basics* (elements common to all process descriptions), and *varieties* (explaining processes, writing instructions, and writing instructions for complex systems). Two examples of complete process descriptions are provided at the end of this chapter: a generalized process description written by a student ("The Process of Seining") and a set of specific instructions written by a professional ("Instructions for Modular Jack Converter"). Within the chapter, short examples are provided to illustrate each point.

1. Basics

The key points of nearly any process description are:

- Put any important principles, especially safety warnings, *first*.
- Be sure you are describing something you know very well, preferably something you can watch or do. Make sure you have access to the process itself as a source of information while you're writing about it.
- Be very specific.
- Keep your audience and your audience's purpose foremost in your mind. How detailed and technical your description should be depends on audience and purpose.
- Use visuals generously.

Any process description will probably have an opening, a body, and a conclusion. Sections 1.1 through 1.3 describe each part in detail.

1.1 The Opening

At the opening of the process description you should provide a brief overview of the process. What is it, who does it, and when, how, and where does it occur? If the process description is not part of some larger document, it also needs an introduction and a specific adaptation to that particular audience. Here is an example of an introduction specifically aimed at a layman:

> **Home Auto Body Repair**
>
> It finally happened. After guarding your new car from scratches and dents for months, you accidentally tried to park just a little too close to that steel post. Can you still avoid the high cost of your local auto body repair shop? Yes! This article explains the process of minor automotive body repair and demonstrates how easy it is to perform at your own home.

Following the introductory paragraph, make a clear statement of the main steps in your process; usually this also forecasts the structure of your report. If you use headings, the main steps of the process should correspond to the main headings. This following extract forecasts the main steps in a process; subsequent major headings in the paper correspond exactly to the steps forecast here:

> The primary steps of automotive body repair are preparing the surface, filling the dent, and repainting the body.

You may want to use a simple flow chart to tell the reader the steps of the process and simultaneously convey the process's dynamic qualities. Each part of the flow chart in Figure 11.1 corresponds to a stage in the process the report describes; each stage in the process has its own heading and section.

The next part of the opening should list all the parts, tools, and supplies needed for the process. This list will vary in complexity and specificity, depending

Figure 11.1 A Simple Flow Chart

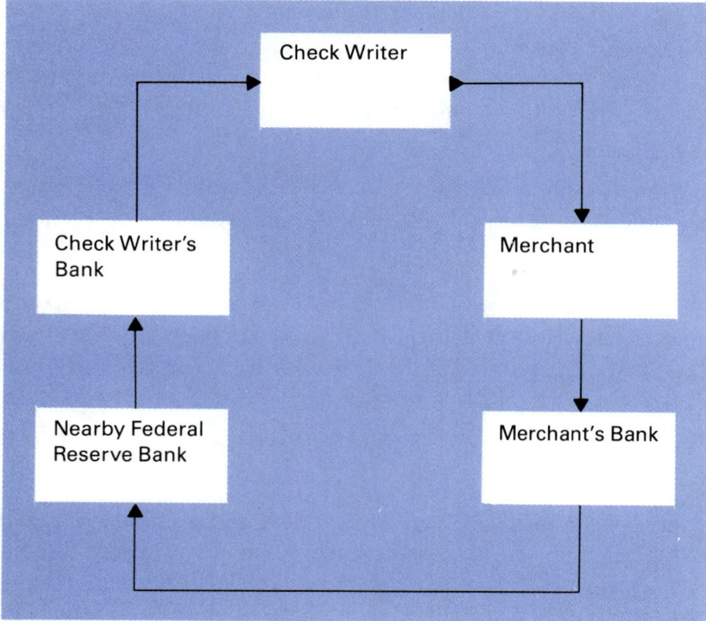

on what kind of description you're writing. The following sample is for a generalized description of the process of making claw hammer heads; a set of directions for the same process would need a much more detailed and specific list.

> The following materials, machinery, and tools are needed in the making of claw-hammer heads:
>
> Round blanks of plain carbon steel (ASTM spec. 1078)
>
> ½ ton (453 kg.) drop-hammer forge
>
> 50 ton (45,000 kg.) trimming press
>
> Induction heat hardener/temperer
>
> Grinder
>
> The process also uses a Rockwell Hardness Tester. This is used between the various steps in the hammer's manufacture to assure that the surface hardness of the hammer-head meets the required specifications.

Just as important as listing parts, supplies, and tools is explaining whatever principles or special conditions apply, *especially safety warnings*. Even in professionally written process descriptions, the failure to indicate principles and warnings at the beginning may be the most common error. A writer may assume that the reader will read the entire set of instructions before starting to perform the process, but experience has proved that assumption false. Put *anything* your reader needs to know throughout the process at the *beginning* of the process description. If there are safety warnings, put them at the beginning, preferably surrounded by some sort of border to call attention to them, as in the following example:

DANGER!

Once X-Rays are being produced, do not open the X-Ray machine. Do not attempt to look at the sample during tests with units running. Do not stand on either side of the X-Ray machine.

1.2 The Body

The parts of your process description usually correspond to the steps in the process. Because the process dictates the structure, writing the body of process descriptions is usually fairly simple—as long as you are sufficiently familiar with the process. You need to have access to the process while you're writing, especially if (as too often happens) it is one with which you are not as familiar as you should be. Keep in mind the key points listed at the beginning of this chapter, especially your audience and its purpose. Notice the different ways in which each of the following examples refers to its audience:

> Once you have acquired the proper materials, you are ready to begin.

> The purpose of this paper is to familiarize the reader with one particular type of manual inventory control process.
>
> The specimen is loaded into the hydraulic test unit and the extensiometer is attached.

The writing in each example makes particular assumptions about the kind of audience involved and their purpose in reading. The first reader needs to know how to *do* the process, whereas the other readers only need to know how the process *works*. In the first example there's a close relationship between writer and reader. In the second, that relationship is more distant. The last example deals with its audience by not referring to it directly at all. Your specific audience and its purposes must be firmly in your mind while you're writing.

1.3 The Conclusion

At the end of your process description you need at least a brief conclusion. Here are five techniques for conclusions that are especially appropriate for process descriptions. These and other conclusion techniques are discussed in more detail in Chapter 9, "Introductions and Conclusions."

- Repeat the major points.
- Emphasize the importance of the process.
- Restate cautions and safety warnings.
- Tell the reader how to evaluate the process—how to tell when it has been done properly.
- Describe alternative steps or troubleshooting procedures.

2. Varieties

Although there are certainly more than three different kinds of situations requiring a writer to write about a process, the ones described here probably cover the majority of situations you will encounter.

2.1 Explaining Processes

Many situations require a writer to explain a process, often for a layman/executive audience. A research-and-development specialist may need to explain a complicated sequence of purchasing orders to an accountant, an accountant may need to explain a financial transaction to a customer, or an engineer may need to explain to a banker the safety-shutdown procedures followed by computer technicians. In these and many more situations, you should explain the process specifically and accurately but not too technically. To discover the right level of detail to use, strike a balance between what you as a writer want to include and what you know the layman/executive reader will accept. Put the process into a frame that will make it appeal to the reader, and be specific without losing your audience.

2.1.1 **Framing the Structure.** Explaining a process to a layman/executive presents particular problems for you as a writer. You cannot assume the reader has either the knowledge or the interest in the subject that an ideal reader might have. The first question a layman/executive reader is likely to ask is "Why should I read this?" You should answer that question in the introductory section of your explanation (see "Reader Benefits," Chapter 4, Section 2.4). The following example shows a writer framing the structure: leading the discussion from the reader's world to the writer's (in this case, a world in which inventory control is a matter of legitimate concern).

> Most businesses in the United States have a substantial portion of their capital invested in inventory. Hence, inventory control has become a necessity for all business sectors of our economy. Inventory and the controls associated with it affect not only the business sector but also the private sector of our economy. Every individual who purchases and consumes goods is affected by the inventory-control policy implemented by the retail firm the individual purchases from. If the business has an efficient policy, then the consumer will find that a substantial number of the items he or she seeks will be in stock.

All the introductory devices listed in Chapter 9, "Introductions and Conclusions" are especially important in this kind of situation.

Once again, making special conditions explicit at the outset is especially important. Writing for an executive/layman you should explain not only the special condition but also *why* it is special (which an expert would probably know). The following example shows a special condition that often occurs in student papers: a specific (perhaps hypothetical) case is used to explain a general principle, and the writer needs to explain that fact.

> So that you will better understand the design process as landscape architects employ it, this report explains how the process would typically be used to create a specific design: a vacant downtown lot is to be turned into an urban park. The lot's location, dimensions, and surroundings are explained in detail, and the project's design criteria (including proposed budget) are also presented.

In this report a general concept—the process of design—is explained by using a description of the creation of one very specific design. Without such a specific case, an explanation of an abstract process (such as the design process) is likely to be too general, too abstract, difficult to write, and even more difficult to read.

2.1.2 **Keeping It Concrete.** In trying to simplify a process explanation for a layman/executive, you must beware of becoming too abstract. However abstract a process you are describing, it's best to tie it to a concrete example (or examples) throughout. As the previous example shows, if you are an architect, don't just describe "the design process," but rather describe how you design some specific project, drawing generalizations about the process when it's appropriate. If you are in management, don't just explain "the problem-solving process," but rather demonstrate it through a specific example. If you are an engineer, don't just explain the process of developing engineered standards, but rather use a description of the development of engineered standards for, say, a knitting mill as the vehicle for explaining the process in general.

Exhibit 11.1 gives an example of a generalized explanation of a process, "The Process of Seining," written by a student for a layman audience (his classmates).

2.2 Writing Simple Sets of Instructions

Because instructions may be written for any kind of audience or combination of audiences, it is especially important for the writer to know what kind of audience is involved. Often, though, you write a set of instructions for a totally anonymous audience, for *anyone*. In that situation you have to write with the assumption that anything that *can* be misunderstood *will* be. You must be especially clear and rely especially heavily on visuals. Whatever the audience, two aspects of the process can present particular problems: dealing with principles and warnings, and maintaining a consistent point of view.

2.2.1 **Principles and Warnings.** Some elements that should go into a set of instructions are not strictly "instructions." Often these are general statements about the idea behind the instructions—something like "Because of its difficulty, this maintenance is only performed once every 200 hours of operation. Because of that, you must be especially careful to perform it exactly as described here. Any variation from these instructions can lead to costly and time-consuming unscheduled repairs." Often the general statements you need to make are safety warnings, such as "For your own protection, you must wear safety goggles any time this machine is in operation." In both cases, the important thing, as mentioned earlier, is to make such statements right at the beginning. Do not assume the reader will read through the entire procedure before beginning to perform it. And in the case of safety warnings, you should have them printed in such a way as to draw the reader's attention to them without fail. As the following extract shows, using a contrasting color to set them off is wise.

> Although the laboratory process of tensile testing may seem routine, catastrophic failure of bridges and walkways may result from a designer not giving careful consideration to a material's properties derived from tensile tests. In view of the potential for human and material losses in such failures, an appreciation of the nature and usefulness of tensile testing is especially important for designers.

2.2.2 **Point of View.** Grammarians call the way you refer to yourself and to your reader in your writing the *point of view*. The most commonly used points of view are: *(continued on p. 224)*

Exhibit 11.1 A Generalized Explanation of a Process

THE PROCESS OF SEINING

As you motor down the lake in your boat, you notice a peculiar sight on the shoreline. One person is standing on the shoreline with a pole in his hand, and about thirty feet from the shoreline another person is pulling a pole through the water. As the person in the water reaches the shoreline, you notice there is some sort of net between the two poles, and now the people are picking fish from the net. This is the process of seining (see Figure One).

The purpose of this report is to describe the process of seining. Safety precautions, types of seines, and the details of the seining process will be described. When you understand how fisheries biologists do seining, you will have learned about one of the most valuable techniques available for measuring (and thus maintaining and improving) the fish population in our lakes and rivers. Maintaining and improving the fish population (and thus the water quality) of our lakes and rivers is important to everyone who enjoys the out-of-doors.

Figure One:
THE PROCESS OF SEINING.
Diagram of Seining a large area.

Safety Precautions

As discussed here, seining is a fish-management technique used in collecting small fish. Although this is a relatively safe procedure, a few safety precautions should be observed:

1. The person who pulls the seine through the water must wear some type of flotation device, such as a life jacket. Pulling the seine can take a lot of energy, and it is also possible to become tangled in the seine.

2. When transporting the seine from one site to the next, put the two poles together and drape the net over them (see Figure Two).

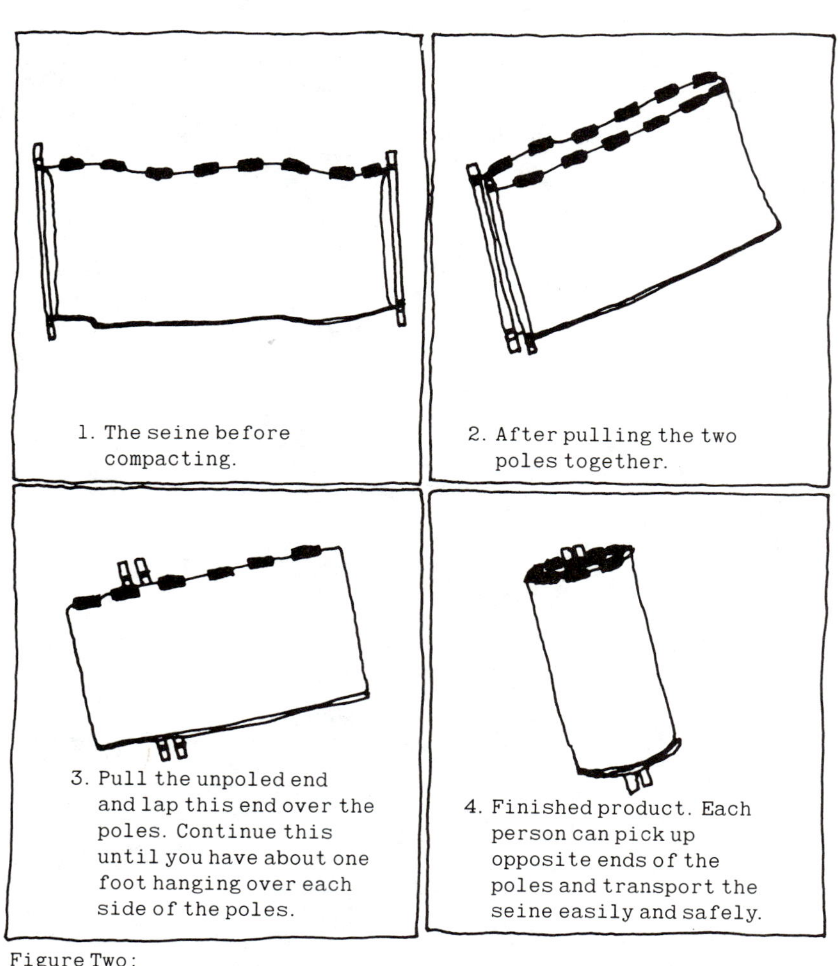

1. The seine before compacting.
2. After pulling the two poles together.
3. Pull the unpoled end and lap this end over the poles. Continue this until you have about one foot hanging over each side of the poles.
4. Finished product. Each person can pick up opposite ends of the poles and transport the seine easily and safely.

Figure Two:
COMPACTING A SEINE.
Steps involved in compacting a seine for easy transport.

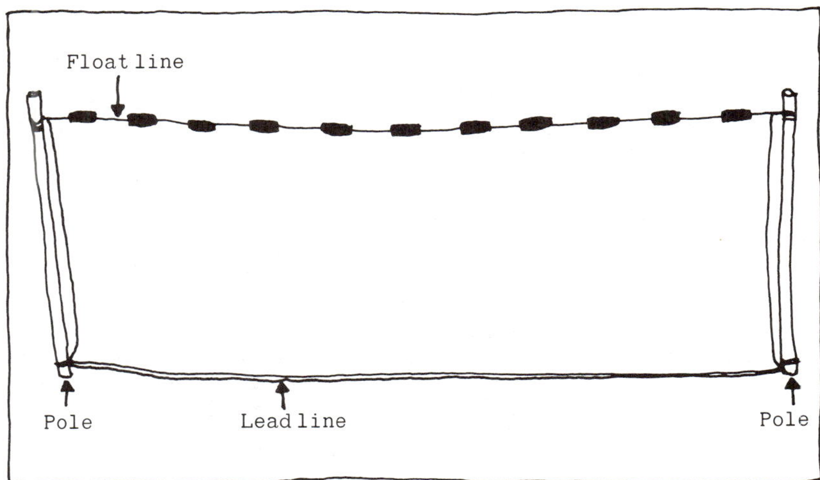

Figure Three:
A SEINE.
Diagram of a seine used for collecting small fish.

3. When seining, always wear a pair of old shoes, preferably tennis shoes. This will prevent cuts from broken glass or jagged rocks.

4. If you plan to seine, contact the State Game and Fish Commission concerning the laws and regulations concerning seining in your state.

Required Equipment and Personnel

Seining can be accomplished by two people, although three are preferable. The materials needed are:

1. A seine—a net connected at each end to a sturdy six-foot pole (see Figure Three).

2. Two or three people

3. A bucket

Types of Seines

There is basically only one type of seine—i.e., a seine by definition consists of two poles and a net between them. But the mesh size and the length of the seine will vary, depending on the type of sampling the seining is to accomplish. The mesh size is the diameter of the holes in the net. Mesh size varies from ⅛″ to 1″.

Areas to Seine

Seining is a procedure that is applicable to all types of aquatic habitats, but it is especially successful in shallow areas, such as streams and ponds.

Steps in Seining

The process of seining may be divided into four stages:

1. placing the net in the water

2. pulling the water end of the net to the shoreline

3. keeping the lead line of the seine on the bottom

4. picking the fish from the seine

THE PROCESS OF SEINING

Seining is one of the sampling techniques of fisheries management that requires a minimum of materials and can be done by anyone. The following discussion will describe in detail the steps of a successful seining expedition.

Step One

Before you begin, it may be important to estimate the area covered in one seine haul. That way, you will know how many hauls you will need to cover the area assigned to you. Figure Four illustrates the calculations involved in estimating the area covered in one haul.

The initial step is putting the seine in the water. If you are the person who will pull the seine through the water, then while wearing a flotation device, swim a straight line from

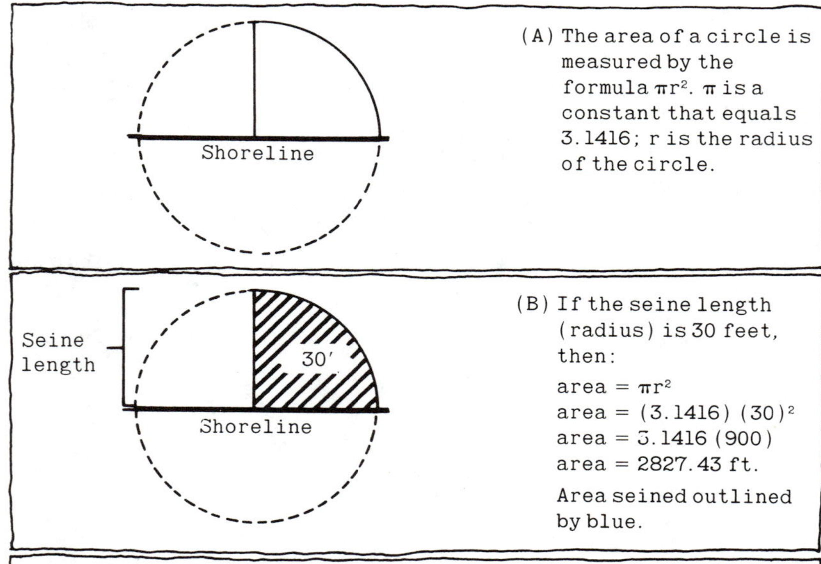

Shoreline
(A) The area of a circle is measured by the formula πr². π is a constant that equals 3.1416; r is the radius of the circle.
Seine length
30'
Shoreline
(B) If the seine length (radius) is 30 feet, then:
area = πr²
area = (3.1416) (30)²
area = 3.1416 (900)
area = 2827.43 ft.
Area seined outlined by blue.
(C) Since the seine haul is only one–quarter of the area of the circle, divide by four:
2827.43 ft² ÷ 4 = 706.86 ft²

Figure Four:
ESTIMATING THE AREA OF A QUARTER HAUL.
Steps involved in calculating the area of a seine haul.

the bank. You can swim a sidestroke and carry your end of the seine in one hand. Or you can fasten a light line to your end of the seine, take the free end of the line out into the water with you, and tow the seine out once you're in position. Make sure you have the seine's edge that is weighted with lead weights at the bottom, then pull the seine taut.

When the seine is taut, begin the quarter-circle back to the shoreline. Maintaining the tautness of the seine is important for covering the area estimated. Because it covers one-fourth of a complete circle, this type of seine haul is called a quarter-haul.

Step Two

When you begin the quarter-circle you usually cannot touch bottom, so it may take time for you to swim the quarter-circle around toward the shoreline. When the quarter-circle is nearly completed, the person standing on the bank should begin to pull gradually on the pole to maintain the tautness of the seine. This will also keep the lead line on the bottom of the seine in contact with the bottom of the stream or pond.

Step Three

It is very important to keep the lead line in contact with the bottom of the stream or pond. If the lead line comes off the mud, fish may escape under the seine. To prevent this, you and your partner should angle the tops of the poles back toward the water (bringing the bottoms of the poles forward toward shore) as the swimmer approaches the shoreline. When you reach the shoreline, one of the two of you should lay the pole on the ground by bringing the bottom forward (trapping the fish in the seine, not under it). This person then begins to pull the lead line, making sure it remains in contact with the bottom because fish are now trapped in the seine and are looking for a way out. If three people are working the seine, the third person would pull the lead line.

Step Four

While the lead line is being pulled, the person on the opposite end should carefully pull the pole up the bank. When the lead line is completely out of the water, both poles may be picked up and held parallel to the ground. Then the seine should be moved farther up the bank. This is a precaution against fish flopping back into the water. It is also easier to collect the fish from the seine when you are on surer footing. Finally, the fish collected from the seine are placed in the bucket for easy transport.

CONCLUSION

The seining process is an important technique for collecting fish. Other possible techniques include electroshocking or gill netting, but both of those are biased toward larger fish. If the steps outlined in this report are followed, seining is an especially successful technique for sampling small fish.

Singular

First Person: *I* next connect *a* to *b*.

Second Person: *You* next connect. . . .

Third Person: *He* next connects. . . .
She next connects. . . .
One next connects. . . .
The technician next connects. . . .

Plural

First Person: *We* next connect. . . .

Second Person: *You* next connect. . . .

Third Person: *They* next connect. . . .

The point of view you write in says a lot about what assumptions you make about your role as writer and your audience's purposes as reader(s). Earlier in this century many writers preferred either the anonymous third person ("One next connects . . .") or the anonymity of passive voice ("Next *b* is connected to *a*"), which avoids point of view entirely. In our time, however, most writers and readers prefer either the second-person ("You connect . . ."), or the second person with the personal pronoun left out ("Next connect . . ."), or a combination of the two. Unless you want your writing to be as formal and stiff as a late-nineteenth-century drawing room, or you are in a specific situation in which you are certain you cannot use personal pronouns (thus usually requiring passive voice), you should stay with some form of second person for your set of instructions.

Exhibit 11.2 presents an example of a very well-written set of instructions from Western Electric, "Instructions for Modular Jack Converter."

2.3 Writing Instructions for Complex Systems: User's Guides

A special instance of writing sets of instructions occurs when you must write procedures for complex systems. This could be routine shutdown procedures for any kind of power plant, an operations manual for an airplane, or a user's guide to a particular piece of computer hardware or software. All of these (and many similar) cases present problems for you as the writer—problems that occur both because of the complexity of the system being operated and because of the operator's attitude toward the process. Because writing computer documentation of one form or another—usually a user's guide—occupies the attention of growing numbers of writers from whatever background, we will use it here as an example of writing instructions for complex systems. Four features of such writing deserve specific mention: the document's overall orientation, its structure, the user's attitude, and the testing of the document. (For more on computer documentation, see Chapter 17, "Varieties of Short Reports.")

2.3.1 **Orientation.** There are two alternatives for the way a user's guide (or any set of instructions for operating a complex system) approaches its subject: the guide can be system (or machine) oriented, or task (or function) oriented.

A *system-oriented* description explains what the system's characteristics are in an encyclopedic manner and describes how the system works using the system as the focal point. Only incidentally does such a document tell a person how to use or operate the system; that information must usually be extrapolated from the encyclopedic description of the system.

A *task-oriented* description takes the *user* as its focal point, and explains in a step-by-step manner each interaction between the user and the system. Only as support for those steps will a task-oriented user's guide explain the system's characteristics or how the system itself works. In writing instructions on complex systems, a task-oriented approach works best.

A simplified hypothetical example makes this distinction clearer: suppose you have come to a world in which elevators had never been invented. Now having invented the elevator, you must write its documentation. Your brochure can look like either Exhibit 11.3 or Exhibit 11.4.

It may seem to you that no one would ever write a user's guide with the kind of machine- or system-oriented approach described in Exhibit 11.3. Unfortunately, it seems the larger the system being described, the greater the tendency to do just that. Perhaps the tendency of an unsure writer to begin any document by telling everything he or she knows about the subject is another manifestation of the encyclopedic tendency described in Chapter 13, Section 1.1. If you are writing *instructions*, take the user as the focal point; write task-oriented instructions, even for complex systems.

2.3.2 **Structure.** Many times, the most usable and thorough way to explain the operation of a complex system is to produce a three-part user's guide. The first section is the user-oriented, "how-to-do-it" set of instructions described above. The second section is a troubleshooting, "what-to-do-if" section. The third section is a brief description of the system's technical characteristics (possibly the system-oriented description) and an indexed reference section.

Suppose, for example, that you are writing the user's guide for a word-processing program your company is marketing. It would be useful to write it in this way:

1. Section 1 would be aimed at beginners. It would have to include even the most basic elements, such as how to turn the computer on and off and how to enter and exit various programs, as well as how to perform basic functions.
2. Section 2 would explain how to solve common problems the user faces—how to copy files, for example. It would also explain errors users often make, such as what to do if you exceed a disk's memory capacity.
3. Section 3 would be the system-oriented description and reference section. It would catalog the program's characteristics and provide an index section as well.

Sections 2 and 3 would have to be cross-referenced to each other, and all sections would have to be organized so that the right pages could be found quickly. Such a guide would be useful to beginners and also give them all the information they would need as their skill levels increase.

Exhibit 11.2 A Well-Written Set of Technical Instructions

INSTRUCTIONS FOR MODULAR JACK CONVERTER SWINGER

1. CAUTION: Your telephone connecting block may have varying amounts of electricity in the wires and screws. Therefore, to avoid the possibility of electrical shock follow the instructions below:

If you have a telephone at a location other than the one you are converting, take the handset off the hook. (This will keep the phone from ringing and reduce the possibility of your contacting electricity. While you're doing this, ignore messages coming from the handset which ask you to hang up the phone.) If you have only one telephone, take the handset of that telephone off the hook.

- AVOID HAND CONTACT WITH BARE WIRES OR SCREWS.
- USE TOOLS WITH INSULATED HANDLES OR USE RUBBER GLOVES.
- DO NOT PLACE THIS DEVICE WHILE A THUNDERSTORM IS IN THE VICINITY.

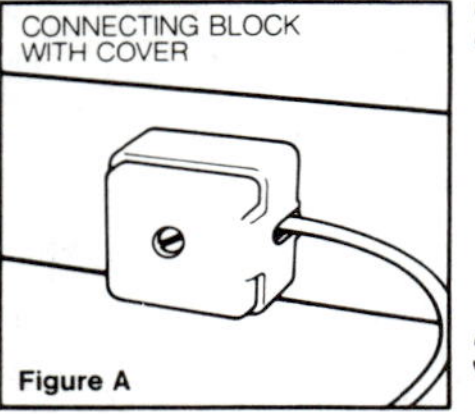

Figure A

2. STOP: Before you go any further, make sure you take the handset of one of your telephones off the hook according to instructions under "CAUTION" above. Then follow steps 3-10 below.

Tools needed: Screwdriver with insulated handle, wire cutters with insulated handles (or scissors with insulated handles).

3. Find the plastic connecting block in the room where the telephone is to go **(Figure A).** Loosen the screw in the center of the connecting block and take off the cover. Discard the cover and screw.

THESE CORDS ARE EXCESS.

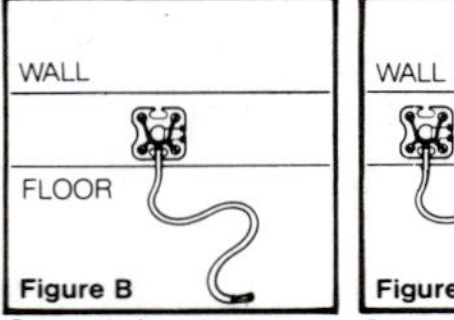

Figure B

One end of cord is lying unatta‿hed on floor.

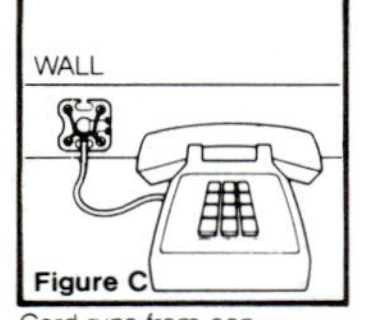

Figure C

Cord runs from connecting block to old telephone.

4. Follow 3 steps below to cut off any excess cords which may be attached to the connecting block:

- Refer to **Figures B-F** to identify which cords are excess and which are not. You may have one or more of these at your connecting block.
- Take each excess cord and gently bend it away from the connecting block so that the wires which make up the cord are clear of all other wires on the connecting block **(Figure G).**
- CUT each of the wires in the cord, one at a time, at the base of the spade tip which connects the wire to a screw. (See enlarged drawing.) Be careful not to cut any wire other than those in the cord being removed.

NOTE: DO NOT UNSCREW THE SCREWS ON THE BLOCK. Leave the spade tips under the screws.

THESE CORDS ARE NOT EXCESS. DO NOT CUT THEM.

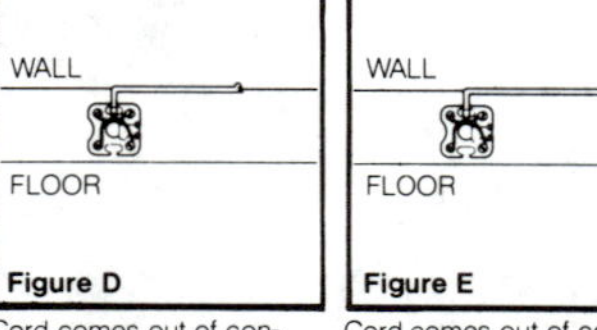

Figure D

Cord comes out of connecting block and goes into wall.

Figure E

Cord comes out of connecting block and runs along wall to another connecting block.

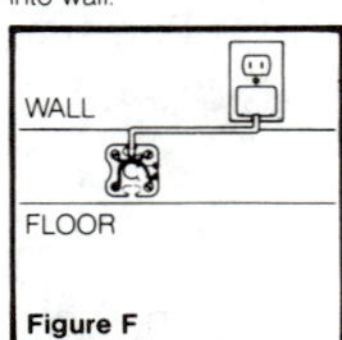

Figure F

Cord comes out of connecting block and runs along wall to a small box which is plugged into an electrical outlet.

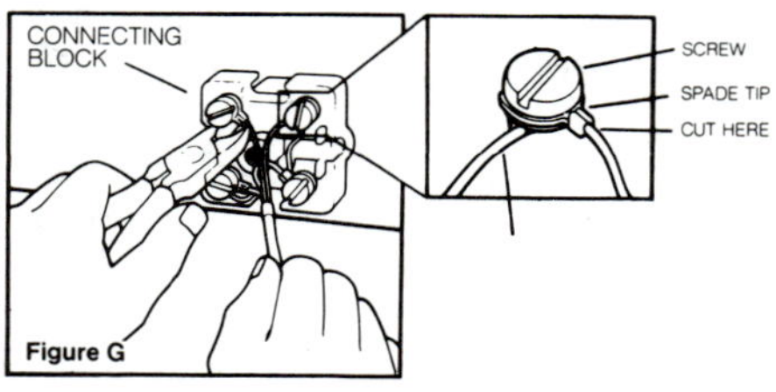

Figure G

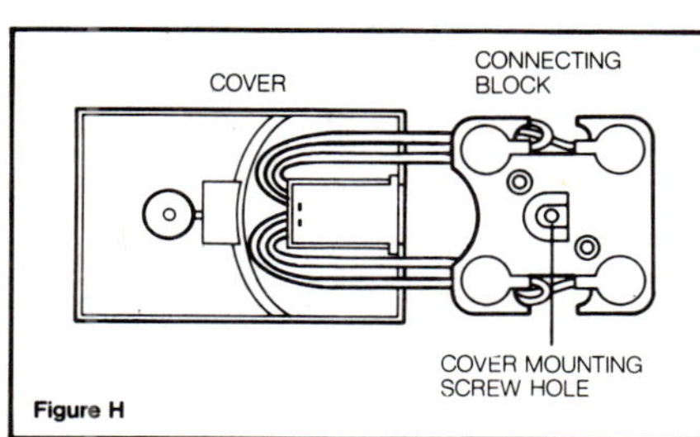

Figure H

5. Snap the four colored buttons of the converter onto the four screws in the corners of the connecting block. **(Figure H)**

- Snap the red button onto the screw which already has a red wire attached to it.
- Snap the green button onto the screw which already has a green wire attached to it.
- Snap the yellow button onto the screw which already has a yellow wire attached to it.
- Snap the black button onto the screw which already has a black wire attached to it.

If the colors of the wires cannot be determined,

- Snap the red button onto the screw marked **R**.
- Snap the green button onto the screw marked **G**.
- Snap the yellow button onto the screw marked **Y**.
- Snap the black button onto the screw marked **B**.

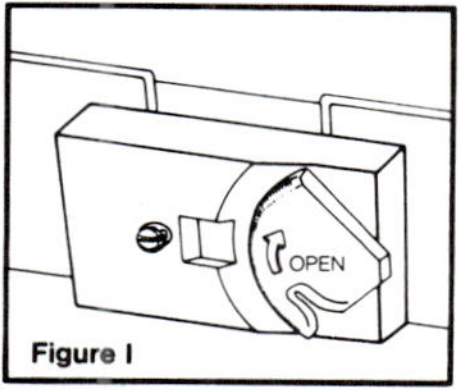

Figure I

6. Attach the converter to the connecting block by fastening the screw in the converter to the hole in the center of the connecting block. Be careful not to pinch any wires between the converter and the connecting block. **(Figure I)**

Give the converter one turn with the buttons in place. This will keep the wires from being pinched.

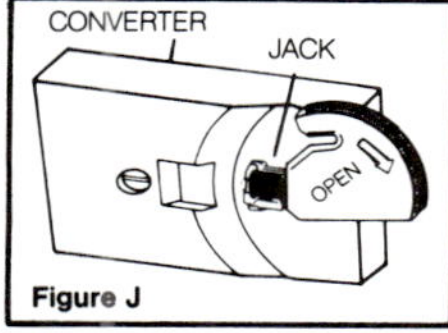

Figure J

7. Plug the end of the cord from the *new* telephone into the jack on the converter. **(Figure J)**

Rotate the cover in a clockwise direction to expose the jack opening.

INSERT FREE END OF CORD INTO OPENING UNTIL CLIP LOCKS

8. Hang up the handset which you took off the hook to keep your phones from ringing.

9. Lift the handset on the new phone and listen for a dial tone. Dial a phone number to make sure the phone works. **If the dial tone does not go off when you dial:**

- Again, take the handset off the hook to keep your phone from ringing.
- Unscrew the converter.
- Switch the red and green buttons.
- Screw the converter back on.
- Hang up the other phone.
- Check the new phone again.

10. If you are attaching more than one converter, follow these instructions again, leaving the handset of the first phone off the hook.

IF YOU NEED ASSISTANCE, CALL THE TELEPHONE NUMBER YOU WERE GIVEN.

Source: Reproduced by permission of AT & T.

Exhibit 11.3 A System-Oriented Description

ELEVATOR

The Orbis elevator is a rectangular chamber 6 feet deep, 10 feet tall, and 8 feet wide. The chamber's face has double sliding doors to allow entry and exit. The doors have pressure sensitive rubber bumpers and electric eyes to prevent injury to people entering and leaving. The chamber will carry as many as 10 to 12 people (1900 lbs.) from one floor to another of the building with a minimum of effort. The chamber carries its own fluorescent lighting system, its own ventilator fan, a control panel with which to select floors (as well as an emergency stop button and emergency phone), and comes equipped with a roof-mounted escape hatch. All Orbis elevators are licensed by the state and inspected yearly. Certificates of inspection. . . .

Exhibit 11.4 A Task-Oriented Description

Tired of walking from floor to floor?

Try taking an elevator instead.

Here's how you do it:

Walk to the end of the hall, and push one of the arrow-shaped buttons—either the one pointing *up* or the one pointing *down* (depending on which way you want to go).

When an elevator arrives at your floor, the door will open, and the lighted arrow over the door will indicate the direction the car is headed. If that's the direction you want to go, step aboard. (If not, wait for one that is headed your way.)

When you step aboard the elevator, push the button on its control panel that corresponds to the floor you want.

When the elevator reaches the floor you want (as indicated by the number over the inside door), the door will open and you simply step out. . . .

Because a three-part structure like this can produce a bulky document, it's good to put it in a format that helps make items within it accessible. A looseleaf notebook with pages reinforced on the inside edges and color-coded index-tabbed (for major sections) on the outer edges makes a good format for such a document. The notebook format also allows readers to insert new or replacement pages as the need arises.

2.3.3 **User's Attitude.** If you are writing instructions for the operation of a complex system, and especially if the anticipated user is a beginner, be particularly aware of the user's state of mind during the operation of the system. Even more than average users, beginners are almost exclusively dependent upon your instructions for their actions. Anything that occurs that your instructions do not explicitly mention may greatly distress the user, even if that occurrence is so totally routine you chose not to mention it. Remember that little things that experienced users deal with routinely can baffle beginners.

For example, if you are writing the word-processing user's guide mentioned earlier, be sure to tell the user how to exit the program! Contrary to the apparent beliefs of many authors of computer manuals, the nearly universal exit codes, such as Control-K, are not widely known outside of computer circles. An inexperienced user, carefully following your step-by-step instructions, can be distressed far out of proportion to the actual seriousness of the situation by being unable to get out of a program, or to solve a grid-lock (the situation in which no key you push seems to stop what the computer is doing), or by any other unforeseen occurrence. Even experienced users of instructions for complicated systems can have incredible tunnel vision when it comes to failing to think of even simple alternatives to an instruction that didn't work the way the guide indicates that it should.

2.3.4 **Testing.** The more complicated the system you write instructions for, the more important it is to test the instructions. To do this, find a person with the same knowledge and experience level as your document's intended audience and persuade him or her to try out your instructions. To make the test even more useful, ask your trial user to tape record his or her thoughts while trying to use your instructions. Then you can alter your instructions as required, based on the trial user's experiences.

EXERCISES

1. Write a brief critique of the excerpt from "Instructions for Modular Jack Converter." How does it employ the principles discussed here? Can you suggest ways to make it a better set of instructions without making it significantly longer?
2. Choose a simple process—changing a tire, tying a knot, or building a birdhouse—and write a 200-word set of instructions for it. Do not assume your reader has any knowledge of the process to begin with. Write a brief sketch of your intended audience—age, purpose in reading, education level, and so forth.
3. Write a description of a process, with your instructor as the audience. Choose an everyday process (baking bread, changing a tire, balancing a checkbook), and try to make your description about half visuals and half words. The description should be about 300 words long.

4. Choose a process that is special to your field of study, one you know very well. Write a description of the process, with your instructor and your classmates as the audience. Make your description as specific and complete as possible. Use a *cpo* introduction, visuals, headings, and a conclusion.
5. Find a set of instructions (perhaps part of a computer user's manual or the instructions for a laboratory) and write a two- or three-page critique of the way they are written. At the end of the critique, rewrite two pages of the instructions incorporating the kinds of improvements you have suggested. Be sure to attach a copy of the relevant pages of the original to your report.
6. Place yourself in this position: It's the summer before your senior year in college, and you've taken a job in your university's Student Counseling Center for the summer. You've been assigned the project of writing a guide for incoming freshmen to use during their first weeks on campus. It should cover such topics as getting used to dorm life, finding your way around campus, making the best use of your time, dealing with your new freedom, and so on. Write the text for that guide (500-1000 words).

12

Abstracts and Executive Summaries

Nearly every professionally written report carries with it an executive summary or an abstract or both. Often one of them is the first element of your report that your reader will see. (Sometimes, it is the *only* thing.) Many times the decision of whether to read the entire report will be based on your executive summary or abstract. The abstract is usually no more than a paragraph long, and rarely more than a page in length. For long reports, the executive summary may be considerably longer. Because the executive summary or abstract shapes key decisions your reader makes about how much attention to give the report, the ability to write a good abstract or executive summary is especially important. This chapter will show you how to distinguish between abstracts and executive summaries and how to write them.

1. Abstracts

Abstracts and executive summaries are brief overviews of the contents of a report. We will discuss executive abstracts later in this chapter. We will first take up the simpler form, the abstract.

1.1 What Are Abstracts?

There are two main types of abstracts, *informative* and *descriptive*. (Confusingly enough, the informative abstract is often also called a "summary"; that will not be done here.) The informative abstract tells the reader what the report says. The descriptive abstract lists the elements the report covers, without discussing what the report says about them. The informative abstract's point of view is *internal*; an informative abstract of Chapter 10, "Definitions and Descriptions," might begin, "There are fourteen different definition-and-description techniques," and then go on to list and possibly to explain them. The point of view of the descriptive abstract, on the other hand, is *external*; the descriptive abstract of Chapter 10 might begin, "This chapter lists and explains fourteen different definition-and-description techniques," but the descriptive abstract might well *not* go on to explain what those techniques are. Of the two forms, many people find the informative abstract more useful. Perhaps the major use of the descriptive abstract today is in library indexing.

To make it easier for you to see the differences between the two forms, Exhibit 12.1 presents a comparison of the basic features of informative and descriptive abstracts, followed by an example of each.

1.2 Why Are Abstracts Important?

Abstracts have important functions for both the writer and the reader. Writing an abstract of the report you have just written helps you to clarify in your mind what the important parts of your report really are. What do you want your reader to see while he or she is deciding whether to read the whole report? Like a topic outline of the report (or its sequence of headings and subheadings), the abstract

Exhibit 12.1 A Comparison of the Two Types of Abstracts

Informative Abstract

- Tells what the report says.
- Uses internal point of view: "Executive summaries and abstracts provide an overview of. . . ."
- Can be useful for all readers.

Example: Most reports carry with them either an executive summary or an abstract or both. Both are brief overviews of the report's contents. There are two forms of abstract: an informative abstract tells readers what the report says; a descriptive abstract lists the elements the report talks about. The abstract is important because the reader usually reads it before deciding whether and how to read the report. Both forms of abstract should be used freely, and both are especially useful to researchers.

Descriptive Abstract

- Names what the report tells about.
- Uses external point of view: "This chapter explains the differences between. . . ."
- Useful mainly for indexers (such as in libraries) and people who use indexes.

Example: This chapter defines the executive summary and the two most common forms of the abstract. It explains their placement in reports, when they should be used, and how they are used in research. The chapter also describes the qualities of a good abstract or executive summary and explains how to write them.

Both kinds of abstract can be written from either an outline or an underlined copy of a report. In both forms the quality of writing is every bit as important as the quality of writing is in the rest of the report.

helps you, the writer, test the organization of your report. It also helps the reader grasp that organization.

Abstracts are especially important for readers. Reading entire reports takes more time than many professionals are willing to spend. Anything you as a writer can do to help your reader make a good decision about whether to read your whole report, read only a part of it, skim it, or send it to someone else to read will usually increase your reader's good will toward both you and your report. Often the abstract is a major factor in that decision.

On a deeper level, a good abstract will help your reader read your report faster and understand it better. When people are given brief, accurate forecasts of what they are about to read, their reading is more efficient. If your abstract is well written, gives an accurate sense of your report's content, and addresses your reader on a level the reader understands, it will help him or her read the report more quickly and comprehend it better and more easily.

1.3 When Should Abstracts Be Used?

You should use an abstract at the beginning of any report you write. Usually the abstract is on a separate page, double or triple spaced, and clearly labeled. (If it's on the cover page, it will be single spaced.) An abstract can be as short as one or two lines or as long as a page.

Abstracts are also used by many as a way of keeping up with current developments in a field. Many journals and other organizations solicit and circulate abstracts of completed work or work in progress as a way of informing their readers or members of reports they need to know about. This is one of the reasons that your abstract must make sense as a separate document. It is more than a miniature of your report; it is a miniature report, self-contained and able to stand on its own. Envision your abstract published with 100 other abstracts, and ask yourself whether it still would accurately and effectively present your report.

Abstracts are often used as parts of proposals; they are often also used by themselves as mini-proposals, as a way of describing a project you would like to undertake (such as a report you would like to write). In that situation it's important to know whether you are expected to submit a descriptive or an informative abstract. The descriptive abstract can be speculative. In it you can, for example, promise to cover a great number of topics even though you may not know exactly what you will say about each one at the time you write it. But the informative abstract requires you to do more than just summarize the points you intend to cover; you must also state the conclusions you intend to reach about those points. Thus the informative abstract requires you to know what points you are going to talk about *and* what you are going to say about them.

1.4 How Are Abstracts Used in Research?

One of the most important sources for scientific, technical, industrial, and business information today is the computerized indexing service. Private companies (and the federal government) collect abstracts of published reports, speeches, and all kinds of research, and organize (or *index*) them in computerized data bases so as to make them accessible in a number of ways, such as by subject, combinations of subjects, and author. For a fee, potential users of that information can access that data base through computer and telephone links anywhere in the world and inquire what is available on a certain subject or subjects, or by certain authors, and so forth. The computer will then send out abstracts in the category requested, and the user then will screen them and decide which reports are worth acquiring. Or users can be placed on regular mailing lists to receive paper copies of abstracts on a certain subset of the larger topic. The users then screen those abstracts and decide which reports (if any) they need to order copies of.

For example, the Office of Scientific and Technical Information, the national information center for the Department of Energy, collects roughly 7000 reports a month. One of its main functions is to maintain the Energy Data Base (EDB), a vast collection of bibliographic citations, abstracts, and indexes to world literature on energy. The EDB contains more than 700,000 entries, and it adds about 150,000 entries each year. For most users, getting even a monthly listing of all the information newly indexed in any particular month would mean getting much too much information. So the Office of Scientific and Technical Information subcategorizes the reports it receives into many different groupings (such as fossil energy, fusion energy, solar energy, etc.) and subgroupings, and then mails out regular summaries of the work done in each area to people who request lists for those areas. An authorized user can also receive more extensive summaries, but for most applications the specific, subcategorized listings are quite sufficient.

This kind of compilation of sets of information into various databases goes on in every field. It has created a totally new research technique, one that takes advantage of computers to scan quantities of information beyond anything any one person could hope to digest on his or her own without the computer. Because of the popularity, speed, and comprehensiveness of this research technique, abstracts have become even more important in research than they were before computers revolutionized the growth of scientific and technical information. The abstract becomes the primary means by which readers select which reports to read and which ones they do not even have to look at.

1.5 What Are the Qualities of a Good Abstract?

From the discussion in this chapter so far, we can see that a good abstract needs to satisfy at least four criteria; it must:

- be well-written
- give an accurate sense of the report's content
- address the reader on a level he or she can understand
- make sense as a separate document

A well-written abstract has the same qualities of style that characterize all effective professional writing: clarity, economy, and straightforwardness (Chapter 3 explains these qualities in more detail). *Clarity* here means choosing the exact words you need to get a precise meaning across to your specific audience. It also means avoiding the telegraphic style that some writers fall into. That is, avoid writing "Report summarizes results of experiments conducted fall, 1981, in game species' native habitat"; instead write "This report summarizes the results of experiments conducted in the fall of 1981 in the game species' native habitat."

Economy in abstracts requires that you be careful about the details you include and exclude, and that you be especially careful about using economical sentence structures. Most readers have an intuitive feeling (reinforced by experience) that

Exhibit 12.2 A Poorly Written First Draft of an Abstract Notice the telegraphic style, the weak verbs, and the way the last sentence comes in almost as an afterthought.

> "The Process of Library Research" (Chapter 16 of *Effective Professional Writing* by Michael L. Keene.)
>
> Chapter is description of library research process. Preliminary planning, card catalogue, periodical indexes, government documents, and technical reports are included. Both research and writing of reports are covered.

abstracts should be no longer than one page (usually about 200 words). That means you must choose your words and expressions very carefully. (You may want to review the section on "Wordy Expressions" in the Appendix when you get to the point of tightening up the wording in your abstract.)

Straightforwardness means that both the sequence of elements in each sentence and the sequence of sentences must be in the order that is easiest for the reader to read, which is not necessarily the order that is easiest for the writer to write. You cannot merely pull one sentence from each major section of your report and string them together into an abstract. You must look at that sequence of sentences as a separate work and ask yourself if that sequence—by itself—will make sense to a reader. Exhibit 12.2 shows a poorly written descriptive abstract. Exhibit 12.3 shows the same abstract revised for clarity, economy, and straightforwardness.

1.6 How Are Abstracts Written?

The easiest way to write an abstract is to work from an outline of the report. If the report makes extensive use of headings and subheadings, they can be the beginning of your abstract. Of course, if you wrote the report yourself, you may

Exhibit 12.3 A Well-Written Abstract Notice the way the style, ordering of elements, and choice of verbs have been improved over Exhibit 12.2.

> **ABSTRACT**
>
> "The Process of Library Research" (Chapter 16 of *Effective Professional Writing*, by Michael L. Keene.)
>
> This chapter describes the process of library research, including record keeping and report writing. It describes preliminary planning, using the card catalogue, searching periodical indexes, accessing government documents, and finding government documents.

well have an outline already available to work from. If you are writing an abstract of someone else's report, the best way to proceed is to reread the report carefully, underlining key sentences and making notes to yourself in the margins. Of course it's easier to write a descriptive abstract than an informative abstract, because the descriptive abstract requires explaining much less about the report's meaning.

Exhibit 12.4 presents a short article, with key lines underlined in preparation for writing an abstract of it; Exhibit 12.5 is an outline made from the underlinings; and Exhibits 12.6 and 12.7 show informative and descriptive abstracts written from the outline.

Exhibit 12.4 An Article to be Outlined and Abstracted Original article.

CRITERIA FOR EVALUATING BINOCULARS

OPTICAL CRITERIA

To estimate optical quality, examine binoculars for each of the following features. Every pair of binoculars will have particular strengths and weaknesses. Focus on an object with fine parallel lines. Do not look through a window. The criteria do not include interpreting the specifications—things like magnification and objective lens size.

Brightness of the Image

A bright image indicates how well the optics gather and transmit light. The lenses and prisms should be coated on all glass-to-air surfaces—100 percent coated.

Resolution of the Image

Look carefully through the binoculars for several kinds of defects in their ability to form a clearly resolved image. Defects in resolution create serious problems in long-term enjoyment of the binoculars in the field. The more severe the defects, the less reliable the optical quality of the binoculars.

Edge-of-field defects. There will always be some lack of resolution around the edges of the field of view, even in sharply focused glasses. But margins should be as sharp as possible, like the center of the field. Edge-of-field defects are a ready guide to relative quality in the optical system of binoculars.

Pincushion distortion. Parallel lines crossing the image may appear to curve slightly toward the center.

Curvature of the image. A flat surface, such as a wall across the street, may appear concave, or slightly bowl-shaped.

Spherical aberration. Caused by imprecise lens grinding, spherical aberration.

Range of Resolution

Excellent optics will seem to go in and out of focus very slowly. This means the optical system has a wide range of resolution. Since binoculars with a wide range of resolution do not have to be perfectly focused to be useful, they are more useful and less aggravating in the field.

Alignment

The images formed by the two barrels of the binoculars should merge imperceptibly into one unified image. Watch especially for a shadow down the center of the image and for vertical misalignment.

Eye Relief

A full field of view should be afforded when the ocular lenses are placed to your eyes or eyeglasses. If dark shadows blot part of the field, and adjustments in the distance between lenses and eyes are required, eye relief is at fault. Eyeglass wearers should rigorously test the retractable cups on binoculars for eye relief. Quality in eye relief for eyeglass wearers varies considerably. Look for a full field of view.

CONSTRUCTION AND CASING

Axis Hinge

A good gauge to the construction of the casing, the hinge should be strong and work smoothly; it should be neither too loose nor too stiff. Compact binoculars often employ double hinges of various design. Double-hinged compact binoculars may be tiring to hold for long periods of time, and it may be difficult to maintain proper alignment.

Focusing Mechanism

A center-focus mechanism is more convenient than the old-fashioned individual focusing mechanisms for each barrel. A well-designed focusing mechanism should be conveniently located, easily reached without having to look for it, and smoothly adjustable.

Balance and Comfort

In well-designed binoculars, weight, size, and balance combine to make an instrument that fits comfortably in your hands and is enjoyable to the feel.

Source: "Criteria for Evaluating Binoculars" from "The Glass of Fashion" by Charles A. Bergman from *Audubon* magazine, November 1981. Reprinted by permission of the author.

Although abstracts take relatively little time to write and very little space to print, their importance continues to increase as our society grows more and more saturated with scientific and technical information and more reliant on computers.

Exhibit 12.5 A Scratch Outline of the Article in Exhibit 12.4

CRITERIA FOR EVALUATING BINOCULARS

I. Optical Criteria
   A. Brightness of the image—indicates how well the optics gather and transmit light.
   B. Resolution of the image—possible defects:
      1. Edge-of-field defects
      2. Pincushion distortion
      3. Curvature of the image
      4. Spherical aberration
   C. Wide range of resolution—goes in and out of focus very slowly
   D. Alignment—images formed by each barrel merge imperceptibly into one
   E. Eye relief—full field of view
II. Construction and Casing
   A. Axis hinge—strong and smooth-working
   B. Focusing mechanism—center focus, well-designed
   C. Balance and comfort—weight, size, and balance combined

Exhibit 12.6 An Informative Abstract of the Article in Exhibit 12.4 Although the following abstract was written from the preceding outline, you may notice that the abstract does not include all of the outline's details, which would have made the abstract much too long.

"Criteria for Evaluating Binoculars," from "The Glass of Fashion" by Charles A. Bergman, *Audubon* magazine, November, 1981, p. 77.

Binoculars can be evaluated on the basis of optical criteria, construction, and casing. Optical criteria include the brightness of the image, the clarity of resolution of the image (absence of edge-of-field defects and other distortions of the image), the range of resolution of the image (it should go in and out of focus very slowly), the alignment of the two images the barrels provide into one image, and the fullness of the binoculars' field of view. Criteria for construction and casing require that the axis hinge be strong and smooth-working, the focusing mechanism be a center focus, and the weight, size, and balance combine to provide good balance and comfort.

Exhibit 12.7 A Descriptive Abstract of the Article in Exhibit 12.4 Compared to the informative abstract, the descriptive abstract is shorter, easier to write, and contains much less information.

```
"Criteria for Evaluating Binoculars," from "The Glass of
Fashion" by Charles A. Bergman, Audubon magazine, November,
1981, p. 77.

This article gives two broad sets of criteria for evaluating
binoculars: optical criteria and construction and casing
criteria. The article gives five different optical criteria
and three different criteria for construction and casing.
```

2. Executive Summaries

Although the word *summary* is frequently used interchangeably with *abstract,* a growing number of organizations use *summary* to mean what is called here *executive summary*.

2.1 What Are Executive Summaries?

An *executive summary* is a brief description of a report's contents in terms of their significance for its readers. The use that most clearly defines the executive summary is in writing for decision makers, such as in a proposal or a problem-solving report. The executive summary is under no obligation to cover *all* the parts of the report, or to cover elements in the same *order* as the report proper, or to cover elements in the same *proportion* as the report proper. It *is* under a strong obligation to answer the questions decision makers will ask about the report, and because of that obligation the writer of an executive summary must know more about the report than just its contents. The writer must know the audience for, and the purpose of, the report. Only then can he or she write an effective executive summary.

Although not all executive summaries are written for problem-solving reports, it may well be that the executive summary, as used preceding a problem-solving report, provides the best example of the spirit in which all executive summaries should be written. In preparing an executive summary to be placed at the beginning of a relatively short (say, twenty-page) problem-solving report, think in terms of a four-paragraph format:

- What is the problem?
- Why does it need to be solved?
- How should it be solved?
- Where in this are the benefits for us?

Exhibit 12.8 An Executive Summary of the Proposal to Create the Science Alliance

> Recent reports from the Energy Research Advisory Board and the Federal Laboratory Review Panel identified the weak link between universities and the major federally sponsored research institutions as "alarming" for the continuation of U.S. scientific leadership. For the continued development of fresh new ideas and a sound technology base, a free academic climate that provides a superior education for the best young minds must coexist with the kind of advanced facilities that are necessary for today's scientific research.
>
> Alone, the University of Tennessee, Knoxville, offers a powerful concentration of scientists and engineers. Alone, the Oak Ridge National Laboratory offers an exceptional resource. Together, these institutions provide an extraordinary concentration of people, facilities, and funds for scientific research and technological development.
>
> The Science Alliance between UTK and ORNL will formalize a strong University/Laboratory bond. It will hire joint scientists of national distinction, create joint institutes, share resources, bring the two institutions together in pursuit of technology transfer, build subareas of common strength, provide incentives to attract and retain the highest-quality faculty and students and strength the educational opportunities for both partners. And it will make that image of partnership visible both to the larger scientific community and to the public.
>
> The Science Alliance is a strong working partnership between the resources of The University of Tennessee, Knoxville, and The Oak Ridge National Laboratory. By uniting these resources, The Science Alliance provides an extraordinary concentration of people, facilities, and funds to support scientific research, technological development, and educational excellence. In each of these three closely related activities, the goal of The Science Alliance is to help ensure continued leadership for the United States.

Exhibit 12.8 presents a short example of just such an executive summary. This was taken from the proposal for The Science Alliance, a research partnership between the University of Tennessee, Knoxville, and the Oak Ridge National Laboratory. The audience is university administrators, university system administrators, and state higher-education commissioners.

Again, not all executive summaries are for problem-solving reports, and certainly they may not be written according to this pattern. But even if your executive summary is not for a problem-solving report, you may well find you can produce a good first draft by using this pattern.

The example in Exhibit 12.9 comes from a report entitled *Value of the Energy Data Base*. The report was written by King Research, Inc. (Rockville, Maryland), under subcontract to Maxima Corporation, for the Technical Information Center (now the Office of Scientific and Technical Information), the national information

Exhibit 12.9 Executive Summary of *Value of the Energy Data Base*

The U.S. Department of Energy currently expends about $5.8 billion annually on research and development in the program areas of defense, nuclear science, basic research, and others. The return on this investment to the nation is basically achieved through the accomplishment of the specific goals and objectives of the R&D and through the use of the knowledge gained from the R&D. There is abundant evidence that energy information plays an important role in current research and development activities. A survey of the 60,000 scientists and engineers funded by the Department of Energy shows that annually they read* about 7.1 million journal articles and 6.6 million technical reports. The total of 13.7 million readings includes 2.5 million by researchers in the defense program area, 2.2 million in the nuclear area, 3.0 million in basic research program areas, and 6.0 million in other program areas.

Clearly, use of existing information saves researchers considerable time and effort. In a survey of DOE-funded scientists and engineers, many indicated that a recent reading of a technical report or article led to a savings of time and/or equipment. For example, from reading a report on steam electric plant construction costs and production expenses which made it unnecessary to repeat the report's calculations, a nuclear scientist reported savings of about $1,000.

The total annual savings attributable to reading by DOE-funded scientists and engineers is estimated to be about $13 billion. This is one estimate of the consequential value of primary energy information found in articles and technical reports. An estimate of the apparent value, or the cost of the 13.7 million readings, is $500 million. One could look at the consequential value from the standpoint of a return on investment. The Department of Energy annually expends about $5.8 billion on research and development. Of that amount, about $500 million is expended in information processing and use, and the remaining $5.3 billion is spent on other research-related activities, which generate information. Thus,

Generation of Information		Information Processing and Use		Future Saving to DOE Scientists
$5.3 billion	+	$500 million	⟶	$13 billion

This suggests that an investment of $5.3 billion in the generation of information and about $500 million in processing and using information yields a partial return of about $13 billion in terms of savings to scientists and engineers in their time and in equipment. Overall, this partial return on investment is about 2.2 to 1. One way of expressing this relationship

*Reading means examining an article or technical report beyond its title.

is that the DOE paid $5.8 billion for the research, information processing, and use, which in turn has been found to be worth at least $13 billion.

The DOE Technical Information Services program managed by the Technical Information Center (TIC) is an Energy Program that has the responsibility of managing the information products from the multibillion-dollar R&D program and maximizing their use by Department staff and contractors. For example, TIC helps increase use of technical reports by making copies available in paper copy and in microfilm. It is estimated that reports distributed by TIC are read [an aggregate of] 6.8 million times by DOE and non-DOE researchers. If $1,280 is the average savings value derived from each reading, then this service has a potential of yielding savings of over $8 billion to the overall energy community. TIC also enhances the use of information through systems that provide effective access to energy-related technical reports, journal articles, and other materials produced worldwide. The major resource containing access information to these materials is the Energy Data Base (EDB). In 1981 it was estimated that the cumulative amount of the international R&D investment represented in the EDB was over $139 billion. The savings value derived by DOE researchers is enhanced by the ability to carefully select relevant items for reading from this data-base resource. A number of TIC products and services are related to the EDB and aid this selection process. These include the published index, *Energy Research Abstracts* (*ERA*), and the on-line bibliographic retrieval system, RECON. In fact, it was found that for DOE researchers, there are about 70,000 searches performed annually using RECON and an estimated 244,000 searches performed annually using *ERA* and other TIC-produced indexes. About 2.6 million of the total 13.7 million readings of energy articles and technical reports are directly attributable to use of EDB secondary information in some form. DOE scientists and engineers also conduct searches using other on-line systems and printed indexes, making a total of 4.6 million readings derived from bibliographic searches.

In determining the value of the Energy Data Base, only those searches and readings that are directly attributable to the EDB are included in the analysis. There are a total of 1.0 million readings from 70,000 RECON on-line searches, 600,000 readings from 40,000 on-line searches of the NTIS data base, and 1.6 million readings from 244,000 searches of *ERA* and other TIC indexes. The values directly attributable to the EDB are given in Table 1.1 [Table not shown here: value to searchers = $20 million; value to readers = $117 million; value to DOE organizations/funders = $3.6 billion.] The numbers given do not include the value associated with reading of technical reports received on standard distribution from TIC. These 3.3 million readings are associated with an additional $122 million in reading value, for a total of $239 million, and $4.2 billion in value to DOE, for a total of $7.8 billion. Of the total funds expended for energy information, the values directly attributable to TIC products and services are 43 percent of the total for searchers, 48 percent for readers, and 60 percent for the funding organization (DOE).

For those funding EDB searchers, one could evaluate searching by treating the $20 million amount paid by searchers as cost and the consequence in readings as benefits. Apparent value of the reading directly attributable to EDB searching is $117 million. The benefit-to-cost ratio of EDB searching is thus 5.9 to 1, and the net value is $97 million. Similarly, evaluation of reading would compare the EDB reading costs of $117 million against the $3.6 billion savings, which results in a benefit-to-cost ratio of about 31 to 1, or a net value of $3.5 billion. For all reading of energy materials, total costs of $500 million can be compared against the $13 billion savings, which results in a benefit-to-cost ratio of 26 to 1 and a net value of $12.5 billion.

The way in which we calculate the apparent and consequential values of EDB products and services is to determine the direct effects of the searches that would be lost by substituting other products and services and assuming a fixed total budget. There are three types of secondary products and services that use the EDB information: RECON, *ERA*, and other printed indexes; other on-line services, such as Lockheed Dialog and others, that have the NTIS data base (which includes many EDB items); and BRS, which provides access to the EDB. By dropping all these products and services and substituting others, there would be 354,000 fewer searches and therefore 2.5 million fewer readings. This results in the reduction of searcher apparent value by $15 million, consequential value to readers by $90 million, and the value of savings in time and equipment by $3 billion.

The latter figure, $3 billion savings in labor and equipment from the EDB products and services, can be roughly translated into productivity. If it is assumed that, with the EDB, research and development costs $5.8 billion for a given level of output, without the EDB the same output would require an investment of $8.8 billion. This is an increase in productivity of about 52 percent. This says that to accomplish the same R&D output without TIC information services, the R&D budget would have had to have been $3 billion higher.

Value assessments were also conducted separately for five major research areas funded by DOE: defense; nuclear science; and basic energy science, fusion, and health and environmental research, components of the basic research program. Separate reports are provided elsewhere for each of these areas with summary results given in this report. Differences were found in the level of reading by researchers in the different program areas, in the methods used to identify materials, and in the value associated with reading. Average annual researcher's readings of technical reports and articles ranged from 203 in the defense area to 276 in the fusion area. Printed index searching was used most heavily in the areas of nuclear, health and environmental research, and on-line searching in the basic energy sciences. Fusion researchers made greater use of standard distribution copies of reports from TIC. Value associated with report reading was estimated to range from $930 in the health and environmental research area to $1,840 in the fusion area. Looking at individual research budgets within the program area, we see that increases in productivity as a result of EDB products and services were calculated as ranging from 24 percent for health and environmental research to 94 percent for nuclear research programs.

center for the Department of Energy. The purpose of the report was to assess the dollar value of the Energy Data Base (described earlier in this chapter; see Section 1.4). The report's primary audience were the individuals in the federal government who make funding decisions about the continuation of the Energy Data Base; its secondary audience were the scientists and technicians who use the data base; its tertiary audience were people such as the author of this book, who are interested in the growth of the information industry. The Executive Summary of the report, shown in Exhibit 12.9, contains a figure and a table not printed here; this version is shorter by about one-third. If you want to see the whole (81-page) report, your librarian should be able to find it for you; its document number is DOE/OR/11232-1 (DE82014250).

EXERCISES

1. Write a descriptive abstract and an informative abstract of Chapter 4 of this text. Assume students like yourself are the audience for each.
2. Write an executive summary of Chapter 4 of this text. Assume students like yourself are the audience.
3. Write an informative abstract of an article in *Scientific American* specified by your teacher. Your teacher will also specify the audience.
4. Using the resources of your school library, write a short report for your teacher on how a person in your field can find abstracts of research articles in your field without having to look up the articles themselves.
5. If your class requires a major report, write an executive summary and a descriptive abstract of it, based on your current knowledge of your subject. It is understood that this summary and abstract will be tentative and speculative, and that you do not know exactly what your report will say until you finish your research.
6. Write a fifty-word descriptive abstract of the executive summary of the *Value of the Energy Data Base* report presented in Exhibit 12.9. Assume the audience is a taxpayer for whom you are preparing a report on how DOE-spent money is justified (or not justified). Then write a 150-word descriptive abstract on the same subject for the same audience.
7. Write an executive summary of the executive summary of the *Value of the Energy Data Base* report. Assume your audience is a group of taxpayers who want an explanation of why their tax dollars are being spent on that kind of information activity. Try for a length of no more than 150 words.

PART IV

Processes in Report Writing

A popular misconception about the writing that professionals do is that it consists of nothing more than reporting facts. Successful writing, according to this misconception, consists of keeping the words out of the way of the facts. If it is that simple, why are the professional journals full of articles made needlessly dense by bad writing? Why are our desks littered with three or four different versions of the user's manual for our favorite computer and its software—manuals purchased in a vain attempt to find one that is *really* "user-friendly"? Why does the student (or professional) who puts off writing until the last minute—on the basis of "I've got all the data together; all I need to do now is write it up"—so often meet with disaster? Effective professional writing is more than just putting down the facts. From the simplest manual to the run-of-the-mill technical report or progress report to the most complex multimillion-dollar proposal, effective writing has an important abstract quality to it. It's that quality that makes the words on the page "say" the same thing to the reader that the facts and data have "said" to the writer. It's that quality that expresses the way purpose, message, audience, and writer's role (the key intangibles in the communication situation) work together to make a successful report. How do we name such a quality? If we were talking about how form and function, practical concerns and aesthetics, come together in an automobile or a building, we would call it *design*. Let us use the same word here, and agree that design is the abstract quality that unites the key intangible elements to produce a successful document, one that goes beyond bare presentation of facts to create successful communication.

In a set of instructions, this quality of design may find its most concrete expression in the selection and placement of visuals. In a technical report, the quality of design may be most operative in the decisions the writer makes about what is a major section or a minor section, what is more important or less important, what comes first, second, and so forth. In a proposal, that quality especially can include hundreds of decisions, large and small, from the entire persuasive strategy right down to specific word choices.

In most college and university settings your writing tasks come to you pretty neatly packaged: Your Freshman English teacher may say, "Write a 500-word paper comparing and contrasting two recent movies." Your Marine Biology professor might say, "Write a 10- to 15-page report on the effect of El Nim̃o on Peruvian anchovy fisheries." Because in these college reports the key intangibles—purpose, message, audience, and writer's role—are so set, beginning writers might naturally think that "just pouring the facts into this mold" is the most important element, and indeed is all that effective writing really requires. But when you move outside of the academic arena into professional life, all of the key intangibles are unknowns, and design becomes critical. When all you know is that you must explain on paper why the Savannah plant is not operating up to par, or that you must convince readers that professional management depends on strict (but not mindless) adherence to policy, you must think about more than "writing as reporting."

In terms of the elements presented in the first twelve chapters of this book, it is *design* that explains how all the skills, ideas, visuals, headings, definitions, process descriptions, and so forth, come together to produce a successful report. The elements that were presented in the first twelve chapters are the building blocks; the next eight chapters provide the design element, the plan.

Chapter 13 shows how audiences and purposes change when you move from school- to work-related writing, how these changes will require changes in your approach to writing, and how careful consideration of audience and purpose, in particular, will help you solve problems in design.

Nothing hurts an otherwise well-written report more than poorly presented, unclear, unconvincing recommendations. Chapter 14 explains how important it is to make the recommendations you include in your reports clear and convincing.

Chapter 15 addresses the situation that most requires the element of design: writing reports that effectively state solutions to hard-to-define problems. The processes described are those that can help you unite, for example, the definition-and-description techniques of Chapter 10 with the clear recommendations of Chapter 13. Of course, every professional field has its own approaches to problem solving—approaches requiring advanced knowledge of engineering, management, medicine, and so on—but the processes presented are valuable additions to your problem-solving approach, no matter what your field.

A final process anyone who writes as part of his or her profession needs to master is the process of library research. Although students often see this as only a school-related skill, most professionals find that they need to know how to use research libraries throughout their careers. The more writing such people do, the more they use research libraries, either those owned by their own companies or those of government or academic institutions.

Using the processes described in Part IV, you should be able to put the elements described in Part III together into effective reports. Part V will then show you some of the forms such reports typically take.

13

Writing Reports in a Professional Setting

1. **Designing Reports for Decision Makers**
   1.1 Catalogical Versus Analytical Reports
   1.2 Varieties of Two-Level Reports
2. **Classes of Reports**
   2.1 Class A Reports
   2.2 Class B Reports
   2.3 Class C Reports
3. **Joint Authorship of Reports**
   3.1 Working with Co-Authors
   3.2 Being the Editor on a Joint-Authorship Team
4. **The Editorial Process**
   4.1 Sizing Up the Manuscript
   4.2 Copyediting
   4.3 Author Review
   4.4 Publications Production
5. **The Automated Office**
   5.1 What It Is
      5.1.1 Word Processing
      5.1.2 Mailing-List Management
      5.1.3 Graphics
      5.1.4 Spreadsheet Budgeting and Statistical Modeling
      5.1.5 Printing
      5.1.6 Internal and External Mail and Document Transfer
   5.2 How It Can Work
   5.3 What Its Problems Are
6. **Coming to Grips with Accountability**
   Exercises

Writing of the kinds this text describes always occurs in the context of someone collecting information, organizing it, and distributing it in written form. The further you go in your academic career, the more time and energy you will put into these three activities. As a professional, you will find that these same activities may well occupy between 30 and 60 percent of your time. As you move from school to professional life, the existence of these activities in your writing remains the same, but there are important changes in the areas of audience and purpose. Chapter 1 discussed the background for this in detail. Let us review that material briefly: In school you write mostly to prove your knowledge; on the job you frequently write not just to provide information but also to guide the thinking of decision makers. In school the people in your audience—your teachers—are paid to read your reports, and they read them in order to measure your mastery of academic subjects. On the job your audience has a choice of whether to read your report, skim it, route it to someone else to read, return it for revision, or discard it! Professional audiences read your reports primarily to make decisions about courses of action, to decide what to do or how to do it, and only indirectly to make decisions about *you*. And professional audiences are likely to be very different kinds of people than your college instructors are. Professional audiences come from all different levels in the organization, from outside the organization, from different educational backgrounds, and even from totally different cultures. Suppose, for example, that your company lands a big contract to supply machinery for fifteen manufacturing plants in Japan. Assuming that the Japanese business people with whom you are dealing read English (generally they do), how will their different backgrounds require changes in your writing? Or suppose your company sells a Middle Eastern state radio parts. How will you need to revise the manuals and other documentation for that special audience? As you move from college to professional life, these important changes in audience and purpose for your writing will require equally important changes in the way you design your reports.

Other features of professional writing will also require changes from the way you write in college. In college you may have a vague idea that one report you do is more important than another, requiring more preparation in terms of a special cover, professional typing, and so forth. On the job, most documents—letters, manuals, reports, brochures, etc.—are usually carefully categorized as belonging to one of several classes, depending on whether they are for internal or external audiences and on the level of formality they are felt to require. In college you are usually prohibited from collaborating with other students on the authorship of papers; in professional life joint authorship is the rule, not the exception. In college your typed report is turned in and that's usually the end of it. In professional life you frequently have an editor, and possibly even a publications production process (professionally done graphics, typesetting, printing, distribution) to deal with. In college your writing almost always has about it the air of an exercise—essentially the same activity being done over and over by different students in order to build their mental muscles. On the job there's an air of reality about the writing assignments that gives new professionals a feeling that they may never have had about their writing as students. Here we will call that feeling *accountability*. When you write on the job you feel your writing *matters*; it matters to you, your business, your career, maybe even to the world. Be prepared for that feeling, because it can change your behavior as a writer in complex ways.

This chapter discusses the aspects of writing that are crucial for students making the transition to professional life:

1. report design for decision makers
2. classes of reports
3. joint authorship
4. the editing process
5. the automated office
6. accountability

Each will have its effect on the process of your writing as a professional. You can begin to prepare for those effects and turn them to your advantage by reading this chapter carefully.

Because it deals with intangible processes in writing as well as finished products of writing, this chapter is somewhat more philosophical than Chapters 2 through 12. In that sense Parts I, II, and III of this text are its first half (with Chapter 1 as that half's introduction), and Parts IV and V are the second half (with Chapter 13 as the second half's introduction).

1. Designing Reports for Decision Makers

Most writing in school operates on only one level, tracing the evolution of a student's understanding of some subject. For example, a typical lab report may well be a strictly chronological account of the activities in the lab: purpose, materials, procedures, results, and discussion. A typical English essay may trace the evolution of a relationship between two characters in a play, building out of that some idea of the relationship's significance. A typical business case analysis may trace the past, analyze the present, and speculate about the future of a company or market. Such writing operates mainly on the level of the *writer's* experience or understanding; it catalogues the writer's activities.

Although that kind of one-level (or *catalogical*) writing is both appropriate and traditional in schools, it is neither in professional life. As a professional person who writes, you will find that your readers expect more of you. Your readers want your experience and understanding sorted out, analyzed, and discussed in terms of *their* understandings and *their* purposes. Rather than one-level, catalogical reports, your readers will expect you to produce *two-level*, *analytical* reports.

1.1 Catalogical Versus Analytical Reports

Earlier chapters have touched on at the distinction between catalogical and analytical writing. The distinction between writer-centered and reader-centered writing, explained in Chapter 10, Section 4.1 and 4.2, is a more general form of this same idea. Compartmentalizing resumés (discussed in Chapter 6) and stair-stepping visuals (discussed in Chapter 7) are also examples of this principle on a lower level. More to the point, the recommendation report with the recommendation at the beginning rather than at the end (developed in the next chapter) is a specific example of using two levels (one for the recommendation, another for the background to it) in a popular and successful application.

The following chart shows some of the distinctions between one- and two-level report writing.

One-level Report	**Two-level Report**
(more writer-centered)	(more reader-centered)
• catalogues writer's experience	• analyzes significance of writer's experience for reader
• example: recommendation at the end	• example: recommendation at the beginning

Did you ever try to figure out the organizational pattern of a catalogue? There may be some broad pattern that is discernible (women's clothes, men's clothes, appliances, etc.), but in general if you want to find anything you must use the index. The organization comes not from any purpose the reader has, but from qualities inherent in the subject matter. This is the sense of the word *catalogical* when applied to reports that pay no heed to their readers' purposes in reading. Analytical, the opposite of catalogical, means that the writer analyzed who the readers would be and decided how their purposes in reading needed to be reflected in the way the report is written—especially in its structure.

The two versions of the same short section of a professionally written report shown in Exhibits 13.1 and 13.2 illustrate the difference between catalogical and analytical report structures: This example is taken from the advanced user's manual for TETRA, a general-purpose management information system. The example has been adapted (by omitting irrelevant sections) to demonstrate the difference between a catalogical and an analytical report structure.

At the end of TETRA's advanced user's guide, the author wants to show readers how to use TETRA to solve a typical (and rather complex) management problem. Here you will see the sample problem (abbreviated to bring its structure more clearly into focus) presented first catalogically and then analytically.

As you may have realized by now, the problem with the catalogical approach to presenting a sample problem is that the writer dives right into the process of explaining the technical content, without adequately preparing the reader for the *significance* of the content (or, in this case in particular, preparing the reader for the fact that, just when the problem gets most interesting, the reader will be referred to another manual to see how to work out the rest of the problem). But these are exactly the things most readers will really want to know before they start into the problem. That is, here we have a fairly typical picture of a writer presenting

Exhibit 13.1 A Catalogical Approach to Writing a Sample Problem

SAMPLE PROBLEM

TETRA can be used in many ways. One question managers frequently must answer is to determine how much is currently available in uncommitted funds. The equation for answering this question is: "Uncommitted funds equals Budget minus Cost-to-Date minus Uncosted Commitments minus the Projected Fixed Costs." Solving this equation is complicated by the fact that each of these data are held in different data bases. The advantage of the TETRA management information system is that it can access a number of different data bases as needed to solve this kind of complex problem.

The first problem is to figure out how much funding is allocated to the project. This information is available in two online data bases, OTTL and SUMMT. In order to access this information, instruct TETRA to. . . . [Two pages omitted here.]

Therefore the project's initial budget is $1,986,000.

Next, you need to determine Cost-to-Date. This information is available in the Ongoing Data Base (ODB). TETRA can access this data base through. . . . [Two pages omitted.]

Thus the Cost-to-Date is $1,087,781. This data can also be used in estimating the projected fixed cost. . . . [One page omitted.] Thus the projected fixed cost is $80,889.

Next you need to take into account any other commitments outstanding. These commitments could be in any of three different data bases: direct outside purchases (DIROPS), subcontracts (SUBS), or outstanding work orders (OWORS). . . . [Three pages omitted.]

Therefore the currently outstanding commitments total $1,023,505.

We now have values for all the unknowns in the equation. That is, . . . [calculations omitted here] . . . the uncommitted funds equals a *negative* $253,540. Obviously, the project is already in trouble. The TETRA management information system will help you isolate the problem. With TETRA, you can determine what specific accounts have problems and specifically where in each account the problem is. TETRA can be used to point out all the key data at these lower areas. This process is explained in the Sample Problem in the TETRA Expert User's Guide.

information in the manner of a catalogue (here a series of steps) without first analyzing what higher-level generalizations or preparations the reader will need in order to be able to understand that series of steps most efficiently.

Compare that approach to presenting TETRA's sample problem with the one shown in Exhibit 13.2.

Only a few lines (specifically, the third paragraph of the second version) separate the ways the two approaches are written. Assuming a manager—a deci-

Exhibit 13.2 Analytical Approach to Writing a Sample Problem

SAMPLE PROBLEM

TETRA is a general-purpose management information system that can provide its users with information in many ways. This sample problem shows you how to use multiple data bases to answer a typical question managers have to deal with: "How much do I have available in uncommitted funds?"

Four variables must be determined in order to solve the problem: the budget, the cost-to-date, the uncosted commitments, and the projected fixed costs. Each of these pieces of information is in a different data base, and it is one of the particular strengths of the TETRA management information system that it can search a number of different data bases to enable you to solve just such a problem as this easily. This sample problem shows you how that is done.

At the end of this process, you will learn that the project in question is several hundred thousand dollars in the red. Just as TETRA can help you determine that important fact through the process shown here, so TETRA can also help you determine exactly where (in what accounts) the specific problems lie. Although this second-stage, lower-level use of TETRA is beyond the scope of this manual (it is explained in the TETRA Expert User's Manual), it is summarized here to give you some feel for how versatile TETRA can be.

The formula for finding uncommitted funds is. . . . [From here the two approaches are the same, until right at the end.]

The calculations show that the project is over $200,000 in the red. The TETRA management information system will help you isolate the problem. With TETRA you can determine what accounts have problems and where those specific problems are. Although this further application of TETRA is beyond the scope of this manual, it is explained in detail in the sample problem in the TETRA Expert User's Manual. But in case you are curious to know just a little more, here is a brief overview of this further application of TETRA. [One page omitted here.]

sion maker—as the reader, which would get a more favorable response? The second, analytical one would. It forecasts the structure of the upcoming problem, and it prepares the reader for the outcome. In the first (catalogical) version, the outcome seems to some readers to be a sort of halfway solution; that is, you know the project is in trouble, but this manual doesn't explain how to find the source of the problem. That frustrates some readers; so does not knowing the structure of the problem-solving process in advance. Because the *analytical* approach foresees and satisfies (in advance) these potentially frustrating points, it is the more desirable of the two. Because its underlying organization is based first and foremost on anticipation of the reader's needs, the analytical approach characterizes the kind of writing you will need to do for decision makers.

The analytical element in writing can take many different forms. In the TETRA manual, the analytical element consisted of anticipating an obvious problem readers would have with the manual's first (catalogical) version (cf. Good Will, Chapter 4, Section 2.7), and dealing with that possible problem by more carefully introducing the report—in this case, by more carefully *framing* the process to be described (cf. Chapter 11, Section 2.1.1). In other reports, the analytical element could be something quite different.

Consider, for example, a proposal. (This example, like the TETRA example, is inspired by problems with an actual piece of professional writing.) In its original, catalogical version, the proposal is eight pages long:

- two pages describing the company proposing to do the work, two pages describing other similar work done by this company in the past
- two pages describing the credentials of the people in the company who will do the work
- two pages describing exactly what the company is proposing to do

Now consider how this same proposal might be rewritten *analytically* by a writer who sets out to create a reader-based version (cf. Chapter 14, Section 1.2), asking from the start, "What will the readers want to see first, second, etc.?" The revised proposal is also eight pages long but with a different composition:

- a one-page list of benefits spelling out what the client company will get if it accepts the proposal
- two pages on what the company is proposing to do
- two pages on the personnel
- two pages on previous similar experience
- one page on the company itself

This analytical version of the report, almost the reverse of the catalogical version, is bound to get a better response from its readers, because it was written with them firmly in mind. It illustrates yet another source for the analytical element—here the distinction between writer-based and reader-based patterns.

There is no particular difficulty or skill involved in writing a two-level (as opposed to a one-level) report. You merely need to size up your purpose and audience accurately and to realize that the situation calls for a two-level design. Typically that situation is characterized by writing for a decision maker. The only additional process required is that of giving consideration to the psychological aspects of your report's design.

1.2 Varieties of Two-Level Reports

If the professional journals in your field print abstracts or summaries at the beginnings of articles, you may already be used to seeing one form of two-level report. The presence of an analytical level, the summary or abstract, assists you, as the prospective reader, in making the decision of whether to read each article.

Another example of the two-level report is the multi-section user's manual (described in Chapter 11). If you write a user's manual with three main sections—a how-to part for beginners, a description of the machine or system explaining each part's capabilities, and a trouble-shooting section—you've written a *three*-level document, each part speaking to a slightly different audience or purpose.

Perhaps the most interesting and important use of the two- or multi-level report structure occurs in long professional reports of the sort described in Chapter 19. In such reports the multiple levels of design include not just the segmentation of the report proper but also the employment of multiple introductory devices. That is, in addition to the report's body being broken into sections corresponding to several levels, the opening pages of the report may include:

- a short statement of authorization (explaining why the report was written)
- an abstract (summarizing the report's scope)
- an executive summary (tying the report's coverage to its significance)
- a formal (*cpo*) introduction to the entire report

This use of multiple introductory devices, explained in detail in Chapter 9, exemplifies the use of multiple levels in report design. The practice is extremely useful for the decision makers for whom professional reports are designed, but it can be extremely frustrating for would-be writers who don't see why or how so many kinds of front-matter need to be used.

2. Classes of Reports

There is no standard classification for naming the degree of formality and finish, the amount of production and expense, needed for reports. Although some reports are merely photocopies of typed pages, others are glossy, multicolor, bound documents. One popular scheme divides reports into three classes—A, B, and C.

2.1 Class A Reports

The Class A report (often called a "prestige" publication) is usually typeset. Its columns may be justified on both sides of the page. There is abundant artwork, and the art is integrated with the text. The report is printed and bound on high-quality paper, frequently in several colors. The format of Class A reports varies widely and is often quite creative. Class A reports are nearly always external communications (directed at people outside the writer's company). Typical Class A reports include annual reports to stockholders, prospectuses, and new product presentations. Exhibit 13.3 shows a two-page spread from a typical Class A report.

2.2 Class B Reports

The Class B report (the kind most frequently seen in business and industry) is usually typewritten (or word processed), with unjustified pages (although the use of word processing has made justified edges available in Class B reports as well).

The illustrations and the text are on separate pages. Although the report is still professionally reproduced and bound, it uses more economical materials than the Class A report. For example, the covers of Class B reports are usually standard, stock covers that the firm has printed in large quantities and uses on all its Class B reports. The format of the Class B report is usually determined by the company involved. Class B reports may be either internal or external communication. Typical Class B reports include technical memoranda, startup procedures, and training manuals. Exhibit 13.4 shows a two-page report from a typical Class B report.

2.3 Class C Reports

The Class C report is typewritten, the illustrations and text are on separate pages (illustrations may be gathered together at the end), the copies are usually done on a departmental copier, and the format is strictly utilitarian. Class C reports are only for internal communication. Business-world examples include travel reports, planning reports, and personnel evaluations. The main elements of an authentic student report, another type of Class C report, are shown in Exhibit 19.6 at the end of Chapter 19.

This classification system is only intended to be representative of the ways reports may vary. The situation you are in will obviously be the primary determiner of the class of report you produce.

3. Joint Authorship of Reports

Only rarely do students encounter a situation in which several people are encouraged to work together on a writing project; in professional life it happens all the time. Joint (or multiple) authorship can take many forms. For example, a large engineering firm, in bidding on a waste-water treatment project, may put together a project team of perhaps five to seven people, each with his or her own staff. This group may include an architect, a mechanical engineer, a civil engineer, and an electrical engineer. Another engineer, one who has risen to the level of management, may well be made team leader. With all these people involved, who writes the reports? Everybody does, working together.

3.1 Working with Co-Authors

Usually the writing of a professional report is broken down into much the same kinds of divisions as are the technical tasks themselves. That is, each person writes the part of the project report that relates to his or her own specialty. With five to seven people involved, you can imagine what kind of report could result, so usually one person is responsible making all the segments blend. Or, if the firm has a technical writer or editor, he or she may perform this function. But most companies choose to have their own technical people do the writing and editing. Sometimes, but not always, the team leader is the editor. More often, the editor is a team member, who then passes the nearly finished report on to the team leader for final approval.

Exhibit 13.3 A Two-Page Spread from a Typical Class A Report

Steam Turbines

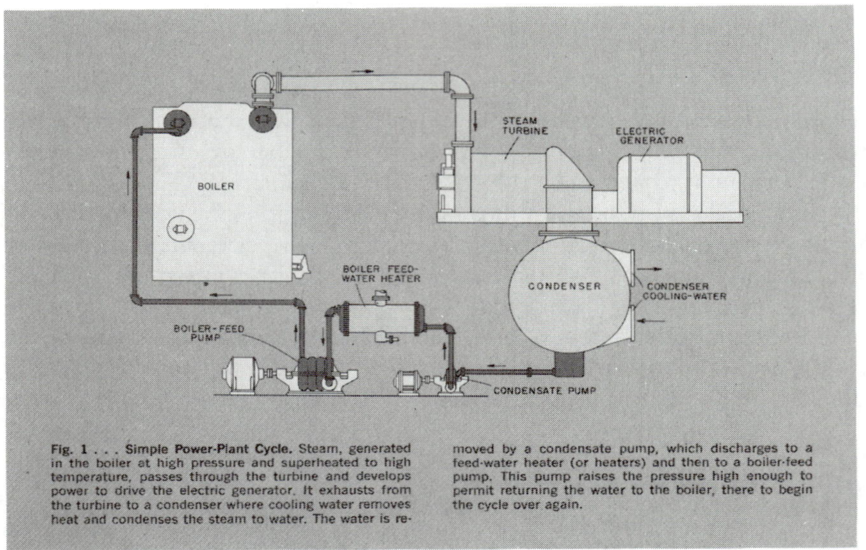

Fig. 1 . . . Simple Power-Plant Cycle. Steam, generated in the boiler at high pressure and superheated to high temperature, passes through the turbine and develops power to drive the electric generator. It exhausts from the turbine to a condenser where cooling water removes heat and condenses the steam to water. The water is removed by a condensate pump, which discharges to a feed-water heater (or heaters) and then to a boiler-feed pump. This pump raises the pressure high enough to permit returning the water to the boiler, there to begin the cycle over again.

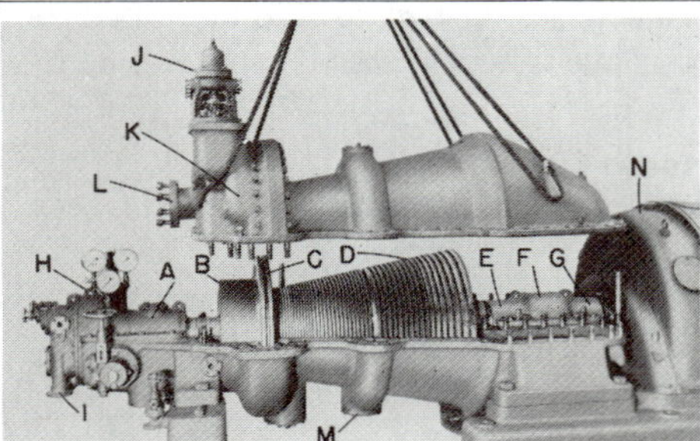

Courtesy of Brown Boveri Corp.

Fig. 2 . . . Single-Cylinder Condensing Turbine. Initial steam conditions for this 2500-kw 3600-rpm turbine are 230-psi (16.2-kg/sq cm) pressure and 580 F (304 C) temperature. Letters refer to the following parts: A, journal and thrust bearing; B, balancing piston; C, impulse blading; D, reaction blading; E and G, journal bearings; F, coupling; H, governor; I, main oil pump; J, steam valve; K, steam-nozzle chamber; L, stop-valve flange; M, bleeder point for feed-water heating; and N, generator.

In a turbine, steam expands in stationary or moving nozzles from which it discharges at high velocity. The force of the high-velocity jets of steam causes the moving parts to rotate, thus making the energy in the steam available to do useful mechanical work—for example, to drive a compressor or generator.

After it has expanded in the turbine, the steam usually exhausts to a condenser, which serves two purposes. First, by maintaining a vacuum at the turbine exhaust, it increases the pressure range through which the steam expands. In this way, it materially increases the efficiency of power generation. Second, it causes the steam to condense, thus providing pure, clean water for the boilers to reconvert into steam. This simple cycle (Fig. 1)—water to steam, power generation, and steam to water—forms the basis on which most steam-power plants operate.

Construction . . . The parts of a steam turbine (Fig. 2) may be thought of as being in four groupings: (1) Stationary parts, (2) the rotor, or spindle, (3) governing mechanism, and (4) lubricating system.

The principal stationary parts are the steam-tight casing, or cylinder, the steam-admission valves, nozzles or stationary blading, shaft seals and bearings. The rotor, depending on turbine type, may consist of wheels mounted on a shaft or may be machined from a solid forging or a forging made up of welded sections. In either case, it carries securely fastened radial blades, or buckets. Turbine governors for small machines may be relatively simple mechanical mechanisms that directly operate a steam-admission valve. For larger machines, they may be very complex hydraulic systems which may not only control speed, by controlling the admission of steam, but also control the pressure of steam extracted for process purposes and the operation of valves or safety devices separate from the turbine. Similarly the lubrication system may be simple reservoirs in the pedestals of ring-oiled bearings or elaborate circulation systems, having pumps, coolers, filters, and devices that automatically shut down the turbine in case of low oil pressure or overspeeding.

Shaft seals at the ends of each casing are neces-

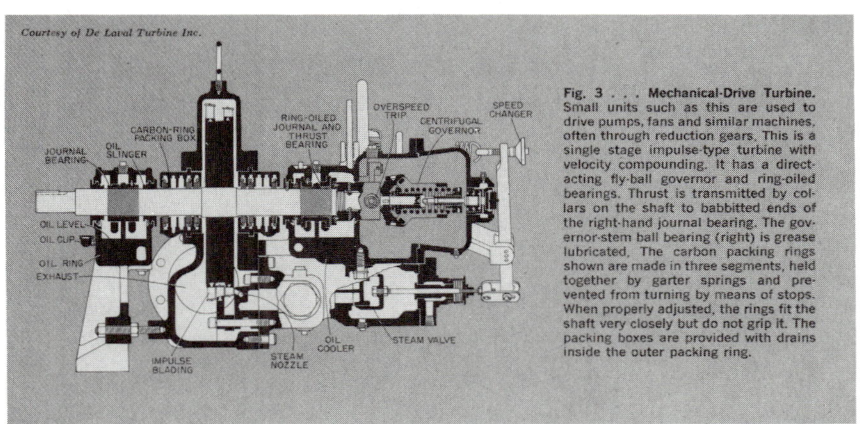

Fig. 3 . . . Mechanical-Drive Turbine. Small units such as this are used to drive pumps, fans and similar machines, often through reduction gears. This is a single stage impulse-type turbine with velocity compounding. It has a direct-acting fly-ball governor and ring-oiled bearings. Thrust is transmitted by collars on the shaft to babbitted ends of the right-hand journal bearing. The governor-stem ball bearing (right) is grease lubricated. The carbon packing rings shown are made in three segments, held together by garter springs and prevented from turning by means of stops. When properly adjusted, the rings fit the shaft very closely but do not grip it. The packing boxes are provided with drains inside the outer packing ring.

Source: Steam Turbines and Their Lubrication, pp. 6-7. Reproduced by permission of Mobil Oil Corporation.

Exhibit 13.4 A Two-Page Spread from a Typical Class B Report

4

2. COMPARISON OF EQUIVALENT ICE AND ELECTRIC CARS

The first tasks were the definition of a typical state-of-the-art electric vehicle and then the selection or development of characteristics of an equivalent ICE vehicle. (The opposite approach was rejected because it appears unlikely that electric vehicle performance can equal that of typical gasoline vehicles.)

The Electric and Hybrid Vehicle Act defines acceptable performance goals for electric vehicles (Table 1).[1] Typical values for today's electric car are compared with goals that were used to establish the performance required from the ICE vehicle.

A goal for the energy efficiency of the electric car is not set forth in the legislative act. This value depends on the car weight, battery/motor efficiency, and recharging rate and efficiency. The relation between weight, range, and efficiency is shown qualitatively in Fig. 1. Numerous tests indicate that the overall electric power use of a 950-kg (2100-lb) curb-weight electric car is at best 3 miles/kWh and more typically only 1.2 to 2.0 miles/kWh.[2,3]

Estimation of the fuel economy of an ICE vehicle of similar acceleration potential can be accomplished by correlating the fuel use and

Table 1. Summary of electric vehicle performance goals

Parameter	Goal	State of art
Acceleration to 50 km/h, s	<15	8–15
Forward speed for 5 min, km/h	80	65–80
Range,[a] km	50	45–70
Recharge time from 80% discharge, h	<10	<10

[a]Using driving cycle in Society of Automotive Engineers Standard J227a.

Source: Ref. 1.

5

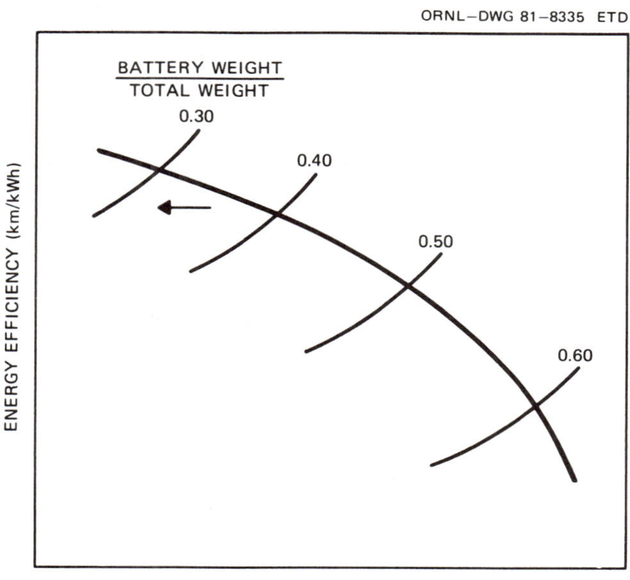

Fig. 1. Illustration of trade-off between range and fuel efficiency.

acceleration of today's typical automobiles (Fig. 2); a direct comparison cannot be made, because no present-day automobile performs as poorly as the goals set for the electric vehicle. An extrapolation to very poor acceleration (0 to 50 km/h in about 12 s, which is still much better than the electric vehicle performance goal) shows that the corresponding fuel economy for a 950-kg (2100-lb) car would exceed 70 mpg over an Environmental Protection Agency (EPA) type driving mode. In fact, the equivalent ICE car weighs even less than this because it does not have the weight of the batteries. Nevertheless, a very conservative value of 60 mpg was used in this analysis. (Note that for a vehicle of this type, fuel consumption is already so low that further increases in efficiency make little difference to the running costs.)

The initial price of a mass-produced electric vehicle is difficult to estimate. Limited production two-passenger electric cars are selling

Source: R. L. Graves, C. D. West, and E. C. Fox, *The Electric Car—Is It Still the Vehicle of the Future?* (Oak Ridge, Tenn.: Oak Ridge National Laboratory, 1981), pp. 4–5.

In other instances, two or three people may actually write a report, or a section of one, together. Even so, there are usually divisions of labor. Two team members may work together to make an outline, but then the actual writing is usually divided up between the two or three members of the team.

Certain problems and pointers apply to both kinds of joint authorship:

1. Most important, *all the people involved in any project must have the same mental picture of the project and the purpose of the report* being written. Depending on the size of your group and the nature of your project, it may well be indispensable to hold a first meeting at which everyone involved works to an agreement on the project, the report's purpose, and the report's audience. Any difference in understanding at this stage will be magnified each day it goes uncorrected.

2. *Everyone involved must agree on a division of labor and a schedule.* The timetable should specify preliminary-draft and finished-copy completion points for each member's contribution, and it should leave time at the end for editing and for a complete technical review by each key team member. Most importantly, once a schedule is arrived at, it must be followed.

3. *Staying within the timetable* is vital to the success of any group project. The kinds of problems that occur when work is late on a single-person project increase exponentially when work is late on a multi-person project. Many teams will specify that one member, usually the editor, check on each member's progress on a regular basis.

4. *Communication* among team members during the course of the project also plays an important role in any project's success. You may want to schedule weekly meetings to review the progress of each member and to provide group support for solving any individual problems that may have come up. In case any members of the group resent the regular meetings, remind them that the purpose is not just to have a meeting but to communicate and to draw on the strengths of the group to solve (and to prevent) problems.

As members complete their projects, they should review the technical content of each piece. Then they should funnel the reports to whoever is designated to be the editor. That person's responsibility (enlarged on in the following section) is to ensure that the various sections fit together into one integrated report. That means controlling style, correctness of grammar, treatment of visuals, and a number of other points, from the kind of typeface to the scope and coverage of the entire document. When these tasks have been performed, review copies of the entire report should be delivered to each team member, and a final meeting should be held to approve the report prior to its publication or delivery to the client.

Although actual practices may vary widely from those described here because of time pressures or other considerations, this process is representative of how joint authorship should function, whether there are two authors or ten. The flow chart in Figure 13.1 summarizes the process for you.

3.2 Being the Editor on a Joint-Authorship Team

Although there are too many complex processes involved in the profession of technical editing to explain here, any professional can profit from some knowledge of how technical editors work. The most important part of any editor's job is to

Figure 13.1 Flow Chart for Joint Authorship of Reports

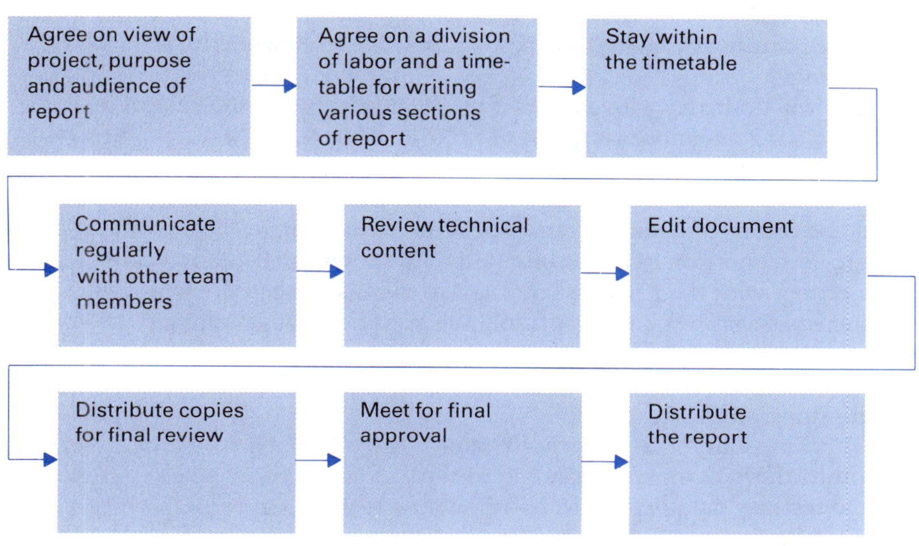

maintain a positive relationship with the author(s). Occasionally an editor and an author will develop an adversary relationship, one in which they are actually working against each other. As an editor, you should go out of your way to avoid conflict with the author(s). Both author and editor have the same goal—to produce the best possible document. Keep that in mind when it seems the authors you work with are making life difficult.

As the person in your group designated to edit the report, a number of functions are expected of you; Box 13.1 lists those functions.

Items 1, 5, and 6 are really administrative functions, matters of efficient communication with other members of your team and of responsible record

Box 13.1 Functions of the Editor on a Joint-Authorship Team

1. Ensure that the various subprojects are completed on schedule.
2. Receive the individual reports and organize them into a coherent whole; take responsibility for the whole report's design.
3. Ensure the stylistic readability and grammatical correctness of the entire report.
4. Review any substantive changes with the appropriate authors.
5. Distribute review copies prior to the final approval meeting.
6. Be responsible for the final meeting; be responsible for the report's production in finished form and its appropriate distribution.

keeping on your part. Items 2 and 3 require writer's skills of the sort described in this text. Item 4 requires some skill at human relationships. Some authors become so ego-involved in their work that they see every possible change in it as a personal threat. A good editor needs to be able to be assertive without being threatening.

You will do better with authors if you avoid altogether the kind of session in which you and an author sit down to go over a bundle of pages word by word. That kind of session not only is immensely (and needlessly) time consuming but also promotes fatigue and frustration that can lead to needless bad feelings. You should be able to take minor grammatical and stylistic changes for granted. If you must review a portion of a report with its author, give the author a copy prior to the meeting, with the passages you want to discuss marked. Invite the author to mark any passages he or she wants to discuss. But do not get into a page-by-page review. Approach such a meeting as a negotiating session, and be prepared to concede on points that are matters of judgment on your part (rather than clear-cut decisions, such as grammar).

The functions of a professional editor are explained in the next section; obviously, they are more demanding of time and expertise than most engineers, or accountants, or other professionals who happen to have been chosen their group's editors can afford. But if you remember the points discussed and listed here, you should be able to function effectively as the member of a project team who is chosen to do the editing. However, if the report you are working on is to be published (rather than merely typed and copied), or if the artwork and illustrations are to be integrated into the text (rather than appearing on pages by themselves), you will probably need a professional editor's assistance.

4. The Editorial Process

You can be a better author and a better editor of your peers' work if you know a little more about how professional editors work, what they do, and the sequence they do it in. Although the exact stages in the editorial process may differ a little from one situation to another (depending especially on the extent to which your editor's company uses computers in the publications-production process), the flow chart in Fig. 13.2 shows its basics.

Briefly, here's how the process works: Before you put any manuscript into production, your peers should review it. After making revisions as required, turn it over to production. Your editor will then copyedit the manuscript (more on this later), and the editor may review any important or technically questionable changes with the author. Then the edited draft is sent for composition and the art sketches go to an artist to be drawn. The editor reviews the galleys and illustrations, and illustrations and text are combined into page masters. The editor makes a final check of the entire package, and turns it over to be printed. After it is printed, the editor will check it again.

When computers and word processors enter the picture, the process is compressed and accelerated. Suppose you start with on-line copy that has already been reviewed by peers and appropriately revised, and you send it (through the phone

Figure 13.2 Flow Chart for the Editorial Process

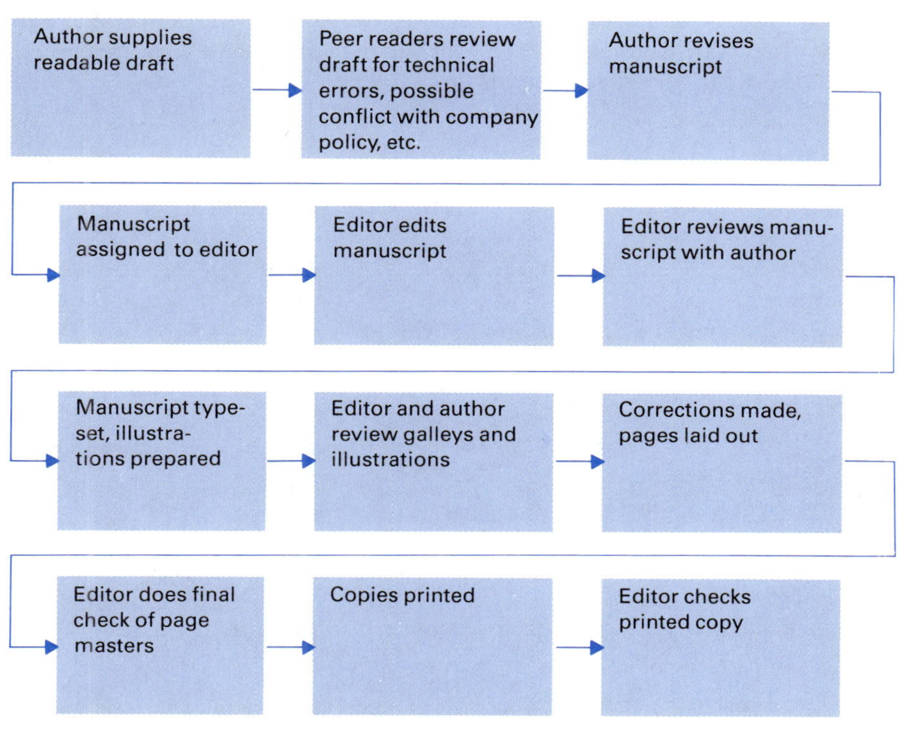

lines, computer to computer) to a publisher who uses computers for typesetting. Your editor will either edit a paper copy of your manuscript or edit it on-line. Once the editor's changes have been made and you have been consulted about any major changes, the copy is marked (on-line) for phototypesetting. The computer file is incorporated with the visuals (which are also computer-generated), and the phototypesetter produces camera-ready copy (page masters), which go directly to the printer.

No matter which variation of the editing process your publisher uses, two important elements remain the same. Your editor will do essentially the same things, and you can help your editor in essentially the same ways. Your editor's job (very much simplified) can be divided into four stages, which are discussed in Sections 4.1 to 4.4.

4.1 Sizing Up the Manuscript

The first thing any good editor does is size up the manuscript. That means reading the whole thing before ever starting to mark it. At this level the editor looks for the manuscript's completeness (Are important parts or visuals, etc., missing?) and overall structure. Does the large-scale arrangement of parts make sense, or should the order of the sections be rearranged? It is the editor's particular function to pay attention to the element of *design* described earlier in the introduction to Part IV. Only when your editor has a "feel" for the manuscript and what it is saying will he or she actually begin to mark it up.

4.2 Copyediting

The functions listed in Box 13.2 are performed by a professional copyeditor.

Box 13.2 Functions of a Professional Copyeditor

- Mark manuscript page numbers.
- Monitor project costs.
- Monitor schedule.
- Edit art sketches to conform to manuscript and design.
- Stay in contact with authors.
- Review manuscript changes with author where necessary.
- Ensure all that manuscript parts are present (cover, title page, etc.).
- Check the table of contents, references, etc.
- Ensure that the author's statements in the report do not contradict company policy or reflect unfavorably on the firm.
- Ensure that all sequences (numbered lists, etc.) are complete and in proper order.
- Check spelling.
- Check subject/verb agreement.
- Check completeness of sentences.
- Ensure that there are no accidental omissions.
- Ensure that figures are of appropriate quality and size.
- Mark mathematics for typesetting.
- Indicate margins, indentions, etc.
- Indicate appropriate type styles (italics, boldface, etc.).
- Indicate form and position of headings.
- Check capitalization, spelling, word compounding, proper use of abbreviations, numbers, bibliographic reference style, grammar, syntax, punctuation, usage, conciseness, and appropriateness of style and tone.
- Code all of the manuscript's parts that are not straight text (lists, headings, formulas, etc.) so that the compositor will know how to set them.

4.3 Author Review

If your editor has made any significant changes in your report, you will be given the opportunity to review them. Do not expect to be part of a line-by-line review. You will only be expected to review the specific sections your editor questions you about. The rest of the report should have been right before you sent it in.

4.4 Publications Production

When you and the editor have agreed on the final version of the manuscript, it goes into publications production. During publications production the pages of text and the visuals are combined into final page proof, it is proofread one last time, and the whole package is sent to the printer.

Perhaps the most important thing you can do to help your editor is to have the manuscript complete and correct in neatly typed form before turning it over. Beyond that, there are a number of things you should *not* expect, which are listed in Box 13.3.

If you provide clean copy that is technically accurate, and if you don't expect the things in the list in Box 13.3, your editor will work for you with a high degree of professionalism to make your report the best possible publication.

5. The Automated Office

If you were to analyze the operation of any office and pare that analysis down to its essentials, you would almost always find that the office's primary purpose is to process information. Because computer technology so readily adapts to the processing of information, and because today's professional world produces so much information to be processed, computers have rapidly entered professional

Box 13.3 What *Not* to Expect of an Editor

Do NOT expect your editor to:

- research references.
- write any of the report.
- search for missing items.
- provide examples of other publications to help you decide how yours should be done.
- edit handwritten copy.
- handle multiple versions of a manuscript or incorporate more than one series of author changes into the manuscript.
- edit for technical content.
- deal with more than one author.

life. An office that uses computers fully is called an automated office. Typically, these functions are handled by computer:

Word processing

Mailing list management

Graphics

Spreadsheet budgeting and statistical modeling

Printing

Internal and external mail and document transfer

Depending on the kind of company, any number of other functions—from employees' schedules to ordering of parts—may be handled by computers as well.

5.1 What It Is

When 701 managers and professionals were polled about how they would spend $10,000 given them by their companies to improve their productivity at work, 82 percent said they would spend additional money on automation: 41 percent said they would use the money to buy a computer.* Most people who have made the transition to word processing estimate that it doubles or triples their productivity, and higher estimates are not uncommon. In terms of the functions listed above, just what is it that the automated office does?

5.1.1 **Word Processing.** Nobody uses a typewriter; rather than typing, operators "key" or "keyboard," and they expend considerable effort to ensure that nothing is ever "keyed" more than once. After the original of a document has been entered into an electronic memory, it may be manipulated, altered, cut up, scavenged, and used in multiple different ways, but it is never to be re-keyboarded. "Capture the original keystrokes" is the motto here. In the past, workers often retyped material, sometimes several times; but they now have compatible computers on their desks at work and at home, so that those original keystrokes are captured. Dictation goes straight from one electronic storage medium (the dictaphone or mini-recorder), through the secretary's ears, and into another electronic storage medium (the computer file).

5.1.2 **Mailing List Management.** All mailing lists are stored electronically. They may well all be part of one large database, accessed differently through several preset subroutines. That is, from that one large database, any particular list is derived on demand—accounts past due, holiday greeting cards, contacts in Seattle, and so on. Keeping the list in one database assures instant updating of *everyone's* version of the address of the Mexico City office once any one person makes a change. (Of course, backup files are kept in case of error, and access to database—required to change anything on it—may be restricted.)

**Modern Office Technology*, Feb. 1985.

5.1.3 **Graphics.** Most of the graphics for the company's reports—all but the very top-of-the-line Class A reports—are done on computers in the office. One support job in large offices is typically dedicated to this, or one secretary may carry knowledge of computer graphics as a special part of his or her resumé. Not only are report graphics done in the office, but overhead transparencies and photographic slides are generated directly from the same computer files. Making the production of sophisticated graphics—including the use of color—more accessible to laymen is one of the hottest fronts in the computer revolution.

5.1.4 **Spreadsheet Budgeting and Statistical Modeling.** There are customized computer software packages available today for nearly any kind of office function, from complex budget processes to ordering food for the cafeteria. There is no logical limitation to the ways in which computers can be used to make *complex* but routine decisions simple—and then print out all the relevant information in appropriate tabular form.

5.1.5 **Printing.** Most work stations in the automated office have their own printers—perhaps an inexpensive dot-matrix printer for internal documents and working drafts but, increasingly a laser printer capable of fast, letter-quality work and the most sophisticated graphics.

5.1.6 **Internal and External Mail and Document Transfer.** Because all of the computers in the office are linked ("networked"), anything in one computer can be transferred to any other computer in the office. If workers want to get the boss's attention as soon as he or she comes to work in the morning, they leave an electronic mail message. When the boss comes in and turns on his or her computer, the message "You have new mail" appears. Similarly, documents and data files can be transferred via the phone lines all over the country electronically, from one computer to another.

These are only a few of the ways automation is revolutionizing the modern office. The next two sections address how these functions affect writers.

5.2 How It Can Work

A typical sequence of steps in writing a report using computers could be:

1. Work out the rough outline of the report on your computer at home with the help of a piece of customized software that facilitates brainstorming, idea generation, and outlining.
2. When you're ready to start writing, transfer that outline directly into the word processing software you use both at work and at home. Keyboard the first draft as fast as your fingers and brain can move; don't worry about mistakes or typos. (You can fix these minor problems later on; right now you're just working to get the raw material down on paper.)

3. At work, print out that file and mark the paper copy for the necessary corrections.
4. Leave the marked hard copy with the secretary, who will make the necessary changes in the electronic version.
5. When the report draft is ready, integrate with it the visuals you and your office's computer-graphics specialist have worked up.
6. After taking another look at a hard copy, make a few more changes in tone and substance, then use the phone lines to send the report—still labeled "draft"—to your boss, who is visiting the Cleveland office.
7. Once your boss approves it, use the office's laser printer to prepare the finished copy.

Using typists, artists, and the mail, this sequence of steps could have taken two weeks or more. Using computers, it can be done in two or three days.

5.3 What Its Problems Are

The process described in Section 5.2 may sound too good to be true and sometimes it is! Too often, the computer hardware and software on different desks—even in the same office, much less at work and at home—are not *compatible*, so that work done on one cannot be used or altered on another. Frequently the personnel involved, both managerial and support staff, lack the necessary training to get the most out of the computer equipment available, much less deal with occasional problems that may arise. (For example, "Just how do we get the visuals off of this graphics software integrated into the word-processing system that contains the electronic version of this report?" Or, "I can't get this computer to communicate with the Cleveland office; is the problem in the modem, my computer, my software, this file, their modem, their computer, their software, or the phone lines?") Not only is the initial cost of such equipment fairly high, but there are sizable maintenance and upgrade costs to bear as well. Despite these problems, the automated office is not just the wave of the future; in most places in the United States, it is here today. As Section 5.2 showed, it can make a writer's life much more productive, by eliminating duplication of effort and speeding up the entire writing process.

6. Coming to Grips with Accountability

Writing you do in college nearly always has about it an air of unreality, a feeling that "this is just an exercise and hence not *real*," which students find both hard to live *with* and hard to live *without*. As much as students and writing teachers dislike this quality of make-believe that haunts much classroom writing, many students find that when their writing really *does* matter, when they have to write job applications, personal statements on medical- or law-school applications, or their first on-the-job reports, they are paralyzed by the realization (or the subconscious recognition) that suddenly their writing *matters*. This quality of work-related writing is what is called here *accountability*. The following pointers will help you to deal with the accountability of on-the-job writing:

1. *Develop confidence in your ability to write effectively* by remembering the lessons presented in this text: If you know your subject matter and adapt it to your audience in light of their particular purposes, you can write effectively. Review the questions for audience analysis and the pointers for audience adaptation presented in Chapter 1, Section 8.

2. Remember that *you don't need to make your first draft of any document perfect.* As Chapter 2 explained, you should plan to write at least two (and quite possibly more) drafts of anything as important as a professional report (or a job application). In the first draft all you need to do is try to get the content into place. Don't worry about stylistic clarity, grammatical correctness, or readability until you get the content right.

3. *Recognize the source of the feeling that makes your writing seem difficult.* The fear comes from your own desire to do well, to succeed professionally. By a conscious act of your will, you can direct the energy you are wasting in being afraid into helping you do well. If you find yourself sitting at your desk paralyzed by fear and frustration, unable to get started, break out of your psychological inertia by putting words on paper. Just start writing without regard for whether it's good or not, and you may find that once you take the pressure off yourself, the writing process will proceed smoothly.

If you know your technical material, the content of whatever it is you're trying to write, you can put it down on paper. Let your concerns about grammar, spelling, and correctness go until later drafts. Don't try to do everything at the same time.

EXERCISES

1. Find a brief piece of writing—either one of your own or one from a textbook or professional journal—that you think fits the criteria established here for catalogical writing. Revise it into analytical writing. Turn both versions in to your instructor.
2. Go to a large administrative office of your university—the Liberal Arts College office, the President's office, the Placement Service, or the Testing Center, for example—and ask to be allowed to study a variety of the brochures, pamphlets, and booklets available there. Select three to five of them that seem to best exemplify a variety of different levels of documents, and write a brief report for your instructor describing and analyzing them in terms of those levels. (This assignment can also be done with corporate publications if you have access to them.) Spell out the level of "gloss," the audience, the use of color, and whatever other qualities clue you in to the report's level.
3. Divide your class into groups of three to five students, all with identical (or similar) majors. Each group is to produce a report of a length specified by your instructor entitled "Careers in (fill in your major)." The audience for the report should be college sophomores considering choosing that major.

Apportion the roles of the various people in the group as you think will work best. Each member of the group should keep very careful records of exactly what contribution *each* member makes. After the group report is submitted, each member should submit his or her own brief (one- or two-page) memo describing the way the group worked together.

4. Find a professional person who has to write as part of his or her job. Interview that person to find out how group writing is handled in that person's company and to what extent that company's writing is automated. Write a brief report to your instructor explaining what you have learned.
5. (This may be done as a class project, or as individual projects visiting various sites.) By prearrangement with the appropriate officials, visit an editorial office, either on or off campus, where you can see the process of editing actually taking place. Follow that with a visit to a printing shop, perhaps where your student newspaper is printed, or wherever the material coming out of the editorial office you visited is printed. After touring the facilities, work individually or in groups to write this report: "How Computer Technology is Changing the World of Editing and Printing." The audience should be laymen—the general public.
6. Recently there has been significant research done on measuring the dollar value of printed information of various types. That is, researchers are now able to come up with relatively concrete answers to questions such as "How much is this particular report worth to our company?" Results of this research are usually printed in important journals in the fields of Information Science (such as the journals produced by the American Society for Information Science) and Technical Communication (such as *Technical Communication* and the *Journal of Technical Writing and Communication*). With help from your instructor and librarians, find an article that discusses some feature of the dollar value of information. Write a brief report detailing what you learn from the article, being sure to discuss its significance for you as a writer. The audience should be your classmates.
7. Between the time the manuscript for this book was completed (December 1985) and the time you read this book, there will have been advances in office automation not even hinted at in this chapter. Write a brief report, for laymen, on recent advances in office automation. Here are some journals you might look in for information:

   Office Administration and Automation

   Online

   PC Week

   Office Automation

   Modern Office Procedures

   The Office

   Personal Computing

   Management Today

14

Making Recommendations

More than any other rhetorical characteristic, weak presentation of recommendations flaws major reports. If no one acts on your recommendation, what good is it to spend six weeks, six months, or a year collecting data and coming to an accurate understanding of a problem? Whether your recommendation is one line, one paragraph, or one chapter in length, and whether it comes in a memo, a letter, or a report, it is usually the most important part of the document. The recommendation will only be as effective as the extent to which your audience puts their faith in it and acts on it. This chapter describes how to present recommendations clearly and persuasively.

This chapter discusses two different ways to structure recommendations: writer-based, and reader-based. It then presents in detail two main kinds of internal organization for recommendations: argumentation and comparison.

1. Patterns for Recommendations

There are two goals you want your recommendations to reach:

- The recommendation is *right* (whatever you are recommending will work).
- The necessary people *endorse* it, *support* it, and *put it into action.*

Of course you will have to pay the necessary attention to ensuring that your recommendation is right. But you also want to ensure that the necessary people endorse your recommendation, support it, and put it into action. Fulfilling this second goal can require some considerable thought on your part as a writer. The simplest pattern for a recommendation to follow is shown in Box 14.1.

All of the other patterns presented here are variations on that one. Like Problem/Solution, several ways of presenting recommendations just seem to make sense to writers. Other methods are less intuitively obvious to writers, but may actually be more persuasive because they appeal more directly to readers. The following two sections describe these two kinds of patterns—writer-based and reader-based—in detail.

1.1 Writer-Based Patterns

Box 14.2 presents what may be, after the simple problem/solution pattern, the most popular writer-based pattern.

Box 14.1 The Simple Problem/Solution Pattern for Recommendation Reports

> Problem: Why do something?
> ("Because Town Lake is polluted, property values are declining. . . . ")
> Solution: What to do?
> ("Continuing pollution of the lake needs to be stopped. This can by done by. . . ")

Box 14.2 A Popular Writer-Based Recommendation Pattern

What is the problem?
("Town Lake is polluted.")

Why is it important to solve it?
("Property values along the lake are declining; new investment along the lake is nonexistent.")

What caused the problem?
("Industrial waste and urban runoff, plus sewage spillover during heavy rains, have caused. . . .")

What are the alternative solutions, in rank-order?
("We have five options: . . . .")

What is the top-ranked alternative, in detail, and how can it be implemented?
("A Water Quality District should be established with the power to. . . .")

This pattern has the strength of being methodical and predictable; each phase of the process seems to be the next logical step. The pattern's disadvantage is that the actual recommendation does not come until the very end of the document. An anxious or impatient reader may want to find out exactly what needs to be done earlier than the end of the report. If you want to include data (for example, facts and figures concerning the nature of the problem, its causes, and how and why that solution will work), that data comes between the reader (who starts at the beginning) and the recommendation (placed at the end). Notice that this pattern allows the writer to present the report in exactly the same sequence as the one the problem was solved in. Exhibit 14.1 shows an example of this writer-based pattern.

Exhibit 14.1 A Writer-Based Recommendation Report

At the request of XYZ Insurance Company, we have evaluated your electrical-service entrance equipment to measure its ability to handle present and projected future loads. This report includes our analysis of your problem and our recommendations on how to solve it.

Here is our analysis of your present and future electrical-service loads:

	Connected	Demanded
Present load	4200 kVA	2207 kVA
Add new computer	86 kVA	86 kVA
Add new building	655 kVA	590 kVA
Total loading	4941 kVA	2883 kVA

As these figures show, a possible peak demand will result in overloading the utility company's 2500 kVA pad-mounted transformer. At the time your building was designed, that transformer was adequate. However, the combination of the new computer and the climate-control equipment it requires clearly means you have outgrown your electrical service.

Four methods of solving this problem were considered:

1. Installing capacitors to improve power factor and to release existing system capacity.

This solution would reduce the possible peak demand to 2550 kVA, which would still be an overload of the utility's transformer. In addition, such capacitors can often be difficult to properly maintain, and when they are switched can cause damaging voltage transients. For these reasons we do not recommend this approach.

2. Asking the utility company to install a one-point 4000 kVA service at 480 V.

The largest pad-mounted transformer your utility can supply is 2500 kVA. Therefore to handle your load would require a substation. You would be required by the utility to provide space (50' by 50'), plus the right-of-way for overhead lines, plus an expensive transition from the delivery point to your service equipment. The higher fault current available from such a substation would also require replacing many circuit breakers inside your existing building. Since this method is by far the most expensive and unsightly, we do not recommend it.

3. Asking the utility to install a new 1000 kVA pad-mounted transformer to serve only the new building.

This 1000 kVA transformer should provide adequate potential for the load growth of the new building. The cost for installing new service equipment to include trenching for underground utility conductors, pad, service switch, and entrance conductors we estimate at $12,500.00. We estimate the power billing for the new building would be $120,225.00. Added to the annual power billing for the existing building ($400,000.00), the total power billing for both buildings we estimate would be $520,225.00.

While this method would have the lowest initial cost, your existing building by itself would still be within 300 kVA of overloading the 2500 kVA transformer. That leaves you almost no potential for load growth in the existing building.

4. Asking the utility to install adjacent to the current 2500 kVA transformer a new 1500 kVA pad-mounted transformer, to divide the load between the two existing service entrances, and to totalize the metering.

Estimated cost of installing this new service equipment, including trenching for underground utility conductors, pad, new entrance conductors, and a feeder to the new building is $34,000.00. We estimate the annual power billing for the two buildings would then be $500,000.00.

We recommend this as the most desirable option for the following reasons:

(a) Although the initial cost is higher, there is a minimum annual savings of $20,000.00. This results from the energy being billed at a more favorable rate schedule the utility makes available for customers receiving such service.

(b) Splitting the service results in some load being removed from the existing substation, which would provide more flexibility for load growth in each building.

(c) With this solution the new building's service can begin immediately, without waiting for the utility to install the new transformer. By the time the peak summer load becomes possible (eight months from now), the new transformer will be in place.

(d) Should you decide in the future to add more equipment, having two separate sources of power will give you improved service flexibility. Having two separate sources of power will also mean more reliability: if one system goes down, the other can handle all but the peak loads.

For these reasons we recommend the fourth option. Should you have any questions about the information in this report, please call us. We will be happy to assist you in this construction in any way.

Another writer-based pattern often used in recommendations is shown in Box 14.3.

14.3 The Basic Three-Part Recommendation Pattern

Introduction

Purpose of the report

("This report examines the scope and significance of the pollution of Town Lake.")

Nature of the problem

("As Town Lake's water quality has declined, parts per million (ppm) of 10 major carcinogenic or otherwise harmful chemicals. . . .")

Scope (criteria) of the solution

("By the year 1995 the lake should be able to pass all standards established by. . . .")

Body

Presentation and interpretation of data

("Tests have been run. . . . As a result of the pollution problem, property values have. . . . New investment has declined to the point that. . . .")

Conclusion

Recommendations and alternatives

("A Water Quality District needs to be established and given the powers to. . . .")

This scheme again has a reassuring, right-at-first-glance appearance. It's predictable and easy to use. The disadvantage, again, is that the recommendation may seem to be buried at the end of the report. Once again the ordering of elements in this pattern of recommendation report has been determined primarily by the ordering of the writer's investigation of the subject. Exhibit 14.2 shows an example of this pattern.

1.2 Reader-Based Patterns

You may find that you need a structure that appeals more directly to your reader than the writer-based patterns. The preceding patterns reflect your need as a writer to produce a document whose structure mirrors the process by which you arrived at your recommendation more than they reflect the reader's need to learn your solution to his or her problem. When you want a structure that responds more directly to your reader's needs than the structures above, it usually means that you need a structure that *begins* with the recommendation, as shown in Box 14.4.

This structure can contain the same parts as the writer-based recommendation, but here those parts have been reordered significantly, with the reader's goals as the ordering principle. Exhibit 14.3 presents the same recommendation as Exhibit 14.1, this time following the reader-based pattern.

You can decide between the two kinds of structures by determining your reader's needs and goals. A reader who is in a hurry, or who may not be especially interested in background information and technical data, may well respond more positively to the reader-based structure than to the writer-based one. However, if you have a reader who will (1) need convincing that there *is* a problem, and (2) need to be shown in detail that your response is the *right* one, then for that reader you may well be better off using one of the writer-based patterns.

Box 14.4 Pattern for Reader-Based Reports

Recommendation: Briefly, what should be done?
("A Water Quality Board should be created. . . .")

Background: What is the nature of the problem?
("Increasing water pollution caused by . . . has led to declining property values to the extent that. . . .")

Foreground: What is the exact nature of the solution?
("Creation of a Water Quality Board will enable us to . . . and to. . . .")

Future: What methods will implement the solution?
("Three areas will be studied and, eventually, regulated by the Board: industrial pollution, urban runoff, and sewage spillover.")

Appendix: Presentation and interpretation of data.

Exhibit 14.2 Another Writer-Based Recommendation Report

This report investigates the availability of information on how to write computer user's manuals. Depending on that availability, I may request your permission to write my major report for English 4140, Advanced Technical Writing, on how to write user's manuals. Part of the report would then be my rewrite of the user's manual for the university's DEC-10.

User's manuals are currently the subject of much attention from both computer manufacturers and computer users. Manufacturers are realizing that many people who buy computers, especially microcomputers, are first-time computer users. Such people often make their decision about which computer to buy based in part on their response to the readability of the user's manual. The buyer's long-term satisfaction with the computer (and thus the manufacturer's chances for resale) also depends in part on the user's manual. Thus manufacturers are looking for people who can write readable user's manuals.

From the computer buyer's point of view, the user's manual can be the primary factor in determining which computer to buy and whether that purchase proves to be a satisfying one. Thus even people who have never seen a floppy disk before are learning to ask—and to test—whether the user's manual for the microcomputer they are considering buying is "user-friendly."

A satisfactory search for literature on this subject should not take more than eight hours in the library, should yield a clear-cut answer, and should be conducted in such a way as to be reliable as a source for deciding whether to go ahead with this topic for a term paper.

I searched the Main Library's card catalogue for books on the subject and found none. In the Main Library's periodicals, searching through three periodical indexes and going back five years, I found eight useful articles. A brief check of the Undergraduate Library's collection showed it has nothing on the subject that Main doesn't have. I worked with reference librarians in both libraries, so I'm reasonably certain these results are reliable. I also interviewed the owner of our local Computerland franchise, who said he knew of nothing devoted to the subject (but he wished there was something written about it).

Based on this search, which took approximately ten hours, I believe there is an even greater need for information on how to write good user's manuals than you and I previously believed. However I do not think there is enough published literature on the subject to make a term paper on it feasible if the paper is mainly to be a review of the literature. There simply is not enough literature to review. While I remain interested in the subject, I recommend we look for ways to modify it, perhaps by expanding the length of the DEC-10 documentation rewrite, before we proceed with our planning.

Exhibit 14.3 A Reader-Based Recommendation Report

At the request of XYZ Insurance Company, we have evaluated your electrical service entrance equipment to measure its ability to handle present and projected future loads. This report includes our analysis of your problem and our recommendations on how to solve it. The Appendix to this report discusses alternative solutions and their drawbacks.

Recommendation

We recommend that you ask the utility to install adjacent to the current 2500 kVA transformer a new 1500 kVA pad-mounted transformer, to divide the load between the two existing service entrances, and to totalize the metering.

Estimated cost of installing this new service equipment, including trenching for underground utility conductors, pad, new entrance conductors, and a feeder to the new building is $34,000.00. We estimate the annual power billing for the two buildings would then be $500,000.00.

Analysis

Here is our analysis of your present and future electrical-service loads:

	Connected	Demanded
Present load	4200 kVA	2207 kVA
Add new computer	86 kVA	86 kVA
Add new building	655 kVA	590 kVA
Total loading	4941 kVA	2883 kVA

As these figures show, a possible peak demand will result in overloading the utility company's 2500 kVA pad-mounted transformer. At the time your building was designed, that transformer was adequate. However, the combination of the new computer and the climate control equipment it requires clearly means you have outgrown your electrical service.

Explanations

Here are the reasons we recommend this course of action:

(a) Although the initial cost is higher, there is a minimum annual savings of $20,000. This results from the energy being billed at a more favorable rate schedule, which the utility makes available for customers receiving such service.

(b) Splitting the service results in some load being removed from the existing substation, which would provide more flexibility for load growth in each building.

(c) With this solution the new building's service can begin immediately, without waiting for the utility to install the new transformer. By the time the peak summer load becomes possible (eight months from now), the new transformer will be in place.

(d) Should you decide in the future to add more equipment, having two separate sources of power will give you improved service flexibility. Having two separate sources of power will also mean more reliability: if one system goes down, the other can handle all but the peak loads.

Should you have any questions about the information in this report, please call us. We will be happy to assist you in this construction in any way.

Appendix

In addition to the solution recommended above, we considered three other solutions. Each has drawbacks, as described here:

1. Installing capacitors to improve power factor and to release existing system capacity.

This solution would reduce the possible peak demand to 2550 kVA, which would still be an overload of the utility's transformer. In addition, such capacitors can often be difficult to properly maintain, and when they are switched can cause damaging voltage transients. For these reasons we do not recommend this approach.

2. Asking the utility company to install a one-point 4000 kVA service at 480 V.

The largest pad-mounted transformer your utility can supply is 2500 kVA. Therefore to handle your load would require a substation. You would be required by the utility to provide space (50' by 50'), plus the right-of-way for overhead lines, plus an expensive transition from the delivery point to your service equipment. The higher fault current available from such a substation would also require replacing many circuit breakers inside your existing building. Since this method is by far the most expensive and unsightly, we do not recommend it.

3. Asking the utility to install a new 1000 kVA pad-mounted transformer to serve only the new building.

This 1000 kVA transformer should provide adequate potential for the load growth of the new building. The cost for installing new service equipment to include trenching for underground utility conductors, pad, service switch, and entrance conductors we estimate at $12,500.00. We estimate the power billing for the new building would be $120,225.00. Added to the annual power billing for the existing building ($400,000.00), the total power billing for both buildings we estimate would be $520,225.00.

While this method would have the lowest initial cost, your existing building by itself would still be within 300 kVA of overloading the 2500 kVA transformer. That leaves you almost no potential for load growth in the existing building.

2. Processes Resulting in Recommendations

Recommendations don't just come out of nowhere; they result from particular processes, such as the problem-solving process described in Chapter 15. Those processes that result in recommendations can be divided into three kinds:

Historical Processes

Methodical Processes

Logical Processes

Each different kind of process has its own implications for the structure of any recommendation the process leads to and for the problems its approval will meet with.

2.1 Historical Processes

Sometimes the historical flow of events merely needs to be observed to lead one to a recommendation. For example, as federal regulations surrounding cigarette smoking become stricter, tobacco companies recommend actions to their stockholders based on the flow of historical events. Similarly, a growing number of state wildlife departments face the problem of acid precipitation and have to come up with recommendations to deal with it, their recommendations again springing out of a historical process. In such cases, the historical pattern needs to be made clear in the recommendation. Do not assume your reader will be as familiar with the flow of events as you are. Frequently someone's partial familiarity with the flow of events leads to one conclusion about what should be done, whereas a full familiarity with that flow of events can lead to another.

2.2 Methodical Processes

It may be that most recommendations are arrived at methodically by some process such as the problem-solving scheme described in Chapter 15. The scientific method is but one of a large number of methods designed to lead to recommendations. In some situations—such as those involving empirical tests—making the methodical process by which you arrived at your recommendation very clear and very convincing (in its apparent reliability and thoroughness) will be crucial to your recommendation's acceptance. In others, the method may be the least of the things the reader wants to know about.

2.3 Logical Processes

Some problems are "thought problems," requiring mainly an ordered set of mental operations for their solution. Einstein is said to have worked best when he worked most conceptually. Many times this kind of process leading to a recommendation poses the biggest problem for a writer. It may be very hard for you (or whoever solved the problem) to come up with a good, convincing explanation of how the problem was solved. And until that process is clear, some people will be reluctant to accept your recommendation. Section 3.1, "Argumentation Leading to Recommendation," gives specific advice on how to approach such a situation.

3. Internal Patterns of Recommendations

How do you go about making your writing as clear internally as using the structures described earlier makes it externally? How do you achieve clear recommendations, clear reasons, and clear connections? The internal patterns of recommendations can take a number of forms; two of the most common are argumentation and comparison.

3.1 Argumentation Leading to Recommendation

Suppose your company asks you to come up with a recommendation on whether they should continue to put money into a certain operation or abandon it. How would you write the report? Obviously you'd have certain facts at hand—a complete accounting of how much has been put into the project so far, how much the project is losing, and projections of its future profitability based on varying levels of new investment from your company. Based on your audience's needs, you can make a choice among the structures presented earlier. But how do you go beyond those structures in making your report's contents logical? How do you present the logic in your report persuasively?

Persuasive logic is a little different from the formalities of induction and deduction that you may have been taught in the past. To be persuasive in writing for business and industry, you need to answer three questions:

1. What do you recommend?
2. What evidence supports your recommendation?
3. What connects your recommendation to your evidence?

Rephrased in general language, these questions become applicable to any situation requiring persuasion:

- What is your claim?
- What is your evidence?
- What connects your claim with your evidence?

Figure 14.1 shows the relationship among these three parts of the persuasive logic pattern.

Suppose you want to recommend that Acme Property Management (your employer) abandon its attempts to make the renovated James Hotel profitable and recoup whatever losses they can from the project by selling the building. How do you put that argument into this pattern of persuasive logic? Here's the persuasive analysis of your argument:

Figure 14.1 A Simple Persuasive Logic The *connection* is the middle step between the *evidence* and the *claim.*

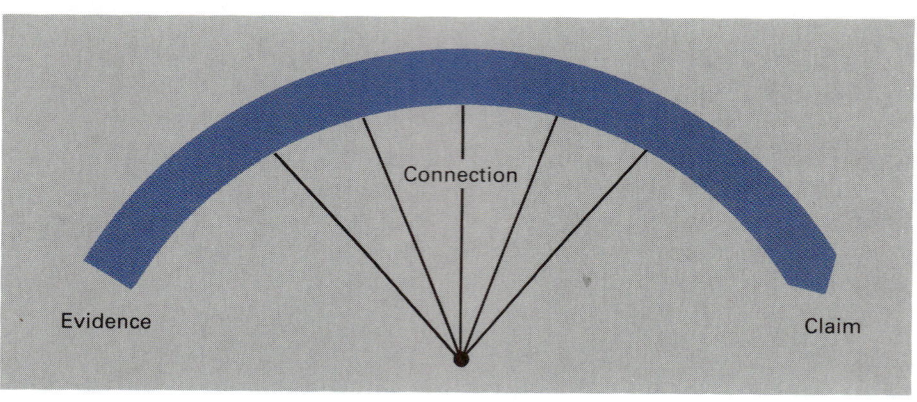

> *Claim*: We should abandon the James Hotel Project.
> *Evidence*: The cost/benefit projections show that it will cost more to operate than it brings in, and that even with a massive infusion of new capital the project may well only break even for years to come.
> *Connection*: The projections are reliable. That is, all of the figures have been checked and double-checked, and they have been worked out under a variety of different economic assumptions (strong economy, recession, and so forth).

Depending on your decision about the report's larger structure, you can organize these as Claim/Evidence/Connection (the reader-based structure) or Evidence/Connection/Claim (the writer-based structure).

The important point is to make the connection explicit. The connection explains why, how, or under what conditions the evidence supports the claim. By performing this function, the connection helps the reader bridge the gap between evidence and claim, which makes your argument more persuasive. At times your reader may simply not know that extra piece of information, or may be too tired (or uninterested) to call that information to mind.

Making the connections explicit also serves to transfer some of the burden of the recommendation from you to the facts. For example, in terms of where the responsibility for the decision lies, there is a substantial difference between stating "The project should be abandoned because the projections show the money won't work out" and stating "The project should be abandoned because the projections show the money won't work out, and these are the most reliable projections available." The second way of putting it places at least some of the responsibility on the reliability of the projections. Exhibits 14.4 through 14.7 show examples of arguments, first *without* the connection, and then—after discussion—*with* the connection.

Exhibit 14.4

FIRST ARGUMENT

Claim: We can encourage people to ride the bus more by selling multi-stop tickets (which allow people to make several stops along one line without buying new tickets).

Evidence: The increased convenience and savings our riders get from multi-stop tickets will encourage more people to ride the bus.

Discussion: Assuming that customers are attracted by convenience and savings, the argument is plausible. It would be stronger if there were some evidence offered that increased savings and convenience really do result in more people riding the bus.

FIRST ARGUMENT REVISED

Claim: We can encourage people to ride the bus more by selling multi-stop tickets.

Evidence: People want increased convenience and savings.

Connection: Our local market research shows that multi-stop tickets will provide riders with increased convenience and savings.

Exhibit 14.5

SECOND ARGUMENT

Evidence: The length of time it takes our draftsmen to produce drawings is holding back our firm's productivity.

Claim: We should begin using computer-controlled drafting.

Discussion: How will switching to computer-controlled drafting increase productivity? That is, will the computers work enough faster to justify their greater initial costs?

SECOND ARGUMENT REVISED

Evidence: The length of time it takes our draftsmen to produce drawings is holding back our firm's productivity.

Connection: Computer-controlled drafting is so much faster than manual drafting that we will be able to at least triple our productivity. This increased productivity should mean that the computers will pay for themselves in a year.

Claim: We should begin using computer-controlled drafting.

Exhibit 14.6

THIRD ARGUMENT

Claim: Chrom-Ex does not induce in any way any type of hydrogen embrittlement (H_2 molecules trapped inside a chrome coating, caused in part by hydrogen being released from the surface to be coated by an acid in the coating).

Evidence: The surface preparation is done manually.

Discussion: Very few people would be able to see the connection between this evidence and the claim in this argument. The audience's lack of knowledge of this coating process makes it necessary to state the connection explicitly: when such coatings are applied manually, acid is not used; therefore, no hydrogen is released from the surface to be trapped under the coating; therefore, no flaws in the coating occur.

THIRD ARGUMENT REVISED

Claim: Chrom-Ex does not induce in any way any type of hydrogen embrittlement (caused by acid).

Evidence: The surface preparation is done manually.

Connection: Manual preparation of the surface means no acid is used.

Exhibit 14.7

FOURTH ARGUMENT

Claim: We can use these plants successfully in interior environments only if they are properly conditioned first.

Evidence: These plants are native to tropical and subtropical regions.

Discussion: Again, the necessity for making the connection explicit comes from the audience's probable lack of knowledge. Plants that are native to tropical or subtropical regions would have to be properly conditioned (slowly acclimated) to any kind of interior environment.

FOURTH ARGUMENT REVISED

Evidence: These plants are native to tropical and subtropical regions.

Connection: Plants native to tropical or subtropical environments must be properly conditioned (slowly acclimated) to any kind of interior environment.

Claim: We can use these plants successfully in interior environments only if they are properly conditioned first.

Figure 14.2 A Fully Developed Persuasive Logic "Reservations" adds an explicit statement of the circumstances that would negate the claim, "Qualifiers" add an explicit statement of the *force* of the claim (*probably, possibly, certainly,* etc.).

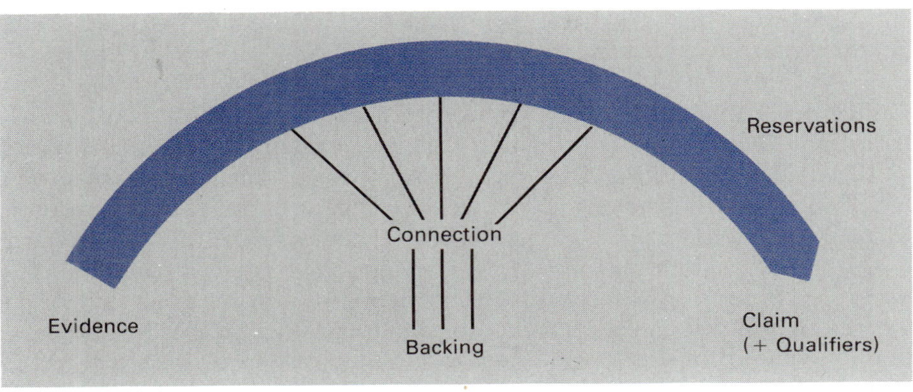

There are three other parts to this persuasive logic. The *backing* for the connection supports it in the same way that the evidence supports the claim. If someone challenges your statement of connection with "How do we know that is so?", the backing will answer that question. *Reservations* add an explicit statement of what circumstances would negate the claim. "If present economic trends continue" would be a statement of reservations. *Qualifiers* add an explicit statement of the force of the claim by bringing in such words as *probably*, *perhaps*, *certainly*, etc.). Figure 14.2 shows how these parts fit into the basic persuasive-logic model.

Adding these other parts to your recommendation continues the process begun by making the connection explicit. By further qualifying your claim, you make the argument tighter, more restricted, and less threatening.

If you will use this persuasive logic as an internal pattern, your recommendations will meet the criteria set out earlier in this chapter: they will be *clear* and *persuasive*.

3.2 Comparison Leading to Recommendation

One specialized kind of internal pattern leading to a recommendation occurs so often it merits special attention here. Over and over again, writers find themselves needing to compare two or more items and come up with a recommendation. There are two basic ways to do this: a two-part pattern and an alternating pattern.

3.2.1 **The Two-Part Pattern.** Suppose you are making a recommendation about a choice between A and B, and you want to compare them on qualities 1–10. The two-part pattern devotes one part to all of A's qualities (A:1–10), and another to all of B's qualities (B:1–10). When A and B have qualities that do not correspond (such as A:11 and B:12), those qualities usually go in a separate section.

3.2.2 The Alternating Pattern. For longer comparisons, you may want to put the comparisons side by side. The pattern then goes A:1–B:1, A:2–B:2, A:3–B:3, etc. Again, when there are characteristics that don't correspond, such as A:12 and B:13, they usually go in separate sections.

3.2.3 Guidelines for Comparisons. Comparisons are relatively easy when A and B have mostly the same kinds of qualities. As long as you can compare A on qualities 1–10 with B on qualities 1–10, the comparison is fairly straightforward, and you can often even use a chart or grid to make the comparison visual. The comparison becomes more difficult to write when A has qualities 1–5 and B has qualities 6–10. Of course, in this situation the alternating pattern is usually ruled out. But despite the necessity here for the two-part pattern, it's usually a good idea to add a part in which you do your best to compare the two head-to-head. Such situations, in which comparisons are being made on the basis of two different sets of characteristics, require special consideration on the writer's part. There are three guidelines to follow in this and any other kind of comparison leading to recommendations:

1. *List the Points of Comparison.* Before you get involved in the actual comparison, let your reader know what you're going to do: Be very explicit in the introduction about which points of comparison you will discuss. Bring up in the introduction any points your reader is likely to think of that you will *not* discuss, and explain in the body the reason for their omission. If you write a *cpo* introduction (as explained in Chapter 10), you will satisfy this criterion.

2. *Maintain a Neutral Stance.* The attitude you have toward your comparisons and eventual recommendations must be neutral. You want your reader to feel (in between the lines) and to see (in the lines themselves) that you have taken a completely fair and impartial attitude into the process of comparing and recommending. Be scientific in the attitude you show in your writing. In writing for business and industry, the most effective way to persuade is through a neutral stance. Of course, you will make your recommendation, and you will hope the reader endorses it, but the way to gain your reader's endorsement is through a nonjudgmental comparison.

The psychologist Carl Rogers (among others) has shown convincingly that when one person explicitly chooses one side of a discussion, it invites other people to take the other side. That is, as soon as I see a report entitled "Whole- Versus Term-Life Insurance: the Whole-Life Ripoff Conspiracy," I immediately lean toward the other side of the issue. If you and I are discussing A versus B, and you open by a strongly biased statement in A's favor, you force me psychologically toward the other side of the issue. The writer of the report who wants to recommend term-life insurance to me would be far better off titling the report "Whole- Versus Term-Life Insurance: A Comparison and Recommendation." Otherwise I suspect the writer has prejudged the issue. Put the facts in your report and let *them* do the arguing for you.

In the "Recommendation" section of your report, you can make the results of the comparison clear; but again, be neutral—a judge, not an advocate. That means you present *the* recommendation, not *my* recommendation; demonstrate that it grows clearly out of the evidence, not out of your feelings.

3. *Make Your Comparison Complete*. It's always tempting to use only the points of comparison that will help you make the recommendation you want to make. But any points you fail to include invite your reader to suspect your work is incomplete, and your recommendation thus may not be fully persuasive. Certainly you can subdivide your "comparison" section into two large groups—one the areas in which there are significant differences, and the other the areas in which no important differences exist. You can often put that second section in an appendix so it won't get in a hurried reader's way. But one way or another you need to account for all the points a complete comparison requires. At the least, if there are obvious points of comparison that you choose not to discuss, explain that fact and the reasons for it in your introduction.

4. Checklist for Effective Recommendations

For your recommendation to be effective, it needs to satisfy at least these three criteria:

- The recommendation *itself* must be clear. *What* do you think needs to be done?
- The reasons *behind* the recommendation must be clear. *Why* do you think this needs to be done?
- The connections *between* the recommendations and the reasons must be clear. What *connects* your reasons to your recommendation?

4.1 Clear Recommendations

Be very explicit about exactly what needs to be done. Do not hesitate to make full and frequent use of charts and other kinds of visuals to spell out your plans. Be very clear with your audience about whether you've come up with a general solution, with details to be worked out later, or you've come up with a very specific, itemized plan of action. If the latter is the case, review Chapter 11 on process descriptions, because part of your recommendation will need that kind of specificity.

4.2 Clear Reasons

You also need to be very clear about the criteria used in choosing this solution: is it the most feasible, the most exciting, the best if cost is no consideration, the most economical, or what? State clearly and explicitly the reasons *behind* your recommendation. Often those reasons will be grounded in history, in your problem-solving method, or in logic, and can be explained in exactly those terms. But the persuasive reasons behind a recommendation may not always be directly or most clearly rooted in *how* the recommendation itself was discovered. Sometimes the most persuasive reason you can offer in support of your recommendation lies not in its past but in its future, not so much in the fact that it was arrived at in a systematic and acceptable way but in the fact that it will *work*. Because you wind up justifying your prediction by explaining in depth how it will work, your prediction really can be persuasive (if it is clear and detailed). It also can seriously endanger your career if your prediction is wrong. For that reason, it's often wise to carefully qualify your prediction ("if present trends continue") and to base it squarely on explicit reasoning. That is, don't just answer the question "How will it work?" Also answer "How do you *know* it will work this way?"

4.3 Clear Connections

It's good to make your recommendation and its reasons clear, but for your recommendation to be fully persuasive, you need to carefully and explicitly connect your reasons to your recommendations. Suppose your recommendation is to centralize all of your firm's purchasing in one department, rather than to continue to allow each separate unit to do its own purchasing. The reasons may be that the current scheme's costs have risen astronomically in the last two years, and you suspect waste, pilferage, and duplication of orders are to blame. To be persuasive, make the connections clear. *How* will centralizing the purchasing functions solve those problems?

Exhibit 14.8 A Sample Recommendation Report

ENERGY CONSERVATION OPPORTUNITIES AT BUILDING TWELVE

Significant opportunities for energy savings exist in Building 12, a 22,680-square foot quonset-hut-type structure with seven air conditioning systems and eleven exhaust air systems. We recommend modifying the three largest systems (AC 1, 2, and 4) to provide night setback controls. This will save $13,028 yearly, with a total payback period of 1.7 years.

Background

Acme Engineering uses Building 12 as a metallurgical and quality-assurance laboratory. To control hazardous contaminants, the work performed in this building requires continuous operation of selected exhaust systems within the building. Providing make-up air to the exhaust air systems requires the continuous operation of the building's heating and cooling equipment. Reheating system fan discharge air accomplishes temperature control of multiple zones served by the air handling system.

The existing make-up air systems are sectionalized, central-station types located in the attic. AC 1 and 4 are equipped with zone steam reheat and are located at the eastern and western extremes of the building. AC 2 is a single-zone system serving the central area of the building. AC 4 handles 100% outside air. AC 1 and 2 mix 58% and 47% outside air by design, respectively, with system return air. All systems are fitted with manually operated outside and return air dampers. The fan discharge temperature is manually reset as the need arises to satisfy building comfort level and is controlled independently of zone reheat demands. The nominal air and tons of refrigeration for systems AC 1, 2, and 4 are 6000 cfm with 28 tons, 10000 cfm with 42 tons, and 3000 cfm with 20 tons, respectively.

Recommendation

By modifying the three largest systems (AC 1, 2, and 4) to provide night setback control, make-up air systems will cycle in response to dedicated night space thermostats. The thermostats should be set seasonally at a moderate temperature, such as 60° F in the winter. This will minimize the operating time and capacity level of these heating and cooling systems. Since at least one of the three systems will probably be operating at any given moment, the possibility of a total absence of make-up air for sustained periods is low.

The major control elements for the proposed night setback mode for each system are electric space thermostats, automatic outside air control dampers, electric-pneumatic relays, or (as in the case of AC 1) a two-position steam control valve to isolate steam reheat. All these space thermostats are programmed by associated time clocks. Steam piping to C must be modified to sub-min service to the central heating coils when the zone reheat is isolated. We recommend that Acme Engineering modify each system as specified here, based on the following conceptual estimates of in-place costs and energy savings:

System	Installation Cost	Energy Cost Saving Per Year	Discounted Payback in Years
AC 1	$9600	$5556	1.5
AC 2	$7000	$3730	1.6
AC 4	$7600	$3742	1.7

Appendix

[The appendix explains how the costs and other data were figured. It consists of about one page of figures, and is not reproduced here.]

EXERCISES

1. Choose a frequently discussed campus problem (parking, the price of athletic tickets, the rising costs of attending college, etc.) and write a recommendation report suggesting a solution to the problem. Write two versions of the report—one in a reader-based pattern, and one in a writer-based pattern. Each report should be about 300 words long. The audience should be the Provost, Chancellor, or President of your campus.
2. Choose a research-oriented journal in your field of study and examine the structures of articles in two or three issues. Can you make generalizations about those structures, especially in terms of their being writer-based or reader-based? Write a recommendation report in which you compile your findings and recommend improvements in the structures that are frequently used in the articles you look at. Make the structure of your report reader-based. The audience should be the people who write articles for those journals, especially entry-level professionals in your field.
3. Assume you work for Smokey's Pharmacy, which runs a very busy delivery service in the Cedar Springs suburb. One of your first jobs as a new Assistant Manager is to recommend to your boss what kind of car to buy for the new fleet of delivery cars. Wanting to make a good decision, you're using as your primary information source the issue of *Consumer Reports* (available at most libraries) that each year compares the new cars. You need to write a 300-word report containing your recommendation. The criteria you want to use are economy, reliability, and durability. Other information you might need: The Cedar Springs suburb is mostly without hills, and the cars need to be air-conditioned. If you want to use other information about the cars you choose to consider, be sure to be able to defend the information's reliability if your instructor questions it.
4. Investigate the career opportunities that will be available to you when you graduate. Based on the results of that investigation, write a report recommending that students follow:
   a. your course of study if they want good jobs upon graduation
   b. a modified variation of your course of study if they want the best chances for jobs
   c. some totally different course of study

   The report can be either reader- or writer-based, depending on what you think is best. The audience for the report should be other students who are in the process of selecting majors.

15

Solving Problems

The most troublesome writing tasks involve one-of-a-kind situations: once in a while you will find yourself writing about a problem that is difficult not just to *solve*, but even to *define*. For this reason, one of the fundamental skills that any writer in business and industry needs in order to be effective is the ability to solve problems. As it is used here, "problem solving" does not refer to a concrete element of writing (in the sense that introductions, conclusions, definitions, descriptions, and process explanations are concrete elements of a piece of writing). Rather, "problem solving" here means a *process* we go through when we write; it's a process that is part of writing, just as the process of sensing when a reader will need more information is a part of writing. Problem solving, like definitions and process descriptions, can appear in any of the types of reports described in Chapters 17–20. This chapter discusses how to do the kind of problem solving that typically goes on when a professional person is doing technical writing; it gives you an inside look at how people create solutions on paper for hard-to-define problems.

Examples of *classroom* problems are: design a particular robot arm end so that the robot can change its own "hands"; analyze an airline's last few years of financial ratios to see whether forecasting its bankruptcy should have been possible; derive a formula to determine limit slope for various shapes of concrete drainage channels; or determine whether radial tires make a big enough energy saving in agricultural use to justify their initially greater expense.

Examples of *professional* problems are: design your company's exhibit for a trade fair; reduce your unit's operating costs by 15 percent without lowering production quality or quantity; explain how your city can successfully operate a mass-transit system with insufficient funds and aging equipment; research how to save energy costs in the operation of a particular building; determine why a particular model of fan brings complaints from so many people who use it (and suggest how to improve its design). When you face assignments like these, you need to go through the steps listed here. The basic procedure for analyzing problems has four steps:

1. Exploring the Problem
2. Finding a Rich Array of Solutions
3. Testing the Best Solutions
4. Making Your Choice

Note that every professional field has its own particular approaches to solving problems. That approach may range from carefully conceived and controlled laboratory experimentation, to computer modeling, to regression analysis, to philosophical inquiry. This chapter is not intended to replace the education your professors in your own field are giving you in problem solving, but rather to add some techniques to those they cover. By demonstrating how to incorporate these techniques into report writing in general, this chapter will help you learn how to work the techniques characteristic of your own field into your reports more effectively.

Box 15.1 Steps in Exploring Any Problem

1. *Define the problem:* What is the conflict or key issue?
2. *Place the problem in a larger context:* Why is it a problem?
3. *Make your definition of the problem concrete and operational:* What specific goals need to be reached?
4. *Assign priorities to your goals:* Which come first in terms of their importance? Which come first in terms of when they must be solved?
5. *Make sure you are aware of all the facets of your problem:* Are there any important features of it that you've failed to consider?

1. Exploring the Problem

Any experienced problem solver will tell you that it's critical not to get locked into thinking in depth about particular solutions before you have made sure that you fully understand the problem. That is, the more you know about the *inside* of the problem—its nature, depth, and complexity—and about the *outside* of the problem—its context, background, and limits—the better you will be able to come up with a good solution. Thus your goal should be to try to understand the problem *before* you let your mind fasten on any one solution. The five steps in exploring any problem thoroughly are listed in Box 15.1.

1.1 Define the Problem: What Is the Conflict or Key Issue?

The first priority is to gather facts. For example, if people are involved, who did what, where, when, how, why, and to whom? Focus on the problem's internal characteristics, and dig into the problem as deeply as you can. Figure 15.1 illustrates this stage.

Figure 15.1 Define the Problem Discover as much information about it as you can.

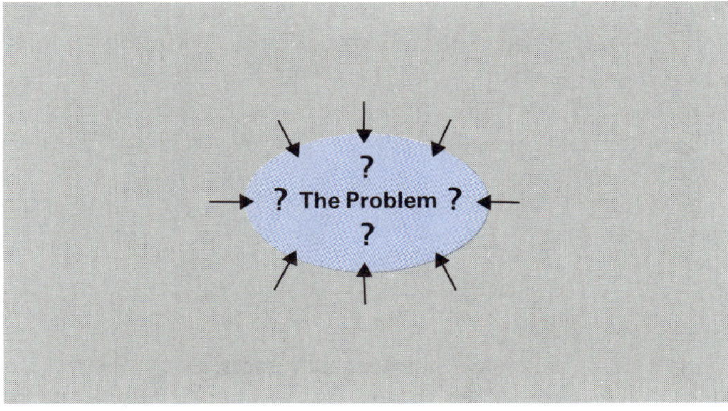

Figure 15.2 Place the Problem in a Larger Context Ask questions, questions, and more questions.

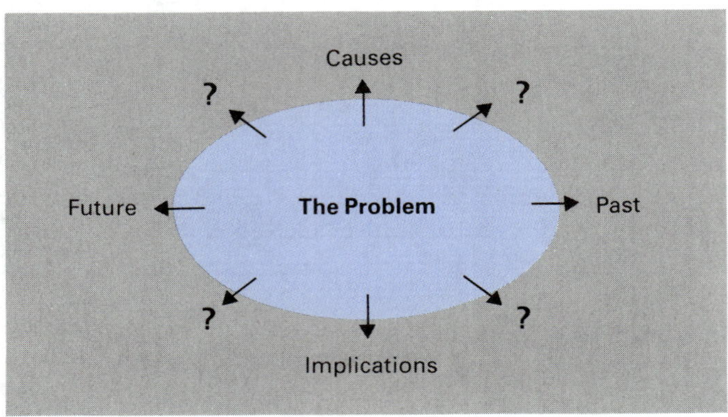

1.2 Place the Problem in a Larger Context: Why Is It a Problem?

In the second stage, work around the edges of the problem, collect background and peripheral information on it, and try to fit the problem into perspective. At this stage it's often useful to talk with other people who may view the problem differently, know more about it, or feel differently about it than you do. Ask questions, questions, and more questions. Figure 15.2 illustrates this stage.

1.3 Make Your Definition More Concrete: What Specific Goals Need to Be Reached?

By this point you should have a clear understanding of the problem. Now you need to envision exactly what the desired state of affairs would be. You're not searching for what the problem's *solution* will look like, but what the problem *area* will look like when it's solved. Figures 15.3 and 15.4 show these two steps.

Making your definition of the problem more concrete and determining what goals need to be reached are especially important. Until you have a really clear idea of exactly what you want, it will be difficult to be satisfied with what you get, or even to know when you've found the best answer. Observe how each of the vague problem statements in Exhibit 15.1 is revised to make it more accurate.

1.4 Assign Priorities to Your Goals: Which Come First in Terms of Their Importance? Which Come First in Terms of When They Must Be Solved?

Often your larger goal will have several smaller parts; one goal may be composed of any number of subgoals. When that is the case, rank the several goals in order of their priority. You can do that two ways—by urgency or by importance. For

Figure 15.3 Make Your Goal Concrete Visualize exactly what the desired state of affairs is. (Adapted from Henry Boettinger, *Moving Mountains.* Reproduced by permission.)

Exhibit 15.1 Clarifying Vaguely Conceptualized Problems

General Problem: How can we solve the campus parking problem?
Concrete Goal: How can we ensure that students and faculty have easy access to campus buildings?

General Problem: How can we improve the marketing of cattle?
Concrete Goal: Will telemarketing improve the marketing of cattle by bringing buyer and seller closer together?

General Problem: What will we do when the federal government reduces the funds they pay our state for highway construction?
Concrete Goal: How can we fund highway construction on the state level?

General Problem: How do incoming industries affect a town's economy?
Concrete Goal: Given a specified town, how will a specified industry affect that town's unemployment rate?

General Problem: What's wrong with the undergraduate biochemistry major?
Concrete Goal: What employment opportunities are there for a person with a B.S. in biochemistry?

Figure 15.4 Visualize the Desired Result Imagine that all you know is that you need to tie the line in **A** into an "eye splice." Without a picture of some sort of what the problem territory will look like after the problem is solved, you simply cannot go on. With some sort of visualization, you can begin to figure our how to get from **A** to **B**. Until you have a very clear idea of what you want, it's hard to know what direction to go. (Adapted from *The Marlinspike Sailor*)

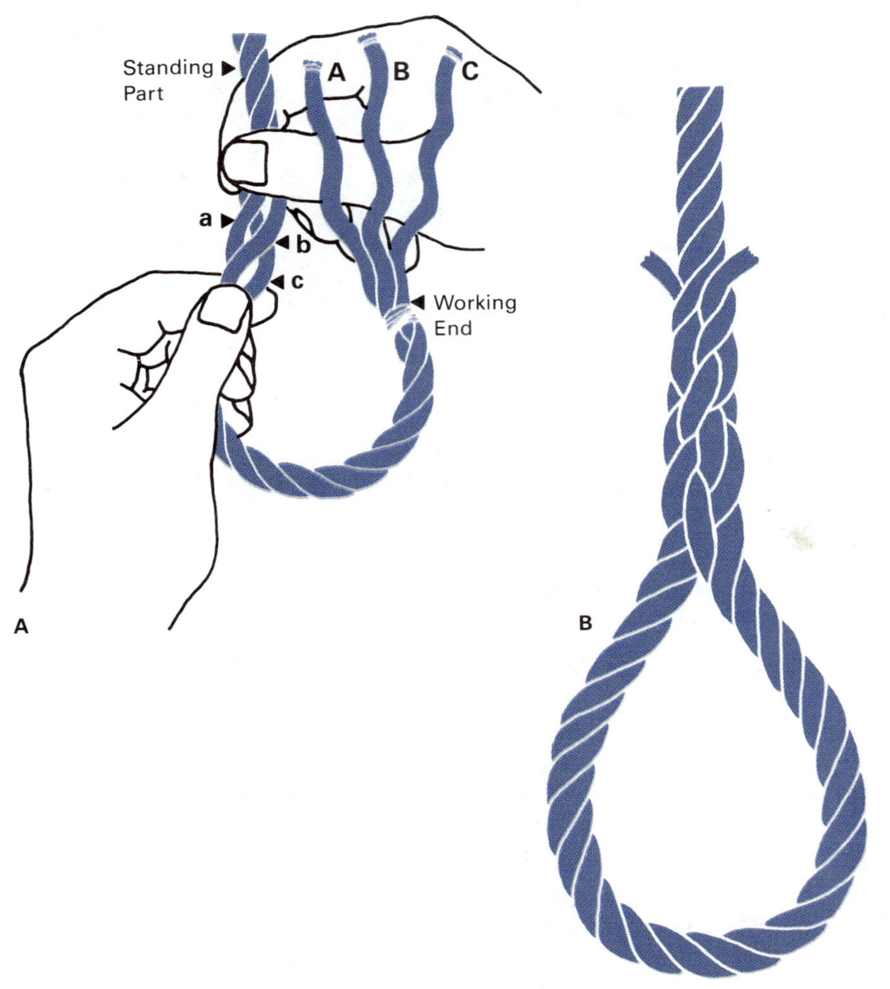

Figure and text adapted from *The Marlinspike Sailor* by Hervey Garrett Smith, *Rudder* Magazine, 1952. Reprinted with permission of Baker-Glazen Publications, Inc.

instance, if you are trying to solve the campus parking problem, you may have the following concrete goals:

- Students and faculty need easy access to classes.
- Parking should be inexpensive.
- The plan should be feasible.
- Delivery, repair, and emergency vehicles need access.
- The parking scheme should work in all weather conditions.
- The parking scheme should be reasonably noise free.
- The parking scheme should get people to and from their cars safely at night.

The way you order these goals—which is most important, next most, next most, etc.—will control the way you solve the problem. Once you have formulated a detailed and ordered list of goals, you may find you are well on your way to solving your problem.

If you organize the goals in terms of which one is most important in an absolute sense, you might choose "Students and faculty need easy access to classes" as the first point to tackle. That would lead your problem-solving process in a very different direction than an ordering of goals based on which one needs to be solved *first*. For example, if you are working in a situation in which there have been recent night-time muggings of people going to and from their cars, you may be pressured to come up with a quick response to "The parking scheme should allow people to get to and from their cars safely at night," and that would lead your problem-solving procedure in a very different direction.

1.5 Make Sure You Are Aware of All the Facets of the Problem: Are There Any Important Features of It That You've Failed to Consider?

Listing the goals will often also mean that you are at least indirectly listing the various facets of the problem, but many times making a separate, deliberate list will help you. Here is a partial list of several facets of the campus parking problem:

- Dorm lots are overflowing.
- Commuters have no parking spaces.
- Faculty and staff cars crowd the campus.
- Exhaust fumes are increasing air pollution.
- Traffic noise is increasing.
- Safety for pedestrians and bicyclers is questionable.
- In bad weather campus traffic is a hopeless snarl.
- People waste too much fuel getting to class.

Notice that a new element, fuel waste, has appeared in the list. If that is to be a part of the problem, then energy efficiency must be added to the ranked list of goals. This is an example of how stopping to consider all of the facets of your problem will help you deal with it more effectively. Another way that identifying the parts of your problem can help solve it is the process called reduction. You may find that only one part of the problem really must be solved. Or you may find that if you solve one crucial part of the problem, solutions to other parts come much more easily. In this way, reducing the problem to its component parts can help you solve it.

While you are exploring your problem, it is important not to get prematurely locked into a solution. Each of us feels the temptation to seize the first solution that comes up, or at least to filter all subsequent exploration through that solution. But to analyze the problem thoroughly and accurately, do not think about solutions until you have completed the exploration phase. Certainly you should jot down possible solutions as they occur to you, but then you should put them out of your mind until you finish fully exploring the problem.

2. Finding a Rich Array of Solutions

Just as you should explore all sides of the problem, so also should you examine a variety of solutions. Just as you should not allow your first *understanding* of the problem to be your *only* understanding of the problem, so also should you not allow the first *solution* that comes into your mind become the only solution that you consider.

Every person has his or her own best ways of coming up with a rich array of solutions. The methods presented in the following pages are among the best used by professional communicators.

2.1 Brainstorming

Brainstorming may be the most commonly taught idea-generation technique. Brainstorming means producing ideas (in this context, solutions to a problem) absolutely freely, not doing any screening, refining, or selecting until some later stage. The idea is to separate the positive, imaginative thinking required to *produce* the ideas from the negative, critical thinking required to *choose* the best idea.

Any number of people can brainstorm effectively. It's helpful to tape record the process so you will not have to stop to write down ideas. The first principle of brainstorming is not to criticize ideas while they are being generated. The second principle is to feel free to piggyback one idea on another; if someone says "paint it green," you piggyback onto that idea with "paint it green with white stripes." In this way, one idea actually helps to produce the next.

2.2 Visual Thinking

Many people find they think much more clearly and creatively when they think visually. One such person typically says, "I just can't visualize what you're telling me—can you put it on paper?" For him, thinking visually means seeing lists, sketches, charts, and numbers. Another person, an architect, sketches everything he talks about, from sailboats, to houses, to the way a foot should hit a soccer ball, to the way a properly smoked turkey should look. You don't need to be an artist to think visually; all it takes is an active imagination and the willingness to try.

What does your problem look like? Give it a shape, a color, a size in your mind. You may find that actually sketching or doodling on a pad while you visualize will be helpful. Or you may just need to lean back, close your eyes, and "conjure up" images in your mind. Whatever it takes for you to think visually, you may find that it enhances your problem solving, making it well worth the time and effort.

2.3 Asking Questions

The solutions you find to your problem generally will be no better than the questions you ask. Working to improve the quality and variety of the questions you ask can thus improve the quality of the solutions you find. There are very few—if any—unsolvable problems, but there are many problems for which the right question has not yet been asked. Box 15.2 lists a few of the most important kinds of questions to remember.

If you will remember not to allow the first questions you ask of the problem to be the *only* questions you ask of it, if you can take the time and trouble to ask a variety of different kinds of questions, you will do much better at problem solving.

Box 15.2 Basic Types of Questions

Basic Questions: Who, What, When, Where, Why, How?

Reminding Questions: "Have we forgotten that. . .?"

Challenging Questions: "If we look at this, being as specific and hard-nosed as possible, . . ?"

Eliciting Questions: "What extra information could we collect that will help. . . ?" or "Can we find three specific examples of. . . ?"

Furthering Questions: "If we follow *X* course of action, what will be the effect of. . . ?"

Clarifying Questions: "What is the evidence that supports this generalization? Does the evidence really connect with that generalization?"

Deflecting Questions: "Can we go around this problem—move in some other direction to avoid it entirely?"

Structural Questions: "What is it that holds the parts of this problem together?"

Testing Questions: "What conditions would have to occur to falsify our current understanding. . . ?"

2.4 Linear Analysis

One of the most commonly used techniques today involves flow-charting (a variant of visual thinking). One special kind of flow-charting, called linear thinking, leads you through an analysis of a problem using a series of yes/no decisions. To perform a linear analysis, you take apart a problem, divide it into its various parts, subdivide the parts, and finally make decisions as to which parts can be dealt with simply and which need more attention. The technique has a double advantage: linear analysis is very systematic, and it makes the problem-solving process easy to visualize. It is also especially useful in the kind of situation that leaves you paralyzed by its complexity. By systematically breaking the problem down into visualizable, manageable parts you may find that you are more able to solve it.

Consider the following simple example, solved here first using words and then using linear analysis. Suppose you find yourself at one end of a strange city with limited funds and no car, and you need to get to the other end of town to attend a meeting. What are the possible solutions? Brainstorm this list:

Taxi	Bus	Combination
Subway	Walk	Hitchhike
Call a friend	Rent a car	Do nothing

Then you can exclude the totally impractical alternatives; here hitchhiking is not safe, and doing nothing is not feasible. Renting a car is too expensive, and you have no friends in this city. That leaves five alternatives, in descending order of preference:

Taxi	Walk
Bus	Combinations
Subway	

You rank Combinations last because it's the most complicated solution. Then you realize the distance is too far to walk. Now you have the following list:

Taxi	Subway
Bus	Combinations

The taxi is too expensive to take clear across town. The bus runs through the part of town you're in, but stops at downtown, and the subway is not in your part of town. This moves you to look at Combinations for a solution. And indeed you discover you can take the bus to the center of town, take the subway from there nearly to your destination, then (depending on how much time is left) either walk or taxi the last ten or twelve blocks from the subway to your destination. Problem solved!

Now consider the linear analysis of the problem (see Figure 15.5). Notice that this particular line of analysis can solve any number of problems. But many kinds of problems require a different line to solve (see the Exercises at the end of the chapter).

This same solution can be flow-charted somewhat differently (see Figure 15.6). Notice also that the choices (to rank-order by preference, and to test by

Figure 15.5 Linear Analysis A Flow Chart for Decision Making

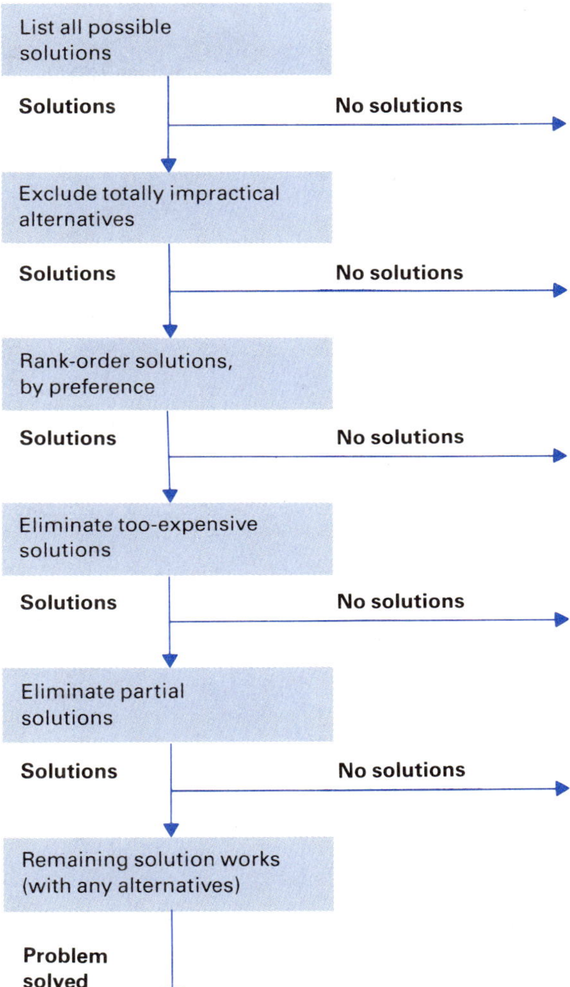

expense) are specific to this problem. One could have rank-ordered and tested according to any number of different criteria (see Section 4, "Making Your Choice").

3. Testing for the Best Solutions

Once you have explored the problem and found a rich array of solutions, you need to test to find the best ones. Much of the time, that testing will be empirical; that is, it involves work in the laboratory, field research, and calculations. More

Figure 15.6 Decision-Making Flow Chart The choices to rank-order by preference and to test by expense are specific to this problem.

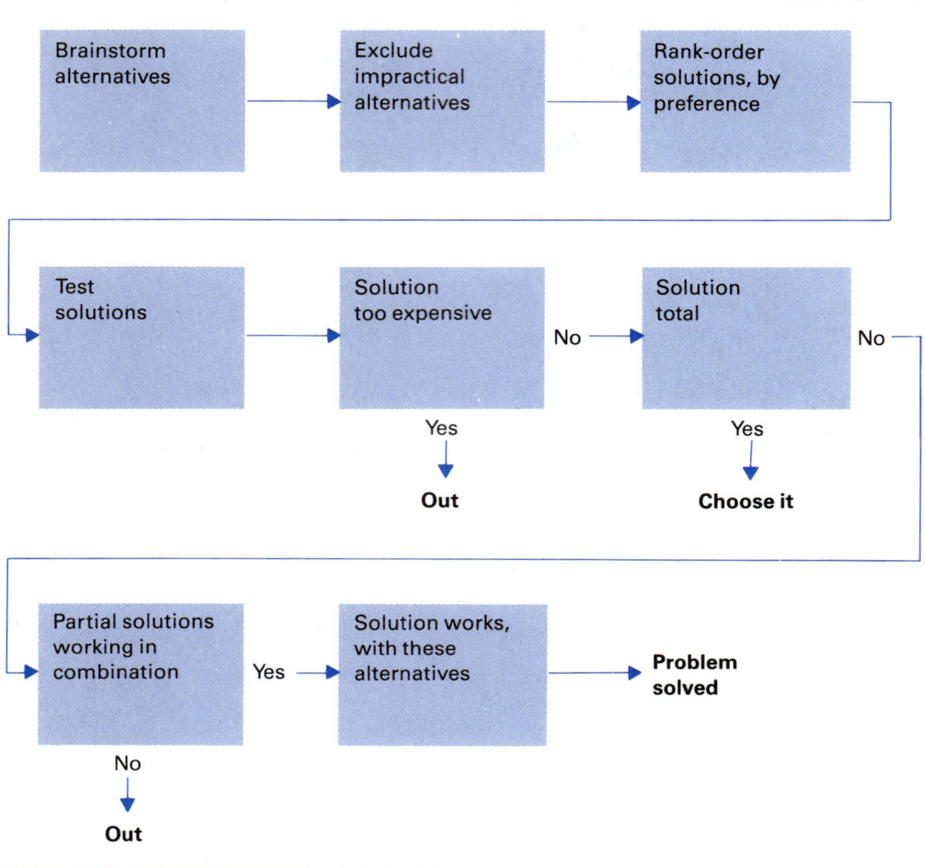

challenging situations occur when you cannot design empirical tests to evaluate the various solutions. Methods of making causal inferences (such as, "If we do this, we solve the problem") are not so well known as methods of empirical testing, nor are they as specific to each field. Yet they can be tremendously useful. Here are seven ways to test solutions, only one of which (number seven) requires empirical methods:

1. Explanatory Power
2. Prior Probability
3. Predictive Power
4. Clarity
5. Provocative Power
6. Falsifiability
7. The Crucial Test

3.1 Explanatory Power

When you are comparing several solutions, which one seems to work on the greatest number of facets of the problem? Which one seems to explain the problem? This is a good way to detect solutions that are smoke-screens that don't really deal with the problem.

3.2 Prior Probability

Which solution seems at first glance to be the best one? That is, if someone just now looking at the problem saw your list of solutions, which would they choose at first glance? This often tells you which solution will be easiest to sell to someone else, or which may be too farfetched to consider further without some good reason.

3.3 Predictive Power

Which solution allows you to plan for the future most effectively? That is, which one will enable you to predict post-solution conditions? Often you can pick a safe solution this way.

3.4 Clarity

Many times lists of solutions include poorly defined solutions, especially those whose limits are impossible to discern. For instance, deficit spending may be a solution to a government's need for capital, or loans may be a business's solution, but where are the limits of those solutions?

3.5 Provocative Power

In some situations you can choose a solution because it seems to open up a number of interesting and potentially attractive possibilities; you choose a solution because it leads you to ask a number of exciting questions. For instance, at the conclusion of the U.S. program to land a person on the moon, those in government who were interested in a continuing U.S. space program had to choose a direction in which to continue. One of the reasons that the reusable shuttle was chosen was the number of doors it would open, the number of interesting and exciting projects it could be used on. (Notice that this is almost the opposite of Clarity.) In some situations, when a number of feasible solutions are competing, the one with the strongest provocative power may be the most attractive.

3.6 Falsifiability

One of the most useful nonempirical tests requires you as the problem solver to describe the conditions that would invalidate the solution you are testing. What would have to happen in order for that solution not to be the right one? Then you check to see whether those conditions do in fact exist, or what their relative probabilities are. You may want to choose a mediocre solution that definitely *will* work over an excellent solution that *might* work.

3.7 The Crucial Test

This is the classical empirical test: can you design a crucial test situation that will allow you to select clearly among the alternatives? Can you design a test that only the right solution can pass?

4. Making Your Choice

The quality of your choice depends mostly on the quality of your work in the previous stages of problem solving; but it is still important to be systematic. Use this simple checklist to keep you on track:

1. Check your work.
2. Rank your alternatives.
3. Get advice.
4. Make your choice and document it.

4.1 Check Your Work

Too often people behave as though "checking your work" applies only in math classes. But successful professionals will tell you that making sure that the earlier stages of problem solving have been done accurately is an important step toward success. It takes much less time to check your work *before* you choose a solution than it will to solve the problems created by making an error that leads to a wrong solution.

4.2 Rank Your Alternatives

To be orderly about problem solving, list your possible (or recommended) solutions according to some clearly explained criterion (or set of criteria). This is necessary to the success of the next two stages.

4.3 Get Advice

When you can, it's a good idea to get advice at this stage. Show a friend at work, your spouse, or maybe your boss your rank-ordered list of alternatives. They can help you catch any errors in your thinking and give you good practice explaining the decision-making process you used.

4.4 Make Your Choice and Document It

If you have followed all the preceding steps, your choice should usually be obvious by now. When you choose, right at that time you should prepare to document your choice. Collect all of your notes, brainstormed lists, data, tests, and so forth—

any elements that contributed to your decision—and arrange them in the right order. At the very least, outline on paper the process you followed, for your own records. Often you will want or need to put together a short written account of how you made your decision. This can then be keyed to the various lists, tests, and data you have gathered, and the whole package stored for future reference. Whether your decision was good or bad, right or wrong, you can count at least on someone asking how you did it, and at most on writing up a full report.

5. Doing the Writing

Solving the problem is one thing; writing up the solution in such a way as to fulfill the report's purpose can be quite another. If you take your reader through the process you used in solving the problem, you may be running the risk of doing exactly the wrong thing. Using the terms developed in Chapter 14, should your report have a *writer-based structure* (as it would if you duplicate the problem-solving process in the structure of your report), or a *reader-based structure* (perhaps beginning with the solution, and then explaining its aptness)?

In terms of the distinction between catalogical and analytical writing developed in Chapter 13, over and over again many writers produce catalogical reports (reviewing problem-solving processes) rather than analytical ones (presenting their solutions in the best possible way). It's not that people are not interested in how a problem's solution was discovered—*some* audiences, for *some* purposes, are—but you cannot assume that interest. For whatever writing situation you are in, you must analyze that specific situation—purpose, message, audience, and writer's role—and make your choices as to what to include and what to exclude, what to put first and what to put last, on the basis of that analysis alone.

EXERCISES

1. Given a cigar box containing a claw hammer, five assorted nails, and a household utility candle, make a design that will fasten the candle to a wooden wall so that the candle will burn in an upright position. Write a report describing your solution and giving a full account of your problem-solving process. The audience is your classmates. (If you experiment, be careful with the lighted candle!)
2. Write a report to your classmates presenting the solution to the Tower of Hanoi puzzle (shown in Figure 15.7). The object of this simple child's game is to restack the rings on another post with the biggest again at the bottom and the others in order so that the smallest is at the top. You can only move one ring at a time, and you can never put a larger ring on top of a smaller one. Include in your report specific mention of any important principles involved. Could the puzzle be solved with seven rings and three posts? How?
3. If your class has as its final requirement a major report, write a problem-solving report detailing your search for a topic to write about. Your report

Figure 15.7 The Tower of Hanoi Puzzle

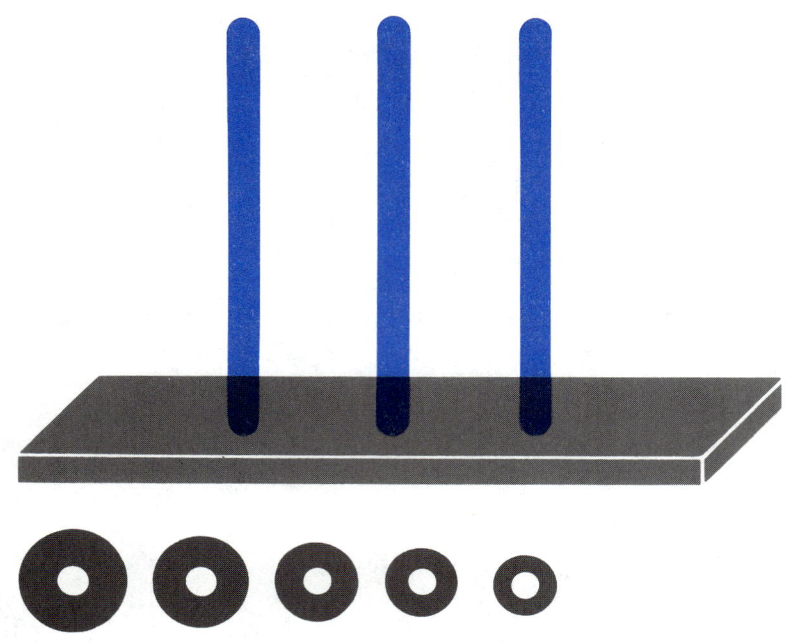

should end by persuasively recommending that your instructor approve the topic you suggest.

4. Do a short report on how problem solving (or decision making) is handled in your field of study. Consult textbooks, your instructors, library resources, and working professionals. How compatible are those methods of problem solving with the one this chapter presents? The audience for the report is entry-level professionals in your field.
5. Sometimes problem solving involves deciding not only *what* to say but also *how* to say it. Do you need a report, a memo, a letter, or what? The following case problem will test both your ability to solve a problem and your ability to decide whom you need to present the solution to and how you need to do it. Solve this case:*

You're a member of the College Arts Committee, which brings in guest speakers, poets, artists, and so on, on a very modest budget (each person is paid $50 for coming). Last week the committee brought in a little-known poet to address some classes and hold a poetry reading in a room at the

*Adapted from *Business Communication Casebook* (Urbania, Ill.: American Business Communication Association, 1974).

Student Union. It turned out that the poet was, apparently, a hobo who used the $50 for buying gin. He was insulting to the classes he visited, his poetry was apparently random words strung together haphazardly, and by the evening poetry reading he was too intoxicated to make any sense at all. Most of the audience left during the first half-hour, and at the end of an hour your "guest artist" fell asleep (or passed out) in his chair. There is now on campus a considerable amount of talk about the incident, and the university president has been heard to say, "We should disband that College Arts Committee and put the money to some more useful purpose." Now the committee has chosen you to deal with this problem on paper. You need at least some kind of letter to the University President, probably a "letter to the Editor" in the university newspaper, and maybe a letter to the committee's faculty sponsor (an English professor who recommended that poet in the first place). You may decide you need to produce other documents as well.

6. Design a container that will hold a fresh egg and protect it well enough that you could drop the container ten feet onto concrete without breaking the egg. The container must be something that will travel with the egg. The optimum design criteria are simplicity, economy, and reusability. As an appendix to the report in which you describe your design, describe your problem-solving process.

16

Using Research Libraries

By this point in your education, you probably have realized how important knowing how to use your university's library is. You need to be able to answer these questions:

- What are the basic reference tools in your field (handbooks, specialized dictionaries and encyclopedias, etc.)?
- What key words does the Library of Congress indexing system use for important subjects in your field?
- What are the three leading professional (or trade) journals in your field?
- What are the periodical indexes for your field?
- Which periodical indexes in your field include abstracts?
- Which periodical indexes in your field can be used via computers?

This chapter will show you (1) how to discover the right tools for library research in your field, and (2) how to accomplish that research.

A Note About Librarians. Your best friend during any library research project is the librarian. *Ask a librarian* is an option you should freely take at any stage in your research process. You should not *avoid,* but rather welcome, situations that require you to get a librarian's help. If you can get a librarian involved in your work, even minimally, your research is well begun indeed. When you ask a librarian for help, however, it is important to ask your question carefully. Box 16.1 lists three important guidelines for dealing with librarians.

1. The Process

As a process, library research in many ways parallels other kinds of fact-finding, information-gathering, problem-solving processes (cf. Chapter 15). Ask the right questions, don't focus on a possibly wrong answer too hastily, keep careful records, weigh the value of your findings carefully, and present those findings thoughtfully. As in other such processes, careful planning at the outset reaps large rewards later on, and errors made at the outset tend to be magnified the longer they continue uncorrected. Most importantly, in library research (as in any research process) you need to be *systematic.*

This chapter explains the process of library research as something that should take place in a particular, especially systematic way. Figure 16.1 shows the broad outlines of the process; fill in the specifics into each cell in the flow chart as the process develops.

Author's Note: I wish to thank Linda Phillips, Byron Stewart, and Vicki Anders for their advice and input regarding the content of this chapter.

Box 16.1 Guidelines for Dealing with Librarians

Be prepared. The librarian may never have heard anything about your topic until the moment you come up and ask about it. Be prepared to give the librarian a good short explanation of what you are trying to do. *Remember:* The answer you get can only be as good as the question you ask.

Be polite. During term-paper season at a university, each librarian may talk to several hundred people each day. Such situations can make for short tempers, and a little courtesy—just "please" and "thank you"—may well get you a more detailed answer.

Be persistent. Frequently a busy librarian will say something like, "it's over on shelf nine," and leave it up to you to find the document in question. If you can't find it in ten minutes of looking, don't hesitate to go back and ask for more help. Be polite, but be persistent.

1.1 The Planning Stage

Before you go into a library, work out a search strategy (See Figure 16.2). A typical university library's collection may contain over a million bound books and another one or two million documents of other sorts. If you wait to begin planning your search until you are physically in the presence of that much information, and *then* try to think of where to go and what to look for, you may well not be able to think as clearly as possible about what your plans should be.

1.1.1 **Develop a Search Strategy.** A search strategy tells you *where* to look and *what* to look for. Begin forming your search strategy as soon as you have an assignment or subject to work on. Refine your search strategy as you define your topic, discover your thesis, sketch your list of main points, and begin to list possible key words.

The flow chart in Figure 16.1 shows a standard (generic) search strategy. Depending on your topic and the reference and research tools in your field, you should be able to make that standard search strategy much more specific for each of your projects. Figure 16.3 shows a tentative search strategy for the sample research topic that will be developed in this chapter, a report on the economic implications of recombinant DNA research.

The *topic* is the subject you want to write about but not necessarily what you want to say about it. For example, the undergraduate student whose research process this chapter follows had become a business student after having been a biology major for three years, and he originally wanted to do a paper on some aspect of DNA research. The writing course he was in, however, required a major report in the student's current major, so in conference with his professor he negotiated the topic "Economic Implications of Recombinant DNA Research." Just what he would say within that topic stayed undetermined for two weeks, while he did preliminary research. During that research he was looking not only

Figure 16.1 The Process of Library Research

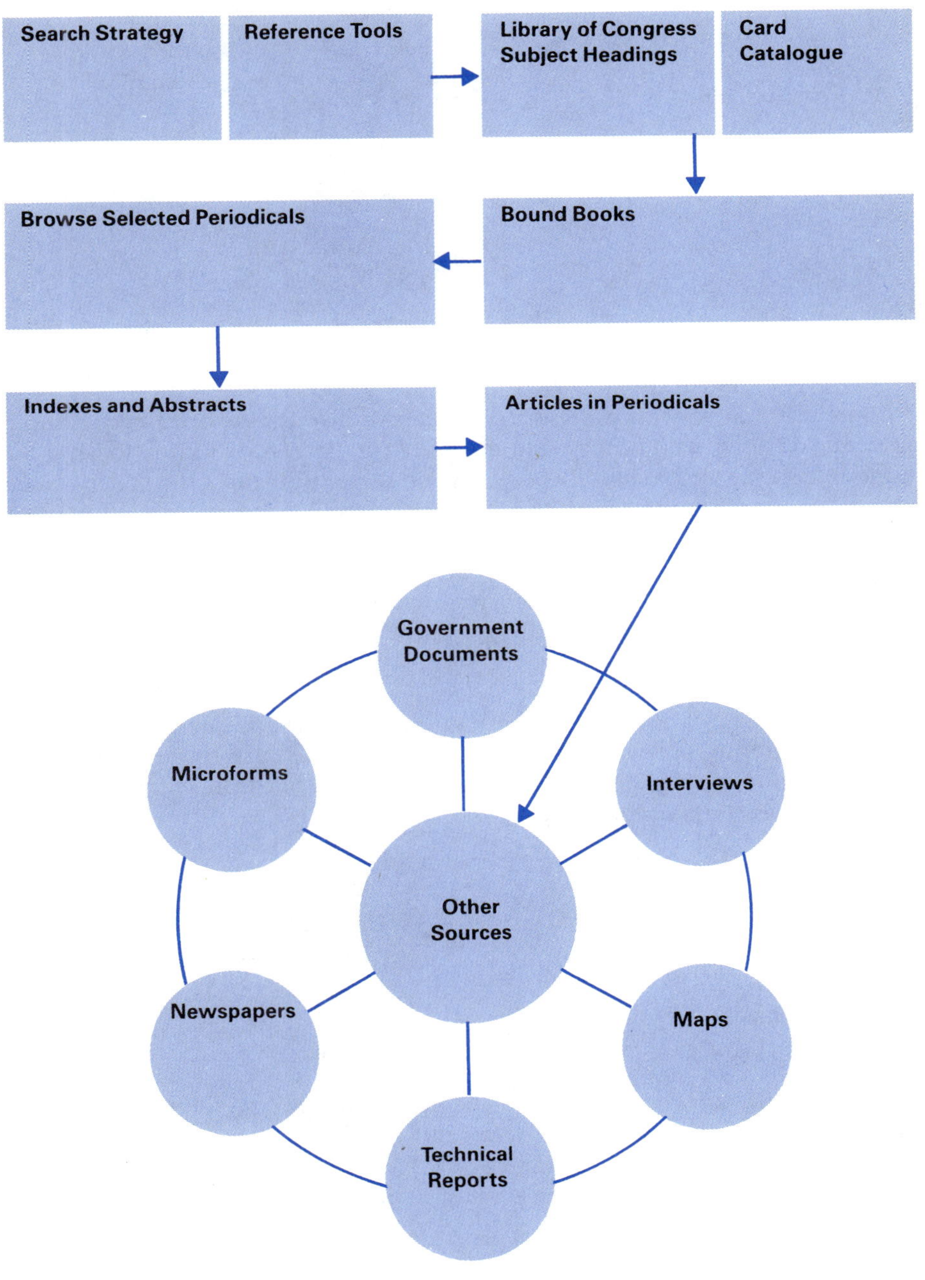

Figure 16.2 The Start of Your Search Strategy This is the beginning of the process in Figure 16.1.

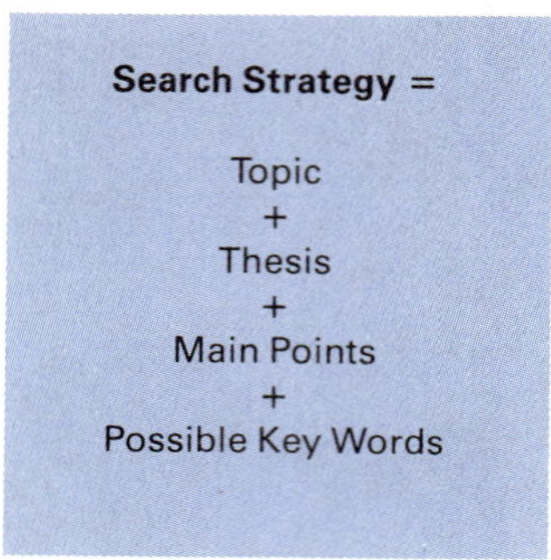

for material, but also for a thesis, something to give the report a beginning, a middle, and an end. (You may find that after you get out of school, looking for a thesis is something you rarely do when you write. But you will still need to be able to collect disparate pieces of information into a coherent whole, one that fulfills a particular purpose for a particular audience, a process that intellectually is recognizably similar to looking for a thesis.)

After two weeks of preliminary research and another conference with his professor, the modified search strategy shown in Exhibit 16.1 was developed.

1.1.2 **Refine Your Search Strategy Using Standard Reference Tools.** One of the ways of making your search strategy more specific is to use the reference tools appropriate for your subject and your field of study. This list names the kinds of reference tools available for many fields:

Generalized Encyclopedias	Specialized Dictionaries
Specialized Encyclopedias	Directories
Almanacs	Gazetteers
Yearbooks	Atlases
Handbooks	Periodical Indexes
Dictionaries	Style Manuals

There are many varieties of the reference tools listed here, and there may be kinds of reference tools in your field that are not listed here. Go to your university library's main reference desk and learn what the standard reference tools for your field are. These three books can help you find out what those reference tools are:

Sheehy's *Guide to Reference Books*
Katz's *Magazines for Libraries*
Ulrich's *International Periodicals Directory*

Figure 16.3 A Tentative Search Strategy This is only a place to *start.*

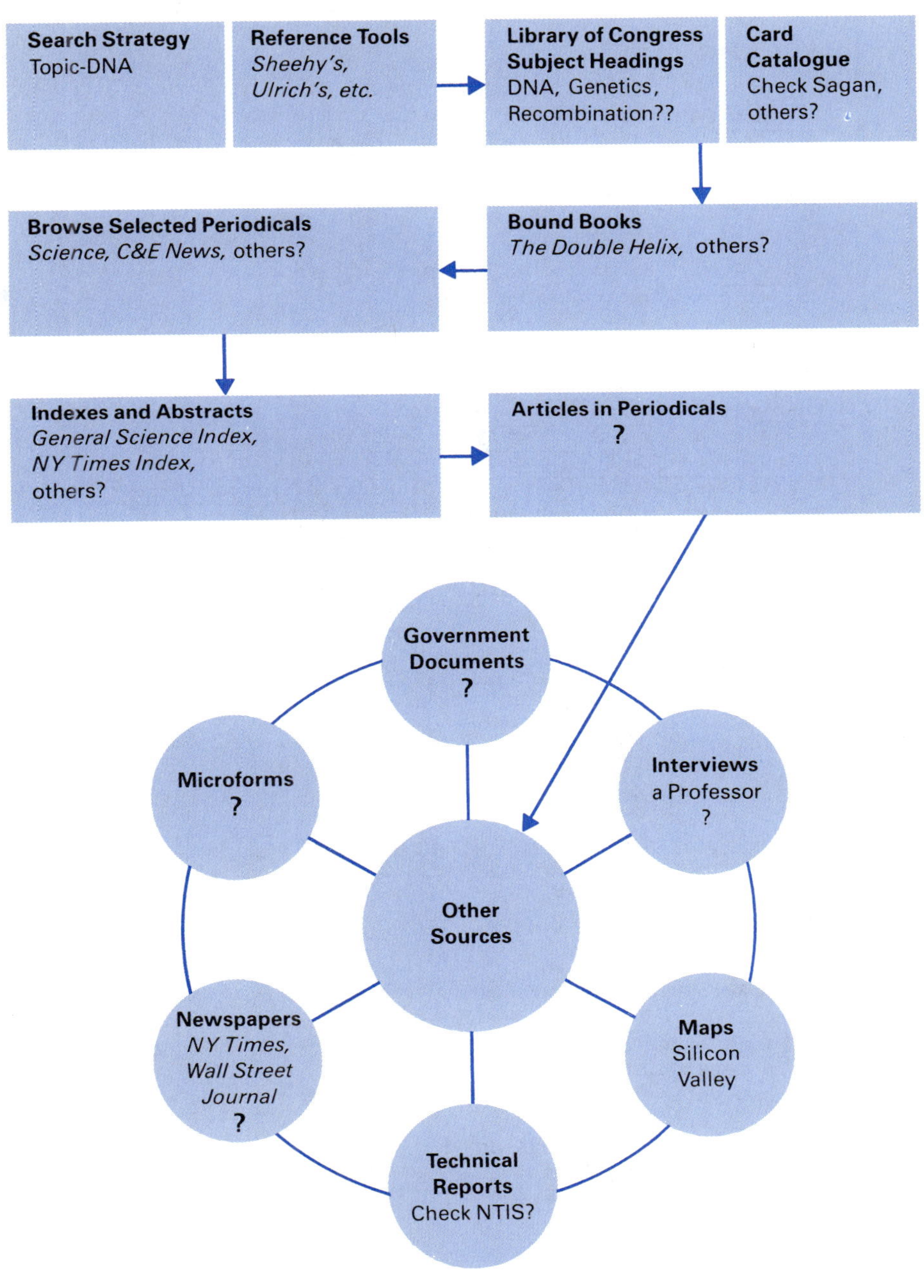

Exhibit 16.1 A Modified Search Strategy At this point, the student has completed several hours of library work; only the "Other Sources" category is left open.

1.a. SEARCH STRATEGY

Topic: Economics of Recombinant DNA Research
Thesis: Recombinant DNA research is already a multibillion-dollar business and is growing rapidly.
Main Points: Explain recombinant DNA research.
Trace its movement into business.
Put dollar value on it.
Key Words: Recombinant DNA research, genetic engineering, biotechnology.

1.b. REFERENCE TOOLS

King's A Dictionary of Genetics
Knight's Dictionary of Genetics
Regar, et al., A Glossary of Genetics
Encyclopaedia Britannica
Williams and Lunsford's Encyclopedia of Biochemistry
More than 85 journals under ''BIOLOGY–Genetics'' in Ulrich's International Periodicals Directory, including:
- Genetic Engineering Letter
- Genetic Engineering News
- Genetic Technology News
- Recombinant DNA
- Recombinant DNA Technical Bulletin
- Biotechnology

Indexes:
- Biological Abstracts
- Index Medicus
- Science Citation Index

2.a. LIBRARY OF CONGRESS SUBJECT HEADINGS

Genetic engineering
sa Cell nuclei–Transplantation
Cloning
Molecular cloning
Recombinant DNA
x Designed genetic change
Engineering, Genetic
Gene Splicing
Genetic intervention
Genetic surgery
xx Genetic recombination

Genetic intervention
See Genetic engineering

Genetic recombination
sa Bacterial transformation
Crossing over (Genetics)
Genetic engineering

Genetic transformation
Recombinant DNA
x Recombination, Genetic
xx Chromosomes
— Research
— Law and legislation (Indirect)
xx Medical laws and legislation

2.b. CARD CATALOG

[This is a list of the books found under the appropriate subject headings of 2.a.]

3. BOUND BOOKS

[This is a list of the books (chosen from the list in 2.b.) to search for in the library.]

4. BROWSE SELECTED PERIODICALS

Science, C&E, Biotechnology

5. INDEXES AND ABSTRACTS

General Science Index
Biological Abstracts
Index Medicus
Science Citation Index
New York Times Index
Wall Street Journal Index

6. ARTICLES IN PERIODICALS

[This is a list of articles (selected from those found in 5.) to search for in the library.]

7. OTHER SOURCES

a. Interviews
Still need to find a professor—check microbiology, botany, etc.
b. Maps
It doesn't seem likely that a map will be relevant to this topic.
c. Technical Reports
Check Government Reports Announcements & Indexes
d. Newspapers
Check The New York Times and The Wall Street Journal Indexes for the financial information.
e. Microforms
These will have been covered in other search steps.
f. Government Reports
Still need to check at least the Publications Reference File and the Index to U.S. Government Periodicals.

While you're working on narrowing your topic, defining your thesis, and shaping your search strategy, work through your field's reference tools to see what they say about your topic. From them you can get valuable background, answering such questions as "What's the current state of knowledge on this subject?" They will also often list the names of authorities on the subject and the sources of more specific information.

Although it is often a little vague in its outlines, this first stage of your research process is especially important. The more *creative* background digging you do on your topic while you're shaping your search strategy, the better focus your topic will have for the remainder of your project. Through background work with reference tools at this stage, you can avoid making false starts on topics that don't work out and traveling up blind alleys of research. And once you take the trouble to learn what the basic reference tools are in your field, you can use them profitably over and over again.

One other point should be made about this first stage in the process of library research. If you were to ask ten randomly selected students how to start working on a library research paper, seven out of ten would probably say, "Begin with the card catalogue." Starting with that step leaves out all of the background information on the topic that reference sources hold. More important, beginning with the card catalogue leaves out all of the topic refining and thesis shaping that go on in the writer's mind during the search through basic reference tools. During that reference search, you learn what questions are the right ones to ask within your topic. And you cannot hope to find the right *answers* unless you ask the right *questions*.

1.2 The Card Catalogue

If you were to put all of the drawers in a typical university's card catalogue end to end, you might well have a row over 500 feet long, with over 6,000,000 cards in it. Out of all this, how do you find the information you want? A little basic knowledge about how card catalogues are organized will help you use them more effectively.

1.2.1 **Library of Congress Subject Headings.** The first obstacle that confronts anyone who tries to look up a subject in a university's card catalogue is the words such card catalogues use to index their subjects. Research libraries generally do not use natural language—words the way you and I use them—to index their collections. Instead, research libraries use a controlled vocabulary—a limited number of words, with meanings especially defined. Generally, it isn't a good idea to guess how the controlled vocabulary indexes the natural words for the subjects you want to research. You need to use the *Library of Congress Subject Headings List*, bound volumes of which should be next to the card catalogue. For example, if you were doing the research paper on recombinant DNA, looking in the card catalogue under "DNA" would at best lead you to look under "Deoxyribonucleic acid." Looking there would lead you to "Recombinant DNA," which would lead you to "Genetic engineering," which, as it turns out, is where most of the appropriate information is indexed. But trying to follow this sequence through the card catalogue would be time-consuming and full of possible errors. Exhibit 16.2 shows you how the *Library of Congress Subject Headings List* is organized. Using it this way, you will be able to find exactly the right vocabulary words to look under in the card catalogue.

1.2.2 **Card-Catalogue Cards.** Some libraries have author/title cards in one place and subject cards in another. Other libraries combine the cards; when they are combined, there is usually a difference in the typeface or a color coding to show you which is which. Exhibit 16.3 shows sample subject, author, and title cards.

When you look at the cards, pay attention to the details beyond author, title, and place and date of publication. To make your research better, you need to look for books published recently, preferably in the last four to five years. You may want to use books with illustrations to give you ideas for your own visuals, and you certainly want books with bibliographies, to tell you about other sources in that subject area. The information on the rest of the card is called "tracings"; it lists the other headings under which to search for information.

As you do your research, especially in its early stages, remember to continue to refine your topic and thesis. Generally, if you can find as much as one current book that exactly matches your topic and thesis, you need to narrow your subject even more. How can you hope to cover adequately in 15–20 pages a topic that someone else required 300–400 pages for? Remember also that the typical card catalogue does not index everything the library holds. In many cases, other important sources of information—such as manuscripts, government documents, technical reports, theses and dissertations, and microforms—will not be included in the card catalogue, and you must access those materials differently.

1.3 Bound Books

Suppose you use the subject headings in the card catalogue and compile a list of thirty books that you might look in to find material on your subject. Although it might be best to at least *look* at all of them, in case you don't have that much time, how do you decide which ones to use and which ones to rank as of secondary importance? From the cards in the card catalogue you can tell whether a book does or does not include a bibliography (the card will say something like "incl. bib."), and because a book's bibliography usually will lead you to more on the subject, you might want to choose books whose cards show they have bibliographies. If you are looking for ideas for visuals for your report, you might want to choose books with illustrations—listed in the tracings on the card-catalogue card as "ill." And you will probably want to choose the more recent books over the older books.

When you find a book on the shelf, take an extra minute and look up and down that shelf for others that might be useful, also. This technique, called *browsing*, can sometimes be very productive. Never rely on it exclusively, but it is a helpful addition to an otherwise carefully directed search.

Exhibit 16.2 The Library of Congress Subject Headings It takes four entries, starting with "DNA," to get to "Genetic Engineering," which proves to be the most productive key words.

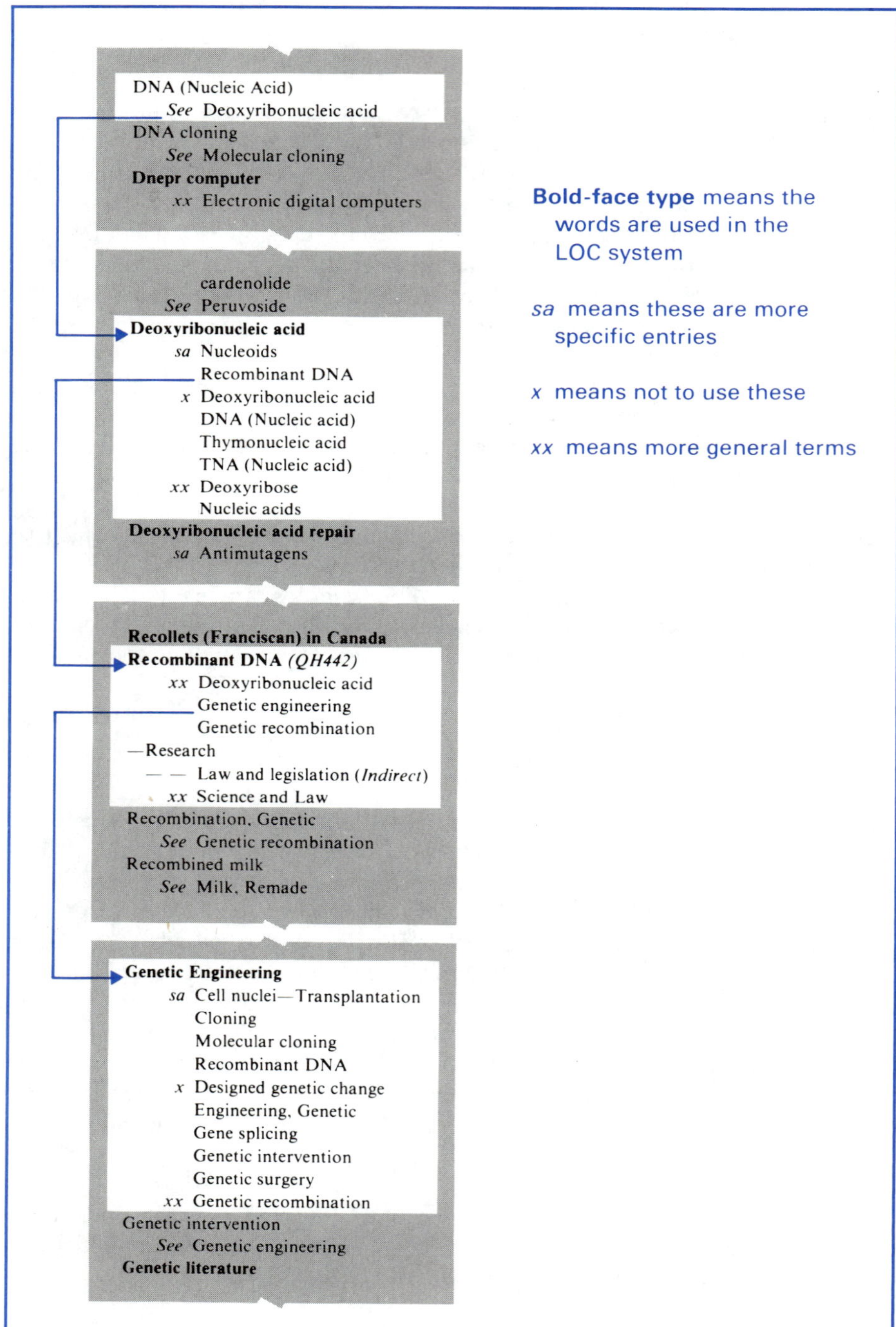

DNA (Nucleic Acid)
See Deoxyribonucleic acid
DNA cloning
See Molecular cloning
Dnepr computer
xx Electronic digital computers
cardenolide
See Peruvoside
Deoxyribonucleic acid
sa Nucleoids
Recombinant DNA
x Deoxyribonucleic acid
DNA (Nucleic acid)
Thymonucleic acid
TNA (Nucleic acid)
xx Deoxyribose
Nucleic acids
Deoxyribonucleic acid repair
sa Antimutagens
Recollets (Franciscan) in Canada
Recombinant DNA (QH442)
xx Deoxyribonucleic acid
Genetic engineering
Genetic recombination
—Research
— — Law and legislation (Indirect)
xx Science and Law
Recombination, Genetic
See Genetic recombination
Recombined milk
See Milk, Remade
Genetic Engineering
sa Cell nuclei—Transplantation
Cloning
Molecular cloning
Recombinant DNA
x Designed genetic change
Engineering, Genetic
Gene splicing
Genetic intervention
Genetic surgery
xx Genetic recombination
Genetic intervention
See Genetic engineering
Genetic literature
Bold-face type means the words are used in the LOC system
sa means these are more specific entries
x means not to use these
xx means more general terms

Exhibit 16.3 Subject, Author, and Title Cards Notice the "tracings" on the author card.

Subject Card

	GENETIC ENGINEERING—SOCIAL ASPECTS.
QH 442 .L4	Lear, John. Recombinant DNA : the untold story / John Lear. New York : Crown Publishers, c1978. 280 p., [4] leaves of plates : ill. : 24 cm. Includes index.

TU 09 FEB 79 3608470 TKNUdc 77-29158

Author Card

QH 442 .L4	Lear, John. Recombinant DNA : the untold story / John Lear. New York : Crown Publishers, c1978. 280 p., [4] leaves of plates : ill. : 24 cm. Includes index.
Tracings	1. Recombinant DNA. 2. Genetic engineering—Social aspects. I. Title

TU 09 FEB 79 3608470 TKNUdc 77-29158

Title Card

	Recombinant DNA
QH 442 .L4	Lear, John. Recombinant DNA : the untold story / John Lear. New York : Crown Publishers, c1978. 280 p., [4] leaves of plates : ill. : 24 cm. Includes index.

TU 09 FEB 79 3608470 TKNUdc 77-29158

1.4 Browsing Selected Periodicals

You can also browse effectively by skimming recent issues of the three or four professional journals most appropriate to your subject. Most university libraries keep the recent issues of journals in a separate place, perhaps called the Current Periodicals Room, and you can go in, take the current issues to a comfortable chair, and scan them pretty quickly. Look for articles on your subject or related to your subject. If you find a few articles that are right, you may have leapfrogged right into the middle of your topic, and you may be able to finish your research much faster. This technique also helps you to refine your own mental picture of your thesis, to have a better idea of what questions you need to ask and what questions you may not be able to answer.

In case you do not know the names of the journals to look in for a particular field of knowledge, the books by Sheehy, Katz, and Ulrich cited earlier (see p. 316) can tell you. Another very complete listing of journals organized by field is the *Standard Periodicals Directory*, which also gives readership numbers for many journals. Another way to find out what the most important journals in your field of study are would be to ask a professor in that field, or to ask a reference librarian.

Once again, you would not want browsing through selected periodicals to be the only way you look for articles, but it's a good way to find out quickly whether there is much current periodical information on your subject, and to find an occasional up-to-date article to help you with the rest of your research.

By this time you should have refined your idea of your topic down to a fairly specific thesis. From here on, be increasingly specific about exactly what you are looking for. Keep an open mind on your topic initially, but focus more precisely on your specific thesis before too much time passes. Many students find that a week or two of preliminary digging will be enough to make their topic and thesis specific.

1.5 Periodical Indexes and Abstracts

There are over 70,000 periodicals in the world, and your university library may well have 15–20,000. How do you find articles on your subject? The most reliable and thorough way to find them is to use periodical indexes. A periodical index organizes the articles in a particular set of journals and during a particular time span into groups by their subjects. You may already be familiar with one periodical index, the *Readers' Guide to Periodical Literature*, from high school or freshman English. The *Readers' Guide* indexes popular journals (listed in the front of each issue), the kind you might subscribe to at home and read for recreation. If you want to know what magazines like *Time*, *Good Housekeeping*, *Road and Track*, or *Cosmopolitan* say about your subject, you can find the bibliographical information on their articles in the *Readers' Guide*. But if you're in a junior- or senior-level college course, you will probably be expected to use considerably more specialized journals than those in the *Readers' Guide*. Yet knowing how to use *Readers' Guide* is useful because many other indexes are put out by that same company (Wilson Indexes) and are organized the same way.

How do you find out what the periodical indexes in your field are? Once again, Sheehy, Ulrich, and Katz will list them. You can also often find the name of the right indexes somewhere on the cover or table-of-contents pages of separate issues of your journals. Or you can ask a reference librarian or a professor in that field. If you want your research to be good, you should plan on consulting four or five indexes covering at least five years back.

If you have seven or eight indexes to choose from, how do you select which one to use first? This is where *abstracts* come in. A growing number of indexes also contain (in the same volumes or separate volumes) a very brief summary of each article cited in the index. An index with abstracts can save you a lot of time. If you have bibliographical information on thirty articles, imagine how long it would take you to find and read copies of each one. But you can read thirty abstracts in thirty minutes, and quite possibly narrow down to five the number of articles you actually need to find.

Most indexes have subject and author volumes; some also have citation volumes. A citation index tells you the names of articles that have referenced a particular name in their bibliography. Thus if I know that Jane Zimmerman wrote a book on my topic ten years ago, I can look in the appropriate field's citation index to find current articles that include a reference to her book in their bibliographies or notes.

Even with Sheehy's, Ulrich's, and similar sources, it is sometimes difficult to find the indexes for your subject. If you have that problem, ask at your library's reference desk to see a list of the indexes that the library has. The librarian will probably only loan it to you, but you can use it to find other indexes to look in.

Some people find their first experiences with periodical indexes a little troublesome. It can take time to find the indexes, and still more time—and a librarian's help—to learn how to use them. Most indexes are generated by computers that seem to have little regard for your ease of using them. However, as long as you stay in that field, what you have learned will remain valid; you don't have to relearn the indexes with every research project. For example, if you are a mechanical engineering student, once you learn the indexes for the field and how they should be used, you will consult the same indexes for doing research as long as you stay in mechanical engineering. And whatever field you are in, using periodical indexes is probably the only really reliable way to find all the articles on your subject.

The list in Box 16.2 contains only a small sampling of the indexes that may be found in most university libraries.

1.6 Articles in Periodicals

You can find the articles you need by browsing, by using periodical indexes and abstracts, and by using your library's own list of periodicals. Once you get to the articles you need, write down all the bibliographical information on each one. Remember that an author who has written one article on a subject may well have written others, so you might want to check that name in the author volumes of a

Box 16.2 Indexes Found in Most University Libraries This list includes only a few of the periodical indexes, to demonstrate the diversity of index topics.

Accountant's Index
Agricultural Index
Animal Breeding Abstracts
Applied Science & Technology Index
Architectural Index
Biography Index
Biological Abstracts
Biological Index
British Technology Index
Business Periodicals Index
Comprehensive Dissertation Abstract Index
Commerce Clearing House
Computer and Control Abstracts
Consumers Index
Current Index to Journals in Education
Education Index
Electrical and Electronics Abstracts
Energy Index
Energy Research Abstracts
Engineering Index
Environment Abstracts & Index
Food Science Abstracts
Forestry Abstracts
F&S Index
General Science Index
Geophysical Abstracts
Hospital Literature Index
Humanities Index
Index Medicus
Index to Legal Periodicals
Industrial Arts Index
Journalism Abstracts
Marketing Information Guide
Metals Abstracts
Moody's Indexes
Oceanographical Abstracts
Index to U.S. Government Periodicals
Personnel Management Abstracts
Petroleum Abstracts
Physics Abstracts
Psychological Abstracts
Public Affairs Information Service (PAIS) Bulletin
Science Citation Index
Social Science Citation Index
Social Sciences Index
Society of Manufacturing Engineers Technical Digest
Sociological Abstracts
Standard & Poor's Index
Target Group Index
Wildlife Abstracts
World Textile Abstracts
Zoological Record

couple of indexes. And a journal that publishes two articles on a subject may well have published others, so you may want to skim the contents of other issues.

1.7 Other Sources

The pages that follow describe six kinds of other sources for information on your subject. Many other kinds of sources are not discussed here, and one of the measures of your resourcefulness and effort as a researcher will be how many and what kinds of other sources you can find.

1.7.1 **Government Documents.** By far the biggest "other source" of information on nearly any subject is government documents. The United States Government Printing Office distributes over 28 million documents annually to its over 1000 depository libraries. How do you find out if there are government publications in your field and on your subject? Some university libraries do not index government documents in their card catalogues at all, and others do so only partially. The kinds of periodical indexes discussed earlier in this chapter typically do not include government publications. The best way to find out whether there are government publications about your subject is to ask a librarian who specializes in government documents to help you. Many people who use government documents regularly still rely on librarians' help, and certainly all researchers who are not familiar with how government documents are organized should. The sources discussed here are the simplest ones available for finding your way around government documents, but to use most of them you will still probably need a librarian's help.

The Monthly Catalogue of U.S. Government Publications. This may be the best way to find non-congressional publications, such as agency reports, pamphlets, and proceedings.

The Publications Reference File (PRF) lists quick access for current government documents still in print.

The Congressional Information Service (CIS) Index lists all congressional publications, including hearings, committee reports, and laws, and includes abstracts.

The Statistical Abstract of the United States contains most kinds of government statistical information.

The American Statistics Index indexes government statistical information and also includes abstracts.

The Index to U.S. Government Periodicals will lead you to articles in government periodicals, indexed by both author and subject.

The Index to Current Urban Documents and the *Urban Documents Microfiche Collection* give you access to documents issued by cities in the U.S. and Canada, incuding annual reports, budgets, environmental impact statements, manuals, questionnaires, and zoning ordinances.

1.7.2 **Microforms.** In many university libraries there are actually more documents on microforms (microfilm, microfiche, etc.) than there are on paper. As with government documents, some university libraries index many of their microforms, and some index very few. Although the list below will give you an idea of the kinds of documents that *may* be in your university library, microform collections vary so much from one school to another that you really need to go explore your school's collection for yourself.

College Catalogues for most colleges and universities in the United States are usually kept in microform.

Special literary collections are often only available in microform. One example is *Early American Imprints*, including all nonserial American publications before 1819.

ERIC, the *Educational Resources Information Center*, indexes many conference papers and otherwise unavailable documents on almost everything concerning any field of education.

Copies of journals. Many university libraries keep second copies of their journals on microforms.

Disclosure System. Often you can find the 10-K and annual reports to stockholders for companies traded on the New York and American Stock Exchanges in microform.

The *Visual Search Manufacturer's File* (VSMF) includes manufacturer's catalogues and industry standards for all types of industrial components.

1.7.3 **Indexed Newspapers and Television News.** Nearly all major city newspapers are indexed, and most university libraries have a very good collection of those papers and indexes. The following list is representative:

The New York Times — *The Washington Post*
The Wall Street Journal — *The New Orleans Times-Picayune*
The London Times — *The Chicago Tribune*
The Los Angeles Times — *The Houston Post*
Pravda — *The Atlanta Constitution*

A number of clipping services regularly collect articles in newspapers on predetermined subjects:

The *Newsbank Urban and Public Affairs Library* clips from 190 U.S. newspapers, including one from each state's capital. This allows you to trace different responses to the same news event around the country. Topics include business and economic development, education, health, transportation, and a number of others.

The *Newsbank Review of the Arts* collects newspaper reviews on books, films, television, art, architecture, and fine arts.

Television news broadcasts represent another source of information for researchers. Increasingly, news broadcasts are indexed, and transcripts are available in university libraries. For example, the *CBS News Index* provides subject-indexed transcripts of all CBS News broadcasts, including morning and evening news and special reports. You should check to see which television news transcripts are available in your university library.

1.7.4 **Technical Reports.** Many libraries contain entire collections of technical reports that are only sporadically included in the card catalogue. These may be from institutes affiliated with the university or from nearby research institutes, and may concern such subjects as water resources, transportation, or wildlife resources. The major source of technical reports is the *National Technical Information Service* (NTIS), an agency of the U.S. Department of Commerce. There are well over a million titles available in this system, including U.S. Government-sponsored research, development, and engineering reports, as well as foreign technical reports. Information about these reports is available through the *Government Reports Announcements & Indexes*, which includes abstracts, and through the NTIS *Weekly Abstract Newsletters*. Many times you may find that your library does not have the report you need, but ordering NTIS reports is a reasonably efficient process, given enough lead time.

1.7.5 **Maps.** Again and again, good maps make the difference between nondescript reports and memorable reports. Most universities have excellent map collections, either in the library or in the Geography department. The standard maps to look for are the U.S. Geological Survey topographic maps for the United States. Ask your librarian where to find local and regional maps as well.

The National Oceanic and Atmospheric Administration (NOAA) publishes nautical and aeronautical charts. Other types of maps to look for are geologic maps, soil maps, highway maps, and the Bureau of the Census's GE-50 series, which includes data on per-capita income, employment in different industries, agriculture, and population trends.

You can also find maps in atlases. The following is a partial list:

The Times Atlas of the World
World Atlas of Agriculture
Oxford Economic Atlas of the World
Atlas of World History
Antique Maps of the World
An Atlas of Fantasy
National Atlas of the United States of America
Rand-McNally Commercial Atlas

There are also indexes to maps, such as the *Index to Maps in Books and Periodicals*, the *Index to Printed Maps*, and the *Guide to U.S. Map Resources*.

1.7.6 **Interviews.** Although they are not part of the information found in libraries, interviews are such an important part of research that it makes sense to discuss them here. Whatever your topic, it is likely that someone at your university is an expert on it. A good interview with such a person can enhance an otherwise run-of-the-mill report. The art of interviewing is too complex to present here, but a few basic guidelines are:

1. Always do such an interview by appointment.
2. Before the interview, do some homework:
   - What is the basis of this person's expertise?
   - Find his or her publications or records of achievement and familiarize yourself with them.
   - Plan your questions before the interview to make the best use of your time and interviewer's time.
3. Send a courtesy note afterward, thanking the person interviewed for his or her time and the information, and perhaps offering to send a copy of the finished report.

2. Primary and Secondary Information

Many people find the distinction between primary and secondary information a useful insight into the process of writing reports based on research. Primary information is information you have collected yourself or you are using directly from its primary source. Secondary information, briefly, is information you have received second hand (say, from reading about it). For example, suppose you were writing a report on the Tennessee-Tombigbee Waterway. If you were to write the report entirely from published information in your university library, it would be entirely from secondary information. But if you were to go out and take pictures of the site, look it over and talk to the people directly involved in the project, then that would be primary information. Many readers value a report that includes at least some primary information more highly than a report that contains only secondary information.

The distinction between primary and secondary is not always easy to see; often it depends on what you are writing about. For example, newspapers are usually considered secondary, but if you are writing about contemporary views of high-technology crime (computer theft, etc.), one contemporary view is certainly the way news media view the subject. Thus for that subject newspapers are primary sources of information.

3. Using Computers in Library Research

Computers play an increasingly important role in library research. The abundance of periodical indexes, and their different varieties, can be traced to the use of computers to compile them. In the next decade an increasing number of libraries will make available to their patrons on-line access to computerized card catalogues. One such system, the OCLC (Online Computer Library Center, Inc.) provides access not only to your own university's records, but also to the records of all libraries in the system (currently over 8.5 million records). You can do author searches, title searches, and author/title searches, and receive paper printouts of the results. OCLC also provides all of the information you would normally get on card-catalogue cards. Eventually some such system will be combined with each library's circulation computer to tell you instantaneously whether the book you are looking for is currently checked out.

Many periodical indexes can already be accessed through computers. This usually will cost you money, perhaps $10-$20 for the average simple search, but it will enable you to search many indexes very quickly. This kind of search is especially valuable when you want to research the convergence of two or more topics. To use a very much simplified example, if you wanted to research pigs, there would be no particular need to use the computer. If you wanted to research pigs in Texas, there is more need for a computer because you would otherwise (theoretically) have to search for everything about pigs and everything about Texas, and then look for instances when sources are identical. The computer can do that much faster. As your topic becomes more and more complicated and specialized—say pigs in Texas who had a certain disease in 1979—the usefulness of the computer grows. For a real example, I wanted to use the Educational Resources Information Clearinghouse (ERIC) computerized bibliography to research whether anything had been written on research on the combination of cloze tests (a measurement of readability) and technical writing. ERIC listed 180 documents on technical writing and over 800 on cloze tests. Without ERIC, I would have had to compare the two lists manually to discover whether any items appeared in both—a very tedious chore. The computer did the same comparison in less than a minute, and the search was performed free as a service of the library's reference department (again, longer searches cost money). Computerized indexes exist for nearly every field of study; ask your university librarian about the availability of such a service on your campus.

4. Keeping Records

The better records you keep of your research, the easier writing your paper will be. Not only does efficient record-keeping make it easier, quicker, and more efficient to retrieve information when you start writing, but also the sooner you begin articulating your understanding of the topic on paper, the better your final version will be.

Perhaps the best way to keep records of your research is to combine your own use of note and bibliography cards with a research notebook, as described in Chapter 18. Such a daily log can be very useful when you begin writing your report. Many students today prefer to photocopy articles to use at their leisure, rather than to take notes directly from the articles when they first read them. The advantage of this is that you have continued access to the article whenever you need it. The disadvantages are that it costs money and does not encourage you to come to your own early understanding of the material the way careful note taking does.

5. Research Structures and Report Structures

A fundamental mistake made by many writers new to writing long reports occurs when the writer unthinkingly confuses the *research* structure—the ordering of a fully developed search strategy—with the structure the *report* should have. It's always tempting to allow the structure the topic took on as you came to understand it to control the structure of the report you write on the topic. To use a computer metaphor, this is letting the structure of the input control the structure of the output. But the typical function of a computer is to change the input structure, to organize the information in new ways. A report writer also needs to take in the research data, make sense of it in light of his or her own thinking, and then reintegrate it into a new structure, one that is best for the intended audience and the report's purpose.

6. Evaluation

After so much attention to the process of library research, you may wonder how your reader, specifically an instructor, evaluates the quality of your research. The following list of questions represents the results of research into how instructors evaluate their students' research:

- Does the report contain enough "hard" information?
- Is the borrowed material properly credited?
- Is there over-reliance on any one source?
- Do the sources include the most recent available?
- Are the sources of a variety of kinds?
- Are the sources of the right level?
- Does the report over-rely on textbooks?
- Do quotations seem artificially inserted, or are they woven into the fabric of the paper?
- Are all references in the proper form for your field?

Of course one must also ask larger, functional questions in order to accurately evaluate the report's total quality. Those questions include whether the report does the job it needs to do for the audience it is aimed at, and a number of other similar concerns. For a brief checklist of those larger questions, see the introduction to Part V of this text.

EXERCISES

On a separate sheet of paper, write the answers to the following questions:

1. On what page number of what generalized encyclopedia can you find information on your research topic?

2. What are the names of the specialized encyclopedias closest to your field?
3. Under what Library of Congress Subject Headings can information on your topic be found?
4. What are the names of three to five leading journals in your field?
5. What periodical indexes are available for your field? Which ones have abstracts?
6. What is the accepted style manual for your field?
7. List three other useful reference works specialized for your field.
8. Create a preliminary bibliography on your research topic. You need to include perhaps two books, five articles, and the names of two local experts you can ask for interviews.
9. Find a periodical index that is appropriate to your field of study and includes abstracts. Use it to make a priority-ordered list of the five articles you listed in the previous question— the most appropriate, the next most appropriate, and so on.
10. Write a brief (100-word) report on the extent to which your library makes computerized database searches available to students and on whether such a search would be advisable for your research project. Be sure to consider key factors (beyond availability), such as the appropriateness of your project for such a search and the cost of the search versus its likely benefits.
11. Choose one of the following topics and prepare a preliminary bibliography for a research report on it:

    Johns-Manville and asbestos health hazards

    Apple Computer's management-succession problems

    Lawsuits concerning the Dalkon Shield

    Marketing strategies cola companies use to achieve Number One status

    Procter and Gamble's logo problems

    The economics of space exploration

PART V

Kinds of Reports

A recent survey of the typical kinds of reports in business and industry reported the following kinds:*

- advertisement
- analysis of complaint
- announcement of price increase
- annual report
- answer to request
- article for professional/trade periodical
- brochure
- bulletin
- business book
- business newsletter
- catalog
- claims adjustment
- collection letter
- complete periodical
- computer documentation
- congratulations
- consumer handbook/manual
- cover/transmittal letter

*From research by Kitty Locker.

- cost estimate
- credit denial
- credit report on customer
- employee reprimand
- evaluation of physical facilities
- evaluation of supervision
- follow-up letter
- forecast
- grievance step response
- housekeeping memo
- house organ for business organization
- industrial handbook/manual
- inspection report
- invitation
- job description
- letter changing price
- letter confirming an order
- letter declining to quote on an order
- letter to union official
- major-expenditure request
- management newsletter
- minutes of meeting
- monthly/quarterly report
- news article
- plant-productivity study
- policy/procedure bulletin
- press release
- procedures
- progress report
- projection of inventory needs
- proposal
- recommendation
- reminder to follow procedures
- report
- report for government agency
- request for credit references
- request to deviate from policy
- request for information
- safety reminder
- safety report
- summary of advantages/disadvantages of service
- 10-K report
- thank-you letter
- training manual
- trip report

Faced with this variety, it's difficult to make definitive statements about exactly what kinds of reports are the most important. There are clearly almost as many kinds of reports as there are report-writing situations.

As with the first four Parts of this book, Part V focuses on presenting key elements that will enable you to respond to each changing report-writing situation appropriately. Chapters 17 and 18 detail a number of specific kinds of reports (especially proposals), and the other chapters present critical features of all professional reports. Once you enter professional life, the kinds and parts of reports described here will become the setting for your use of the principles and skills presented in Parts I–IV.

Each of the four chapters in Part V presents patterns and outlines for reports and parts of reports. People use patterns like these to assist in their report writing every day. But remember to use all such models and patterns intelligently. It doesn't make sense to use a prefabricated model *unchanged* in a complex report-writing situation. To use such a model intelligently, you must consider the important ways in which each specific audience, purpose, and message—and your own role as a writer—requires alterations in the model. As your needs and abilities as a writer grow and change, you should find yourself increasingly modifying and combining the patterns presented in this book. Remember that the principles behind the patterns (principles such as audience analysis and adaptation) are much more important than the patterns themselves.

Many principles are important to your success as a report writer. Four of the most important are:

1. Always have in mind a specific reader for your report. Do not overestimate your reader's knowledge of (or interest in) your subject.
2. Ensure that your report's purpose is explicitly stated and that every part of the report clearly contributes to fulfilling that purpose.
3. Reread your report with a critical eye before you submit it; clarify passages in which your reader may misunderstand your meaning.
4. Ensure that the final version of your report is in a style and form that will meet or exceed your reader's expectations.

17

Varieties of Reports

For professionals who write as part of their jobs, each day brings new kinds of problems to solve on paper and new demands on their writing skills. Many situations require a unique kind of report, one whose structure and approach are tailored specifically to that situation. But many other situations require a routine report format. Just as there are many routine kinds of business letters, so there are many routine kinds of reports:

Progress reports	Periodic reports
Lab reports	Meeting reports
Inspection reports	Travel reports
Trouble & accident reports	Estimates & Appraisals
Evaluations	Survey reports
Preliminary reports	Planning reports
Policy reports	Cost reports
Design reports	Recommendation reports

See also the list in the Introduction to Part V. There are as many common kinds of reports as there are common kinds of situations in business and industry. In fact, it often seems like there are many *more* kinds because there is no standard terminology. Thus a "periodic activity report" and a "progress report" are frequently different names for the same thing.

This chapter's goal is to familiarize you with some of the many of kinds of reports that commonly occur in business and industry. First it discusses two typical *formats* that any kind of report can appear in—the letter report form and the formal report form (discussed in more detail in Chapter 19). It then presents in detail a number of the most common kinds of routine reports:

Periodic Activity Reports
Lab Reports
Manuals:
- Personnel
- Hardware
- Repair
- Software

This chapter also suggests guidelines for creating tailor-made (unique) report forms, guidelines that can also be used for creating new formats that may then become routine.

1. Report Forms

Reports can appear in many different forms. Three of the most frequently used are discussed here: the letter report, the fully compartmentalized report, and the formal report.

1.1 Letter Reports

One of the most convenient ways to present a short report is called the *letter report*, which is used frequently with reports that are only a page or two long. If the entire document (letter plus report) will be more than three or four pages long, you should probably use a different format. (For example, rather than put the report inside the letter, use a cover letter and accompanying report, as in the formal report described later in this chapter.) But if you want a convenient way to put a short report on paper, you may want to consider the form known as the letter report.

Exhibit 17.1 shows the conceptual outline of a letter report.

The letter report contains all of the typical elements of a business letter, but it has a short report sandwiched between the letter's opening and closing paragraphs. The letter should satisfy all of the requirements for an effective letter

Exhibit 17.1 The Conceptual Outline of a Letter Report

```
                                          inside heading

inside address

subject line

salutation

   Introductory paragraph of letter—may be written in a less
formal style than that used in the report proper.

First Heading of Report
   First paragraph of Report

Report continues one or two pages, with more headings.
```

```
              [Continuation page format, as on p. 72]

Last paragraph of Report.

                        * * * * * *

Concluding paragraph of Letter. Again, the tone may be
somewhat less formal than in the report proper.

                                          Signature block
```

(covered in Chapter 4), and the report needs to satisfy all the requirements for a good report (covered in the introduction to Part V).

1.1.1 **Strengths and Weaknesses.** The letter report form makes your letter and your report inseparable. Its advantage over simply writing a long business letter is that you can change your tone and stance within the document. The letter part can be reasonably personal and sometimes even a little judgmental, while the report remains impersonal and objective. In fairly informal situations, such as when there will probably be only one reader, the letter report offers a convenient format. Exhibit 17.2 shows such a case; here the letter report is a progress report, but contained within it is the early draft of a technical report.

The letter report's advantage over the letter-plus-report is also its weakness. If the report will need to be passed on through an organization, the letter report format may not be right. You may say things in the letter parts of the report that would just be inappropriate for readers other than the one to whom the letter is addressed. This can also apply if the report will be kept on file; you may not want the letter's life to be that long.

1.2 Fully Compartmentalized Reports

A report form that is growing in popularity for all kinds of reports is the fully compartmentalized report (also called the programmed report or the modular report). Its main distinctive feature is that there is a systematic relationship between the length of the report sections, the use of visuals, and the places where page breaks occur (places where the reader has to turn the page). Figure 17.1 shows the conceptual design of a fully compartmentalized report.

This pattern goes through the entire document. That is, each new section of text starts a new page, and most, if not all, of those sections have visuals of some sort associated with them. That way the reader is always looking at the appropriate visual at the same time as he or she is reading the matching text. When a page must be replaced (as in the looseleaf binding that is commonly used in repair manuals), there is usually room for the text on that page to get longer or shorter without materially affecting the rest of the report. With this form you lose the economy of having every page filled with text; instead, you have lots of short pages (pages with several inches of extra white space). What you gain is a one-to-one match of visuals and text, a match achieved effortlessly, and the ability to change sections, to let them grow (or shorten) without having to change the rest of the text. (Incidentally, an interesting question on this format is whether to put the visuals on the left and the text on the right, or vice versa. There is no professional consensus on this point as yet.)

1.3 Formal Reports

The alternative to a letter report is the formal report; what you may have known up to now as the "term paper" format is a recognizable derivative of the format widely known as a formal report. Chapter 19 discusses this format and all its parts

Exhibit 17.2 A Typical Letter Report

Dear Fred:

Here are the preliminary findings for the report on manpower requirements, 1985–2000. Take a look at the areas I've covered and tell me if I've left out anything major that you think we'll need.

<u>Background</u>
Table S.1 shows the employment of technical personnel in the energy program at the present time. Engineers make up about 60% of the total professional employment but only about 30% of the total doctoral employment. In Table S.2 these data are broken down by budget category.

[Tables not reproduced here]

These data on current employment were used to model staffing patterns . . . .

.
.
.

[Five paragraphs omitted]

.

<u>Conclusion</u>
This report suggests that we foresee several kinds of manpower problems. Spot shortages of highly specialized, experienced workers in fields such as cryogenics and superconducting magnets are expected. Temporary shortages caused by sharp increases and decreases in the program's required staffing will probably occur. General shortages in certain disciplines, such as nuclear engineering and computer science, are almost certain. And the university programs in energy technology may require additional support.

For a long-range activity like this one, these can be viewed as ordinary operational problems that can be expected to be adequately managed, given the energy program's already demonstrated sensitivity to manpower and education issues.

* * * * * *

That about wraps it up. Anything else you want covered in the final report, let me know in the next week or so. Otherwise I'll proceed to write it up as outlined here.

Sincerely,

David

Figure 17.1 Conceptual Design of a Fully Compartmentalized Report

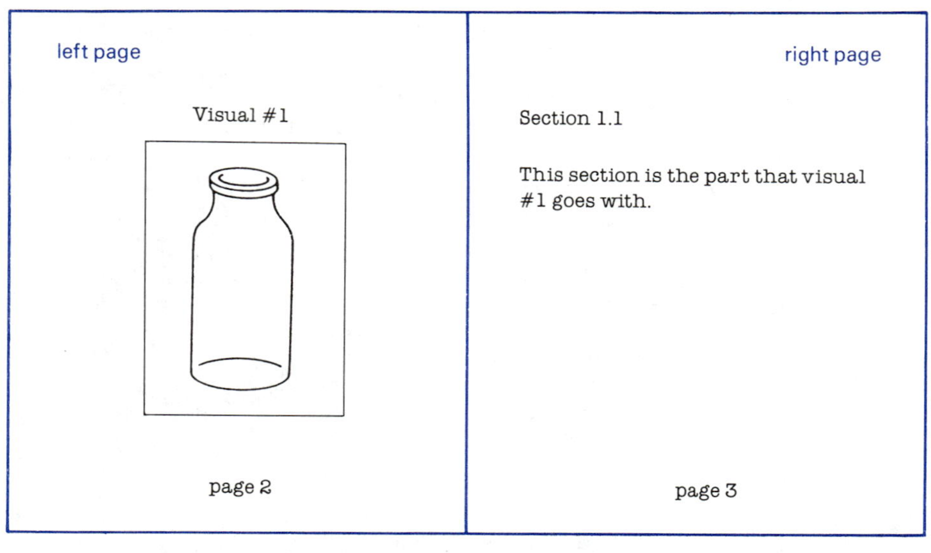

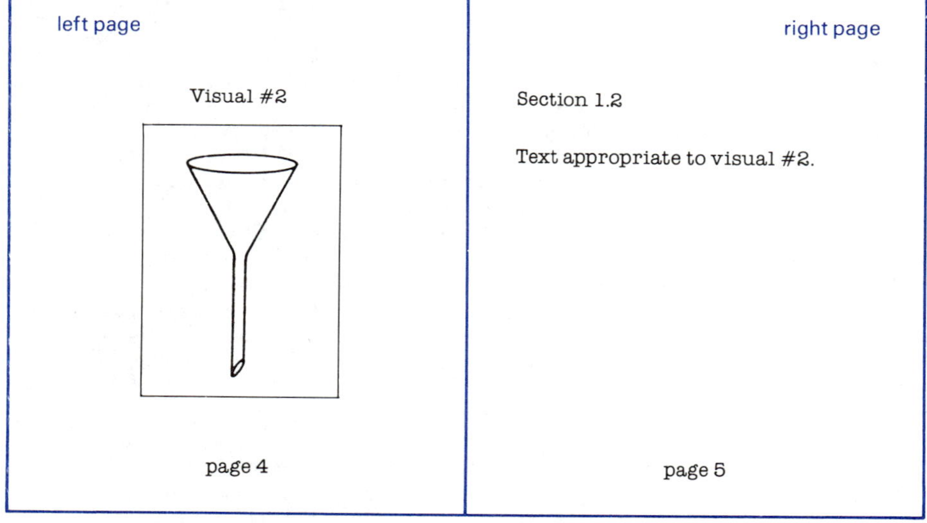

in complete detail, but you'll understand more about the varieties of reports presented here if you know a little about the format of a formal report. Here is an outline of the parts of a very complete formal report:

Letter of transmittal
Distinctive cover
Executive Summary (or abstract)

Title page
Distribution list (optional)
Table of Contents
List of figures and illustrations (may be two separate lists)
Introduction
The body of the report
Conclusion
References
Appendixes (if needed)

Of course, not all formal reports have all these parts, and a few have more.

2. Types of Reports

There is no comprehensive and authoritative list of all the types of reports, or of the standard types of reports, nor is there agreement among authorities about what should be the "basic" kinds. The types presented here are the ones that occur most often, but do not be surprised if someone someday asks you to write a type of report not covered here. The only thing authorities agree on is that, however the names may change and come into and out of vogue, the only really new form of report is the proposal. Because proposal writing is so important, it is given its own chapter here (Chapter 18).

2.1 Periodic Activity Reports

Periodic Activity Reports (also called progress reports) give employers, customers, supervisors, or investors necessary information about how work on a particular project has gone. Such reports can be turned in at intervals determined by time (such as weekly or monthly) or by task (completion of planning, completion of preliminary site work, and so forth).

2.1.1 **Organization.** Your reader's purposes should help shape the organization of your progress report. Three elements usually appear in progress reports:

1. an explanation of the relationship between the part of the project this report covers and parts earlier reports covered
2. an explanation of the project's recent developments
3. at least some mention of the project's next phases.

These three elements—the looks backwards, at the present, and to the future—are present one way or another in most progress reports. But they appear in so many different ways that to be more specific about them would be misleading. Some reports carry all three, some only two, and some only one.

2.1.2 **Functions.** Besides keeping others informed of your progress, progress reports force you, the writer, to focus systematically on how your project is going. Progress reports can also form the first draft of your final report. In many cases progress reports are the only contacts between the person doing the work and the one for whom the work is being done. In view of all these functions, the length and organization of your progress reports are especially significant.

2.1.3 **Length.** Most readers expect progress reports to be short. But you can't decide what "short" means without some fairly precise knowledge of your reader's purpose in requiring the report. Is the report totally routine, done solely for record-keeping purposes? Or is the report significant in that it will contribute to future decision making, maybe even decisions about whether to continue to support the project? To know what "short" means, you have to know what your reader expects in the report and how your reader will use it. Only then can you tell what level of detail to use, what to include and what to exclude. As in other kinds of writing for business and industry, concern for your reader's purpose should shape the way you write progress reports. Exhibit 17.3 shows a typical progress report, written regarding the student report at the end of Chapter 19.

2.2 Lab Reports

This section describes elements common to reports of routine laboratory testing. When your goal is to report on original research, you would normally use a much fuller format, such as the one presented in Chapter 19, "Long Reports."

2.2.1 **Pattern for Lab Reports.** Many times routine laboratory work is written up on preprinted forms. There's not much to say about using such forms, except to remind you that when you need to go into more detail than the form allows, remember that you can nearly always attach a supplemental letter or short report to the standard form. When a preprinted form is not used, you are usually given a set of headings, such as the ones in the following list, to structure your report around. You can cover other areas as well, but you'll usually be expected to include at least these:

Purpose		Purpose
Results	or	Procedures
Discussion		Results
Procedures		Discussion

Purpose of the Test. Why is this work being done? To determine the compression strength of a particular sample, to determine the cause of failure of a certain structural element, to isolate and identify a particular enzyme? Be very explicit in your lab report about why the test is being done. That way, when your reader sees your report, he or she will not think you did more than you actually did or mistakenly fault you for doing less than you actually did.

Most readers will check to see whether your purpose and results are on the same scale. For example, if you set out to determine why a certain sample of steel

Exhibit 17.3 A Typical Progress Report

This report presents my progress on the English 4140 major report, "Economic Implications of Recombinant DNA Research," from the time of our last conference (Jan. 20, 1983) to this date (Feb. 15, 1983). At that time, we agreed that the report would have two major sections: the first on current research and recombinant DNA technology, and the second on the economic implications of that research and technology. The research for those two sections is well under way; a major change in the report's focus, if you approve, will be to add a new section at the front of the report that presents the basics about recombinant DNA.

Research is well under way on the section on current research and technology regarding recombinant DNA. Attached to this report is a list of books and articles that have been consulted so far, as well as a second list of sources yet to be read. The material on economic implications presents no problems at all; it is quite accessible and easy to read. The material on current developments in research and technology, on the other hand, is somewhat harder to find and much harder to understand. Even for a person with a college-level background in biology and a special interest in genetics, the typical article in, for example, Biotechnology is nearly impossible to understand, much less interpret.

The extremely technical and difficult nature of literature on current research and technology in recombinant DNA has two implications for this project: (1) it will not be possible to give quite so full a presentation of the current research and technology as originally conceived, and (2) I propose the addition of a new first section to the report, one that presents the basic elements of DNA recombination. Thus the report will have three sections, proceeding from the basics of recombinant DNA to a section on the current state of research and technology (slightly shorter than originally proposed, but easier to understand because of the presence of the new Part One), to a section on the economics of recombinant DNA. For an executive/layman reader, this three-part structure will make the report much easier to understand.

The remaining work to be done mostly involves the exploration of other sources (government documents and interviews, especially) and the actual writing of the report. With your approval of the changes described here, writing can begin almost at once. Current plans are to finish writing by Feb. 23, type on the 24th and the 25th, and have ample time left over for careful proofreading before the due date (March 1).

pipe has stress fractures, you can legitimately conclude something like "The stress fractures are caused by prolonged exposure to (a particular chemical) under (a particular pressure)." You *cannot* conclude, however, that that is the reason a certain pipeline exploded. Your lab report might well be a part of that larger investigation into the pipeline's explosion, which would then become a long report of the sort shown in Chapter 19, but you still have to keep the scope of your results comparable to the scope of your purposes.

Results of the Test. Many readers like to see *results* right after *purpose*, and will use what you say there to decide whether or not to read your procedure. Others will feel the order of purpose-procedure-results (which mirrors the steps the experimenter goes through) should be kept intact. You, as the writer, have the choice of using a reader- or writer-based structure. You should make the decision about which structure to use based on the nature of your subject, your purpose, and especially your audience and their purpose in reading. An expert may be as interested in the procedure as in the results, so writing for an expert audience you would put procedure *first*. An executive/layman might only be interested in procedures if something in the results piques that interest, so writing for that audience you would keep procedure *last*. When in doubt, you're probably better off to stay with the more traditional pattern, purpose-procedure-results.

Be careful how you phrase your results. Let the reader know explicitly when you are merely reporting the test's results and when you are drawing conclusions from those results.

Discussion of the Results. If you want to add more information to the report that does not spring directly from the test itself, you can add "Discussion of the Results" as an optional section. Here you would discuss any anomalies or unexpected results. You might, for example, mention how the results fulfill (or fail to fulfill) the test's purpose, or recommend whether and which further tests should be performed. Here you can also enlarge on the implications of the test results.

Procedures. Under "Procedures" you might write a narrative description of the tests that were run and under exactly what conditions. Use visuals to help explain what was done, but remember that you have to explain in words all of the content of the visuals. You cannot just say "I placed the sample on the plate as shown in Figure 3"; you must first explain just how the sample was placed on the plate, and then refer the reader to Figure 3.

General instructions for writing up procedures in laboratory reports are the same as those for processes, described in Chapter 11. Be specific, and be sure you don't lose your reader in the process. You probably know all of the steps in the process before you begin the report, but your reader (outside of college) probably doesn't. Those steps should be forecast at the beginning of the procedures section. Break the test into steps, forecast them, and use subheadings to help your reader follow the steps. Most important, be specific: *exactly* what materials were used, *exactly* what machine, *exactly* how long, and so forth.

2.2.2 **Style in Laboratory Reports.** Most writing works better if it uses present tense and active voice and includes personal pronouns. That is, in most situations most readers would rather read "Next I place the sample on the plate" or "Next I placed the sample on the plate" than "Next the sample was placed on the plate." Although present tense, active voice, and personal pronouns can make laboratory reports much more readable, the tradition requiring past tense, passive voice, and omission of personal pronouns is still quite strong. It can be persuasively argued, on historical evidence, that past-passive-impersonal is *not* the essence of scientific style (*clarity* is); on psychological evidence, that past-passive is harder to read and increases reader errors; and, on philosophical evidence, that impersonal style falsifies the experiment's reporting (because the experiment was conducted by a human agent, the report should show it). Nevertheless, the majority of readers of lab reports seem to want past-passive-impersonal, forcing the majority of writers to deliver it. The person writing a lab report is usually not in a position to select the style it is to be written in. As a writer, be aware of the problem and do your best to give your reader the best possible report within the bounds of what your reader will accept.

Exhibit 17.4 shows a fairly typical laboratory report. But remember that, other than preprinted forms, there is no one standard format for laboratory reports. Generally, each laboratory has its own form for such reports.

2.3 Manuals

Manuals are a type rather different from most other kinds of reports. A manual is a document used to instruct or remind people how to do something. Because manuals must be replaced or have sections updated frequently, they are usually done in a looseleaf-notebook format; increasingly they are done in the form of the fully compartmentalized report described earlier in this chapter. There are many kinds of manuals; we will discuss four of the most common: personnel manuals, hardware manuals, repair manuals, and software manuals. All of these types of manuals are, to some extent, process descriptions; review Chapter 11 "Processes and Instructions," in connection with writing any kind of manual.

2.3.1 **Personnel, Hardware, and Repair Manuals.** In 1971, Stello Jordan's *Handbook of Technical Writing Practices* presented a general outline for manuals that can still be adapted to serve for most kinds of manuals. The *Handbook* suggests the following organization:

Front matter
Introduction
General description of product
Theory of operation
Description of the operation controls
Adjustments and operator's activities prior to actual operation of equipment
Actual operation instructions and operation technique
Troubleshooting section
Emergency or standard servicing
Index

Exhibit 17.4 A Typical Laboratory Report

CONTROLS FOR ENZYMATIC AND NON-ENZYMATIC BROWNING

In food systems several types of browning reactions occur which may be favorable depending on the food product being produced. Browning reactions are enzymatic or non-enzymatic in nature. Enzymatic browning occurs in some fruits and vegetables when they are cut or damaged. Non-enzymatic browning includes carbonyl-amine browning, caramelization, and ascorbic acid browning. In this experiment the factors which inhibit or control these reactions were demonstrated in apples, chocolate cakes, and caramels (Campbell et al., 1979).

Method

Slices of apples were treated with different solutions to illustrate the inhibition of enzymatic browning. The treatments used are listed in Table 1. Untreated cut apples served as the control. The samples were evaluated one hour after treatment.

Table 1. Treatments used on apples to retard enzymatic browning.

	Treatment
A.	No treatment[a]
B.	Water
C.	50% Sucrose solution[b]
D.	Ascorbic citric acid solution
E.	Lemon juice
F.	0.05% KH Sulfite solution

[a]the control
[b]50g sugar dissolved in 50ml water

Five chocolate cake batters were prepared to show the effects of pH on carbonyl-amine browning and the crumb color of the baked product. The proportions of the leavening agents, baking soda, baking powder, and buttermilk were modified in each batter to yield a different pH concentration. Two of the cake batters were neutral, one was acidic, one was basic, and the final one was extremely alkaline. The formulas for the cake batters appear in Table 2. The procedure for mixing was that of Campbell et al. (1979). The pH of the cake batters was determined with pH paper. The color of the batter was also noted. The cakes were evaluated on the basis of crumb color, grain, volume, and flavor.

Table 2. Formulas for cake batters with different pH.

	Formulas				
Ingredient	Acidic	Neutral[a]	Neutral[b]	Basic	Alkaline
Cake flour, g	100	100	100	100	100
Sodium bicarb, g	–	–	0.7	1.3	5.0
Baking powder, g	5.0	5.0	2.2	–	–
Salt, g	1	1	1	1	1
Cocoa, g	18	18	18	18	18
Sugar, g	150	150	150	150	150
Shortening, g	66	66	66	66	66
Eggs, g	100	100	100	100	100
Milk, g	–	68	–	68	68
Buttermilk, g	68	–	68	–	–
Vanilla, ml	2	2	2	2	2

[a]neutral with 5.0g baking powder and no baking soda.
[b]neutral with 2.2g baking powder and 0.7g baking soda.

Caramels were made using two different sugars, sucrose and glucose, to demonstrate carbonyl-amine browning. The basic formula for caramels appears in Table 3. The formula containing sucrose was heated to a boiling point of 120°C, whereas the formula with glucose was heated to 138°C.

Table 3. Basic formula for caramels.

Ingredient	Quantity
Sucrose[a]	200g
Margarine	14g
Milk	127ml
Half and Half	110ml

[a]Repeat substituting glucose for sucrose.

Results

All the solutions used to treat the apples were effective in stopping enzymatic browning. The apples treated with lemon juice were slightly yellow while all the others remained white (excluding the control).

The evaluation of the cake batters and cakes appears in Table 4. The pH readings for the supposedly neutral batter containing 0.7g baking soda and 2.2g baking powder and for the batter with 1.3g baking soda are both too acidic. The inaccuracy in pH may be attributed to human error when taking the pH. The crumb color of the cakes turned darker as the pH increased.

The caramels containing sucrose were lighter in color and hard in nature. The ones produced with glucose were darker in color with a more desirable texture.

Table 4. Evaluation of chocolate cakes based on batter color, batter pH, crumb color, grain, volume, and flavor.

	Formulas				
Characteristic	Acidic	Neutral[a]	Neutral[b]	Basic	Alkaline
batter color	light	medium	medium	medium	darker
pH	5.5	6.4	5.5	5.5	8.0
crumb color	light	light	darker	darker	darkest
grain	poor	excellent	very good	good	poor
volume (cm)	5.5	6.5	7.0	5.0	5.5
flavor	good	very good	excellent	good	good

[a]Neutral with 5.0g baking powder and no baking soda.
[b]Neutral with 2.2g baking powder and 0.7g baking soda.

Discussion

Enzymatic browning is inhibited by inactivating the polyphenoloxidase (the enzyme responsible for the reaction), altering the substrate, or eliminating oxygen. Polyphenoloxidases, present naturally in fruits and vegetables, transform the polyphenolic compounds (in fruits) in the presence of oxygen to quinones. The quinones polymerize, and thus the fruit turns brown (Campbell et al., 1979). In this experiment the water and the 50% sucrose solution treatments prevented browning by eliminating the fruit's contact with oxygen. Ascorbic citric acid and lemon juice retarded browning by producing a pH medium (pH 4 or less) in which polyphenoloxidases do not function. The final treatment of 0.5% kH sulfite solution stops the browning process by repressing the enzyme system (Campbell et al., 1979).

The darkening which occurred in the cakes is primarily due to the increase in pH by manipulation of the leavening agents. Basic pH mediums increase crust browning as carbonyl-amine browning is accelerated (Campbell et al., 1979), and they alter pigments found in cocoa. Thus a darkened and red crumb color results (Lee, 1975).

Carbonyl-amine browning results from the condensation of a carbonyl group of a reducing sugar and an available amino group, followed by a series of reactions which ultimately produce brown pigments known as melanoidins. High temperatures, high pH's, and low moisture levels accelerate the reaction. Sucrose was ineffective in producing satisfactory caramels since it is not a reducing sugar and does not participate in carbonyl-amine browning. This accounts for the light product produced. Glucose, on the other hand, is a reducing sugar, participates in carbonyl-amine browning, and consequently darker caramels resulted. The hard consistency of the sucrose product (caramels) is due to excessive crystal formation since sucrose is unable to invert (Campbell et al., 1979).

Conclusion

The results of this study have shown that enzymatic and non-enzymatic browning can be inhibited or controlled in order to produce a desirable food product. Conditions which affect browning include pH, the availability of oxygen, and inactivation of enzyme systems.

References

Campbell, A.M., Penfield, M.P., and Griswold, R.M., 1979. "The Experimental Study of Food." Houghton Mifflin Co., Boston.
Lee, F.A., 1975. "Basic Food Chemistry," p. 331. Avi Publishing Co., Inc.

Source: Reprinted by permission of Gina Marlowe.

Although many manuals may not need quite so full a treatment, this list—with proper modifications—can serve as an outline for the content and structure of most such manuals. Beyond that, the particular content of any manual you may be involved in producing will probably dictate its structure to a large extent.

Another area of special interest to a technical writer producing any kind of manual is the way the words and pictures are laid out on the pages and the way the pages are bound together. This text has stressed that the purpose, message, audience, and situation in which any technical document will be used should have a strong influence on how that document is written. Manuals provide particularly vivid examples of the ways in which those factors can affect the way a technical document is done. Some critical questions for the writer or editor of a manual are:

- What kind of person will be using this manual?
- What environment will this manual be used in?
- What will be the goal of the person using this manual?

Answers to these and other similar questions must be taken into account if a manual is to function effectively.

For example, consider the binding of the manual. If the manual is glued, stapled, or stitched, it will be difficult to use with no hands; such bindings do not allow the document to lie flat. If, on the other hand, it is bound with a spiral binding or three-hole punched to be put into a looseleaf notebook, the manual can be laid flat, freeing the operator's hands for technical work. The looseleaf

Exhibit 17.5 A Page from a Typical Personnel Manual

GROUP INSURANCE PLANS

Basic Plan

All full-time faculty and staff members and regular part-time employees who are scheduled to work at least 30 hours a week are eligible to participate in the basic group hospitalization plan. Academic appointments must be for at least 75% time and for a minimum of one semester or 2 consecutive quarters in order to meet eligibility requirement. If both the employee and spouse work for the state, both must elect to be insured under separate policies. No person eligible for coverage as an employee may be included as a dependent. Coverage under the Group Program will become effective the first day of the calendar month coinciding with or following completion of one month of active service provided the employee has completed the necessary enrollment forms. Under this plan, the individual pays 40% of the premium and the University pays 60%. (This is the only insurance coverage for which the University may legally contribute toward premiums.) The monthly contribution of the individual varies, depending on salary and coverage of dependents. The basic group-insurance package contains hospital and surgical insurance, major medical insurance, emergency accident expense benefits, term life insurance, and special accident insurance. The plan also has an additional optional special accident insurance (payable upon death or dismemberment), which can be elected by the individual. Details of all benefits under this program are set forth in the Group Insurance Booklet issued to all participating employees.

format also allows the operator to replace pages that carry out-of-date or no-longer-accurate information with new pages, without replacing the whole volume.

For another example, consider the way words and illustrations are laid out on the page. Exhibit 17.5 shows a sample page from a typical personnel manual.

Exhibit 17.6 shows the same information, reworked to take more into consideration that the document is a manual and will be used differently from other kinds of reports.

These kinds of variations in the way each page looks—use of typefaces, chunking of information, careful cross referencing, and so on—are characteristic of the kind of thought and work that needs to go into many different kinds of manuals. By enhancing the text's visual qualities, the writer makes the material within it more accessible to the reader.

2.3.2 **Software User's Manuals.** One of the most rapidly growing areas of report writing is software manuals (also called software documentation). (These were covered briefly in Chapter 11, Section 2.3.) This documentation typically takes several different forms:

Exhibit 17.6 Reworked Version of the Page in Exhibit 17.5

BASIC GROUP HOSPITALIZATION PLAN

WHO'S ELIGIBLE?	The following University employees are eligible for the Basic Group Hospitalization Plan: • All full-time faculty • All full-time staff members • Regular part-time employees who work a minimum of 30 hours per week
RESTRICTION ON ELIGIBILITY	Academic appointments must be for at least 75% time and for a minimum of one semester or 2 consecutive quarters.
RESTRICTION ON SPOUSE COVERAGE	If both employee and spouse work for state, both must be insured under *separate* policies.
WHEN DOES COVERAGE BEGIN?	Upon applicant's submission of all necessary forms and the completion of one month of active service, COVERAGE BECOMES EFFECTIVE THE FIRST DAY OF THE CALENDAR MONTH.
PREMIUMS	Under the Basic Group Hospitalization Plan, • you pay 40% of the premium, • the university pays 60% of the premium. • (Your monthly contribution varies, depending on salary and coverage of dependents.)
WHAT DO YOU GET?	Under the Basic Plan, you get the following coverage: • hospital and surgical insurance • major medical insurance • emergency accident expense benefits • term life insurance • special accident insurance • additional special accident insurance (optional). This insurance is payable upon death or dismemberment.
COMMENTS	Details of all benefits under this program are set forth in the Group Insurance Booklet issued to all participating employees.

Source: Michael E. Hall, "Improving the Readibility of Training Manuals," unpublished M.A. thesis, the University of Tennessee, 1984.

New user's guides
Advanced user's guides
Programmer documentation

These three types of software documentation provide perfect examples of the importance of audience analysis and adaptation. Although the three types of documents cover many of the same areas of a program, the way each does it is completely different from the way the others do it. For example, a new user's guide has to focus to a great extent on the user's lack of experience with the system, and this limitation affects everything the guide does and how it does it. The writer of such a guide has to resist the temptation to be catalogical (or encyclopedic) about what the system is and what it can do, and realize that the reader wants to know first how to access the relevant programs (this may even include something as basic as turning the computer on and logging on), and then how to get started in a simple routine. Similarly, a new user will feel considerable discomfort if something does not go just the way the instructions suggest. Discussion of more complex procedures has to wait until the reader has learned the basics.

An advanced user's guide, on the other hand, can be more theoretical and comprehensive. Advanced users have the time, inclination, and courage to try new procedures, to understand considerations beyond those currently being discussed, and to experiment on their own.

Programmer's manuals, on the other hand, work in almost the reverse manner to the way user's manuals work. Where the user's manual is taking an incremental approach, trying to build up an understanding one piece at a time, the programmer's manual takes a catalogical (or encyclopedic) approach, laying out the whole system, not according to the logic of a user (who looks at the system from the bottom up), but according to the logic of a programmer or systems analyst (who looks at the system from the top down).

Let's assume you are the manager of a small business, and you have just purchased a software package called "Paymaster" to serve as your business accounting system. What will its structure look like? Exhibit 17.7 offers a sample outline of a typical new user's manual; you may want to compare it to the Stello Jordan manual outline given earlier in this chapter.

Although this structure or format will vary considerably from one user's manual to another, it is typical of what you will see. Notice that the user is introduced to the system with the briefest of all overviews, instructions on how to use the manual, and a short tutorial on a simple problem. Notice, too, that technical information of any kind of detail or complexity at all is placed at the back of the manual.

3. Creating Report Formats

There are conceivably as many kinds of short reports as there are recurring situations in business and industry. Many times you may have to construct the report's format from scratch, with no routine or model to work from. The next two sections offer guidelines for situations in which you have to create your own

Exhibit 17.7 Outline of a Typical New User's Manual

- Clipped to the inside front cover is a "ready reference" card, for quick reminders of frequently used commands and routines.
- Before the title page is a page listing the numbers and titles of all the chapters, in big print.
- The title page has a copyright notice and a "proprietary information" notice on it.
- The Table of Contents is quite detailed, using different typefaces, perhaps even different colors, to give readers quick access to particular parts of the manual.
- A one-page piece called "About the Paymaster Manual" tells who it is for, what its parts are, and how to use it. It also reminds the reader that there is a reader-response card at the end of the manual to fill out and send in with comments about the manual.

Chapter One: Before Starting
This chapter introduces the system; gives a one page-overview of the whole system, possibly in the form of a flow chart; describes a shortcut that experienced users who may happen to get this manual can take; and gives a quick overview of what the system will do for its users.

Chapter Two: Getting Started
This chapter explains what the system needs in terms of software, hardware, and supplies; how to load the disks and copy them; and how to set up Paymaster.

Chapter Three: A Practice Run
This chapter sets up a simple trial problem and explains how to solve it using Paymaster.

Chapter Four: Setting Up Paymaster
This chapter explains the different options available and procedures used to set up Paymaster in its basic form.

Chapter Five: Running Paymaster
This is the most detailed chapter, explaining each function of the software in detail.

Appendix A
This section explains possible error messages and how to deal with them.

Appendix B
This section gives paper copies of the various formats used to enter data into Paymaster, so that users can marshall the appropriate data in proper form before they start keying it into the computer.

Appendix C
This section gives technical information on Paymaster.

Glossary

Index

report format, first for tailor-made, one-of-a-kind reports, and then for new routine formats.

You may have to write a report for a new or different situation, and the newness or uniqueness of the situation is what makes it reportable. In such a situation your report can be tailor made; you create a structure that may never be used again. Or you may need to create a pattern—a routine—to be used from now on by anyone in your organization who needs it. The two situations are different in important ways.

3.1 Creating Tailor-Made Reports

For most reports you write without a model, you can easily construct an outline. To do so, combine three lists:

1. the list of topics you want to cover
2. the list of questions your reader will want answered
3. the list of topics that need to be included for record-keeping purposes

Combine items from the three lists when you can, and then organize the resulting list into a coherent structure, one that makes sense from the reader's point of view.

Consider the following example: Suppose you're the Minnesota/Wisconsin Regional Manager for XYZ Kitchen Implements, assigned to write a report for the national office of a situation that occurred in your region. Jones Cafeteria in Duluth, a large and successful cafeteria in a major suburban shopping center, uses six of your machines, worth more than $150,000, including a food slicer. On Jan. 7 they reported to your office in Minneapolis that their slicer had stopped working, and you dispatched a service representative, who reported by phone that a new motor was needed. He told Jones Cafeteria it would take three to five days to get a new motor from Chicago, and they agreed to slice by hand for that time, which uses more food (the slices aren't nearly as thin) and takes much more time. Then the serviceman went on vacation, you were out for three days with the flu, and Chicago somehow lost the order. Nine days later you got a furious call from Jones Cafeteria, realized what had happened, and frantically called Chicago. They said they could have a new motor in Duluth in one day, so you got another one-day extension from Jones Cafeteria. The motor didn't show up. So twelve days after they reported the breakdown, you personally brought Jones Cafeteria a new slicer to use free of charge while you personally see to getting theirs fixed. They were happy to have a functioning slicer again, but still understandably angry about the poor service they received.

Now you have to write a report to the Marketing Vice-President in the national office about the whole situation. Here are the three lists you come up with:

Topics you want to cover
What happened—background
What you did

What went wrong
How you dealt with it
How to prevent future occurrences

Topics the reader wants
What happened—background
What went wrong
Analysis of why the problem occurred
How it was handled
How to prevent future occurrences

Topics for record-keeping
What went wrong
How it was handled
How to prevent future occurrences

Here is the composite list of topics, which will then become the outline of the actual report:

The Background

The Problem
What Went Wrong
How It Was Handled
Analysis of Why the Problem Occurred

The Future
How To Prevent Future Occurrences

In a similar way, you can make a structure for any report you need to write, even when you cannot find a model.

3.2 Creating Routine Formats

You may be called on to create a format to be used regularly for a certain kind of report in your organization. Usually this will mean someone is looking for a one- or two-page form to use every time a particular situation comes up. The process you should follow is an extension of the one described in the preceding section. Begin by making three lists (topics you want to cover, questions your reader will want answered, and topics you need to include for record-keeping purposes). Combine and organize those three lists into one form for a report, just as was done in the preceding example. But the next step is different. Through your company's records, trace the accounts of previous similar situations, and try writing them up on the draft of your form. You can also test your form by sharing it with people who have dealt with such situations in the past. A third alternative is to monitor the first uses of the newly designed routine form, to continue to refine it through its first year of use. Your goal should be a form that is short, easy to use, and designed to prevent its users from making mistakes in its use. To accomplish the goals, design the form carefully and test it thoroughly.

EXERCISES

1. Write a progress report describing your progress on the major report described in Chapter 19.
2. Design a two-page routine form for the telephone company to use in handling customer complaints.
3. Write a short (200–250 word) progress report to the Dean of your major's academic college detailing your progress toward a degree.
4. Find a lab report you have already completed for another class and rewrite it for this one. Pay particular attention to the ways this class's setting, purpose, and audience require changes in what you had already written. Be sure to consult with your instructor about the desired length.
5. Find an example of one of the kinds of manuals discussed in this chapter and write a brief report on it. The focus of the report should be on how well or poorly written the manual is, judged by the principles presented in this book. The audience is your instructor.
6. Write a short (4–5 pages) report on one of the topics listed in the "Exercises" at the end of Chapter 16. The audience is laymen.

18

Proposals

What mechanism connects people who can do a job with the people who need the job done? In business, in science, or in engineering, your way of communicating with the people you want to work for will usually be a *proposal*. For example, if your company does business with the federal government, you may begin projects by responding to an RFP (Request For Proposals) in *Commerce Business Daily*. If you are an architect preparing a design for a new city hall, a researcher requesting funding for a new project, a production or maintenance engineer suggesting a way to deal with an engineering problem, or a student suggesting a term paper project to a teacher, the proposal is probably the required format.

There are many different varieties of proposals. They may vary in length from short (a page or less) to long (400–500 pages for a proposal for a major government contract). And proposals can address any kind of audience: an engineer proposes a new maintenance procedure to management, a manufacturing company proposes a new product to its customers (who may be private individuals or the staff of a government agency), or a research scientist proposes federally funded research in a document that will be reviewed by grant administrators and other research scientists.

Proposals may also be *solicited* (in response to a request) or *unsolicited*. As in unsolicited letters of request (such as job applications), the unsolicited proposal usually emphasizes reader benefits right from the start much more strongly than does the solicited proposal. And as in unsolicited letters of request, unsolicited proposals usually do not get what they are asking for.

1. Elements of Proposals

Despite all the different varieties of proposals, there is a set of elements common to nearly all of them. When you write a proposal, you should choose its elements from the list in Box 18.1. Of course, depending on your topic, purpose, and audience, you may omit some elements or change their order.

Before going into a more detailed discussion of the typical parts of proposals, it is useful for you to see a sample. Exhibit 18.1 shows a student's proposal for her major report project in a typical Advanced Technical Writing class.

As you can see, this student's proposal follows very closely the outline suggested in Box 18.1. In many cases the writer will expand some areas of the outline and condense others, and of course proposals written by practicing professionals are usually considerably more complicated. But the parts, with minor changes, are the same.

1.1 Introduction

The opening sections of a proposal typically explain the motivation for the project and give a brief overview of it. Write these opening sections as though your audience will make up its mind on the basis of them alone. Although we hope that every line of any proposal we write will be read and considered carefully, the opening section establishes in the reader a tendency to approve or disapprove the rest, and thus its importance cannot be overstated.

Box 18.1 Elements of Proposals

- **Introduction**

Need: Explain why the project you are proposing needs to be undertaken—what is the problem?

Goals: What is it you want to do, specifically?

Benefits: What will be gained by the successful completion of your project? (Remember to take the reader's point of view here.)

- **Body**

Detailed Description: Explain fully what you intend to do and how you intend to do it.

Personnel: Explain who your people are—their qualifications, experience, and references. If you need to include resumés, these should be in an appendix (appropriately cross-referenced in this section).

Facilities and Equipment: Explain what facilities and equipment you will use, with specific attention to what is already on hand and what needs to be bought.

Budget: In most cases there will be a prescribed form for the budget. Whatever form you use, check your figures and your math very carefully.

- **Conclusion**

Typically, the conclusion will be a restatement of the proposal's needs and benefits. Reemphasize:

- why this project should be done
- why you and your firm are the ones to do it
- what its benefits will be
- the project's longer-term or larger implications

Depending on whether your report will be long or short, you would go into each section in more or less detail. The order of elements may also change from that presented here.

Exhibit 18.1 An Example of a Proposal

PROPOSAL FOR TERM PAPER

Computers play a major role in today's technologically advanced society. Use of computers for design, manufacturing, distribution, and management continues to grow at an amazing rate. As more people's jobs involve using computers for several to many hours each day, the subject of the efficiency of the computer system's interface with the user becomes more and more important. In response to your request for a term paper, I propose to write mine on the human-factors approach to designing computer systems.

The goal of this project will be to identify the ways in which the new field of human-factors engineering is being used to improve the quality and efficiency of interactions between people and computers. After summarizing the growing importance of human-factors engineering on such areas as computer languages, programs, and systems, the report will focus in on the physical relationship between the video-display terminal (VDT) and the operator, with specific attention to avoiding possible health hazards for operators and promoting ease of use.

The report's benefits include increasing your own awareness and knowledge of an area that affects all of us who are involved with computers on a daily basis. For you, the report will bring you up to date on the most recent research about what constitutes the most efficient configuration of operator, keyboard, screen, lighting, and seating. For me, the report lets me increase my knowledge in a field that may well be an important part of my career.

Specific Plans and Schedules

In order to investigate and fully report on the role of human-factors engineering in designing computers, especially computer work stations, I propose to follow this seven-week plan:

Week 1: Perform preliminary library search; ensure that there is enough material for this report to be feasible.
Week 2: Continue preliminary library work; confer with my technical writing instructor to narrow the topic.
Week 3: Perform the second stage of library research; focus on background information—books, articles, and so forth.
Week 4: Perform the third stage of library research; focus on current periodicals, newspapers, government documents.
Week 5: Confer again with technical writing instructor to review progress; discuss tentative outline; consider the advisability of interviews with computer users.
Week 6: Conduct interviews with computer users and write first draft of report.
Week 7: Revise, type, and proofread report.

As an industrial engineering major with a strong minor in computer science, I am qualified to carry out this kind of research and to write this report. Because I hope to have a career in industrial design, specifically as it relates to computers, I have even more motivation to do well on this report.

Because this report is primarily a library report, special facilities and equipment are not necessary to carry out the project. The library has many computer and industrial-engineering journals, so finding up-to-date articles should be relatively simple.

Estimated expenses for this project are minimal. The major cost incurred will be the typist's fee, estimated at $30, for which I already have money set aside.

CONCLUSION

Your approval of this topic will mean we can both learn more about a topic that will affect the lives of every worker in the United States in the decades to come. I will gain valuable experience in writing the kind of report my future jobs will require, and you will be able to evaluate my skills in writing on a significant topic at some length. The project awaits only your final approval to proceed.

1.1.1 **Need.** If your proposal is short, all of the opening sections (need, goals, benefits) might well combine to form an introduction to the proposal. If the proposal is long, in addition to these opening sections being separate, the proposal may well have a separate executive summary of the sort described in Chapter 12.

The "need" section explains what the occasion for the proposal is. Is it in response to a request, is it provoked by a problem, or made possible by the availability of new techniques and procedures? What is it that brings this proposal up, to this audience, now? This section also makes explicit any earlier connection you might have had with the people or agency you are writing to. Have you worked for them before, talked with them about the project, read a brochure they sent out describing the problem?

1.1.2 **Goals.** The second part of the proposal, still often within the introductory sections and thus still relatively short, consists of a brief overview of your project, expressed in terms of its goals. The way you explain the goals should not only convince the audience to accept your proposal but also show them that you understand the project's requirements (how long the project is to last, other limitations, criteria, and so on). Get to the essence of the problem, to show your reader you have thought through carefully exactly what should be done. Don't limit yourself to echoing the words of the announcement you are answering. Don't run the risk of suggesting that all you have done is read the announcement; show quite clearly that you have understood the problem behind the announcement and have devised a solution.

1.1.3 **Benefits.** The last of the proposal's opening sections should list what the benefits to your reader will be from accepting (agreeing with, funding) your proposal. What, specifically, will result? You may want to use a short-term, long-term approach here.

These three introductory sections should be short, perhaps three paragraphs in a three- to five-page document, or a page or two in a ten- to twenty-page proposal. Many times these sections will be done as lists, with each item introduced by a number if the ordering of items is significant, or some such typographic convention as a bullet (•) if the ordering is not significant.

1.2 Body

The body of your proposal should go into more detail than the introduction, and will thus be longer. If the opening section has gained your reader's interest, then this section will have a chance to do some convincing. The detailed description, list of personnel, explanation of facilities and equipment, and budget constitute the body of your proposal. Make these sections detailed and specific. Although you may have used some generalizations in the introduction, use specifics in the body.

1.2.1 **Detailed Description.** In the detailed description, explain the project's *scope*, in terms of both its time and its tasks. When would it start and finish? What event will mark the project's beginning and ending? Explain what *methods* you will be using. Will they be traditional or innovative? Another important part of many proposals is an account of how you propose to solve the problems you encounter within the project. What preliminary problems do you anticipate, and how do you intend to solve them? How have you broken down the separate *tasks* within your project, and how do you expect to accomplish each?

For many research proposals, this opening section also includes a review of (or at least reference to) earlier studies or approaches. This may be a review of the background of the problem, or of previous approaches to solving the problem, or both.

The detailed description should also include a detailed time schedule for your project, including among other things a schedule for your preliminary and progress reports (and an indication of what their distribution will be).

1.2.2 **Personnel.** The second part of your proposal's body should focus on the people who will be working on your project. Who are your personnel and what are their qualifications? What previous experience on similar work do the people in your group have? What are the references for the people on your team? What is the match-up between your people's qualifications and the approach you will take?

1.2.3 **Facilities and Equipment.** Discuss in this section the facilities and equipment that will be used in your project. What facilities and equipment are currently available, and what remains to be acquired? Will the equipment have to be leased, bought, or designed from scratch? Who will pay? And who will get the equipment at the end of the project?

1.2.4 **Budget.** As you might expect, the budget is an important part of your proposal. Depending on how long, detailed, or expensive your proposal is, your budget section may well need a short summary in words in addition to a detailed tabular presentation. You may also want to break the budget down in several ways—certainly by year, but possibly also by source of funds (such as requested funds, matching funds, etc.). Whatever other parts of your proposal may or may not be examined closely, you know your budget will be, so make it a careful and visually attractive presentation. Even if all you are doing is one simple table for the budget, remember to make sure that each horizontal row is accurately totalled in the right-hand column, that each column is accurately totalled in the bottom row, and that the bottom row of totals and the right-hand column of totals both add up to the same amount. Doing so will show the readers of your proposal that you are careful and thorough—and possibly make the difference between having your proposal accepted and having it rejected.

1.3 Conclusion

At the end of your proposal, you can take one more opportunity to convince your reader that you are the right person for that job. A restatement of needs and benefits usually will function as your proposal's conclusion. It is one last chance to convince your reader that you have anticipated and can deal with foreseeable problems, to restate the merits of your project (or your approach), and to urge the reader to take the action you're requesting.

Not every proposal will have all the parts mentioned here; a few proposals will have more. Every time you write another proposal, you should make slightly different decisions about which elements to include or to exclude and the order in which to put your elements.

2. Proposals as Problem-Solving Reports

Comparing proposals to problem-solving reports may help you to understand the internal logic of proposals. Although not all proposals are really done in response to problems, viewing proposals that way for a few minutes may help you to better appreciate what proposals are all about. The clearest comparison between proposals and problem-solving reports may well involve the introduction's three sections—need, goals, and benefits. In the "need" section, explain what the problem is: Has water quality in Town Lake deteriorated to the point that fish kills are becoming commonplace? Has new technology made it possible to retrieve and repair malfunctioning orbiting satellites? Has the increase in suspended particulate matter in the atmosphere made studies of particulate deposition on tree leaves in the mountains necessary? The problem should be something that the reader will either recognize immediately or that he or she can be educated to appreciate relatively quickly. Making it that way is a matter of careful writing on your part.

If the "need" section explains *what* the problem is, then the "goals" section discusses *how* to solve the problem: Do you propose a study of upstream sources of pollution, with an eye toward increased regulation of their discharges into the lake? Do you propose a space shuttle mission to retrieve and repair hitherto-inoperative satellites? Do you propose establishing measurement techniques and base information for levels of particulate matter deposition on tree leaves at various elevations and locations in the mountains? Your reader will look particularly carefully at the match (or lack of match) between what you propose to do and what the reader has requested be done. If the government has requested proposals for a new plane to replace the T-28 basic jet trainer, you cannot submit a proposal for both a new plane and a new fleet of aircraft carriers from which to launch them.

The final section of your introduction, "benefits," tells the reader how your solution of the problem will help him or her. The introduction already has sections on what the problem is and how it should be solved; this section is on *why* it should be solved. Remember to look at the benefits from the reader's point of view (just as you did in the "reader benefits" part of Chapter 4 on business letters). There may well also be benefits for you in the project, and in some cases you may make them explicit, but they must take a definite back seat to the benefits for the reader.

If the first three sections of the proposal (need, goals, and benefits) explain *what* the problem is, *how* it is to be solved, and *why* it should be solved, then what does the rest of the proposal do? In terms of our problem-solving example, the rest of the proposal presents specifics to support the generalizations made in the introduction. Write the first three sections so well and so strongly (though not at such length) that by the time the reader has finished the introduction, he or she is already looking favorably on your request. If the problem-solving essence of the introduction has been done properly, the remainder of the report simply fills in the details.

3. Questions About Proposals

In *The Winning Proposal: How to Write It* (New York: McGraw-Hill, 1981), Herman Holtz and Terry Schmidt offer the following seven questions as those on which customers/evaluators make their decisions about proposals:

1. Do you (the potential contractor) fully understand our problems and needs?
2. Are you expert enough at whatever skills and technologies are needed to furnish the planning and performance to satisfy our needs and solve our problems?
3. Will you provide fully qualified staff people to do the work?
4. Have you done such work successfully before?
5. What, specifically, do you promise to deliver?

6. Do you have a track record of success to prove that you can and will deliver?
7. Can you prove your abilities at all of the above?

One last problem should be mentioned, and that is the tendency of proposal writers to give in to writing encyclopedic proposals rather than analytical ones. Encyclopedic proposals include everything; analytical proposals include only the information the reader wants or needs. For example, if you see a proposal that begins with the history of the project in question, you should immediately suspect the writer of encyclopedic writing. It's true that there may be projects whose histories are important in relationship to their proposals, but most of the time a proposal writer who begins with history is not oriented toward what the *reader* wants or needs, but rather is concerned with the showing what he or she, the *writer*, knows about the project. (Chapter 14 discusses reader-based versus writer-based writing in more detail.)

4. Examples

Two more examples will demonstrate the principles we have discussed as they appear in action. Exhibit 18.2 presents a proposal written for a high-technology, energy-related engineering firm. Exhibit 18.3 is an in-house proposal.

Exhibit 18.2 A Proposal Written for a High-Technology Engineering Firm

PROPOSAL FOR PREPARING A STYLE GUIDE FOR XYZ ENGINEERING

Based on our discussion last Thursday, May 20, I would like to propose the preparation of a report style guide to be used specifically by XYZ Engineering in the preparation of their reports for commercial clients. This style guide will promote more efficient production of reports, reduce the cost of those reports, and improve their quality.

Brief Overview

Technical reports prepared by XYZ Engineering are written by nuclear engineers as the result of their analyses of nuclear power plants and chemical refineries. Customers often judge the engineering accuracy of the report's results and recommendations by the writing quality of the report. Sloppiness, inconsistencies in format, stylistic flaws, and grammatical errors detract from the report and lessen the firm's credibility in the customer's eyes. The elimination of such problems will be the major goal of this report guide. Secondary goals include standardizing the process of document production and establishing a clear system of document review for quality control.

I plan to use three major sources for this guide. Many of XYZ's engineers are graduates of State University and are familiar with the *University Thesis and Dissertation Manual*.

To the extent that XYZ's current reports have a model, it is that document, which I will also use as a basis. Supplemental information will come primarily from two sources. Because many of our reports are done for the National Laboratory, I will consult the Laboratory's *Technical Reports Preparation Manual* when necessary. Additional stylistic information will be taken from *The Chicago Manual of Style*, perhaps the most widely used style manual.

The style guide will have three parts:

*A full description of the document production and review process, by task and time.
*Guidelines for the treatment (including format and placement) of each component of a report, from the title page to the list of references.
*A handbook with rules for consistent punctuation, abbreviation, capitalization, pagination, typing of equations, enumeration, and referencing in reports from XYZ Engineering.

Timetable. This style guide should take fifteen weeks to complete, followed by a two-month trial period, and two weeks of revisions. If I begin work on it June 1, you should have a trial document on or about September 15, and a finished document in use December 1.

Personnel and Facilities. Because I worked as Office Manager for XYZ Engineering for two years before returning to school to work on my Master's degree, I am already familiar with the nature of these reports. I understand that as part of this agreement I am to have after-hours and weekend access to XYZ's CPT 8100 or Olivetti TES 401 and all paper supplies needed for this project. I have enclosed a copy of my resumé for your review.

Both the State University Manual and the Laboratory Manual are currently undergoing revision. I have contacted the head of each committee to be assured of current information concerning any important changes in those documents.

Fee. As we discussed, my fee for this work will be $1500.00, payable upon your acceptance of the finished, trial-tested document.

Conclusion

A report-writing style guide for XYZ Engineering will make your reports more efficient and less expensive to produce while improving their quality. If you have any questions about this proposal I will be happy to answer them. I look forward to providing this service for XYZ Engineering.

Exhibit 18.3 An In-House Proposal in the Form of a Memo

TO: J.T. Lomax

FROM: Susan Jones

SUBJECT: Discussion of 8/14/85 (recarpeting of P-3)

DATE: 8/18/85

The carpeting in P-3 should be replaced as soon as possible. Its poor condition creates several safety hazards in this heavily traveled area, and its continued deterioration (despite repeated requests to have it replaced) adversely affects the morale of all the employees who work in that room. Two alternatives exist for replacing the carpet: new carpet or new tile. Given that the tile under the current carpet is already broken beyond repair and would have to be replaced, a procedure more expensive than putting down new carpet would be, I recommend we replace the old carpet with new carpet.

The current torn carpet presents two kinds of safety hazards. In many places the carpet is pieced together, with the seams joining the pieces directly under desk chairs. Several of those seams have opened up, creating a situation in which chair legs (or wheeled rollers) and employees' feet can catch in the carpet. A fall in this room, with its many desks, tables, and dividers, could lead to serious injury. The second source of hazards is the many large wrinkles in the current carpet. Again the potential exists for falls that could injure employees. These conditions become worse each day.

The tile under the current carpet is already broken and patched, so we cannot simply remove the carpet. Between new tile and new carpet, the advantage is clearly with new carpet. It is quicker and cheaper to install, and it offers other advantages (such as sound absorption) not offered by tile.

According to Maintenance, recarpeting will cost $18.75 per square yard (installed), for a total of $1518.75. Because the carpeting can be done in one day, we can do it on a Saturday and thus cause a minimal disruption of the work in this room. Retiling, on the other hand, will cost $5500 for labor and materials alone. It would require three days to do, resulting in a total cost (including materials, labor, and lost time for the work that should go on in that room and cannot be moved) of almost $7500.

EXERCISES

1. Write a proposal for the major report you are writing for this class.

2. Combine with two or three of your classmates to write a proposal to put on a workshop, "Effective Writing," for high school students at a local school. The purpose of the workshop—to be held on two consecutive Saturday

mornings for three hours each morning—is to give high school students who intend to attend college extra training in the kinds of writing they will have to do in college. The audience for the proposal should be the high school principal.

3. Pick a university procedure that you think isn't handled as well as it should be—enrollment, student parking, allocation of football game tickets, etc.—and write a 300–500-word proposal to the appropriate authority recommending a specific change or changes in the procedure.

4. The short proposal in Exhibit 18.3 is written from the section head of a company to her superior, the division head. As in-house communication, it is in the form of a memo. Rewrite it so that it more clearly reflects the key elements of proposals discussed in this chapter.

19

Long Reports

(continued)

1. The Importance of Long Reports

Writing a long report as part of your professional employment is the major test of any professional's writing skills. Whether 20 or 200 pages long, the major report gives you a chance to take a significant topic and give it a thorough treatment. Success can mean much more than personal satisfaction for a job well done, and failure can mean much more than simply having to do the report over. Writing an effective major report can require you to employ any and all of the skills and knowledge presented in earlier chapters, but most of all it requires your determination to produce a document that clearly presents its subject for its specific reader(s). With skill and determination you can write a report that will fulfill its purpose and make you proud of being its author.

1.1 Types of Long Reports

Any of the types of reports discussed in earlier chapters of this text can appear as a long report. Long reports can include proposals, feasibility studies, problem-solving reports, progress reports, lab reports, meeting reports, trouble or accident reports, and most other typical kinds of reports. But many long reports cannot easily be classified as one "kind" or another: the report is a unique structure of thought, tailor-made to present a specific subject to a specific audience. Particular sections within such a report may be readily identifiable as this "kind" or that "kind," but the report taken as a whole is unique.

1.2 Parts of Long Reports

Most long reports have these basic parts:

Distinctive cover
Letter of transmittal*
Title page
Abstract or Executive Summary
Table of Contents
List of Figures and Illustrations

Glossary*
Introduction
Body
Conclusion
Appendixes
References*

*These items are less frequent than the others.

These individual parts can be grouped together into three sections: *front matter* (everything up to and including the glossary), the *report proper* (the introduction, body, and conclusion), and *back matter* (the appendixes and references). It's not unusual for the front matter and back matter to include more pages than the rest of the report. This happens especially when the report proper merely lays out a problem and presents conclusions or recommendations, and the appendixes contain all of the technical data (this is discussed further in Section 2.5, "Typical Structural Patterns," later in this chapter).

1.3 Characteristics of Long Reports

Besides a distinctive cover, often with artwork on it, long reports usually share a number of other features: good paper quality, crisp and careful typing, 1- to 1 1/2-inch margins on every page, extensive use of headings and subheadings, and full and frequent use of visuals. Although student reports are always double spaced, professional reports are occasionally typed single spaced (or space and a half), with double spacing between paragraphs. Usually reports are bound, especially if they are to go outside the company, and at least several copies are printed. Of course, these elements also depend on whether the report is Class A, B, or C (see Chapter 13, Section 2, for more on this).

1.4 Assumptions About Long Reports

Perhaps because of tradition, people assume several important qualities about long reports: some are obvious, such as that the content will justify the length, or that the report's structure will make sense to its reader. But the biggest assumption is less than obvious: that the report is *self-contained.*

"Self-contained," as used in this context, means a number of different things. It means that anything that your reader needs to know about the circumstances of the report's composition in order to read and understand the report, should be in the report. For example, if you decided to focus only on data up to 1980, perhaps because more recent data is not available, you should state that explicitly somewhere in the report, probably in the letter of transmittal. Or if you decided to put all of the technical data into appendixes at the end of the report, resulting in a report with a very short body but long appendixes, you should explain that in the report, probably in the introduction. Do not force your reader to try to figure out what the report's structure is or why.

"Self-contained" also means that you cannot assume that the reader you have in mind for the report is the *only* reader who will see it; your report's circulation and lifespan may be much greater than you expected when you wrote it. Do what you can to ensure that the report explains itself to *whoever* reads your report, and *whenever* they read it.

2. Techniques for Producing Long Reports

In terms of producing the document, the biggest difference between the long, or major, report and other reports you may have written is its length. Many writers find that producing a report with fifteen or twenty (or more) pages of report proper—not counting front- and back-matter—presents not just a different *degree* of difficulty, but a different *kind* of difficulty, than writing shorter reports. Because of its length, producing a long report requires a special emphasis on planning.

People approach planning the process of producing a long report in a variety of ways. Some writers take voluminous notes, make extensive outlines, write many rough drafts, and plan their projects extensively. Other writers write as they research, and plan as they write, counting on doing substantial revising later on to draw the document's scattered pieces together. Neither process is ideal. The techniques involved in producing a long report include planning, researching, and writing.

2.1 Planning Long Reports

Planning for producing long reports falls into two distinct areas: Defining the Purpose and Scope, and Using the Calendar.

2.1.1 **Defining the Purpose and Scope.** You and the person for whom you are writing the report must agree in detail on what your report will do and won't do, what it will and will not discuss. For example, reports written by juniors and seniors in an advanced report-writing class may have any of several different purposes: you may want to present the results of original research on a subject, or you may want to use the library to define the current state of knowledge on a subject. You may want your paper to solve a problem, to lead to a recommendation, to point to a prediction, or merely to present the facts. You and your reader should specifically discuss which of those purposes your paper is to fulfill—whether it is to be persuasive or merely expository.

Just as you and your reader must clearly understand the purpose of your report clearly, so you must also agree on its scope. What years are you covering? what countries? How do you define your topic's boundaries, and what will be your criteria for including one fact and excluding others? Are your resources to be limited somehow—say to those in your university's library—or are you allowed to find information wherever you can? To what extent are you encouraged, or expected, to find information outside the library?

Purpose and scope are overlapping aspects of reports, and they both must be clearly understood, in order for you to write a good report. One of the best ways to ensure this understanding is to plan at least three meetings with the person you're writing for, in order to accomplish three purposes:

1. Determine the topic initially, to find what "ballpark" you'll be working in.
2. Narrow down the topic's scope—what you'll include and exclude—by defining the paper's purpose and approach to the topic in some detail.
3. Discuss your progress and test whether reader and writer are still in agreement on purpose and scope.

The First Meeting. For example, suppose your instructor requires a major report with fifteen to twenty pages of body on a topic relating to your major field of study. In your first conference, you explain that although you're a business major, for your first three years at college you majored in biology, and you'd like to do a paper in that field—specifically, "something with recombinant DNA research". Your instructor further stipulates that the paper have something to do with business (the college you're enrolled in and the area you'll be writing in when you leave college). So the two of you agree on the topic "Economic Implications of Recombinant DNA Research." At that point, with a partial idea of purpose and scope, you have a general area within which to work, and you and your reader have agreed on enough for you to begin collecting information on the subject.

The Second Meeting. In the second conference, you work out with your reader more precisely the purpose and scope of your report. In English classes this step is often called "determining a thesis." To the extent that "thesis" only means a point you're trying to prove, "determining a thesis" is a misleading name for this step. During this second conference, you work out the details of purpose and scope. For example, on the topic "Economic Implications of Recombinant DNA Research," you may decide that you will first explain the biology of recombinant DNA, then follow a couple of cases of university researchers forming private companies to develop their research, and then, for the paper's last ten pages or so, trace the financial growth of several companies involved in capitalizing financially on recombinant DNA research.

During this second meeting, you discuss with your instructor the paper's purpose. The two of you agree that the paper should do more than just trace the subject's history; because you're working in a past/present/future structure, anyway, one logical conclusion would be to predict the financial future for such companies. Your instructor points out that there are several other issues involved—the relationship between big business and university research; the financial soundness of a firm that may only consist of six people, some laboratory equipment, and a patent, but which begins trading on the stock market with six million dollars worth of shares; and so forth. The two of you agree that both of these would be legitimate topics to include in the paper but that to orient the report toward making a judgmental statement about either topic would require totally rethinking the entire paper. At this point, by the end of the second conference, as a result of negotiations between you and the person you're writing the report for, you have the paper's purpose and scope fully defined.

The Third Meeting. In the third of this series of three conferences, you report to your instructor that you have finished the research for the discussion of the biology of recombinant DNA, that you've found plenty of information on the

Box 19.1 Schedule for Producing a Typical Long Report

Week 1: Topic-clearance conference. Collect preliminary bibliography.

Week 2: Continue preliminary bibliography and ensure that available sources can supply enough information.

Week 3: Second conference, to establish purpose and scope. Do research for Part I, "Biology of Recombinant DNA."

Week 4: Begin writing first draft of Part I and research Part II, "University Research Meets Big Business."

Week 5: Write the first draft of Part II and research Part III, "The New Companies."

Week 6: Progress report conference. Research Genentech.

Week 7: Write Genentech section and conclusion.

Week 8: Revise all sections and produce visuals.

Week 9: Type and proofread final manuscript, copy it, and turn it in.

current status of companies involved in marketing the results of DNA research. But you think that the last section is a little thin—too thin to support any prediction about the future. Your instructor is pleased with your progress, and suggests that you select the company for which the most information is available and develop your prediction based on that company's situation. That way, even if you cannot find enough information on all of the companies, you can still construct a reasonable estimate of the future based on one company's performance.

Less dialogue between you and your reader risks your writing a report that doesn't satisfy your reader's need. More dialogue can be helpful, but isn't really necessary. However many times you meet with your reader, discuss the subjects of purpose and scope in at least as much detail as we have gone into here.

2.1.2 **Using the Calendar.** Because of the major report's length, you need to plan carefully how to use your time. The best way to do that is to establish the set of tasks that producing the report requires and to plot those tasks out on your calendar. The list of tasks will be different for each writer and each project, but the list in Box 19.1 can be taken as representative. It allows the writer nine weeks to produce the paper on "Economic Implications of Recombinant DNA Research" discussed here.

Notice that this task-based calendar breaks the larger project down into four Parts, and you research one Part while writing the previous Part in rough-draft form. This method spreads the actual writing of the report out over almost the entire nine-week span, and is usually more effective than the alternative of leaving all the writing for the last week. If you leave all the writing for the last week, you run a number of needless risks: if you catch the flu that week, or another instructor surprises you with a major exam, or if you find you haven't done enough research, or if the words just won't come, you don't have the time to do a good job of writing the report. Subdividing the long paper into several smaller papers means that whatever problems you encounter in any one week, you still have the majority of the paper—the result of all the other weeks' work—well in hand.

These two techniques—dividing the paper into sections, and writing the sections separately (not waiting until the last week to write)—will enable you to handle any long report more efficiently and with less stress. The sooner you begin putting words on paper for your report, in however rough a form your first draft is, the better your final report is likely to be.

2.2 Researching Long Reports

The research that goes into long reports can be of any variety, including physical research (such as laboratory tests), original investigation (surveying the territory or talking to the people yourself), and library research. The techniques of good physical research and original investigation are too varied to detail here, and the process of library research is thoroughly presented in Chapter 16. But to do *any* kind of research well you must do two things: keep records, and be thorough.

2.2.1 **Keeping Records.** The best way to keep records, regardless of the kind of research you do, is to keep a notebook. This technique applies to library research as well as to laboratory research. The notebook should contain dated and timed entries summarizing each block of time you spend on research (see Exhibit 19.1).

Although the entries certainly need not be grammatically correct, they should be written clearly. Each entry should summarize what you did in that time: for example, if on the date specified you found five journal articles, took notes from two and copied one, the notebook entry should list the names and other bibliographic information on all five and in one or two sentences summarize each of the three you found usable. The research notebook does not, however, replace other methods of keeping notes such as bibliography cards and note cards (see Exhibits 19.2 and 19.3).

But those cards do not help you control the process of your research, so that you know what you have done and what you have not yet done, the way the research notebook does. The research notebook also can serve as a way of guaranteeing the authenticity of your work.

2.2.2 **Being Thorough.** The second key ingredient to good research of any variety is thoroughness:

1. Follow up all of the leads your research uncovers, even when you suspect that what you find may challenge your understanding or working hypothesis about your subject.
2. Accept the appearance of phenomena you haven't predicted, follow up on them, and analyze them.
3. Try to use the best-quality materials and information, not simply that which is easiest to come by.

Exhibit 19.1 A Typical Research Notebook Entry

February 26, 1986
Went to the Main Library at 10:00 to take another look at the September, 1981 Scientific American, looking especially for the article on microbial production of pharmaceuticals. Shocked to see someone had taken that bound volume off the shelf and the librarians were unable to find it. Talked with the librarians about my problem, and one pointed out that they have the same issue on microfilm. Went to the microfilm/microfiche collection, found the right film, and copied all of the pages of that article (even at 10 cents a page, it's worth it to have my own copy). It looks like big chunks of the article will be useful in my major report—have to be careful about quoting, paraphrasing, references, etc.

When you think about how thorough your research needs to be, remember that thoroughness of research is one very common measure of the quality of any kind of research project, especially in academic settings. Professionals read the abstract of a report and then immediately turn to its bibliography or references section, and look for a number of qualities. A thorough bibliography:

- Cites the standard works on the subject.
- Cites the most recent works on the subject.
- Cites a variety of different kinds of sources.

Exhibit 19.2 Sample Bibliography Card

Scientific American, September 1981, Volume 245, Number 3 pp. 65-75, "Industrial Microbiology," by Arnold L. Demain and Nadine A. Solomon
T1. S5 Main Library Basement
This whole issue contains articles that may be useful. Note especially the lead article, "Industrial Microbiology," which surveys the whole field. Pay attention also to "The Microbiological Production of Pharmaceuticals," which should be right on target.

- Cites works that cover a good span of time.
- Cites works in proper form.
- Cites works on the appropriate levels.
- Does not over-rely on any one or two works.

Many times people make snap judgments—rightly or wrongly—about the quality of your research process on the basis of such a quick examination of the bibliography, an element of the report that you may have seen as relatively less important than many others. It's a good idea, therefore, not only to be thorough in your research but also to ensure that your bibliography (as well as the other aspects of your finished report) clearly reflects that thoroughness.

2.3 Writing Long Reports

Writing twenty-or-more-page reports requires different kinds of skills than writing papers three to five pages long. Breaking your long report down into several major parts will help you to deal with its length. Also separate the writing you do to *understand* your subject from the writing you do to *explain* the subject, and adjust the report's structure to help your *reader* deal with the report's length.

Exhibit 19.3 Part of a Typical Note Card

"Industrial Microbiology," by Arnold L. Demain and Nadine A. Solomon. Pages 66–75 in <u>Scientific American</u>, September 1981, Volume 245, Number 3.

p. 67 Started with fermentation (yeast to make alcohol) (Babylonians before 6000 B.C.)

p. 68 Pasteur's role

pp. 69–70 General discussion of nature of microorganisms that make the process possible

p. 70 Four products: microbial cells, large molecules (i.e., enzymes) that they synthesize, primary metabolic products, secondary metabolic products

<u>N.B.:</u> This article is mostly useful for general background, definitions, etc. The issue contains another article, "The Microbiological Production of Pharmaceuticals," that is more to the point.

2.4 Exploratory and Presentational Writing

Keeping a research notebook and writing the entries in it only for yourself is a different kind of writing from the kind appropriate for your report. The notebook sample in Exhibit 19.4 shows the kind of *exploratory* writing characteristic of a person who is still thinking his or her way through a subject. The writing is *writer-centered*, characteristic in tone and structure of a person who doesn't yet know where the topic is going.

Exhibit 19.4 Writer-Based Prose This is how one passage looked in its first draft, which came right out of the writer's research notes.

Industries want to keep up with what is going on in recombinant DNA research; it has industrial, commercial, and scientific applications, both positive and negative. Positive applications include pharmaceutical, agricultural, and chemical ones. Negative applications include biological warfare, accidents, or use by terrorists.

Readers of reports expect writing different from exploratory writing. The differences in tone and structure on both the sentence and paragraph level can be seen by comparing the exploratory, writer-centered writing in Exhibit 19.4 with the presentational, reader-centered writing in Exhibit 19.5.

The kind of thinking that goes into doing research for a major report can cause problems in the report's finished version in yet another way. A common error that inexperienced writers make is to allow the sequence in which they *learn* the data to dictate the sequence in which they *present* the data. The order that your subject has when it first becomes clear in your mind is probably *not* the best order for you to use to make that subject clear to your reader. The structure of

Exhibit 19.5 Reader-based Prose This shows the same passage as in Exhibit 19.4 revised once to make it fit the particular report's purpose, message, audience, and situation. For the finished version of this passage, see the sample student report, page 391.

It is natural for industry to follow greatly the achievements required in recombinant DNA research. As with nuclear science, recombinant DNA procedures have industrial, commercial, and scientific applications. As with nuclear science, scientific knowledge about recombinant DNA can apply positively or negatively. Positive applications include developments in the pharamaceutical, agricultural, and chemical industries. The negative applications include biological warfare or use by terrorists.

your long report should be the one that is most appropriate for that topic and your expected audience; that structure may not resemble at all the order of your research.

Allow some time at the end of your research to consider the way your paper represents your subject. Is the structure you have been using so far really the best way to present that topic to that reader in order to fulfill that purpose? Most writers become committed to a certain structure rather early in the research process, and it's tempting to become unthinkingly committed to that structure for the duration of the project. It may well be that the structure you became committed to early was the best way for you to understand the subject and around which to organize subsequent research and writing; but it may well *not* be the best structure in which to present your report to your reader. Student writers are often afraid to even *question* their structure, fearing that the answer to the question may mean that they may have to write the whole paper over again with a different structure. But professional writers know that doesn't necessarily mean rewriting the whole paper, though it may mean reorganizing already-written sections and perhaps writing a new introduction and a few new internal summaries. That kind of reorganization takes relatively little time, and it can be well worth the effort to restructure the paper so that it is really right for the reader, the subject, and the paper's purpose.

2.5 Typical Structural Patterns

Certain structural patterns occur over and over again in long reports. Some reports have only one of the structures listed in Box 19.2; other reports will use a combination of two or more.

There are many other types of structures. The subjects of other parts of this text could be structures, also: proposal, recommendation, problem-solving, and various definition techniques. Deciding which organization is right for your subject depends on the topic, your purpose, and the nature and purpose of your audience.

2.6 Audience-Centered Structural Adaptations

Adapting the structure of a long report to a particular audience makes a big difference in the audience's response to the report. Your report should unfold and open itself up to its reader; the reader should not have to struggle to understand what you have written. If your audience is composed of one kind of person, that structural adaptation is fairly straightforward. If the audience is more complex, such as executive/layman, adapting the structure to it is still fairly simple. If, however, the audience is both complex and multiple—for example, composed of some executives, some experts, and some technicians—adapting the structure can be more of a challenge. Three ways to accomplish such a structural adaptation to a complex and multiple audience are:

- Write for the lowest common denominator.
- Write several different versions.
- Compartmentalize the report.

Box 19.2 Typical Structures for Long Reports

Chronological Describing a chemical process, the story of a space flight, or the evolution of a problem.

Pros and Cons Examining whether to invest in a new plant or operation.

Order of Importance Presenting goals that need to be met.

Classification Inventorying a varied stock.

Spatial Describing the distribution of different types of vegetation.

Analysis Breaking a problem or situation into its various parts.

Functional Organization Explaining the different parts of a situation by the way in which each one works.

General to Particular (or vice versa) Leading a reader from a general background to a specific point, or starting with a specific example and building to an understanding of a generalization or abstraction.

Simple to Complex Explaining a complex organization, starting with one fixed point of reference and building on it.

Organization by Association Leading a reader naturally from one part of a subject to another; useful when your subject has lots of disparate elements.

Task-Oriented Organization Arranging the topic in sequence of what needs to be done.

2.6.1 **Writing for the Lowest Common Denominator.** Writing for the lowest common denominator is generally the least satisfactory technique. By lowering the level of the concepts you use, your choice of vocabulary, and the kind and amount of detail you use to the level of the least-interested and least-informed audience, you run the risk of all your other audiences losing interest.

2.6.2 **Writing Multiple Versions.** Writing several different versions of your report is probably the best solution to the problem of a complex and multiple audience—if you can successfully direct a different version of the report to each audience. Unfortunately, this solution is not always possible.

2.6.3 **Compartmentalizing the Report.** A good solution to the problem of a complex, multiple audience is to compartmentalize your report—that is, to put each part in a clearly labeled section, and to organize the sections so that each reader can easily find the section or sections most appropriate to that reader. (You may recall "the compartmentalized report" as a type of report discussed in Chapter 17. The kind of compartmentalization discussed here is a less fully developed application of the same principle.) Thus, for example, in a problem-solving report, the first major section may describe the solution, for executives who are interested only in that. The next section may describe the implementation of the solution, for the technicians who will have to apply it on the practical level. Final sections on the method of solving the problem and on technical data or calculations are available for experts who may want to know the "how" and "why" as much as the "what." Thus, you have produced, not a one-level report, but a two-(or more)-level report (see Chapter 13, Section 1.2).

Any well-written report will be compartmentalized to some extent, but when faced with a complex, multiple audience, you will find that thorough compartmentalization is a good practice. In such a situation, the letter of transmittal and/or the introduction to the report should make the structure clear to all of the readers.

3. Basic Elements of Reports

Certain elements are common to nearly all major reports. Those elements can be conveniently discussed as front matter, the report proper, and back matter. (Refer to the student report at the end of this chapter for examples of the elements in the following discussion, as used in a Class C report.)

3.1 Front Matter

Included in front matter are the cover (with art and label), the letter of transmittal, the abstract, the table of contents, the list of figures and illustrations, and (optionally) the Glossary.

3.1.1 **Cover (with Art and Label).** Reports usually have a distinctive cover, or binder, often of a sort specified by the company that the writer works for. Cover art is becoming more and more common as a way of making the report distinctive. Usually the cover also has a label giving the report's title, the date, the author's name, and the name of the person or company for whom the report was written. Page i of the sample student report at the end of this chapter (page 391) shows a typical cover, with art and label.

3.1.2 **Letter of Transmittal.** Most major reports contain at their beginning a letter from the report's author to the report's reader, called a letter of transmittal. It officially submits the report to the reader. This letter should not be treated as a totally routine or trivial piece of communication, but as the writer's first chance to talk to his or her reader, as an introduction to the whole report that goes in front of the report's formal Introduction. In the letter of transmittal, the writer typically mentions a number of relevant details concerning the report—explanations of its structure, details about what it includes and what it excludes, and often a brief summary of the report. If, as the result of ongoing conversations between reader and writer, there are special characteristics of the report's content and structure (such as a certain year's data omitted, or engineering specifications moved into appendixes), that should be explained in the letter of transmittal. The attitude the writer establishes toward the reader (good will, positive emphasis, and "you" attitude) is especially important in the letter of transmittal. Page ii of the sample student report (page 392) shows a letter of transmittal.

3.1.3 **Title Page.** Like a book, the major report carries a title page, with the report's title, the author's name, the name of the person, agency, or corporation the report is written for, and the date. Often the title page carries a list of the people or offices the report is being sent to, called the report's *distribution*. (The title page is not shown, because it is almost identical to the cover.)

3.1.4 **Abstract or Summary.** The first page after the title page usually will be an abstract or summary of the report. The abstract or summary should be typed triple-spaced for easy reading, and should be no longer than a page. Page 393 shows a sample abstract.

3.1.5 **Table of Contents.** The report's table of contents should list the report's sections, down to the level of at least B- or C-level headings. The important thing here is to visually organize the table of contents page(s) so that the reader sees the report's structure at a glance. To do this use vertical and horizontal spacing on the page, different kinds of typeface for emphasis, and the general ordering of elements to organize the table of contents. Page 394 shows a sample table of contents.

3.1.6 **List of Illustrations.** Most reports have a list of illustrations separate from the table of contents. Page 394 shows one such list.

3.1.7 **Glossary.** If your report is being written for a layman, it's often wise to include a glossary for your reader. If you can define eight to ten words at the front of the report and make the reader's understanding of the whole document easier, taking a page to do it can be a good idea. This usually would only be done for layman readers, however. (The Glossary is not shown.)

All the pages of the report's front matter should be counted, and all but the letter of transmittal and title page usually carry lower-case Roman numerals (i, ii, iii, iv, etc.). Use Arabic numbers for the body of the report (beginning with 1 for the Introduction) for every page, right on through whatever endnotes, bibliography, or appendixes you use.

3.2 The Report Proper

The report proper usually will have at least three parts: the introduction, the body, and the conclusion.

3.2.1 **The Introduction.** This section should be on a separate page or pages, with its own A-level heading. The *cpo* model presented in Chapter 10 is a good model for this introduction. Its length should vary, depending on the length of the report. For a twenty-page report, an introduction of one or two pages is appropriate. The Introduction of the sample student report at the end of this chapter is one good example; notice its extended use of the *cpo* structure.

3.2.2 **The Body.** This section usually begins on a new page following the Introduction, beginning with the report's first heading (for example,"Background" or "Statement of the Problem"). The report should use headings and subheadings throughout, and make extensive use of visuals. The sample student report (pp. 396–398) provides examples.

3.2.3 **The Conclusion.** This section of your report, like the Introduction, should be clearly labeled as a separate section, beginning on a new page. Conclusions to reports, however, take many forms and different names, from "Conclusion" to "Recommendations," to "Feasibility," to any number of other possibilities. Whatever title you use, ensure that your reader will be able to find your report's "bottom line," and that it is clearly labeled and marked as a separate part of the report's structure. The sample student report provides an example (p. 399).

3.3 Back Matter

Any number of different kinds of elements can appear after the Conclusion of a major report. If the report is written in an academic setting, the writer will usually include some form of endnotes and/or a bibliography. The way these two parts of the report's documentation are done varies widely from one field to another; the Appendix discusses different documentation styles in detail (see pp. 436–39). The sample student report provides examples of one popular form of documentation (page 399).

You may elect to include an appendix or appendixes at the end of the report, containing such elements as specifications, alternate solutions, technical data, drawings, personal recommendations by the author, or suggestions for the future. The assumption about such appendixes is that the reader can read them if he or she is interested, but that the appendixes are not essential to the meaning of the report. The choice of what to put in an appendix versus what to include in the report proper is one of the writer's main opportunities to adapt the report's structure to its specific reader.

4. Evaluating Reports

Learn how to evaluate the quality of the reports you write, so that you *know* the report is good *before* you turn it in. The form shown in Box 19.3 is a modification of one used by judges in report-writing competitions sponsored by the East Tennessee Chapter of the Society for Technical Communication.

Box 19.3 A Form for Evaluating Reports

Score only those items which are applicable to this particular document. Scores: 1-2 = below average; 3-5 = average; 6-8 = excellent; 9-10 = outstanding.

Part One: Purpose and Effectiveness

____1. Does the document fulfill its purpose effectively by providing material that can be easily assimilated by the intended reader?
____2. Are the central ideas or the purpose clearly stated, and does the content carry out the stated purpose?

____*Total Score*

____*Total Score divided by 2*

Part Two: Writing and Editing

____1. Is the text easy to read and understand?
____2. Does the text use appropriate grammar, syntax, spelling, punctuation, and capitalization?
____3. Are nomenclature, abbreviation, and capitalization consistent?
____4. Is there a variety of sentence structure and originality of expression?
____5. Are the words well chosen and used in their correct meanings, without continuous repetition of the same words and phrases (except where required)? Has jargon been held to a minimum?
____6. Is the pattern of organization logical and easily recognized from headings and other organizational dividers? Is continuity evident throughout?
____7. Are text headings, figure captions, and table titles well written? Do the figure captions support the illustrations well? Do the text headings effectively describe the sections?

____*Total Score* ____*Total Items Scored*

____*Total Score* divided by *Total Items Scored*

Part Three: Graphics, Layout, and Production

____1. Do the illustrations contribute to the usefulness of the document and provide adequate detail for the purpose of the document?
____2. Are the illustrations legible, neatly constructed, and properly sized?
____3. Are the photographs in sharp focus, do they have a good range of tones, and are they properly cropped?
____4. Does the artwork show imagination and creativity where possible?
____5. Is the type easy to read?
____6. Do the size, shape, and binding of the document fit its intended purpose? (As applicable:) Is the document easy to handle for constant use and reference? Is it of appropriate size for use and storage in the field? Are mailing pieces designed for convenient mailing?

____7. Is the overall design layout effective and well executed?
____8. Is the printing of good quality?

____*Total Score* ____*Total Items Scored*

____*Total Score* divided by *Total Items Scored*

In each section, arrive at a score ranging from 1 to 10. Now add those three section averages together, divide the sum by 3, and you have a numerical evaluation of the whole document.

____Score on Part One

____Score on Part Two

____Score on Part Three

____Total Score (sum of scores on Part One, Two, and Three)

____Total Score divided by 3

Judge's Comments:

5. A Sample Long Report

Exhibit 19.6 presents the main elements from a sample Class C report, "The Economic Implications of Recombinant DNA Research," written by a senior business student who had recently changed his major from biology and wanted a paper topic that would combine both fields of study.

Exhibit 19.6 Main Elements from an Authentic Student Paper, a Class C Report

THE ECONOMIC IMPLICATIONS

OF

RECOMBINANT DNA RESEARCH

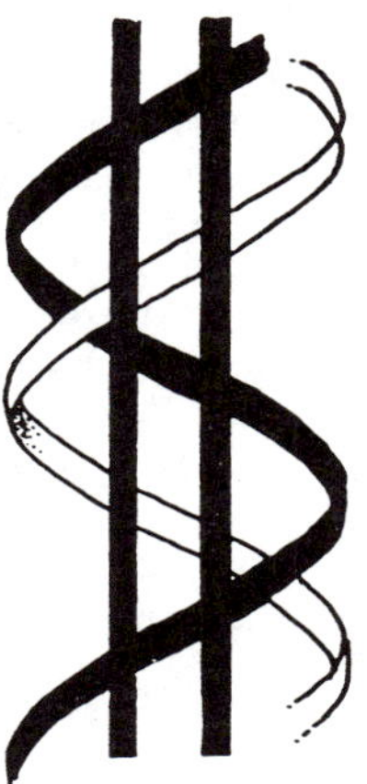

By
Terrell Alverson
For
Dr. Michael L. Keene
English 4140
March 1, 1983

1600 West Sylvan Boulevard
Knoxville, TN 37919
March 1, 1983

Dr. Michael L. Keene
Department of English
The University of Tennessee
Knoxville, TN 37916

Dear Dr. Keene:

As you requested, I am submitting the following report on the economic implications of recombinant DNA research. This area of biotechnology is receiving a great deal of attention from scientists, industrialists, and Wall Street analysts. Investment opportunities are rapidly increasing in the young area of genetic engineering.

This report is organized as you suggested in our planning conferences, with an opening section on the basics of recombinant DNA, a second section on research and recombinant DNA technology, and a third section on its economics. The report has three appendixes, providing the results of the Asilomar Conference, the NIH guidelines on DNA research, and a listing of DNA-related patents.

This report provides useful information for anyone interested in recombinant DNA research or for anyone curious about the links between big science and big business. Thank you for all the help you have given me in preparing this paper. If you have any questions regarding this report, please call me at 555-1250.

Sincerely,

Terrell Alverson
Business student

ABSTRACT

One of the most widely reported but least understood areas in which high technology is affecting the marketplace is recombinant DNA research. Gene splicing, in its simplest terms, is easy to understand, but its possible dangers have alarmed the scientific community. These risks can take many forms, but so can the benefits of the many possible applications of recombinant DNA technology. As a result of the opportunities for profit, biotechnology has become big business.

TABLE OF CONTENTS

iv

[The List of Illustrations would normally begin on a new page.]

LIST OF ILLUSTRATIONS

v

INTRODUCTION

The acknowledged landmark date for biotechnology is June 16, 1980, the date the U.S. Supreme Court struck down the Patent and Trademark Office's stipulation that there was a patent law distinction between living and nonliving matter. One of the most important effects of this decision was its psychological effect on the business community, especially on potential investors in research and development. This decision, a result of Diamond vs. Chakrabarty, opened the door for biotechnology to become a billion-dollar industry. Stock market analysts project that by 1987 total sales in the genetic engineering market may reach $3 billion.

The general public will be affected by these developments in many ways. As recombinant DNA technology is refined and turned to large-scale production techniques, new medicines, foods, and chemical products will be increasingly apparent. The general public also has the opportunity to participate in this phenomenon by becoming investors in the rapidly growing genetic-engineering industry. Genentech initiated this investment opportunity by being the first genetic engineering company to make its stock available to the public, and most other companies in the field have now also gone public.

The purpose of this report is to inform the general public and potential investors about recombinant DNA and its economic potential. The report is broken down into three sections. The first section explains the basic process of DNA recombination. The second section details some of the more recent technological applications of recombinant DNA technology. The third section analyzes the relationship between big business and the big science of biotechnology. Three appendixes offer further details on specific points mentioned in the report: the results of the Asilomar conference, the NIH guidelines on recombinant DNA research, and a list of DNA-related patents and their holders. Based on this report, readers should have the knowledge to allow them to understand a subject that will soon shape the lives of all of us.

1. SCIENTIFIC BACKGROUND OF RECOMBINANT DNA

In 1972 Jackson, Symons, and Berg described the biochemical method for cutting DNA from two different organisms and recombining the fragments to produce biologically functional DNA molecules (Johnson and Burnett, 1978). This method, known as gene splicing or DNA recombination, depends on using certain enzymes to cut and splice the DNA at specific points in the molecule's structure. DNA is the genetic coding for all living organisms. Recombination of DNA gives us the ability to take genes from one organism and splice them into the gene set of another organism. These spliced genes are then reintroduced into a living cell and become a normal part of the cell. The cell then begins to synthesize the products of the foreign genes.

1.1 The DNA Molecule

The DNA Molecule consists of two nucleotide chains which twist around each other, forming a double helix (Figure 1). DNA's chains contain alternating sugars and phosphates. The four chemical bases, Adenine (A), Thymine (T), Cystosine (C), and Guanine (G), bond to the sugars in the nucleotide chain. The bases in one strand then match with the base partner in the other strand. Adenine pairs with Thymine, and Guanine with Cystosine. When one of the code words (A–T, C–G) matches incorrectly, genetic diseases such as sickle-cell anemia occur.

Recombination of DNA depends on restriction enzymes and vector systems (bacterial plasmids). Restriction enzymes break or cut up DNA at specific sites along the base sequence. These restriction enzymes leave sticky ends and unmatched bases on the broken DNA molecule.

Plasmids are small circular molecules of extra chromosomal DNA capable of replicating themselves inside the bacterial cell. They can be inherited when the bacterial cell divides. A plasmid is a useful vector because the biologist can hook a desired gene into a plasmid and take advantage of plasmid biology to get copies of the desired gene.

1.2 The Procedure for Gene Transfer

The following steps explain the procedure for transferring genes to a foreign cell using plasmids:

1. Plasmids are isolated from the bacterial cell.
2. The restriction enzymes break the plasmids leaving sticky ends and unmatched bases on the DNA molecule.
3. The desired foreign gene is chemically sequenced using methods that determine the order of the base pairs.

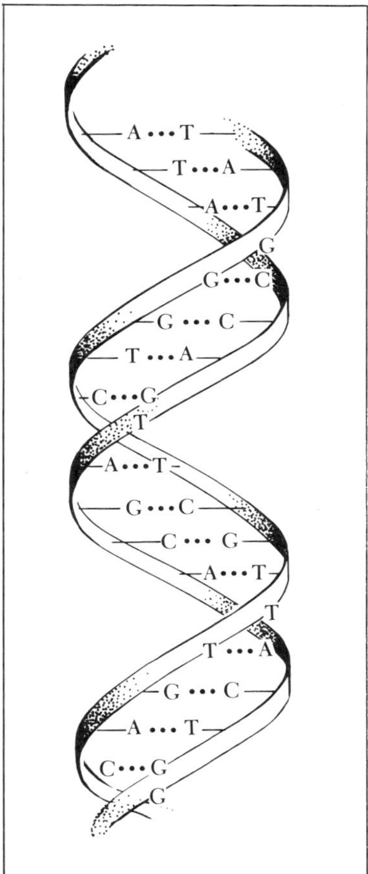

Figure 1. Diagram of the DNA Double Helix showing the base pairing.

3

Source: Gary E. Maciel, Daniel D. Traficante, and David Lavallee, *Chemistry* (Lexington, Mass.: D.C. Heath and Co., 1978), p. 379.

(The remainder of the body of the report occupies pp. 10–19.)

CONCLUSION

Although some of the initial euphoria has dwindled, enthusiasm still prevails in the genetic engineering field. Even though stock prices have settled from the original first-day excitement, projected sales are still into the billions by the mid-1980s. Those sales rely on the markets created by products such as antiviral or anticancer interferon.

Because the NIH heavily funds medical research and the pharmaceutical industry already has large-scale facilities, pharmaceuticals will be the first genetically engineered products available. Research and development in the agricultural and chemical fields are taking place with more results daily. Through the benefits of genetic engineering, our generation may eventually have the ability to end famine and disease. Even cancer may become a disease of the past.

BIBLIOGRAPHY

Agricultural Microbiology. Winton J. Brill in Scientific American, Volume 245, No. 3, pp. 199–212; September 1981.

Asilomar Conference on Recombinant DNA Molecules. Berg, et al., in Science, Volume 188, pp. 991–994; American Association for the Advancement of Science, 1975.

Bringing Biotechnology to Market. Steven J. Hochhauser in High Technology, Vol. 3, No. 2, pp. 55–60; February 1983.

Cell Biology: Structure, Biochemistry, and Function. Phillip Sheeler and Donald E. Bianchi, pp. 134, 443; John Wiley and Sons, 1980.

Cloning Gold Rush Turns Basic Biology Into Big Business. Science, vol. 208, pp. 678–681; May 16, 1980.

Dangers of Legislative and Regulatory Approaches Concerning the Hypothetical Risks of the Recombinant DNA Technique. W. Szybalski in Genetic Engineering, pp. 253–276; Elsevier/North Holland Press, 1978.

Genentech: Is Its Glamor Gone? Marjorie Sun in Science, vol. 211, p. 262; January 16, 1981.

Genetic Engineering: A Key to Innovation in Industrial R&D. J. Boldingh in Genetic Engineering, pp. 203–208; Elsevier/North Holland Press, 1978.

Genetic Engineering: Building New Profits. Yale L. Meltzer in Chemical Marketing Reporter, pp. 34–41; April 6, 1981.

21

Source: Used with the permission of Terrell Alverson.

EXERCISES

1. As you complete your own long report (assignment in Chapter 19), arrange with another student in the class to trade next-to-last drafts prior to the final typing. Write a one-page report about what you learned about your own report from looking at someone else's.
2. Compare the student report in Exhibit 19.6 with the excerpts from the professionally written long reports in Chapter 13. In what ways are they similar, and in what ways are they different? Write a short report about what that tells you about popularized science writing.
3. Popularized science writing is one of the most important (and abundant) types being done in the United States today. Find three popularized science articles from different sources (perhaps three different magazines, or a magazine, a newspaper, and a brochure or pamphlet), and compare their audiences, purposes, and messages.
4. One of the most interesting applications of technical writing for laymen is in the advertising done to sell high-tech equipment to the public. Find an advertisement and write a short (300–500-word) report about how it exemplifies the principles presented in this book.

20

Oral Reports

Once you have a well-written report, one that fulfills your audience's purposes and is adapted to their needs, how do you go about turning it into an effective *oral* report? Although the art of public speaking has its own college courses, textbooks, and principles, for most people the ability to make a five- to-ten-minute oral presentation lies within easy reach. As a speaker you need only to remember a few principles and to make sufficiently careful preparations, and you can make oral presentations a strong part of your communication skills.

The important intangibles? Purpose, message, audience, and the *speaker's* role. As usual, the most important element is to focus squarely on adapting what you want to say to the specific audience that will hear it.

1. Preparation and Organization

How should you prepare for your oral report? There are three key elements: keep your audience first, simplify your message's content, and reinforce the structure.

1.1 Keep Your Audience First

How many times have you seen speakers get so absorbed in something they are reading, or so caught up in the message they are delivering, that their eyes seem to glaze over and they lose all contact with the audience? In classrooms, professional meetings, boardrooms, and banquet halls, the speaker who gets totally absorbed in what he or she wants to say and totally ignores how the audience is responding is a recognizable species. This kind of speaking can be called "writing off the audience." (It's exactly the same phenomenon as the catalogical, writer-based kind of writing described in Chapter 14.) Although such speakers get through their messages, their messages never get through to their audiences! No one likes to be ignored, and when an audience senses the speaker is writing them off, they will respond by writing off the speaker—making noise, dozing off, and in some cases, leaving. Such a speaker has violated the first rule of making oral presentations: *Keep the audience first.*

In order to keep your audience first, tailor your presentation just for them. Think about whether they are there voluntarily or on orders, whether they may feel threatened by anything you may say, whether they will be tired of sitting and listening, and what their questions might be. Think through these points, and deal with them in the content of your talk and in the way you present it. The generalizations about audience in earlier chapters are equally true of audiences for oral reports, and the analysis techniques offered in Chapter 1 work equally well for audiences of oral presentations.

Don't get locked into a particular amount of detail or method of presentation before you analyze your audience. For a five- to ten-minute presentation, you should have a very few key points in mind that you want to make, but the way you make them should depend on your audience. You cannot make the best decision about how to approach your audience until you have analyzed that audience.

One specific mistake speakers often make deserves particular mention here. Especially in a short presentation, there is no reason to read a speech word for word, or to deliver it verbatim from memory. A few lucky people can do that successfully, but most of us cannot avoid seeming like robots when we follow a prepared speech word-for-word. The best ways to deliver a short presentation all involve knowing the subject matter thoroughly and preparing for delivery by practicing but not memorizing or reading the speech. *Know* what to say because you know the subject thoroughly. Then you can use either a brief outline on note cards or a more detailed outline on paper to help you remember what point to go to next. If you know your subject well enough to make a speech about it, you should be able to *talk* your speech through, working from no more than an outline. Reading a speech word-for-word is the surest way to write your audience off—and to invite them to write *you* off.

1.2 Simplify the Content

How many key points can you make, effectively, in seven minutes? Probably no more than five. And if the subject matter you're speaking on is in an area the audience is not familiar with, thus requiring more introduction and explanation, probably no more than three.

It does not matter much how important *you* think all your topic's parts are; limited time means a limited number of points you can make. Most people agree that it makes much more sense to present five points well, in a way that the audience understands, appreciates, and remembers, than it does to rush through ten or fifteen or twenty (and have your audience grasp few or none of them). Simplifying the content of your presentation is an important way to keep your audience first. It shows that you understand the difference between an oral presentation and a written presentation, and are willing to modify the way you express yourself, based on your audience's needs.

One good way to simplify your report's content is to make an outline of it, with upper-case Roman numerals (or decimal numbering) for each major point, and with supporting elements arranged appropriately under those major points. Then choose the five or six major points that are most essential, and eliminate the rest. For supporting material under those major points, select as much as you think you can cover easily in the time allotted, eliminating levels from the lowest up to adjust to your time requirements.

If you don't have time to do all of the supporting material under I, first take out everything at the lowest level (maybe a, b, c, d); if you need to cut more, take out the next lowest level (1, 2, 3, 4); and keep trimming under the various upper-case Roman numerals until you've adjusted the presentation to the time you have. While you're cutting you may feel some pain, but the result will be worth it. Successfully cutting your speech to fit your time limit tells your audience that you are more interested in their understanding what you *do* cover than in your need to tell them *everything* you know about your topic.

1.3 Reinforce the Structure

Because your presentation is oral rather than written, your audience can neither scan ahead to see where you're going nor look back to see where you've been. Because of that, you should reinforce the structure of your presentation. The easiest way is to put your presentation in the form of a number of key points, and to use visual aids (discussed in Section 2.2) to emphasize these points. Don't hesitate to use the *cpo* introduction (see Chapter 9): forecast the key points, work through them, and then summarize the points in your conclusion. The more technical, specialized, or possibly confusing your subject is, the more important structural reinforcement becomes. First, build a strong structure into your presentation; second, use visual aids to reinforce that structure in the minds of your audience.

2. Presentation

If you do a good enough job preparing for your report, and then practice it enough, presenting it can be both enjoyable and rewarding. If you are nervous or unsure about your upcoming presentation, prepare it some more, and practice it some more. The best solution for nerves is over-preparation.

2.1 Making It Easy On Yourself

You can make your presentation better by making yourself more comfortable; preparing more thoroughly and practicing it is one way to do this. Another way is to make sure that you know the environment you'll be speaking in—when, where, and to whom. Find out exactly when you are to speak, and get a look at the room in advance. If you can, while the room is empty, stand in the front of it and try out the sound. And the more you know about how many and what kind of people will be in your audience, the better your adaptation will be. Practice and preparation are two good ways to make delivering your oral presentation more comfortable for you and therefore better.

When you practice your presentation, be careful to practice it out loud, at the same speed and volume and with the same expressiveness you intend to use for the actual presentation. Practicing saying the words over in your mind, or mumbling the words in a monotone, is too different from public speaking to be very useful as practice. And if you can get a chance to practice in the room you will speak in, your practice will be much more productive.

2.2 Using Props and Visuals

One of the ways the talks you may give in professional life will usually be different from speaking situations you may have experienced in school is that you will use props and visuals much more frequently. Props include models, pieces of equipment, or anything you use as an example. Visuals include overhead-projector transparencies, slides, flipcharts, poster boards, chalkboard drawings, and any of a number of media you might use to help you present information. Used wisely, props and visuals can be a speaker's best friends.

2.2.1 **Props.** You can get your points across clearly and more vividly to your hearers by using models and actual examples as illustrations in your speech. You might have scale models or mockups of the subjects you are discussing, you might have actual examples of the electrical device in question, or you might have the implements used in the process you are explaining. If your hearers can actually *see* what you're talking about, your speech will be much more effective.

Although props are nearly always a good idea, passing a prop around in the audience while you speak is generally not a good idea. This inevitably causes more distraction than the knowledge the audience gains from it is worth. A good alternative to passing the prop around is to invite interested people in the audience to come up and examine the props after the presentation is finished.

A hidden bonus of using props is that nervous speakers often find that handling the props calms their nerves. For example, an architect whose voice has quavered through the first two minutes of speaking picks up the architectural scale model of the house he is discussing and suddenly becomes self-assured and a much better speaker. Again, if you *know* your topic thoroughly, your speech will be much better; if you can bring part of that topic that you know so well up to the front of the room with you, your speech can be better still.

2.2.2 **Visuals.** Visuals may be even more common than props among speeches in business and industry. Types of visuals can range from the simplest poster boards and flip charts to the most complex multi-media presentations, but for this chapter we will concern ourselves only with the simpler forms: poster boards, flip charts, overhead projectors, and slide projectors. Use of the more complex forms of visuals, especially when attempted by people who are not professional speakers, usually demonstrates an important truth: the more complicated the form or medium you use for visual aids, the more you can impress your audience *if* everything goes right, but the more chances there are for everything *not* to go right. The more complicated forms of visual aids bring possibilities for greater success; they also bring possibilities for greater failure.

Many speakers are comfortable using *poster board visuals* (See Figure 20.1). Using poster boards—either on a stand especially designed for them or, in a classroom, on the chalktrays at the blackboard—can help a speaker reinforce the structure of a short presentation very effectively. For example, to describe a process, you can have the speech's outline on one poster board, with subsequent steps and a summary each on separate boards. Using chalk trays you can display the entire process right across the front of the room. Poster board is relatively cheap, available in a variety of colors, and relatively foolproof.

Poster boards have several inherent disadvantages. The poster board rigid enough to stand on its own is fairly small, and thus the size of your visuals—and your audience—is relatively limited. The size of the poster board also limits the complexity of the visuals; everything has to be very simplified, and words come across better than all but the simplest drawings.

Figure 20.1 Poster Boards To explain a four-step process, use five boards—one for an overview, and one for each step.

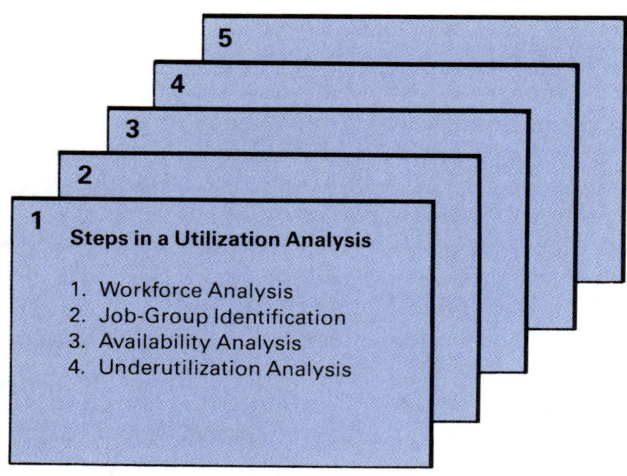

5
4
3
2
1
Steps in a Utilization Analysis
1. Workforce Analysis
2. Job-Group Identification
3. Availability Analysis
4. Underutilization Analysis

Flipcharts are a time-tested and popular medium for speakers (See Figure 20.2). The flipchart should be big enough for all of your audience to see its message, and you need a stand especially designed for its use. Using a flipchart allows you to use a number of different visuals—as many pages as the flip-chart has; the visuals can be any color and can be words, simple cartoons, or fairly complicated drawings. The flipchart has a nice simplicity, even a spontaneity to it that many kinds of visuals lack. Many people like to use contrasting colored markers to highlight the flipchart pages as they speak. Although a little less portable than poster board, the flipchart's increased size also makes it usable in more situations.

The flipchart's main disadvantages are that it is relatively large and requires a proper stand. Some people claim to be bothered by the sound of the pages flipping, but they are in the minority. Other people think using a flipchart is trite or old-fashioned, but most believe flipcharts have been used so much and so long precisely because they are so effective.

Overhead projectors bring us to higher-technology visuals, those with more possibilities and more problems. In addition to the machine itself, the overhead projector requires transparencies, a screen, and a power source. These in turn require extension cords, bulbs, and the apparatus for constructing the transparencies. Many things can go wrong, but also a great deal can go right. Using the overhead projector gives you light, color, a very large image, the possibility for as many visuals as you want, and the ability to be very detailed—and you retain the ability to mark on the visuals as you go.

Overhead projectors have other disadvantages besides their complexity: Inevitably you lose some eye contact with your audience. Many overheads are noisy in operation. Transparencies can be difficult to handle, especially if you use them

Figure 20.2 A Flip Chart This may be the most versatile form of visual aid.

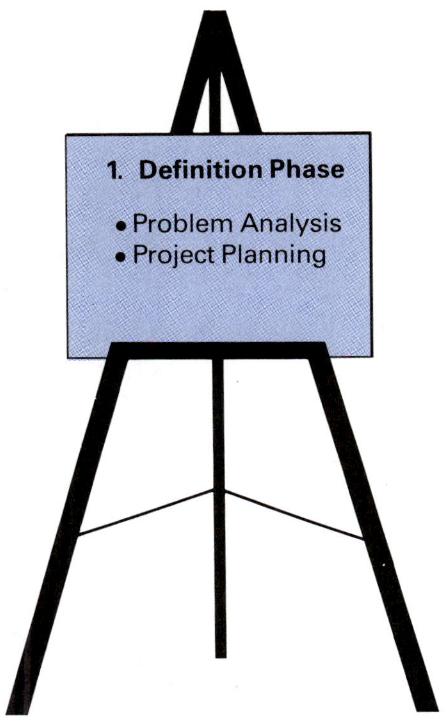

without frames. And some people think that for a short, five- to ten-minute talk the overhead projector is, in general, too much trouble.

Slide projectors give you beautiful light and colors, big images, fast-changing images, and a chance to really impress an audience with the kind and amount of preparation you have done. However, slides take careful preparation, slide projectors can malfunction, and you cannot use one without a screen. You lose eye contact with your audience, and again, this may be just too much trouble for a short talk.

No matter what kinds of visuals or props you use, certain principles apply, as listed in Box 20.1.

2.3 Tips

A number of elements of making oral presentations can be learned through practice. Like skill at writing, skill at public speaking comes naturally only to a few, and the rest of us must work at it. The most important thing to remember in any kind of public-speaking situation is that *long after your audience has forgotten what it is you said, they will remember what kind of person you seemed to be.* In many

Box 20.1 Principles for Using Visuals or Props in Oral Presentations

- Use visuals or props when the subject cries out for it, when a point is particularly complex, or when a point is particularly important.
- Never fail to *double*-check the availability and working order of your visual or prop. Ensure that the projector is there and works, that the screen is there, that the cord is long enough, and, if necessary, that there is someone to run the machine while you speak. Ensure that the flipchart and poster boards are on hand, and that the kind of stand you want is available. Never take for granted that someone else will do or has done these things for you. As the speaker, they are *your* responsibility.
- Whatever kind of visual you use, look at your audience, not at the visual. If you use an overhead projector, look at the audience, not at the machine or its screen. This usually means that you need someone else to change the transparencies for you.
- If you use a slide projector, position yourself in front of the audience, looking at them. If you want to operate the machine yourself, use a long extension cord and a remote control switch. If you don't want to, arrange for someone else to operate it for you.
- Finally, regardless of the kind of visuals you use, specifically adapt them to the situation you are in. Consider the room, the nature of your audience, their purpose, your purpose, and the nature of your subject. And consider whether the amount of energy you invest in preparing your visuals is justified by what they could add to your speech.

ways, the way you present yourself may be as important in the long run as any particular thing you say. Over and again, you will hear people say things like "Yes, I heard Joe's talk last week. He seemed like a pretty sharp fellow." Or "Yes, I heard Joe's talk last week. He didn't really seem much interested in what he was doing." So think carefully about the way you present your material. The tips for speakers listed in Box 20.2 are like tips about writing: you can learn them, but only experience can really teach you their value.

2.4 Answering Questions

One of the most important parts of any presentation in a professional setting is answering questions. Your audience has listened to you, and now you must listen to them. To answer questions well, you must first *listen* well. Establish eye contact with your questioner, and don't begin to answer until the person has finished asking the question. Give the question as thoughtful an answer as you can. Give special treatment to all questions, but especially to difficult questions, those you can't answer, or those that are challenging or threatening.

Box 20.2 Tips on Making Oral Presentations

- Bring enthusiasm to your talk; your audience's attitude will mirror your own.
- Be well-dressed and well-groomed; look the way you want your audience to envision you when you're at your best.
- Save your mouth for talking; don't chew gum or smoke while you're speaking. Some people find it merely distracting, and others find it offensive.
- Decide in advance what to do with your hands. It's fine to rest them on a lectern, but don't put a death grip on it.
- Plan how you will stand. Don't fall into shifting from one foot to another or standing only on one foot.
- Concentrate on speaking slowly. Most speakers go too fast, trying to do too much.
- If you use notes, prepare them neatly. Speaking from tatters and scraps of paper isn't effective.
- Beware of passing things around while you're speaking. Handouts and props are distracting to you and your audience if they're moving around the room while you're speaking.
- Establish and maintain eye contact with your audience. People like to feel that you are talking to *them*, and the way to do that is to look at their eyes. Look briefly at your visual aids occasionally, but spend most of your time looking at your audience.
- Monitor your word choice. Use words appropriate to your audience in both formality and level of technicalness.
- Ensure that your visuals are ready. If you're using a chalkboard, draw the figures on it in advance. If you're using poster board or a flip chart, set up the stand in advance. If you're using an overhead or slide projector, focus the machine ahead of time.
- Avoid asking opening questions of a "cold" audience. It only works on talk shows, where a comic has been out "warming up" the audience for fifteen minutes before the cameras are turned on.
- Never start by saying "This will be easy" or "This will be hard." The first statement invites the audience not to listen, and the second invites them not to understand.
- Be aware of the importance of your listener's questions. Anticipate the obvious ones and have answers ready. And answer all questions carefully (discussed in the next section of this chapter).

2.4.1 **Dealing With Questions That You Can't Answer.** Sometimes you will be asked a question you just can't answer. Usually this means you don't have the right information. You can deal with the situation by saying, "I'm sorry—I just don't know the answer to that right now, but I'll find the answer and give you a call on it as soon as I do." Or you can refer the question to someone else who you think may have the answer.

Another way to deal with a question you can't answer is to deflect it back to the person who asked it: "That's a question I hadn't anticipated at all, and I don't know the answer right now." Then say either "What do you think the answer is?" or "It's an unusual question—why do you ask it?" Many times a questioner who asks an unusual or very particular question will either have his or her own idea of the answer or a specific reason for asking. Given a chance to express their idea of the answer or their reason for asking it, some of these questioners will be satisfied.

2.4.2 **Dealing With Threatening or Challenging Questions.** Occasionally, you will be asked a question that tells you the questioner is challenging or threatening you. When you detect a hostile attitude in a questioner, you can deal with it more effectively if you follow this advice: Listen carefully to the questioner, keeping eye contact and a closed mouth. When the questioner finishes, the first thing you should do is to make sure you understand the question: "Let me be sure I understand your question. As I understand you, you want to know. . . ." Then do your best to restate and rephrase the question. This technique gives you a number of advantages. By carefully *listening* to the entire question, you show the questioner that you take him or her seriously. By carefully *restating* the question, you ensure that the question you *think* you heard is really the one the questioner asked. And you also give yourself extra time to formulate a satisfactory answer. Your answer should show that you take seriously:

1. the *question*
2. the *questioner*
3. the questioner's *attitude*

If the person is frustrated, you need to say something like, "I can understand how you feel frustrated that. . . ." Of course, at some point you will have to answer the question, but this approach will establish some good will in your audience, so that both the questioner and the rest of the audience will more readily accept your answer.

EXERCISES

1. Adapt one of the papers you have already written for this class as the basis of a five- to seven-minute oral presentation. If your teacher was specified as the only audience for the paper, giving a speech to the whole class means adapting the paper to suit your classmates as well as your teacher. Plan also on using at least one form of visual aid or prop.

2. Give a speech in which you introduce yourself to your teacher and classmates. Topics to cover might include your name, the name of your home town and one interesting fact about it, your major, your area of specialization within that major, your reasons for choosing that area of specialization, your job plans, and one personal fact (hobby, etc.).

3. Adapt the content of your major report for a seven- to ten-minute speech to your class. Use at least one visual aid. Either summarize your whole report or focus on one aspect of it in detail.

4. Choose an on-campus speaker, attend the speech, and write a critical analysis of the speaker's abilities. Because your reader will not have heard the speech, describe in your report what the speaker did as well as analyze it.

5. Make modified versions of the audience-analysis and audience-adaptation lists in Chapter 3, tailoring them specifically for speaking (rather than writing) situations.

6. Interview three professionals in your field about the demand in that field for public-speaking skills. Give a short speech to your class about what you learn.

Appendix

Writing Better Sentences

(continued)

Sooner or later we all have to learn grammar. You can't hope to write at a professional level in any field if you still make basic errors in such areas as sentence structure, punctuation, and usage. Although it may not seem logical, it is nonetheless true that professional audiences frequently make decisions about the technical merit of reports based on the grammatical correctness of the reports.

1. Parts of Sentences

The grammar presented here is designed to help you learn to use the basic elements of sentence construction more correctly in order to produce more effective sentences. This grammar, a combination of traditional and generative approaches, divides sentences into sentence bases, openers, closers, and interrupters.

1.1 Sentence Bases

The basic building block of any sentence is a sentence base—a noun/verb unit (also called a *clause*).

> A sentence base consists of a noun, a verb, and (optionally) an object or other kind of complement.

$$SB = SV(O)$$

Sentence bases can be independent or dependent. Independent sentence bases can stand alone as sentences; dependent sentence bases cannot.

> *Independent* sentence bases (complete sentences):
> The information is in a different data base.
> Enter a carriage return and the monitor returns.
> The user must have a unique PPN number.

Author's note: For many parts of this chapter, I am particularly indebted to the Union Carbide Corporation–Nuclear Division's *Document Preparation Guide,* especially Chapter 6, "Usage." That document defines the "house style" for the Oak Ridge National Laboratory.

Dependent sentence bases (sentence fragments):
that the program identified
where you were before using the Select command
which can be obtained from the CSD

The difference between the two kinds of sentence bases is easy for some people to judge by intuition. An English instructor might say, "The first three strings of words can stand alone as sentences; the next three can't. It's common sense." In case your common sense doesn't work that way yet, here's how to tell the difference: dependent sentence bases begin with words that signal their dependency. Those words may be *relative pronouns* or *subordinate conjunctions*.

If the sentence base you are looking at begins with one of the words listed in Box A.1, it is a dependent or subordinate one, and it cannot stand alone as a

Box A.1 Relative Pronouns and Subordinate Conjunctions

Relative Pronouns

which	that
what	where
when	how
who	whoever
whom	whomever
whose	

Subordinate Conjunctions

if	because
after	although
as	because
before	if
once	since
that	though
till	unless
until	when
whenever	where
wherever	while
as if	as soon as
as though	even though
in order that	in that
no matter how	so that

Box A.2 Two Tests for Distinguishing Sentences from Sentence Fragments

1. Ensure that the series of words has a noun and a verb.
2. Ensure that the series *does not* have a subordinate conjunction or a relative pronoun at its beginning.

Only if the string of words passes *both* tests can it be called (and punctuated as) a sentence.

sentence. If you have a series of words that you want to test to determine whether or not it constitutes a grammatical sentence, there are two tests you must apply (shown in Box A.2).

Several things can be done to sentence bases. We can add a group of words:

- to the front of the sentence base—an *opener*.
- to the end of the sentence base—a *closer*.
- to the middle of the sentence base—an *interrupter*.

If the addition is an essential part of the sentence (if its meaning is necessary), and if it is not an opener, joining it to the rest of the sentence requires no punctuation. Otherwise (if the addition's meaning is not necessary, or if it is an opener), it must be spliced on with a comma. (Combining two independent sentence bases has its own rules, discussed in Section 3.)

1.2 Openers

An *opener* is a word or group of words added to the beginning of a sentence base. Openers are usually connected to the sentence base with a comma. The longer the opener, the stronger the need for a comma. With more than one opener, each one gets a comma.

EXAMPLES:

1. *A sentence with an opener*: With more than one opener, each opener gets a comma.
2. *A sentence with more than one opener*: With more than one opener, and with long openers, be sure to use commas.
3. *A sentence with a short opener and no comma*: Today you need to learn grammar.

1.3 Closers

A *closer* is a word or group of words added to the end of a sentence base. Closers can be spliced on with a comma, a dash, or parentheses. Although there is no theoretical limit to the number of closers you can use, as a practical generalization you probably shouldn't use more than one at a time.

EXAMPLES:

4. *A sentence with a closer*: A closer is something added at the end, often to pack more information into the sentence.
5. *A sentence with too many closers*: A closer is something added at the end, often an afterthought, sometimes an important qualification, probably a place for revision, and especially a nuisance when there are too many of them.

When the closer is a group of words (such as a dependent sentence base), you must decide whether to join it to the rest of the sentence with a comma. This depends on whether the group of words to be added is *restrictive* (essential) or *nonrestrictive* (nonessential). "Restrictive" means that the group of words is essential to the meaning of the sentence. "Nonrestrictive" means that the group of words is nonessential. Sometimes this is a judgment call on your part, and sometimes the distinction is clear cut. In one notable instance, custom rules: In most scientific and technical writing, if you introduce the string with *which*, it's nonrestrictive. If you introduce the string with *that*, it's restrictive.

EXAMPLES:

Nonrestrictive: You next must access the HELP program, which tells you the allowable input.

Restrictive: You next must access the program that tells you the allowable input.

1.4 Interrupters

An *interrupter* is a word or group of words placed within the sentence base to clarify and specify the ideas in the base. Interrupters are spliced in with paired commas, parentheses, or dashes. Interrupters also can be classed as restrictive or nonrestrictive, and once again the restrictive ones are not set off from the rest of the sentence. *Which* again typically signals that the interrupter is nonrestrictive, and *that* signals that it is restrictive.

EXAMPLES:

Nonrestrictive: This file, which can be accessed at any level, tells you the current status of the system.

Restrictive: A file that can be accessed at any level is called a common file.

When the interrupter is nonrestrictive, commas, dashes, or parentheses may be used.

EXAMPLES:

6. Some elements of sentences—such as interrupters—can be punctuated in several ways.
7. Some elements of sentences, such as interrupters, can be punctuated in several ways.

Box A.3 Four Rules for Building Better Sentences

1. Prefer straightforward sentence bases and sentences (SVO order).
2. Shorten your sentence bases and sentences.
3. Use openers; prefer them over closers and interrupters.
4. Use grammatical parallelism whenever you can.

8. Some elements of sentences (such as interrupters) can be punctuated in several ways.

1.5 Sentence-Base Rules

As Chapter 2 explained, the time to consider style is when you are revising. Don't worry too much about the elements presented here while you are writing your first draft. When you turn your attention to revising, you will find that with only the building blocks of sentence base, opener, closer, and interrupter, you can already begin to make better sentences. Box A.3 gives four rules for building better sentences, using the changes in sentence bases suggested here.

1.5.1 **Prefer Straightforward Sentence Bases and Sentences.** Written English is primarily a language that relies on the order of subject, verb, and (optional) object or complement, abbreviated "SV(O)" here. Although having every sentence written in the same order would be very tedious for readers, many times problem sentences have at their heart an accidental and unwise alteration of the SV(O) order. Such alterations can come from sentence inversion—putting an object (or other complement) first—or from making too big an interruption between subject and verb. Another unwise alteration of SV(O) straightforwardness is placing a part of the sentence last when that part is necessary for the reader to understand the first part of the sentence.

EXAMPLES:

9. The GAO reports that after examining 111 federal consulting contracts valued at $20 million these services weren't needed.

Revised: After examining 111 federal consulting contracts valued at $20 million, the GAO reports that the services in those contracts weren't needed.

10. There will be more regulations as oil prices continue to rise.

Revised: As oil prices continue to rise, there will be more regulations.

11. Into Zoffer's category of administrative skills fit creativity, clarification, organization, and invention.

Revised: Creativity, clarification, organization, and invention fit into Zoffer's category of administrative skills.

1.5.2 **Shorten Your Sentence Bases and Sentences.** Analysis of confusing and jumbled sentences written on topics in business and industry shows again and again that length is frequently a major factor in the problems in such sentences. Although such sentences may have other problems as well, it is their length that usually makes them unintelligible. It would be an incredibly hasty generalization to suggest a maximum number of words per sentence, but a good rule of thumb to follow is: *If your rereading of your first draft reveals a sentence that is confusing, you should first suspect its length, especially if it's over fifteen words long.* Try breaking the sentence into two shorter sentences; that may well solve the problem.

EXAMPLES:

12. The judicial system contains the symbols of all the great principles that give dignity and honor to the individual, independence to the businessman, and that gives the title of Righteous Protector to the state while performing the dual duty of keeping it in its proper place.

Revised: The judicial system contains the symbols of all the great principles that give dignity and honor to the individual and independence to the businessman. The judicial system gives the title of Righteous Protector to the state at the same time that it keeps the state in its proper place.

13. Viewing this statement of a man who has been in the insurance business for over thirty-five years and being pro–term insurance indicates that there should be more comparative information given to the consumer and letting him make the decision between whole- and term-life insurance for himself.

Revised: This man has been in the insurance business for over thirty-five years and is in favor of term insurance. This indicates that more comparative information should be given to the consumer, so that the consumer can make the decision between whole- and term-life insurance for himself.

14. Pyrimidine bases contain a single heterocyclic ring, and purine bases contain two rings that are fused together, heterocyclic being a molecule with a circular arrangement of atomic elements.

Revised: A heterocyclic molecule has a circular arrangement of atomic elements. Pyrimidine bases contain a single heterocyclic ring. Purine bases contain two rings that are fused together.

1.5.3 **Use Openers; Prefer Them Over Interrupters and Closers.** First-draft writing often arranges the elements in each sentence in the order in which the writer thought of them. That sequence frequently is not the best order for the reader to read those elements in. As a writer, you frequently will find an interrupter in one of your sentences that would be better as an opener or a closer, or a closer that should be an opener. The question to ask about interrupters is whether putting something in between subject and verb sidetracks the reader's thoughts; if you're in doubt at all, move the interrupter to the beginning or end of the sentence. If the interrupter or closer contains information that the reader must know in order to understand the rest of the sentence (such as a logical, temporal, or causal precondition), it would probably be better as an opener. The extent to which you reorder such elements for your reader's convenience is one important measure of your concern for audience adaptation. Once again, the time to make such decisions is when you are revising.

EXAMPLES:

15. These supplies can be purchased separately, because they are not on public display.

Revised: Because they are not on public display, these supplies can be purchased separately.

16. The combine's reliability will suffer if daily preventive maintenance is inconvenient to do.

Revised: If daily preventive maintenance is inconvenient to do, the combine's reliability will suffer.

17. Please let me know if I can provide you with any additional information if the position is still open.

Revised: If the position is still open, please let me know if I can provide you with any additional information.

1.5.4 **Use Grammatical Parallelism Whenever You Can.** Using grammatical parallelism means putting sentence elements that are roughly equal in importance and logically parallel (such as items in a series) into similar (parallel) grammatical structures. Using parallelism allows you to say more with fewer words and greater clarity.

EXAMPLES:

18. My background in communication includes several job interviews and writing letters to get information.

Revised: My background in communication includes having several job interviews and writing letters to get information.

19. The rewards to the hobbyist are money saved, satisfaction of accomplishment, and a unique piece of furniture.

Revised: The rewards to the hobbyist are saving money, satisfying a desire for accomplishment, and owning a unique piece of furniture.

2. Kinds of Sentence Bases

There are four different kinds of sentence bases:

Active bases

Passive bases

It . . . that bases

Is bases

During revising, work on using more *active* bases and fewer of the other kinds.

2.1 Active Bases

An active sentence is one in which the subject does something and the verb tells what the subject did. The action is straightforward through the sentence, from beginning to end:

S to V to (O)

As the typical sentence in written English for business and industry, and as the most easily understood structure, active sentences are the ones you should use most.

EXAMPLES:

21. A search strategy makes your research process more efficient.
22. Thousands of larvae hatch simultaneously.
23. The chief programmer codes ten to twenty times faster than the other programmers do.

2.2 Passive Bases

The passive sentence is the reverse of the active. In the passive sentence, the verb explains something that is, or was, done to the subject. The *doer* (called the *agent*) may or may not be named in the sentence. The flow of the passive sentence is usually backwards:

Subject (S)having something done to it (V) by (agent)

The file was coded by the client.

Passive sentences require more words than active ones do, take readers longer to read, and increase the chances of misunderstanding. They increase the possibility for grammatical mistakes, and they encourage vagueness. An occasional passive verb is acceptable, but avoid long strings of passives. If you tend to write such long strings of passives, build one step into your revising process in which you check only for them. Then eleminate them.

2.2.1 Recognizing Passives.

Some students have trouble recognizing passives. First, passives have nothing to do with present and past *tense*. A passive can be in any tense. Box A.4 explains how to recognize a passive sentence.

2.2.2 Revising Passives.

Once you have recognized a sentence as a passive and decided to change it, how can you revise it into an active sentence? First you have to find the agent (insert one if it isn't there to begin with but is understood or implied).

Box A.4 How to Recognize a Passive Sentence

All passives use a form of the verb *to be* (*is*, *are*, *was*, etc.) plus a past participle. (A *past participle* is anything that can fill the empty slot in this sentence: "I had ____ it.") Some passives also have agents expressed in the sentence.

Passive = subject + form of *to be* + past participle (+agent)

The agent is the person or entity by whom (or by which) the action of the sentence is being done. With the "by + agent" in place at the end of the passive sentence, you can then change the sentence from passive to active by rotating it around the verb:

By positioning the (former) agent first and the (former) subject last, and then reshaping the verb to match, you can change a passive sentence to an active one.

EXAMPLES:

24. Houses were destroyed by the storm.

Revised: The storm destroyed houses.

25. Your proposal has been turned down.

Revised: Our committee has turned down your proposal.

26. The experimental rationale was summarized in the Foreword and detailed in Chapter One.

Revised: The Foreword summarizes the experimental rationale, and Chapter One explains it.

2.2.3 **Necessary Passives.** One special situation does justify using the passive. When there is no actor or agent, or when the actor or agent is either unimportant or unknown, you may need to use the passive. Here is an example:

The wind flows were divided into three categories.

To introduce an actor or agent ("we" or "the research group," for example) into this sentence would place the emphasis in the wrong place. In addition, in the organization for which this sentence was written, it is customary for quarterly progress reports (from which this sentence was taken) *not* to mention human actors or agents in such sentences.

2.3 *"It . . . That"* Bases

People sometimes write "throat clearing constructions"—that is, sentences that wander around aimlessly before they decide what to say. These sentences often begin with either an "*it . . . that*" structure or some similar unnecessary construc-

Box A.5 *"It . . . That"* Openers and Alternatives to Them

Avoid	*Use*
It can be seen that	Note that
It can be shown that	We have shown that
It is apparent that	Apparently
It is assumed that	We assume that
It is clear that	Clearly
It is natural to expect that	One could expect
It is possible that	Possibly
It is proposed that	We propose that
It is shown herein that	We show that
It is worth noting that	Note that
It might be thought that	One might think that
It should be noted that	Note that
It will be remembered that	Remember that; recall that

tion. You can nearly always revise such a sentence for economy by deleting that entire construction.

EXAMPLES:

27. It goes without saying that productivity measures the economic progress for a whole nation.

Revised: Productivity measures the economic progress for a whole nation.

28. The reason for this is that the strip of unplowed land will help prevent water erosion.

Revised: The strip of unplowed land will prevent water erosion.

29. What many people do not realize is that there are many benefits derived from using fire in the forests.

Revised: Many benefits are derived from using fire in the forests.

Box A.5 presents a list of frequent "*it . . . that*" openers and the alternatives to them.

2.4 "*Is*" Bases

Written English draws most of its strength and vigor from the verbs it uses. Inexperienced writers often produce first drafts that contain many weak verbs, especially forms of *to be*, *to have*, and *seem*. We call sentences that employ these weak verbs "*is*"-base sentences. They are very tedious to read, especially when they occur in chains (see Exhibits A.1, 10.8, and 10.9).

Exhibit A.1 A Paragraph Containing a Chain of Weak Verbs

> In foods, the rate of evaporation is dependent upon the moisture content of the foods. Because no food is composed of a free surface of water, there is great variation in the amounts of water available for evaporation in foods. Some sort of measuring tool for the amounts of evaporatable water present is needed. This tool is known as free water content. Free water is all moisture in a product which is not "bound" to the proteins or other molecular structures in the food, and can be evaporated. Bound water is defined as all water that remains unfrozen at −30 C. This water is closely tied up with the substrate and cannot be evaporated out. So free water is all evaporative water within a product or cell, except the bound water in the food.

When you see such a chain of weak verbs in your writing, revise at least some of those sentences—the easy ones—into action bases. Revising an *is* base into an action base can happen in several different ways. Sometimes simply rotating the sentence around the verb will make the new verb obvious. Sometimes if you look past the *is* verb you can find another word in the sentence that is a verb that has been changed into another part of speech. Convert that word back into a verb, and you usually have a strong verb. This same pattern for revision will also alert you to passives, which can then also be revised in the ways discussed here under *is* bases.

EXAMPLES:

30. The profit is dependent on the government's stimulation of the economy.

Revised: The profit depends on the government's stimulation of the economy.

31. The purpose of this paper is to measure the potential usefulness of replacement-cost data.

Revised: This paper measures the potential usefulness of replacement-cost data.

32. When a Harley-Davidson Sportster engine is in need of major repair, it most commonly is the cylinder that must be fixed.

Revised: When a Harley-Davidson Sportster engine needs major repair, commonly the cylinder must be fixed.

By revising "*it . . . that*," "*is*," and passive bases into active bases, you will make your writing clearer, easier to read, and more vigorous stylistically. You do not have to make *every* sentence in your writing active, but a strong majority of them should be.

3. Combining Sentence Bases

You can combine independent sentence bases in two different ways: by putting them together side by side, or by putting one inside the other (using a relative pronoun or subordinate conjunction, as demonstrated in Section 1.1). Combining independent sentence bases on an equal level can be done in two ways (see Figure A.1):

1. Use a comma plus a linking word such as *and*, *but*, or *or* (coordinate conjunctions).
2. Use a semicolon with either no linking word or a word such as *therefore*, *thus*, or *however* (conjunctive adverbs).

EXAMPLES:

33. Designing large components is challenging. Much time is required to develop such skills.

Revised: Designing large components is challenging, and much time is required to develop such skills.

Figure A.1 Combining Two Sentence Bases

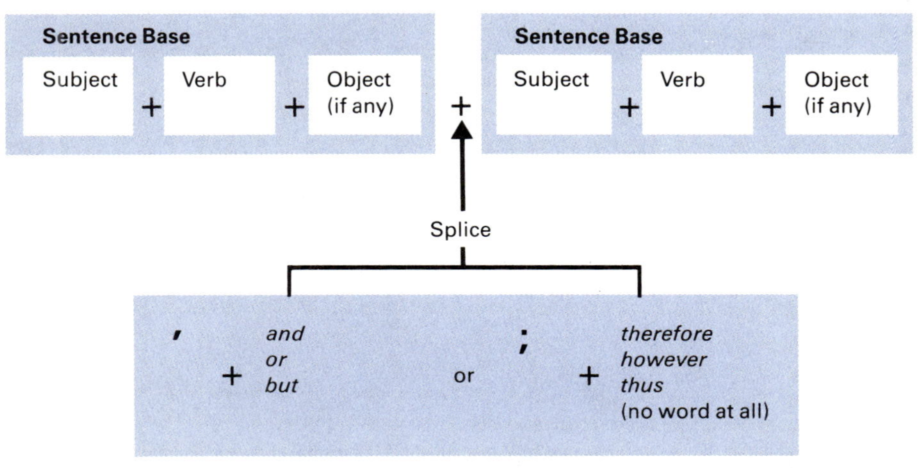

34. Turbocharging can provide more passing power. Diesels are traditionally slow to accelerate.

Revised: Diesels are traditionally slow to accelerate; however, turbocharging can provide more passing power.

35. Some expenses can be related to revenue. These expenses are called product costs.

Revised: Some expenses can be related to revenue, and these expenses are called product costs.

You can also combine independent sentence bases by placing one inside the other, which is called *embedding*. Doing this puts the embedded sentence in a particular subordinate relationship to the main sentence. Embedding uses words such as *that*, *which*, *when*, or *where* to introduce the newly embedded base. This is the same process (using relative pronouns or subordinate conjunctions) discussed in Section 1.1.

svo embeds in SVO:

S (<*that* or *which*, etc.> vo) VO

There are too many other embedding patterns to list here, but they all follow essentially the same method.

EXAMPLES:

36. *Embed a. in b.:*

   a. The device requires a source of potential heat to produce power.

   b. The words *heat energy* imply something.

Revised: The words *heat energy* imply that the device requires a source of potential heat to produce power.

37. *Embed a. in b.:*

   a. When young the mass has no organization.

   b. The callus is a mass of cells.

Revised: The callus is a mass of cells that when young has no organization.

38. *Embed a. in b.:*

   a. Tasks were once thought difficult.

   b. Hydraulic systems make tasks easy to perform.

Revised: Hydraulic systems make tasks that were once thought difficult easy to perform.

4. Separating Sentence Bases

Sometimes during revision you will find a sentence (or at least a string of words beginning with a capital letter and ending with a period) that just doesn't seem to make sense. To make such a string make sense, find the subject and put it first, put the verb next to it, and the object (or complement), if any, next. With the sentence base united, sort out the rest of the sentence as openers, closers, and interrupters, and place them accordingly.

EXAMPLES:

39. He will be able to see potential problems that might result from too great a reliance on short-term financing, an excessive investment in inventory or accounts receivable, or an over-generous dividend policy may be spotted readily through analysis of a sources-and-uses statement.

Revised: Through analysis of a sources-and-uses statement, he will be able to see potential problems that might result from too great a reliance on short-term financing, an excessive investment in inventory or accounts receivable, or an over-generous dividend policy.

40. Cytoplasmic male sterility is a genetic character in which male sterility is carried in the female cytoplasm, as opposed to the normal situation of genetic characters being carried in the male and female germ plasm.

Revised: In the normal situation the genetic characters are carried in the male and female germ plasm. In cytoplasmic male sterility the male sterility character is carried in the female cytoplasm.

41. Computer system documentation is a relatively new idea and lacked real direction until in 1974, four years after it was organized, the Documentation Subcommittee of the American Society for Testing Materials formed the concept of CSD.

Revised: Four years after it was organized, the Documentation Subcommittee of the American Society for Testing Materials formed the concept of computer-system documentation, a relatively new idea that had lacked real direction until that year (1974).

5. Grammar and Usage Problems

A number of kinds of minor grammar problems and usage conventions can become major problems if left uncorrected or handled incorrectly. The following sections discuss how to deal with twelve of those kinds of problems.

5.1 Sentence Fragments

A sentence fragment has no independent sentence base in it; it's a string of words that begins with a capital letter and ends with a period, question mark, or exclamation point, but that lacks a subject, or a verb, or both. If a sentence fragment has a noun/verb unit, the unit has usually been introduced by a relative pronoun or a subordinate conjunction, which disqualifies it from being a sentence. When upper-division students write sentence fragments, the fragment usually conforms to one of two patterns:

1. The *-ing* pattern (Example: Being a pilot.)
2. The noun-phrase pattern (Example: That the thruster rotates.)

The *-ing* pattern is a sentence fragment because *-ing* forms of words cannot function as verbs without help from another word, such as *is* or *are*. Carefully scrutinize any "sentence" that begins with an *-ing* form of a verb and consider splicing that group of words (the fragment) onto the previous sentence.

EXAMPLE:

Being a pilot, I have travelled extensively around the country.

Recognize *noun-phrase* fragments as being introduced by relative pronouns (*that*, *which*, *where*, etc.) or subordinate conjunctions (*after*, *because*, *when*, etc.)—words that make whatever follows them depend on some other sentence; the noun-phrase fragment just doesn't make sense standing on its own:

EXAMPLES:

That the thruster rotates.

What the manual says.

Where the moisture persists.

As with the *-ing* pattern of fragments, noun-phrase fragments must be connected to another sentence in order to become grammatically complete.

EXAMPLE:

The Harrier gets its unique abilities from one fact about its engine arrangement—that the thruster rotates.

5.2 Fused Sentences and Comma Splices

When you join independent sentence bases on a side-by-side level, connect them with a conjunction, such as *and*, *but*, or *or*, and insert a comma before the linking word. Failure to do so results in the error called a *fused sentence*.

EXAMPLE:

The heavy fighting that characterized this conflict has now ceased the war-weary population now can begin to assess the damages.

(The fusing of the two sentence bases occurs between *ceased* and *the*.)

To remedy the fused sentence, merely insert a comma and the word *and*. (If you use the comma but no conjunction, you still have an error called a *comma splice*.) Be sensitive to the length of your sentences when you revise, and check long sentences for these problems.

5.3 Semicolons

There are two situations in which you should use semicolons:

1. When you join two independent sentence bases on a side-by-side basis and do not use a linking word, or when you join them with a word like *thus*, *therefore*, or *however*, use a semicolon between the bases (and *before* the linking word).

EXAMPLES:

The image is transmitted in digital code; therefore it must go through a computer to appear as a visual image for analysis. The image can also be enhanced by the computer; the result can be something clearer than any normal camera could produce.

2. When you have a list of long items in a series, and some of those items have commas in them, use semicolons to separate the items from each other, for clarity:

EXAMPLE:

The following students will work together in groups: Smith, Wilson, and Nunley; Thompson, Davidson, and Derrick; and Freid, Wells, and Hernandez.

5.4 Colons

Use a colon to introduce a quote, a list, or an example. When you use a colon, be sure that the words in front of it comprise a complete sentence base. The following paired examples illustrate this point:

EXAMPLES:

Ungrammatical: Two possible problem sources are: overlubrication and lubricant contamination.

Grammatical: There are two possible problem sources: overlubrication and lubricant contamination.

or

Two possible problem sources are overlubrication and lubricant contamination.

5.5 Hyphens

The use of hyphens is not standardized in English; authorities disagree about when to use them, when not to use them, and when using them is optional. In a recent article in *Technical Communication*, Lindsay Murdock (an editor for the National Oceanic and Atmospheric Administration) suggested the guidelines listed in Box A.6.

As you may have guessed, the rules for hyphenation are complex (in addition to varying from field to field). A good guide to consult is your dictionary. An even better guide is the appropriate style manual for your field or firm (see Section 5.12.1 of this chapter).

5.6 Subject-Verb Number Agreement

In English, subjects and verbs must agree in number; if the subject is singular, the verb must also be singular. The most common problem that advanced students have with subject-verb number agreement is when another noun occurs between the subject and the verb, and the second noun is of a different number.

Box A.6 Guidelines for Using Hyphens

Hyphens are properly used in some kinds of "unit modifiers"—pairs of words that work together to modify another word.

1. If the unit modifier consists of two nouns, do not use a hyphen. Examples: *avalanche prevention program*, *heat exchange capacity*.
2. When the unit modifier consists of an adjective and a noun, or a noun and an adjective, or an adverb and an adjective, use a hyphen. Examples: *happy-face shirt, hand-blown glass, round-bottom flask.*

Exception: If the first element of the unit modifier is a comparative or a superlative, omit the hyphen, as in *lower order problems*.

3. Use a hyphen when you combine two color terms to make a unit modifier. Example: *rosy-red heat*.
4. Use a hyphen in unit modifiers that contain numbers. Examples: *four-way intersection, 10-m board.*
5. When a connecting word between the words in the unit modifier is implied, use a hyphen. Example: east-west air traffic.
6. When the unit modifier is a one-of-a-kind construction and contains a verb, or when it contains three or more words, use a hyphen. Example: *his run-for-glory attitude*.
7. When the unit modifier contains a present or past participle, or when it contains words ending in *-ed* or *-ing*, use a hyphen. Examples: *free-running river*, *forced-convection flow*.
8. Proper names (words that are capitalized) don't use hyphens, even though the same words when not capitalized would use hyphens. Examples: *a First Stage Alert* versus *a first-stage-alert, the New York office*.
9. If the unit modifier contains an adverb ending in *-ly*, do not use a hyphen. Use a hyphen in unit modifiers containing *well*, *still*, or *ever*. Examples: *a happily married man, a well-worn path, wholly owned subsidiary*.

Exception: Do not use a hyphen with *well*, *still*, or *ever* when the word is modified by another adverb.

Example: *fairly well worn tires* (not *fairly well-worn tires*).

EXAMPLES:

Ungrammatical: The angle of the vanes are crucial to the turbojet's operation.

Grammatical: The angle of the vanes is crucial to the turbojet's operation.

Even though the plural noun *vanes* is closer to the verb, the other noun, *angle*, is still the subject of the sentence, and it still controls the number of the verb: singular.

5.7 Abbreviations and Acronyms

Professional writing in business and industry abounds with abbreviations and acronyms. Some are standard throughout entire fields, and seldom require explanation within their particular fields. Others, such as the ever-changing ones in government and the military, should nearly always be explained at least once (typically at their first use, sometimes in a glossary) in each document that uses them.

EXAMPLES:

The annual meeting of the Southeastern Conference of Teachers of English in the Two-Year College (SECTETYC) will be in Atlanta this year.

The Executive committee put Paul Blakely in charge of the Strategic Planning Committee (STRAPLCOM).

The operation of the Long Island Lighting Company's (LILCO's) power plant is frequently studied.

Whether or not you explain the abbreviations you use is another measure of how carefully you adapt your writing to its audience. If there is any doubt in your mind about whether your reader will immediately know what your abbreviation means, explain the abbreviation.

5.8 Confusing Words

Some pairs of words are very easy to misuse because they look or sound very much alike. Consider the pairs of words in Box A.7 and make sure you choose the right one of each pair for the meaning you want.

Box A.7 Often-Confused Words

advice/advise
adapt/adept/adopt
allusion/illusion
affect/effect
principal/principle
cite/site
to/too
its/it's
alternate/alternative
among/between
less/fewer
among/number
assure/insure/ensure
capital/capitol
complement/compliment
consists in/consists of
continuous/continual
device/devise
discreet/discrete
farther/further
imply/infer
personal/personnel
practical/practicable
precede/proceed
respectively/respectfully
stationary/stationery

Box A.8 Phrases to Avoid

Avoid	*Use*
agree with the idea	agree
at the present time	now
at this point in time	now
by means of	by
demonstrates that there is	shows
during the time that	while
for the purpose of	for
for this reason	therefore
if the developments are such that	if
in all cases	always
in a similar fashion	similarly
in order to	to
in the course of	during
in the event that	if
in the neighborhood of	about

5.9 Complex Words and Phrases Versus Simple Ones

Avoid many word traps by using simple, concrete, specific words. Avoid cliches, complex phrases, and pompous expressions. In the list in Box A.8, avoid the words in the left column.

5.10 Lists

The kind of writing that people do on the job tends to employ lots of lists. One particular kind of list that especially concerns writers and editors is called a "where" list. The following example shows how to do a "where" list.

EXAMPLE:

In one computer program, the user needs to type in

ATT RO VAL

where

ATT = any attribute,
RO = any relational operator, and
VAL = a specific value.

Several important things should be noted about the way this list is done. Because the sentence that introduced it is incomplete, no colon is used. When you introduce a list with a complete sentence, use a colon.

EXAMPLE:

In one computer program, the user needs to type in the following:

ATT RO VAL

The subject of the "where" list here is a piece of computer syntax; it could equally easily be a chemical formula or a mathematical equation. In any case, the subject of the "where" list is centered on the page. The "where" itself is back at the left margin, and the explanations of each term are indented five spaces from the left margin. When the explanations are complete sentences, they are followed by periods. Otherwise they are followed by commas or semicolons. Authorities disagree on whether or not to use *and* before the last line.

The "where" discussed in the previous paragraph is one example of a larger group of lists called "displayed" lists. Displayed lists include any kind of list that is set off from the rest of the text. This could also include bullet lists (in which each item is introduced by a "bullet" (•), or alphabetical lists (items introduced by a, b, c, etc.), or numbered lists (items introduced by 1, 2, 3, etc.). Displaying your lists is especially useful if the list contains information that your reader may want to be able to find easily by skimming your material.

5.11 Quoting Borrowed Material

Proper use of other people's words and ideas is important both in and after college. Box A.9 lists four guidelines that will help you avoid accidentally using someone else's work without proper credit. Exhibit A.2 presents some short examples to illustrate the four points listed in Box A.9.

Version A is unacceptable, because it is not a true paraphrase, and because it doesn't credit the source. Although B credits the source, it is still too close to the words of the original. Version C is in the student's own words and credits the source, so it is acceptable. Version D is in the student's own words, credits the

Box A.9 Guidelines for Using Quoted Material

1. Whenever you can, *introduce* the borrowed material in your report with the name of the authority from whom it was taken ("John Smith, project engineer, says that if we. . . . ").
2. Put *quotation marks* around all quoted material, even in your note cards.
3. When you paraphrase someone else's words, be sure you *really* have put the thought into your *own* words.
4. For everything you borrow, whether it be quoted or paraphrased, *document* its source.

Exhibit A.2 An Original Passage and Some Student-Paraphrased Versions of It

The Original (quoted from *Steam Turbines and Their Lubrication*, p. 5; see p. 260):

Because it can readily be built in units of large capacity, and because it is highly efficient and extremely reliable, the steam engine is supreme as the prime mover in the central-station field.

Student Version A (Unacceptable):

The steam turbine is supreme as the prime mover in the central-station field because it can readily be built in units of large capacity, is highly efficient, and is extremely reliable.

Student Version B (Unacceptable):

The steam turbine is supreme as the prime mover in the central-station field because of its high efficiency, extreme reliability, and because it can readily be built in units of large capacity.[1]

Student Version C (Acceptable):

As a central power source the steam turbine is without equal. For power generation its efficiency and reliability, coupled with the ease with which it can be built in units of large capacity, make it the first choice.[1]

Student Version D (Acceptable):

As Mobil Oil Corporation points out, the reliability, efficiency, and easily attained size of steam turbine units make them the most popular choice for central power stations.[1]

[1]From *Steam Turbines and Their Lubrication* (New York: Mobil Oil Corporation, 1965, 1981), p. 5.

source, and *tags* it as well ("As Mobil Oil Corporation points out"), making it the safest use of someone else's material.

In order to make the best use of other people's material in your own writing, you should be aware of three other useful techniques: assimilation, reduction, and insertion. Assimilation and reduction are methods of making long material short enough to use; insertion is a method of introducing quoted material smoothly and gracefully.

5.11.1 **Assimilation.** When the quoted material you want to use is too long, one way to incorporate it into your own material is to assimilate it. State the core of the borrowed passage in your own words but present enough of the key phrases or expressions as quotes to give your readers a feel for the force and flavor of the original. Although the original passage about steam turbines was certainly not too long to quote in its entirety, we can still use it to illustrate assimilation:

> As Mobil Oil Corporation points out, the steam turbine is "supreme as the prime mover in the central-station field."

5.11.2 **Reduction.** Another useful way to shorten a quotation down to a usable length is to use ellipsis dots (three or four spaced periods) to indicate that you have omitted words or phrases. When you omit words in the *middle* of a sentence, use three spaced periods to indicate the omission. When you omit words at the *end* of the sentence, use four spaced periods (with the first one right after the last letter of the last word) to indicate it. (The first dot is the period for the sentence, and the other three are ellipses.) This kind of reduction is common in scientific and technical writing. An abuse of it that, although not common, still happens too often occurs when a secondary author uses reduction to change the meaning (by shifting the emphasis) of the primary author's words. For example, it would not be ethical to reduce the original report on steam turbines in this way:

> Because it can readily be built . . . the steam turbine is . . . in the central-station field.

This reduced version makes it appear that Mobil was really saying that ease of construction put steam turbines into the central-station field, which is not at all what the original version said.

5.11.3 **Insertion.** Insert quoted material into your report so that it does not impair your report's continuity. The worst violation of this rule is the too-common practice of writers saying what they want to say three times: in their own words, in the quoted material, and then again in their own words.

EXAMPLE:

> Mobil Oil Corporation points out that the steam turbine is the best power source in the central-station power field: "the steam turbine is supreme as the prime mover in the central-station field." Thus we see the supremacy of the steam turbine in the central-station field.

5.11.4 **Limitations on Quoting.** In some fields, quotation (especially direct quotes) is almost never used in formal reports. Even if quotes are sometimes used in your field, it is likely that there is an unwritten policy dictating that they be used sparingly. Box A.10 lists some good guidelines for when to use quotes in technical material.

5.11.5 **Punctuation.** One point about quoting material: remember that in most fields—

- Periods and commas go *inside* the quotation marks,
- Colons and semicolons go *outside* the quotation marks, and

Box A.10 Guidelines on When to Use Quotes in Technical Material

- Quote only when your own words will not do the job as well (or better).
- Use only as much material for your quote as you need—the bare minimum.
- Be sure that, whether you use a direct quote or not, you credit the source for all borrowed material (unless you are absolutely certain that the material is common knowledge).

- Dashes, question marks, and exclamation points go *inside* the quotation marks when they pertain only to the quoted material and *outside* when they apply to the whole sentence.

5.12 References

In Section 5.11, the superscript number ([1]) in student versions B-D could lead the reader to a number of different kinds of source notes. Those different kinds of source notes all come under the general heading of "reference styles"—methods you use to mark in the text your use of someone else's material and to give your reader the information needed to locate that original material. Reference styles vary from field to field. Although in your previous schooling you may have been required to use MLA, Turabian, or the *Chicago Manual* style, by the time you are a junior or senior in college you should be learning your own field's reference style, which may be quite different from those you've used before. Exhibit A.3 shows a few examples of how the last line of student version D might look in different reference styles.

Exhibit A.3 Examples of Various Reference Styles

Example A: A Footnote. Note appears at the bottom of the page.

. . . the most popular choice for central power stations.[1]

[1]Steam Turbines and Their Lubrication (New York: Mobil Oil Corporation, 1965, 1981), p. 5.

Example B: An Endnote. Note appears with other notes on separate page at end of report.

. . . the most popular choice for central power stations.[1]

1. Steam Turbines and Their Lubrication (New York: Mobil Oil Corporation, 1965, 1981), p. 5.

Example C: One Form of Parenthetical Documentation. Note appears with other notes on separate page at end of report.

```
. . . the most popular choice for central power sta-
tions (1).

1. Steam Turbines and Their Lubrication (New York: Mobil
   Oil Corporation, 1965, 1981), p. 5.
```

Example D: Another Form of Parenthetical Documentation. The first number inside the parentheses—assigned in order of occurrence in the chapter or in the book—indicates the source; the second number gives the page number within the source. By using this system, you can make subsequent references to that document without repeating the entire note: (1:455), etc.

```
. . . the most popular choice for central power sta-
tions (1:5).

1. Steam Turbines and Their Lubrication (New York: Mobil
   Oil Corporation, 1965, 1981).
```

Example E: Another Parenthetical Form. A short title or author's last name, plus the year of publication, may save most readers from ever checking the note itself, which is an entry in the report's bibliography.

```
. . . the most popular choice for central power sta-
tions (Steam Turbines, 1981: 5).

Steam Turbines and Their Lubrication (New York: Mobil
Oil Corporation, 1965, 1981).
```

Example F: Another Parenthetical Form. This one uses a long entry for first full reference. It makes subsequent references easy, and a "Notes" page unnecessary.

(1st reference)

```
. . . the most popular choice for central power sta-
tions (Steam Turbines and Their Lubrication, Mobil Oil
Corporation, 1981, p. 5).
```

(subsequent references) . . . water contamination which may be traced to the cooler itself (*Steam Turbines*, p. 16).

Most other forms of referencing are variants of one of the styles shown in Examples A–F.

5.12.1 **How to Find Your Field's Reference Style.** Most fields of study in college have their own reference styles, established either by the leading journal in that field or by the professional association representing the field. Sometimes a particular academic department will have its own guidelines for reference, and when

Exhibit A.4 Sample Instructions to Authors on Citation Style

GUIDELINES FOR AUTHORS

professional
ters, editors,
ers involved
ı article, look
re your topic

and cite any
and extends
vious issues
International
Transactions
ınical Writing

form, not im-
ormal style,
e and usage
ɔst common,
mation? Our
Heritage Dic-
nual of Style.
st. The most
way that im-
ers *his* com-
' Easy ways
rs take their
ı second per-
the secretary
y types each

s (about 16
er double- or
ıper. Please
ɔu want itali-
the back of

paragraphs

itself)
ɔy itself)
lics, as part
ıaragraph)
ay you want
imited space
ɔr 29.5 picas
although the
ɔn occasion.
in choosing

REFERENCES, NOTES, AND BIBLIOGRAPHY

Reference and notes are identified in the text by sequential superscript numerals, except that the original numeral is used when the same page of a previously cited source is cited again. All references and notes are then listed in numerical order at the end of the article, using *Chicago Manual of Style* format:

1. Bergan Evans and Cornelia Evans, *A Dictionary of Contemporary American Usage* (New York: Random House, 1957), pp. 387-88.	*Book*
2. Don Bush, "The Passive Voice Should Be Avoided—Sometimes," *Technical Communication* 28, no.1 (First Quarter 1981): 19-20	*Article in a professional or scholarly journal*
3. "Hurtling Through the Void," *Time*, 20 June 1983, p. 68.	*Article in a popular magazine or newspaper*
4. Paul M. Postal, "On So-called Pronouns in English," *Readings in English Transformational Grammar*, ed. Roderick A. Jacobs and Peter S. Rosenbaum (Waltham, MA: Ginn and Company, 1970), p. 57.	*Article in an anthology or conference proceedings*
5. Evans and Evans, p. 409.	*Shortened form for different page in a previously cited work*

Sources listed as references do not need to be repeated in a bibliography. If, however, you wish to include a bibliography of other related sources, arrange the entries in alphabetical order, again using *Chicago Manual of Style format:*

Fowler, H.W. *A Dictionary of Modern English Usage*. 2nd ed. Revised and edited by Sir Ernest Gowers. New York and Oxford: Oxford University Press, 1965.	*Book*
Held, Julie Stusrud. "Teaching Writers How to Write: What Works?" *Technical Communication* 30, no. 2 (Second Quarter 1983): 17-19.	*Article in a professional or scholarly journal*
Lu, Cary. "Second-generation Microcomputer Report." *High Technology*, June 1983, pp. 28-30.	*Article in a popular magazine or newspaper*
Creager, Cynthia. "Format Design: Help Your Readers Use Your Manuals." In *Proceedings* of the 30th International Technical Communication Conference, pp. W & E 147-150. Washington, D.C.: Society for Technical Communication, 1983.	*Article in an anthology or conference proceedings*

Note: Some regular columns—such as Book Reviews and Recent and Relevant—use other formats that are better suited to their purposes. Contact the column editor (listed inside the front cover of the journal) for guidelines.

COPYRIGHTS

The Society for Technical Communication holds the copyright on all material published in *Technical Communication*. (The Society grants republication rights to authors on request.) If your article has been previously published or presented elsewhere, please tell us when you submit your manuscript it comes to theses and dissertations most universities have schoolwide guidelines. In writing for business and industry, you will often not need references at all. When you do, your employer may well have a specified form. To find out what reference style you should use, either ask a professor in your field (if you're in school) or check the leading journal in your field to find out what it requires. That information is usually printed in small type on a page labeled something like "Notes for Contributors," as Exhibit A.4 shows.

To give you an idea of how many different reference-style manuals there are, Box A.11 lists some of the more commonly used ones.

5.12.2 **Publication Style Versus Manuscript-Submission Style.** Suppose that in your attempt to use your field's reference style you take a copy of an article from your field's leading journal and merely imitate the way it does references. Will you be right? It depends on whether your reader wanted publication style or manuscript-submission style. "Publication style" means the way references finally appear in printed pages of the journal. "Manuscript-submission style" means the way the reference appeared in the manuscript the author sent in to the journal. (This same distinction affects visuals; see Chapter 7, Section 5.2.) The two styles can be very different. For example, many journals still print bibliographical references as footnotes (as in Exhibit A.3, Example A), but most such journals require the references in manuscripts submitted for publication to be in end-note form (as in Exhibit A.3, Example B).

5.12.3 **Guidelines for References.** Whatever reference style you use, there are at least these three guidelines for using it properly: *clarity*, *consistency*, and *common sense*. The main purpose of references (beyond acknowledging that certain material is borrowed) is to enable a curious reader to find your original source, either to check your accuracy or to learn more about the subject. If your reference style is clear, a reader can easily find your original source. Review your own references and ask yourself if a reader could trace your borrowed material back to its source from the information you've given. Once you establish a pattern for your references, follow it consistently, so that your reader only has to figure out the pattern once. Finally, use common sense in selecting your reference style; if what you are doing seems strange, it's probably wrong, and you've probably misinterpreted something. If your use of a particular reference scheme employs clarity, consistency, and common sense, it will function adequately for you.

5.12.4 **Using Bibliographies.** Most reports written in academic settings require some sort of bibliography, a compilation of all the sources consulted in the production of that report. The bibliography may be alphabetized, or items may be numbered in order of appearance in the report. Some bibliographies are ordered chronologically. If a bibliography lists everything the author so much as glanced at, it should be labeled "A Complete Bibliography"; if it lists only the most important sources, it should be labeled "A Selected Bibliography."

Sometimes you may be asked to use shortened forms of bibliographical citation in your own notes, and complete forms in your bibliographical entries. A

Box A.11 Some of the Many Different Style Manuals

The APA Style Sheet

The Chicago Manual of Style

Kate Turabian's *A Manual for Writers of Term Papers, Theses, and Dissertations*

The MLA Handbook

William Campbell, Stephen Ballou, and Carole Slade's *Form and Style* (often called "Campbell/Ballou")

American National Standards for Bibliographic References

Eugene Fleischer's *A Style Manual for Citing Microform and Nonprint Media*

The U.S. Government Printing Office's *Style Manual*

The American Psychological Association's *Publication Manual*

The *Council of Biology Editors Style Manual*

The American Chemical Society's *Handbook for Authors*

The American Institute of Physics' *Style Manual*

The American Medical Association's *Stylebook*

Harvard Law Review's *A Uniform System of Citation*

The Royal Society's *General Notes on the Preparation of Scientific Papers*

The American Society of Agronomy, Crop Science Society of America, and Soil Science Society of America's *Handbook and Style Manual*

The American Journal of Medical Technology's *Handbook for Authors*

The American Society for Testing Materials' *Manual for Authors of ASTM Papers*

The Engineers' Joint Council's *Recommended Practice for Style of References in Engineering Publications*

The American Society for Mechanical Engineering *MS-4: An ASME Paper*

The American Institute of Industrial Engineers' *The Complete Guide for Writing Technical Articles*

A recent reference book, *Business and Technical Writing: An Annotated Bibliography of Books, 1880–1980*, by Gerald Alred, Diana Reep, and Mohan Limaye, also describes a number of typical reference styles.

reasonable compromise between no bibliography and a full bibliography is to include in your bibliography only those items that (1) are important for the reader to know you consulted, and (2) do not appear in the notes. Such a bibliography should have a title that indicates its unusual nature, such as:

A Selected Bibliography
(Important Sources Not Otherwise Cited)

What kind of bibliography to use, or whether to use one at all, depends on the field you are writing in, and your purpose, subject, and audience. Many kinds of writing for business and industry require neither notes nor bibliography. When referencing *is* required, a growing trend among journals leads away from bibliographies entirely; most journals can afford only the space for notes.

5.12.5 **A Note on "Notes."** If you consult the "Guidelines for Contributors" page of the leading journal in your field, it talks about two different kinds of "notes"—literature citations (called "references" here) and notes in which you as author comment on some point.* Manuscript style occasionally treats the two kinds of notes differently, with references on a separate page at the end of the article and authorial comments at the bottoms of pages. But most journals also discourage all such authorial comments. Most editors probably would delete a note like the one below, feeling that if your comment is worth making, it should be worked into the text. So when you read the "Guidelines for Contributors," do not be confused by the ambiguous use of the word *notes*; although authorial notes may be discouraged, in many fields (and especially in academic settings), bibliographical notes ("references") are expected.

EXERCISES

1. Find a copy of the reference style guide for publishing in your field. Make two copies, one for yourself and one to turn in to your teacher. Note: if the page you find refers you to some multipage document (ASME Report 4, for instance), you only have to copy that page, not the entire document.
2. Correct the grammar and style errors in the following sentences.
   a. There are two types of combines. The pull-type combine which is pulled by a tractor. The power to operate the combine is taken from the tractor. The second type is the self-propelled type. The operator rides on the combine itself. It has its own engine to move it through the field and harvest the grain.
   b. To maintain productivity, farming requires modern, efficient machinery. Machinery which means big investment for the farmer.
   c. The self-propelled combine is the type most commonly seen in grain fields today. And the self-propelled combine is the type I will be describing.
   d. Needed proteins can be separated from a donor's blood. When a person's body cannot produce needed proteins.
   e. About 48% of all the consumers surveyed indicated that they like Coors. Only 26% indicated that they disliked Coors. A surprisingly large amount of those surveyed indicated that they had no opinion about Coors, 25%.

*For example, this style of note—the asterisk in the text with the note at the bottom of the page—is called a "natural footnote."

f. Advertisers are able, by use of various methods such as sociopsychological tactics, to force opinions and beliefs on others that is against their own better judgment.
g. The social and economic impact, together with the environmental effects of airport development and operations, should be evaluated in order to guide development to make the airport environs compatible with airport operations and physical development and use of airports compatible with existing and proposed patterns of use.
h. Unfortunately, there is not much that consumers can do to prevent credit-life insurance abuses. The reasons being that the ordinary borrower is so pressed for time and the transactions are so small that the fuss and trouble of trying to evade the credit-life scandal is not worth the trouble.
i. The Douglas Amendment directs that no application for approval of a non-exempt transaction shall be approved which will permit any bank holding company or subsidiary thereof to acquire, directly or indirectly, any voting shares of, interest in, or all or substantially all of the assets of any additional bank located outside the State in which such bank holding company maintains its principal office and place of business, or in which it conducts its principal operations; unless such acquisition is specifically authorized by the statute laws of the State in which such bank is located, "by language to that effect and not merely by implication."
j. The saprophytic *Escherichia coli* can turn into pathogenic *Escherichia coli* under certain conditions and produce toxins.
k. Rather than dealing heavily with lobbyists, through previous contacts and selective advertising, sales are directed toward private industry.
l. This corporation needs an experienced (with corporate finances) accountant to insure proper financial records.
m. The government operates on a relatively fixed budget whereas a private company's budget is flexible. Flexible in the sense that if more funds are needed, sales can be increased to increase revenues.
n. The restrictions removed were primarily those requiring research with small amounts of bacteria, that would not grow outside the laboratory, to be reported.
o. Two varieties of costing, the historical method and the predetermined method, exist.
p. By defining the term "bid," giving bid contract information sources, and analyzing an actual government bid solicitation package; businessmen will have a clearer view of the bid process.
q. The estimate of credit losses are usually based on past experience, with some consideration given to projected sales.
r. Pyrimidine bases contain a single heterocyclic ring, and purine bases contain two rings which are fused together. Heterocyclic being a molecule with a circular arrangement of atomic elements.
s. By purchasing software, almost any business activity can be handled by a computer.
t. It goes without saying that to a certain extent productivity indicates the economic progress for a whole nation or for a particular industry.

u. The other category called fixed assets are assets that are valued at their depreciated cost.
v. I am presently attending State University in the capacity of a senior. My graduation date is May, 1987. My major being Engineering Technology.
w. I spent two quarters studying the government securities market and three quarters of computer (Basic, Fortran, and Cobol) which will allow me to handle your data processing.
x. An indication of a food's textural characteristics is obtained from the measurement of the distance that a penetrometer's probe falls through or against a food material during a specific period of time.
y. Computer system documentation is a relatively new idea and lacked real direction until in 1974, four years after it was organized, the Documentation Subcommittee of the American Society for Testing Materials formed the concept of CSD.

Suggestions for Further Reading

If you want to learn more about effective professional writing, your best sources of specific, up-to-date information are articles in these journals:

Technical Communication

The Journal of Technical Writing and Communication

The ABCA Bulletin

Journal of Business Communication

Each of those journals has its own method of indexing the articles it publishes. There are also a number of more or less standard bibliographies in the field, including:

An Annotated Bibliography on Technical Writing, Editing, Graphics, and Publishing, 1966–1980. Edited by Helen V. Carlson, Ruth Hersch Mayo, Theresa Ammannito Philler, and Douglas J. Schmidt. Washington, D.C.: The Society for Technical Communication, 1983.

Research in Technical Communication: A Bibliographic Sourcebook. Edited by Michael G. Moran and Debra Journet. Westport, Conn.: Greenwood Press, 1985.

Business and Technical Writing: An Annotated Bibliography of Books, 1880–1980. Edited by Gerald J. Alred, Diana C. Reep, and Mohan R. Limaye. Metuchen, N.J.: The Scarecrow Press, 1981.

Written Communication in Business. Edited by Mary Ann Bowman and Joan D. Stamas. Urbana, Ill.: ABCA, 1980.

Business Communication: An Annotated Bibliography. Edited by Ruth M. Walsh and Stanley J. Birkin. Westport, Conn.: Greenwood Press, 1980.

Abstracts of Studies in Business Communication: 1900–1970. Edited by Jane F. White and Patty G. Campbell. Urbana, Ill.: ABCA, 1982.

There are also a number of more specialized books on particular kinds of professional writing or aspects of professional communication:

- Proposals—*The Winning Proposal: How To Write It*, by Herman Holtz and Terry Schmidt. New York: McGraw Hill, 1981.
- Graphics—*Pocket Pal: A Graphic Arts Production Handbook*, Thirteenth Edition. New York: International Paper Company, 1984.

- Computer Documentation—*How to Write a Usable User Manual*, by Edmond H. Weiss. Philadelphia: ISI Press, 1985.
- Persuasion—*An Introduction to Reasoning*, Second Edition, by Steven Toulmin, Richard Rieke, and Allan Janik. New York: Macmillan, 1984.
- Office Automation—*The Office Automation Primer*, by Carolyn J. Mullins and Thomas W. West. Englewood Cliffs, N.J.: Prentice Hall, 1982.
- Grammar—*The Heath Handbook*, Eleventh Edition, by Langdon Elsbree and Gerald P. Mulderig. Lexington, Mass.: D.C. Heath, 1986.

Index

1 2 3 4 5 6 7 8 9 0